Methods of
Life Course
Research

Methods of Life Course Research

Qualitative and Quantitative Approaches

Editors

Janet Z. Giele
Glen H. Elder Jr.

SAGE Publications
International Educational and Professional Publisher
Thousand Oaks   London   New Delhi

286210

For information:

SAGE Publications, Inc.
2455 Teller Road
Thousand Oaks, California 91320
E-mail: order@sagepub.com

SAGE Publications Ltd.
6 Bonhill Street
London EC2A 4PU
United Kingdom

SAGE Publications India Pvt. Ltd.
M-32 Market
Greater Kailash I
New Delhi 110 048 India

Printed in the United States of America

Library of Congress Cataloging-in-Publication Data

Main entry under title:

Methods of life course research: Qualitative and quantitative approaches / edited by
   Janet Z. Giele and Glen H. Elder, Jr.
      p.   cm.
   Includes bibliographical references (p.   ) and index.
      ISBN 0-7619-1436-6 (cloth: acid-free paper).—ISBN 0-7619-1437-4
   (pbk.: acid-free paper)
      1. Social sciences—Biographical methods.   2. Life cycle, Human—
   Research—Methodology.   I. Giele, Janet Zollinger.   II. Elder, Glen H.
   H61.29.M47   1998
   300'.7'2—dc21   97-45466

00   01   02   03   04   10   9   8   7   6   5   4   3

Acquiring Editor:	C. Deborah Laughton
Editorial Assistant:	Eileen Carr
Production Editor:	Astrid Virding
Production Assistant:	Denise Santoyo
Typesetter/Designer:	Marion S. Warren
Indexer:	Juniee Oneida
Cover Designer:	Ravi Balasuriya
Print Buyer:	Anna Chin

Contents

This book is dedicated to the memory of John A. Clausen (1915-1996), pioneer in life course research, mentor, and friend.

Foreword

Crafting Life Course Studies

ANNE COLBY

In addition to grappling with some of the central conceptual issues in life course research and its development as a field, this book serves as a comprehensive and practical handbook, to be consulted over and over by anyone conducting research who takes seriously the interconnectedness of the various eras of the life course. Its importance rests on the tremendous impact on social science that the life course approach has had in the past three decades. This approach has affected several disciplines and many fields of study, bringing a developmental perspective to issues that had been conceived in terms of cross-sectional slices of life and bringing a greater awareness of social and historical contexts to developmentalists. Fields that would not have been developmental in focus at all came to look at lives over time. The study of particular developmental periods began to take seriously the groundwork laid earlier in life and the outcomes to emerge later. As the editors say in their introductory chapter (Chapter 1), "Any point in the life span must be viewed dynamically as the consequence of past experience and future expectation" (p. 19). Equally important is the recognition that individual and social change are interconnected through mutual influence.

The impact of the life course/life span approach has itself taken time to develop. The framework was controversial when it was introduced in the

1960s and continued to be for some time. The reasons for this were different in different disciplines and subdisciplines, and communication sometimes was impeded by the difficulty of translating ideas across fields. The emphasis on human plasticity and on the historical contingency of age-related patterns called into question the regularities and continuities in development that many observers had documented. To some extent, this simply reflected new findings yielded by better research methods. However, the debate arose from miscommunication due to different ways of using some of the same terms. For example, one use of the term "development" (generally favored by sociologists) focuses on temporal norms and expectations related to age, life stage, and social transitions, whereas others (most of whom are developmental psychologists) reserve the term for regularities in ontogenetic changes indicating increasing complexity, functional adequacy, and sophistication within a specified domain. These two are quite different, as are their relationships to historical changes in age norms for common life events. Another of the several controversies stimulated by the life course approach concerned development in adulthood about which some theorists were skeptical. This debate also was tied to the complexities of defining exactly what constitutes *development*.

For reasons that have more to do with the influence of cross-cultural research than of life course research, there has been a move away from universal stages of development within psychology. Over the past decade or so, the field has moved to a more contextual view of adaptation that is more consistent with the core principles of the life course perspective. Thus, the claim that the form of development is (at least to some extent) historically and culturally contingent and that *adaptation takes different forms depending on the social context* no longer is as controversial as it once was.

Now the controversies surrounding the introduction of the life course approach are mostly forgotten, and the approach is widely seen as providing an accepted set of background assumptions that guide and provide common ground for research on a great number of issues across virtually all of the social sciences. Younger readers may find obvious and unsurprising insights such as the historical and social embeddedness of development, the fallacy of using cross-sectional data on different cohorts to assess change within individuals, the potential for development across life, the importance of human agency and the bidirectional relationship between individuals and their settings, and the plasticity of human behavior. It is important to remember, however, that the widespread acceptance of these positions has been hard won. In fact, I believe that the establishment of this approach, which is widely shared internationally as well as across disciplines, is one of the most important achievements of social science in the second half of the 20th century. It is, therefore, very appropriate that this book appears now, as the century draws to a close.

Unfortunately, these insights are considerably easier to appreciate than to operationalize, and the actual practice of life course research has lagged behind the conceptual advances. This is so in part because the designs most suited to life course study—such as long-term longitudinal studies, cohort-sequential designs, and the comparative study of cohort subgroups—are resource-intensive methods.

There are several ways in which to mitigate this problem of collecting and reconstructing relevant research data on the life course. One way is to collect biographical history at a single point in time and at repeated intervals. Another is to find and resurvey individuals who were studied at an earlier point in time.

A third strategy that is particularly promising but that has been developed only recently is to use existing archival data sets. Using archival data can provide a great advantage in the implementation of life course research, but many investigators are unfamiliar with the techniques needed to fruitfully mine archival data. Of course, if a goal of one's research is to illuminate the impact of historical context on the life course, then using data collected in the past is almost unavoidable. Elder's (1974) groundbreaking study, *Children of the Great Depression,* is a well-known exemplar of this approach. Of course, longitudinal research, even cohort-sequential studies, can be and often is conducted without the use of archival data. But given the great deal of time and money that this type of study requires, it is greatly advantageous if one can find an existing data source on which to build.

Several chapters demonstrate the value of existing data sets such as the Gluecks' study of delinquency and the Berkeley and Oakland studies of children born in the 1920s. Especially useful are those that include open-ended material that can be recoded and recast in terms consistent with the investigators' new research questions. Giele and Elder, in their opening chapter (Chapter 1), and a number of other authors in this book point to the importance of archival data sources for their works, mentioning some of the well-known longitudinal studies that represent another unique achievement of social science in the past half century.

Many of these landmark studies are archived at the Murray Research Center at Radcliffe College, where several authors in this book have done research. Like the Inter-University Consortium for Political and Social Research at the University of Michigan, the Murray Research Center is a national archive of social science data sets, especially longitudinal studies, but it is distinctive in being the only data bank in the United States that offers a wide range of data sets with original *qualitative* records. It also is unique in that samples from many of the studies it holds are available for further follow-up by the new investigators. The use of existing data sets also allows for the addition of a new cohort to a single cohort longitudinal study or for the integration of two data sets into a multicohort study.

For such archives to be maximally useful, there must be provision for organizing and documenting the data carefully and for assisting researchers in learning how to use archival data. Instruction is needed because methods for secondary analysis, especially secondary analysis of qualitative data, are unfamiliar to many researchers and not taught in most graduate study programs.

In addition, the availability of data cannot alone drive the research. To recast an archive or collect relevant new data, the life course researcher needs to begin both by specifying a problem and by understanding how to organize the data using key concepts such as events, timing, the impact of historical period, and the distinctive experience of particular cohorts. The crucial phase of problem specification can be done in a variety of ways, as shown in several chapters here that, for example, focus on the ups and downs of life satisfaction, success in adult life, or times when an innovation has occurred. Open-ended questions also can be useful as a means of capturing unanticipated insights such as the importance of Vietnam veterans in the Iowa Farm Crisis. For the historic studies conducted over the past several decades to remain active and productive sources of new insights, we need to bring to them powerful conceptual frameworks, fruitful and imaginative questions, and creative ways of operationalizing new concepts with material collected for other purposes.

This book provides theoretical insights and practical guidance that should help with every phase in this process. It is rich with lore on many aspects of the craft of conducting life course studies, how best to use and interpret life stories, conditions under which prospective and retrospective methods are most appropriate and useful, how to assess data quality, how to track study participants for longitudinal follow-up, and many aspects of the analysis and interpretation of life course data. This distinguished collection should help to ensure the continued progress of the field as we move forward into the next century.

Preface

This book is intended to fill a gap in the research on the human life course by focusing on *how one does life course research*. Our focus is particularly on the art and method of the appropriate research design, the collection of life history data, and the search for meaningful patterns to be found in the results. This focus is justified because the life-span approach to human development has become well established in the past two decades, but the conceptual advances in life course theory (Elder, 1998) have outstripped advances in research design and method, measurement, and data analysis.

To be sure, there are specialized accounts of how to analyze longitudinal data in qualitative form; how to conceptualize the interaction of age, period, and cohort; and how to locate respondents for a follow-up survey. But the neophyte might not know that a key issue is how to organize life events data (as done in this volume by Karweit and Kertzer in Chapter 4) or how to record data on a calendar retrospectively or prospectively (as shown by Scott and Alwin in Chapter 5), least of all where to look for an answer. Thus, this book is aimed at social scientists and students from every discipline who are interested in collecting or analyzing for themselves the varieties and themes of life course patterns and life paths in the populations that they want to study. However, because we are both sociologists, our editorial focus has been primarily on methods of life course research in sociology. We have cited a number of methodological works in life span psychology (e.g., Baltes, 1968; Magnusson & Bergman, 1990; Schaie, 1977), but we do not claim to do justice to that large and important field.

The first part of the book introduces the life course approach and shows how it developed and what it entails. The second part considers how to collect and organize longitudinal data and contains very practical and specific nuts-and-bolts advice on ways in which to code and store life events data, whether to use a retrospective or an ongoing method of data collection, how to find a respondent for a follow-up interview, and how to design a regional or national study (using Germany as an example). The final part of the book introduces several analytic perspectives, for example, what one discovers if the analytic focus is on the individual's life review, on objective change between adolescence and adulthood, on the amount and location of innovation in the life course, or on the connections between historical change and personal change. Although these questions are by no means exhaustive, they suggest some rewarding possibilities for newcomers as well as interesting points of comparison for those researchers already in the field.

This book began as the result of several streams of research interest and professional association coming together. The first connection was a long-standing professional friendship between the editors; each of us has used the life course perspective (Giele to study midlife women and Elder to study children, adolescents, and adults). Each of us also has served for an extended period on one of the interdisciplinary Social Science Research Council committees that studied and stimulated new research on middle years and the life course (Giele with the Committee on Work and Personality in the Middle Years in the 1970s and Elder with the Committee on Life Course Perspectives on Human Development from 1977 to 1987). In the course of that 15-year period, we literally saw the life course perspective take shape before our eyes and influence a whole wave of new studies in the social sciences, including our own (Giele, 1982b).

The Murray Research Center for the Study of Lives founded at Radcliffe College, Harvard University, in 1976, became another meeting place for sharing our work and the works of other life course scholars. Giele was a visiting scholar there in 1987. Elder served in various advisory capacities and conducted two workshops on analysis of life course data in 1989 and 1991 that began to codify some of the procedures for analyzing archival data on human lives (Elder, Pavalko, & Clipp, 1993). A conference at the National Academy of Sciences conference center at Woods Hole, Massachusetts, in September 1990 became the occasion for our first discussion of a future book to assemble papers by experts *on how to do life course research.* Among the participants at the conference, Erika Brückner and Karl Ulrich Mayer, who later became contributors, also took part in these preliminary talks.[1]

Our discussion at Woods Hole was in large part the result of an event that occurred just one month earlier, in August 1990, at the American Sociological Association meeting in Washington, D.C. On that occasion, Giele organized and chaired two sessions on the life course that brought together a number of leading researchers to discuss their methods of work in doing life course studies.[2] A number of authors who are represented in this volume (Brückner, Clausen, Karweit, Dempster-McClain and Moen, and Laub and Sampson) were among the presenters. As the book took shape and papers were recast into chapters, we determined that it should have three major parts or sections: the first on the history and development of the life course perspective, the second on measurement and methods of data collection, and the third on modes of analysis. To round out the first part, we invited Riley's autobiographical account of how the life course perspective had developed and O'Rand's analysis of life course methodology using the sociology of knowledge. To complete the second part on measurement and data collection, we asked Scott and Alwin to compare retrospective and prospective alternatives for the collection of longitudinal data, and we invited Brückner and Mayer to describe the methods of the massive German Life History Study.

Now that our original idea has come to fruition, we have many to thank. Anne Colby and the Murray Research Center fostered the research, workshops, and conferences that helped make this book become a reality. Margie E. Lachman, Paul Baltes, and Lars R. Bergman generously agreed to review the manuscript prior to publication. Nancy Marley and Susan Schantz at Brandeis University and Aline Christoffelsz at the Carolina Population Center (CPC-Chapel Hill) helped with many technical tasks in getting the manuscript to press. Lynn Igoe, also of CPC, carefully checked and ably consolidated all the references to create a unified references section. Our contributors, whose work represents some of the finest in the field, have given their time to this work and have patiently endured the inevitable delays of bringing a multi-authored work to publication. We dedicate this book to the memory of the late John Clausen, a mentor and friend, who was one of the pioneers of life course research and who completed his chapter shortly before he died.

As editors, we both are grateful to those institutions that have furthered our own work on life course studies. Giele is indebted to the Ford Foundation, Lilly Endowment, National Institute on Aging, Rockefeller Foundation, and German Marshall Fund for support of her studies of women's changing lives since 1972. She began writing Chapter 10 during her 1993 fellowship at the Rockefeller Center in Bellagio, Italy. The Heller School at Brandeis has provided a stimulating environment through its Policy Center on Aging and its Family and Children's Policy Center to study the lives of families and children. Elder expresses his gratitude to the Institute of Human Development at the University of California, Berkeley, and its staff and directors for all of their encouragement across a long research career. In addition, he wishes to thank the National Institute of Mental Health, the National Science Foundation, the MacArthur Foundation, and the U.S. Army Research Institute for generous support of his life course studies. At his home in Chapel Hill, the Carolina Population Center, the Center for Developmental Science, and the Institute on Aging have made the University of North Carolina an invigorating place for longitudinal studies of human development and aging.

➤ NOTES

1. The conference, sponsored by the Murray Research Center for the Study of Lives, was titled "Bridging Levels of Analysis in the Study of Women's Lives Across Three Longitudinal Studies."

2. The sessions were titled "Life Course: Innovations in Reconstruction of Life Histories" and "Life Course: New Applications of Life Course Methodology."

Part I

The Life Course Mode of Inquiry

> ➤ INTRODUCTION

The following chapters in Part I of this book ask the question of how the life course perspective came into being. Together, they suggest several general principles to guide life course research, in particular, a bidirectional focus on social change as studied through life events and transition rates of particular individuals and groups. Questions ask how certain individuals have been affected by social change and also how the life course situations of some groups actually help to produce social change.

In Chapter 1, Janet Z. Giele and Glen H. Elder trace the confluence of four streams of social science inquiry following World War II that helped to create the life course field. Historical studies in both Europe and America became more demographic and shifted the focus from wars and heroes to the ordinary events of daily life such as births, deaths, and the bequeathing of property. The sociology of age gradually shifted its focus from particular stages of life, such as old age and youth, to a view of the process of aging as both more continuous than thought before and more difficult to classify in terms of expected roles. Developmental psychology similarly discovered that universal stages of development were difficult to discern and that, in fact, great variation existed by gender, race, and individual background and experience. Methodological advances paralleled these substantive developments in the conception of age and development. Panel studies and massive longitudinal surveys that were government sponsored stimulated growth in a technical understanding of how to interpret the interactions of many different effects and their impact on life events over time. Giele and Elder articulate what they believe to be an implicit four-part paradigm that has emerged from the past several decades of life course research. *Location* in time and place refers to history, social structure, and culture. *Linked lives* are the result of the interaction of individuals with societal institutions and social groups. *Human agency* is embodied in the active pursuit of personal goals and the sense of self. *Timing* covers the chronologically ordered events of an individual's life that simultaneously combine personal, group, and historical markers.

In Chapter 2, Matilda White Riley provides an autobiographical window on how the field developed. Through her account, it also is possible to reconstruct the institutionalization of aging and life course research. Informal support for Riley's work began with friendships formed during her graduate work at Harvard University in the 1930s (with Sorokin, Parsons, Merton, and others). Stouffer and Lazarsfeld's pioneering work on survey design and panel analysis in the 1940s and 1950s carried into Riley's (1963) two-volume *Sociological Research* (Volume 1, pp. 560-561), in which she explained the use of transition rates as a technique for assessing change in individuals or groups by comparing observations made at two different times. Coleman and Merton were her mentors in this work, and through it she began to realize her goal of understanding social change "from a non-Marxist perspective."

That new perspective was the sociology of age. Key concepts were age structure and the dynamic of aging as explications for the differences in consciousness and status that bring about social change. Riley's students (Anne Foner, Beth Hess, and Joan Waring) ensured continuity of the emerging paradigm. Validating support from the Russell Sage Foundation for three volumes on aging (Riley & Foner, 1968-1972) helped to legitimate the new endeavor. Further steps in the process of institutionalization came with the work of two successive committees of the Social Science Research Council (SSRC): the Committee on Work and Personality in the Middle Years (established in 1973) and its successor, the Committee on the Life Course Perspectives on Human Development (1977-1987). With Riley's move to the National Institute on Aging and work there with Ronald Abeles, former staff associate of the two SSRC committees, the new perspective on aging and the life span would shape the field of aging research from the 1980s on.

Chapter 3 uses the methods and tools of the history of science and sociology of knowledge to dissect the many technical and theoretical steps that had to be taken for a paradigm shift to occur that would replace older deterministic and stage concepts of human development with the life course perspective. By using Merton's insights into the mutual influence of research on theory and theory on research, Angela O'Rand outlines the major breakthroughs that have occurred. Of particular importance is the focus on *time* and *temporal organization* as the common denominator that allows cross-disciplinary communication and the accumulation of scientific data in a form that lends itself to a search for the interconnections between individual life change and dynamic fluctuations in larger social systems.

The key building block elements of the new life course paradigm are *events* combined in *event histories or trajectories* that are then compared across persons or groups by noting differences in timing, duration, and rates of change. O'Rand demonstrates that data must be recast not only to permit comparison based on timing and duration of events but also to permit comparison across both individuals and higher order systems. The organizing questions also have changed. No longer are the principal questions ones of comparing static qualities such as how many and which people are poor; rather, the new dynamic questions focus on both individual characteristics and system properties. For example, typical questions that are encountered in cross-national comparisons of panel studies ask how life experiences differ by gender and cohort, which people are more likely to remain poor, and how the United States compares to other countries in the persistence of inequality. These new questions, in turn, require a new type of research design that, as Riley points out in Chapter 2, is based on a *combined social system* approach that makes it possible to address both person dynamics and system dynamics simultaneously. By contrast, the *constituent* (or structural) approach observes systems through the properties of their members (events, rates of change, background characteristics), and the *contextual* approach studies individuals through the properties of the groups to which they belong. Only the combined social system approach is concerned with both groups and individuals as research units and proceeds by identifying which individuals belong to which groups. If one considers the four aspects of the life course paradigm as a hierarchy of generality, one can find a rough correspondence between them and these different approaches. *Location* in time and place corresponds with the *combined social system* approach that focuses on which individuals belong to which groups. *Linked lives* are especially visible through a *constituent or structural* approach that compares similar systems through properties of their individual members. To focus on *human agency,* one uses the social *context* as a backdrop for understanding individual action. Finally, an attention to *timing* requires use of *events as elemental data* to link information and analyses to ages, dates, and co-events.

Chapter 1

Life Course Research

Development of a Field

JANET Z. GIELE
GLEN H. ELDER, JR.

One of the most vital new arenas of social science research since World War II has been the impact of massive social change on people's lives. *The American Soldier* documented the positive impact of racially integrated fighting units on racial attitudes of white soldiers (Stouffer, Suchman, DeVinney, Star, & Williams, 1949). *The Authoritarian Personality* suggested the different types of child rearing and socialization that bred rigid and punitive attitudes (Adorno, Frenkel-Brunswik, Levinson, & Sanford, 1950). Erikson's (1950) *Childhood and Society* and later works (Erikson, 1958, 1969) asked what cultural and psychological factors made persons such as Hitler, Luther, and Gandhi the leaders of giant movements for social change. Since then, tremendous advances have occurred in the ways in which to study changing lives over time. Many disciplines are involved: anthropology, history, psychology, sociology, and medicine. At the same time, longitudinal projects such as the Terman studies of gifted children begun in the 1920s (Terman, 1925; Terman & Oden, 1947, 1959), the Grant study of Harvard University men (Vaillant, 1977), and the Gluecks' accounts of adolescent delinquents begun in the 1930s (S. Glueck & E. Glueck, 1934b, 1950) have now run for decades and demonstrated what valuable insights can be obtained from following respondents over time.

This book represents a stage in the maturation of life course inquiry in which it is possible to assemble and disseminate both lessons and skills that researchers have learned. The chapters document the use of both retrospective accounts and prospective surveys, novel methods for finding respondents who had not been contacted for years, and different ways of recording event histories in a variety of domains. The purpose of this introduction is to provide an overview of the major methodological issues in life studies by showing how all share in a new paradigm. The life course model arose out of the confluence of several major theoretical and empirical streams of research connecting social change, social structure, and individual action. This chapter makes explicit the new life course paradigm, especially as it has come to be understood in sociology, shows how it developed out of empirical discoveries after 1950, and then introduces the methodological innovations in data collection and analysis that are reported in the rest of the book.

➢ EMERGENCE OF THE LIFE COURSE PARADIGM

Before the articulation of the life course idea, social scientists generally followed one of two broad methods for observing human behavior: (a) a snapshot "social relations" or structural approach that viewed the impact of the social surroundings on the individual and (b) a movie-like "temporal" or dynamic approach that traced the story of lives over time.

The social relations approach generally focused on either the interconnections of the macro social order (the whole society) or the micro level (small groups and face-to-face interaction) and often was associated with functionalists such as Durkheim (1893/1933) and Parsons (1961, 1966) or exchange theorists such as Mauss (1925/1967) and Lévi-Strauss (1949/1969). In addition, within psychology, Bronfenbrenner (1979) emphasized the importance of the surrounding environment for the individual in what he termed an "ecological" perspective.

The dynamic or "temporal" orientation tended to concentrate on special subgroups or individual actors. At the macro level, it was associated with conflict theories of Marx. At the micro level, it appeared in the life history tradition advanced by W. I. Thomas and the Chicago School. In addition, Mead (1934) developed a theory of socialization and growth of the self resulting from social interaction and internalization. Blumer (1969) extended symbolic interaction theory to explain how new cultural and social movements arose.

The difficulty was to integrate the structural and dynamic approaches in a comprehensive way that took into account the many levels of social structure and, at the same time, comprehended dynamic change. Numerous critics of functional theories such as Collins (1994) have faulted functionalism for overlooking conflict as an engine of social change. Conflict theorists, on the other hand, have explained stability by the manipulation of power and failed to account for voluntary reproduction of custom or tradition through shared values or mutual investment in social capital (Coleman, 1990).

Fresh answers to these questions of social change gradually began to appear in work on social structure and personality (Inkeles & Levinson, 1954). At the macro level, cross-national research uncovered changes in orientations and attitudes across cohorts in countries undergoing rapid social change. Bauer, Inkeles, and Kluckhohn (1956) described the emergence of a "new Soviet man," and Inkeles and Smith (1974) began a search for "modernization" of personality structure in developing countries. At the micro level, Elder (1974) began to reconstruct longitudinal data on children's lives that had been collected since the 1930s and that would constitute one of the first systematic studies of change in families and children over time. Further research by Elder and others on individual life records would connect the trajectory of personal lives to large cultural and economic changes such as depression and war.

As co-authors, each of us brings a somewhat different intellectual formation and research experience to this introductory chapter. Yet, we have discovered a convergence in what we regard as common elements of the life course paradigm. Giele, trained at Harvard under Parsons, Homans, Inkeles, and Stouffer, has been interested in how social system needs become articulated with individual goals through the connections between social structure and personality and how, in turn, individuals consciously try to change the larger society. Her research began with her 1961 dissertation on the 19th-century American women's movement and from there moved to cohort comparisons of women's lives. This research raised more general questions of innovations in women's life patterns—how they first change their roles and then begin to change the larger institutions of work and family of which they are a part.

Giele's (1988) model of role and life course change is bidirectional; that is, societal values and institutions and informal groups transmit influences to the woman that affect her life pattern. The individual may, in turn, retreat or conform to past standards or, as in the case of reform leaders, attempt to transform the social structure "upward" by changing group norms, institutional rules, and societal values. This bidirectional model of interrelated life course change and feminist activity grew out of Giele's research on Wellesley College graduates and other college alumnae groups in the 1970s and 1980s. By comparing the timing and concurrence of retrospective life histories across different birth cohorts, she discovered a clear shift toward multiple roles among women born since 1930. Further comparison of data from the United States and Germany pointed to changes in education, jobs, and family life that already had begun in the 1940s and 1950s and contributed to the resurgence of feminism in the 1970s.

Elder's early work, like that of Giele, came out of a social structure and personality tradition but concentrated on the micro level. His graduate work at the University of North Carolina was shaped by the early Chicago School of sociology and focused on socialization more than on the relation of careers and life history to the larger social structure. His transition to the University of California, Berkeley, and his work with Clausen (1972) and others at the Institute of Human Development were instrumental in moving him toward life course studies. His work with life records and longitudinal samples immersed him in the age grading of life events. As a result, he began to integrate social structural and temporal (age) perspectives through an explicit study of the life course. This work led him back to the theory and research of Thomas and Znaniecki (1918-1920/1927). His first major articulation of a life course perspective appeared in *Children of the Great Depression* (Elder, 1974), an account that traced the adolescent and adult life patterns of children to the different adaptations made by their families in Berkeley and Oakland.

As a result of his accumulated findings and research experience, Elder (1994, 1997) identified four key factors that determine the shape of the life course: historical and geographical location, social ties to others, personal control, and variations in timing. To Giele, these propositions appear to be an independently derived variant of Parsons' (1966) four-function model of the social system (the familiar AGIL in reverse—Latent pattern maintenance, Integration, Goal attainment, and Adaptation) as applied to the life course and social change. In *Two Paths to Women's Equality,* Giele

(1995, pp. 18-23) used the four elements of cultural background, social membership, individual goal orientation, and strategic adaptation to describe the ways in which the historic women's temperance and suffrage movements carried life course change of leaders into the broader social structure.

How is it that the elements of the Elder and Giele paradigms correspond with each other? Elder's four elements of life course analysis are filtered through the individual, whereas the corresponding dimensions named by Giele are focused on the relations between the individual and the surrounding social structure. Linking the two frameworks is a useful device for tracing the interplay of person and setting and of dynamic change by the individual in a context of structural leads and lags, as spelled out in the following paragraphs.

Location in time and place (cultural background). Individual and social behavior is multilayered involving several different levels of the social and physical context. Yet, each individual's experience in its totality is of necessity particular in some respects. Both the general and unique aspects of individual location affect personal experience and thus can be understood as being socially and individually *patterned* in ways that carry through time. Thus, children who lived through the Depression experienced a historical era that was distinctive compared to that experienced by children born later, and they suffered differentially depending on the severity of conditions where they grew up. In the case of the early feminist leaders, their regional and historical backgrounds set them apart from the general mass of women. To create a new order, they developed an ideology that would promote new cultural patterns.

Linked lives (social integration). All levels of social action (cultural, institutional, social, psychological, and sociobiological) interact and mutually influence each other not only as parts of a whole but also as the result of contact with other persons who share similar experiences. How well these different expectations, norms, or social institutions are *integrated* or internalized will vary. Some will show discontinuity and disruption, and others will show a smooth interweaving of individual attainments with social and cultural expectations; in any case, one expects to find differences among persons with different family backgrounds or experiences in work, education, or other domains. The children of deprived families in the

Depression had a different experience from that experienced by the nonde-prived. In the example of the feminist leaders, their family, religious, and educational networks were distinctive and supported them in becoming reformers but were somewhat different for the women who focused on charitable work compared to those who wanted to change the laws.

Human agency (individual goal orientation). Any dynamic system persists through time and adapts its behavior to the environment to meet its needs. The motives of persons and groups to meet their own needs result in their actively making decisions and organizing their lives around *goals* such as being economically secure, seeking satisfaction, and avoiding pain. The girls from deprived families in the Depression grew up to seek out traditional homemaker roles, whereas the nondeprived were more likely to get further education and be interested in combining paid work and family life. The feminist leaders who experienced some personal loss were more likely to be interested in temperance and charitable work, whereas those who had been denied higher education, work opportunities, and/or political voice because they were women were more likely to support the suffrage movement.

Timing of lives (strategic adaptation). To accomplish their ends, persons or groups both respond to the timing of external events and undertake actions and engage in events and behavior to use the resources available. Thus, the timing of life events can be understood as both passive and active *adaptation* for reaching individual or collective goals. How and when a person accumulates or deploys wealth or education, takes a job, or starts a family are examples of various possible strategies. Marriage and homemaking came earlier in the lives of the girls who came from deprived families in the Depression. For the early feminists, a number were interested in temperance early in their careers and then graduated to suffrage, a pattern that was reflected in feminism as a whole as temperance became the most popular women's reform movement in the 1890s, whereas suffrage came to dominate in succeeding decades.

As shown in Figure 1.1, the way in which we picture that all these elements come together is through the funnel of timing. Whatever a person's social location and cultural heritage, friendships and networks, or personal motivation, all come together and are experienced through the individual's adaptation to concrete situations and events. Thus, as is shown

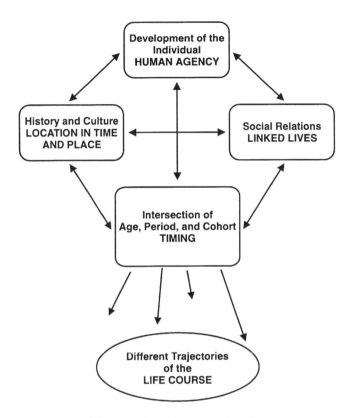

Figure 1.1. Four Key Elements of the Life Course Paradigm

later in this chapter, the use of life events and their timing as a means of organizing data on the life course makes sense both theoretically and practically.

➤ EMPIRICAL BREAKTHROUGHS AFTER 1950

The insights that generated the four-faceted model of the life course have come as much from empirical research as from abstract theorizing. In his perceptive essay on the bearing of empirical research on sociological theory, Merton (1948) noted that research pushes forward theory by exerting pressure to elaborate and clarify concepts and by refocusing theoretical interest. The life course model draws on the two main traditions in social science—one focusing on the ecological and "age norm" context surrounding the individual, the other focusing on the longitudinal trajectory connecting roles and events in a person's life over time. The flowering of social science research during and after World War II produced disparate discoveries across the social science spectrum, from history and demography to psychology, that further united these two traditions. Ethnographic accounts from simple societies and developing nations expanded the horizons of American researchers. New survey techniques were piloted and generated vast stores of data. A complicated array of findings became a reservoir of experience and understanding that helped to shape and enrich the conceptual framework of the life course.

Four types of empirical study have particularly benefited life course research: historical demography, sociology of aging, life history, and longitudinal surveys. Each of these, in turn, roughly corresponds with one of the four elements in the life course paradigm. Reconstruction by French and English historical demographers of births, deaths, and fertility patterns in pre-industrial villages helped to pinpoint the importance of regional and historical *location* in the shape of individual lives. Cohort comparisons of Depression and baby boom children, or of army recruits who experienced some level of racial integration in their units, demonstrated *linkages* of various institutions and expectations to the individuals' attitudes and life patterns. Life histories and biographies constituted stories of perseverance against odds and documented the role of *human agency* in the face of social constraints and opportunity. Finally, panel studies and longitudinal surveys helped to sort out antecedents and consequences and suggested the variety with which individuals *timed* their life events and adapted to current circumstances.

Developments in life course methods described later in this book are predicated on discoveries made by each of these research traditions, although the connections between contemporary methodological advances and these precursors remain largely implicit. Historical accounts, demographic projections, life histories, and panel studies all were contributing different levels of data and analysis to the growing corpus that would turn into research on the life course. Because one of the tasks of this book is to make more explicit and codify the theoretical and methodological elements of the life course paradigm, we begin by summarizing the major lessons to be learned from each of these research traditions.

Historical Demography

After World War II, both French and British historians began to develop a new type of "total" history that shifted the focus from leaders and battles to ordinary people. Through family reconstruction and use of archival parish registers, historical demographers reconstructed births, deaths, and marriages and the economic and political factors that shaped the key demographic events of everyday life. The English stream centered at Cambridge University, where Wrigley (1969) and Laslett (1972) made clear that the modern family predated industrialization in Western Europe although it might not have done so in Eastern Europe. The French, beginning with Ariès (1962), examined family structure. Through painstaking research in local archives, they examined intricate details of inheritance from the Middle Ages to the Renaissance and discovered a wide range of consequences for social structure that stemmed from a fall in death rates or a rise in births. French historians, in a special 1972 issue of *Annales, Économies, Sociétés, Civilisations,* traced the impact of population change on inheritance laws and the structure of the family (Forster & Ranum, 1976). Ladurie (1972/1976), for example, showed how the egalitarian nuclear family tradition of inheritance gained ascendancy in northern France over an older seignorial tradition of the extended family; by 1510, because of lower population pressure, there was less need to keep the patrimony intact by passing the land to only one child and forcing the others to take their portions and leave.

When similar methods of archival reconstruction were applied in America, they helped to illuminate the family as the important mediating institution between economic and social change and the shaping of individual lives. Moreover, the family managed the transition to adulthood. Demos (1970), in *A Little Commonwealth,* reconstructed family life in colonial New England and showed that although it was largely nuclear in form (except for children and servants "bound out" to other families), the family had a much broader range of functions as "business," "school," and "welfare institution." Children after the age of 7 years or so were treated as "little adults." By reconstructing census records from Philadelphia after the Civil War, Modell, Furstenberg, and Hershberg (1976) were able to piece together a shift in the nature of the transition to adulthood—from a linear or serial pattern of finishing school, getting a job, leaving home, and getting married to a pattern of concurrent or even "disordered" events that reflected the likelihood of leaving home earlier and finishing school, finding employment, and getting married, all at about the same time. Hareven (1982) demonstrated how families synchronized household formation, placement of family members in jobs, and their daily routines, all the while taking into account the exigencies of factory life in Manchester, New Hampshire. In a three-generation reconstruction of family life in Casalecchio, Italy, Kertzer and Hogan (1989) traced the impact of the transition from agrarian life to industrial life on migration, marriage, and fertility of family members. Numbers of children and old people, the age structure of the population, and the timing of births and marriages through the life cycle all affected the family's decisions about fertility and mobility in relation to economic opportunity.

Authors of these European and American studies were beginning to construct an implicit model of individual and family decisions that were affected by many levels of experience in which changes in population and social structure were tightly bound together. This model was a system with positive and negative feedback loops such that negative conditions such as poor soil, plagues, depression, war, and political chaos limited growth and reproduction and kept population stable, whereas positive trends such as improving health, economic growth, and expanding communication caused population increases that forced the social structure to change (Wrigley, 1969).

An important byproduct of historical demography was a new importance that it accorded women's lives. In the words of Rabb and Rotberg (1971), "Perhaps the happiest result of this new genre has been its illumination of the single most neglected historical subject—women" (p. vii). Women's importance in the family illuminated their decisive roles as marriage partners, mothers, and workers. Tilly and Scott (1978) detailed the intricate connections in France and England between industrialization and the recruitment of women from villages and farms into domestic service, marriage, or the factory.

The general principles of historical demography identify the distinctive features of the individual or community. Among these special characteristics is a particular *location* in time and place, one of the four key elements of the new life course paradigm. In France, for example, family forms and individual life patterns varied by century and region. The contribution of this new total history (*histoire totale*) was to illuminate general processes and principles so that what was unique in the individual life span would become visible. In the words of Willigan and Lynch (1982), "The identification of long-standing demographic, social, or biological conditions in human societies is a necessary precondition for the identification of the historically unusual or unique" (p. 434).

Sociology of Aging

A whole new field of study of aging and the aged burst onto the scene in the 1960s with the widespread growth of the older population in all advanced industrial societies. The new understanding of age put forward primarily by Riley and Foner (1968-1972) rejected a focus on age as dealing primarily with the end of life. The authors argued instead that aging starts at birth and constitutes one of the two principal dynamisms for all social change (the other being change outside the person in the surrounding social structure). Rich new empirical studies of variations in life patterns among different birth cohorts helped elaborate a multidimensional model of aging and the life course, the principal elements of which are *age* of the individual (time since birth), historical *period* describing the larger society (e.g., the 1930s), and *cohort* (the aggregate of persons of the same age).

The new cohort studies demonstrated the powerful connections between the two forces of individual aging and historical period by showing that the shape of the life course was different depending on one's year of birth; that is, age, period, and cohort *intersect* with each other to produce different life patterns among different age groups or "generations." For example, Uhlenberg (1969), in a study of the life patterns of women before 1900, discovered that only a fraction ever lived to marry or have children; earlier birth cohorts had largely experienced a "truncated" life pattern because of early deaths. Among elderly persons, Schaie (1977, 1989) demonstrated that more recent birth cohorts of old people had higher scores on inductive reasoning and verbal meaning, probably because they had more education. Bennett and Elder (1979) discovered that mothers' employment during the Depression had more direct effect on the life patterns of Berkeley study children (born in 1928-1929) than on the lives of Oakland study children who were 8 years older when their families experienced economic deprivation. Featherman and Sørensen (1983) observed that three cohorts of Norwegian men (born in 1921, 1931, and 1941) revealed different patterns in the transition to adulthood, the younger showing more simultaneous and complicated ways of integrating schooling, employment, and military service than the older. Likewise, Perun and Giele (1982) and Giele (1982a) found different life patterns predominant among Wellesley College alumnae who graduated after 1930 from those who graduated before 1930. Fully 25% of the 1911-1915 graduates had received postgraduate degrees, been employed professionally, and never married compared to only 7% of the post-1930 graduates.

Other cohort differences in life patterns were discovered by demographers, demonstrating what Riley, Johnson, and Foner (1972b) identified as the interaction between aging of the individual and structural change of the social order. Oppenheimer (1970) connected the increase in women's labor force participation in the United States in the 1950s to several interlocking forces—the growth in female-labeled occupations, the small birth cohort of the 1930s, and the mismatch between demand and supply. The result was a redefinition of married women as acceptable workers in occupations such as teaching from which they once had been excluded after marriage. Hogan (1981) traced the changing lives of blue-collar and farm men born between 1907 and 1952 whose Depression and wartime experiences and use of veterans' benefits for higher education resulted in combining marriage with education and employment rather than in waiting for school completion or secure jobs. Harris (1969), Waring (1975), and Easterlin (1980) linked cohort size and opportunity and predicted two general patterns of adaptation: Small birth cohorts were likely to experience unprecedented demand for their skills and career success, whereas large birth cohorts were apt to wait in line for openings to preschool, college, and retirement communities.

These intriguing findings about cohort differences in life patterns, and the expansion and contraction of opportunities with cohort size and economic cycles, gave impetus to theoretical and methodological developments in studies of aging. Mannheim (1929/1952a) first formulated the connection between differential opportunities and the distinctive ideology of different "generations" by showing regular patterns of correlation. Conceptual synthesis began with Cain's (1964) use of the term "life course" to encompass anthropological, sociological, and psychological concepts of aging, particularly as they were related to the maturing individual's movement through an expected sequence of social roles. Two other milestones in postwar theorizing were Ryder's (1965) discussion of the cohort as a principal concept for understanding social change and Riley and colleagues' (Riley, Foner, & Waring, 1988; Riley et al., 1972b) formulation of the sociology of age to reflect the growing conceptual codification of the field and the idea of the "two dynamisms" of age and structural change. On the methodological side, Boocock's (1978) discussion of various strategies for interpreting cohort, period, and life pattern data provided a prescient synthesis. The net impact of the sociology of age on the life course paradigm was to elaborate the various mechanisms by which aging processes are integrated with existing role opportunities and yet, at the same time, push forward structural changes in the larger social order. The sociology of age and cohorts views the process of change from an aggregate or macro perspective, whereas life history is focused primarily on the individual level of action. But neither personal nor social change is understandable without the other. The sociology of age helps us to comprehend the many possible ways by which the life course of one person is linked to the fate of both age peers and the larger social order.

Life History

Of all the studies associated with the life course, it is life history and the psychology of developmental stages that are most commonly identified with it. Beginning with Freud and Erikson, various scholars have tried to describe the typical life cycle that begins with birth and moves through adolescence, young adulthood, and the middle years to old age and death. Life history offers an elaboration of the third major life course concept, *human agency*, as a key element in shaping and directing an individual's life path.

Following World War II, Erikson's (1950) elaboration of Freud's theory of psychosexual stages provided the reigning scheme for interpreting maturation and development. Erikson made clear that the child's maturation through control of oral, anal, and genital orifices actually was a metaphor for summarizing the child's interpersonal and physical modes of interaction with the environment at any given stage. Erikson then extended the application of these patterns to the entire life span by showing the ways in which they were combined and recapitulated through stages such as "identity formation" and "generativity" in adulthood and old age. Numerous further attempts by Levinson (1978), Gould (1978), and others (e.g., Smelser & Erikson, 1980) spelled out various ways of conceptualizing development in adulthood.

Cognitive psychologists, starting with Piaget, also strove to delineate regular stages of intellectual and moral development. Kohlberg (1969) amassed evidence and constructed tests to support a scheme of six major stages of moral development beginning with "egocentric," passing through "conventional," and culminating in "principled" and "autonomous." The universality of these stages was challenged, however, particularly in the case of women. Gilligan's (1982) *In a Different Voice* suggested that women's concern for others' needs and opinions (termed "Stage 3: conforming to persons" in Kohlberg's scheme) actually might represent as mature and complex a morality as "Stages 5 and 6: principled-autonomous," which focused on justice and individual rights. Subsequent work, particularly in the gender field by Thorne (1994), suggests that differences such as being a boy or girl affect play group size and, in turn, the moral order that is internalized. Thus, if gender differences are any sign of a more general process, then it is that stages may be different according to personal characteristics and life circumstances that vary by gender, race, ethnicity, class, and national origin.

A way out of the universal stages box is to define the developmental challenges of an individual's life in much more general terms—as issues of achieving "competence," "personal control," or "successful adaptation." White (1960) was a pioneer in pointing to the intrinsic personal reward of feeling competent. A sense of competence derives from dealing successfully with other persons and the environment and becomes its own reward.

With the work of Paul Baltes in the new field of life-span developmental psychology, the study of individual lives has broken out of the idea of developmental stages and been replaced by a more flexible and continuous concept of the life span. Baltes focuses on adaptation by the individual to the dual nature of human aging in which the person experiences biological losses but cultural gains. By selection, optimization, and compensation, the person psychologically manages these changes. In his interview with the pianist Artur Rubenstein, Baltes discovered these processes at work. Rubenstein was able to maintain his concert activity into old age by performing fewer pieces (selection), practicing each more frequently (optimization), and leading up to fast sections by playing the preceding sections more slowly (compensation) so that the contrast would make the fast sections sound faster (Baltes, 1993, p. 590).

Similar themes shine through *Adaptation to Life*, Vaillant's (1977) analysis of the 1930s and 1940s Harvard graduates, Clausen's (1993)

American Lives, and autobiographical accounts such as Rossi's (1983) *Seasons of a Woman's Life* and Bateson's (1989) *Composing a Life.* All demonstrate the satisfaction that comes of mastering complexity, living in friendliness with one's neighbors, and, at the same time, feeling a sense of autonomy, confidence, and self-esteem.

The developmental psychology of the life span slowly has become more closely intertwined with the history and sociology of age. Recognition that there may be diverse developmental trajectories related to gender or race, or that adaptation and competence will take different forms depending on the social context, has shown the importance of integrating the study of individual aging with the examination of the surrounding social order. Two important way stations in this process were the study of socialization beyond childhood (Brim & Wheeler, 1966) and the study of the middle years sponsored by the Social Science Research Council through its Committee on Work and Personality in the Middle Years (established in 1972 and chaired by Orville G. Brim, Jr.). This committee sponsored a special study group on Women in the Middle Years that met at Brandeis University in 1977-1978 (Giele, 1982b). Since that time, the study of the life course has perceptibly moved from a tendency to divide up the study of development into discrete stages to a firm recognition that any point in the life span must be viewed dynamically as the consequence of past experience and future expectation as well as the integration of individual motive with external constraint.

At the same time, a new methodology of collecting life stories has arisen. The method had been important in the work of W. I. Thomas and the Chicago School of sociology before World War II. But then, according to Bertaux and Kohli (1984), "sociologists turned their backs on the method altogether," and it was marginalized when "survey research became the dominant paradigm" (p. 232). With the growth of life course studies has come a new development in collective biography and methods for collecting life stories as a way of capturing the subjective meaning of experience that cannot be wholly represented by quantitative survey methods (Denzin, 1989).

Testimony to the reformulation of life history is the replacement of the term "life cycle" with the more continuous concept of the "life course." By the same token, the level of analysis also has shifted from the individual case to groups of individuals who were born at roughly the same time and experienced approximately the same historical events at the same time of

life. Key examples are the intensive studies of some 500 California children
born in the 1920s who have been followed for more than 60 years by the
Berkeley Guidance Study and the Oakland and Berkeley Growth Studies
(Clausen, 1993; Elder, 1974).

Panel Studies and Longitudinal Surveys

If human agency is one of the primary interests of life course scholars
and they discover, as we have just seen, that regularities flow from both the
structuring of the environment and the maturation process, then the methodological challenge is to observe the ways in which detailed transactions
between self and other and between person and context are both involved
in steering the life course in one direction or another. Techniques and
models for addressing these questions gradually have emerged from widespread experience with panel studies and longitudinal surveys that collect
information from individuals at discrete points over a period of years or
decades.

Some of the earliest attempts to pinpoint individual change over time
came from analysis of survey data that found associations between antecedent and consequent variables. Using methods of interpretation and specification, Stouffer et al. (1949), Kendall and Lazarsfeld (1950), and Hyman
(1954) developed principles for sorting out the time order of variables and
examining differential effects of longer or shorter exposure to some experience such as serving in the army. One of the key inventions of the period
was the "panel" study, whereby the same individual respondents were
surveyed at successive points in time to gauge changes in their attitudes.
In 1940, between May and November, Lazarsfeld, Berelson, and Gaudet
(1944) surveyed a representative sample of 600 people in Erie County,
Ohio, regarding their voting intentions in the November elections. The
technique made it possible to identify influences from both reference
groups and background characteristics such as education, occupation, and
religion that predisposed one to vote Democrat or Republican. Voters who
remained undecided the longest were those caught in cross-pressures
between their predispositions to vote Democrat or Republican and the
predominant views of their reference groups.

Beginning in the 1960s, two major national longitudinal surveys were
launched using the panel method. The National Longitudinal Surveys,
funded by the U.S. Department of Labor, followed roughly 5,000 persons

in each of four nationally representative samples with biennial surveys of older men, mature women, young men, and young women (Center for Human Resource Research, 1989). The Panel Study of Income Dynamics studied a nationally representative sample of 5,000 families and their members by yearly questioning them concerning income, occupation, unemployment, and family changes (University of Michigan Survey Research Center, 1972-1990). On a more modest level, many social scientists undertook numerous smaller longitudinal studies to track child development, health, and various effects of education (e.g., Young, Savola, & Phelps, 1991).

Widespread sharing of the data from many of these studies stimulated development of mathematical models for explanation and statistical methods for estimating significance. Coleman (1981), Tuma and Hannan (1984), Allison (1984), and Yamaguchi (1991) spelled out techniques of event history analysis and methods for calculating the hazard and survival rates for remaining in a given state versus undergoing a transition to some other state. The key question is how to identify the principal influences in prior states or events that affect the rate of a given behavior at a later time. Mayer and Tuma (1990) demonstrated the versatility of the method in their collection of studies ranging from job histories and occupational careers to family events such as childbearing and marriage.

Another technique known as LISREL (Linear Structural Relations) was put forward by Jöreskog and Sörbom (1979) to distinguish causal and reciprocal influences from measurement error and to estimate the strength of links among antecedent, concurrent, and consequent events. Kohn and Schooler (1983), in a detailed investigation of work environments and intellectual flexibility, found important reciprocal effects between personal style and occupational choice. Those with greater intellectual complexity sought out more interesting jobs and, in turn, were pushed to ever greater heights of cognitive functioning, whereas those with simpler cognitive styles accepted less demanding jobs.

These methodological developments have produced a more precise picture of how individual lives are mutually shaped by personal characteristics and social environment, and they are in line with theoretical developments that picture change of the individual and the social order as a bidirectional process. In the terms used by Featherman and Lerner (1985), the life course paradigm is moving toward a "metatheoretical perspective" to combine ontogenetic and sociogenetic ideas. The result is a "developmental contextualism" in which the phenomenon to be studied is a "person-population process." By using duration-dependent rates of change as a major way of characterizing different persons in a population, and by sorting out endogenous from exogenous and reciprocal effects, it becomes possible to distinguish the impact of biological change ("age grade") from the impact of socialization and experience ("event grade") or cultural and institutional change ("history grade").

The central contribution of these various longitudinal surveys, as well as the methods associated with them, has been to operationalize the emerging theoretical model of the life course. Whether one uses regression, hazard rates, or LISREL, the findings all point toward the mutual influence of person and social context over time. Background characteristics, the social context, and the person's current states combine to produce personal histories with considerable variation but also some regularities. Individuals appear to adapt to the challenges confronting them by timing the events of their lives—in work, education, family behavior, and leisure—so as to make the most of opportunity and suffer the least frustration and failure. Thus, the invention and elaboration of longitudinal study has become the primary method for studying the fourth dimension of the life course paradigm, adaptation through *timing* of major life events.

➤ CONVERGENCE ON THE LIFE COURSE CONCEPT

The superiority of the life course idea is in its flexibility and capacity to encompass many different types of cultural, social, and individual variation. Earlier depictions of the life cycle that came from anthropology, family sociology, and psychology expressed the normative expectations of a particular culture, class, or cohort or purported to describe an innate developmental dynamic. The life course idea, by contrast, freed theorists and researchers from single-factor explanations and introduced a combinatorial model with many variables.

Life course refers to a sequence of socially defined events and roles that the individual enacts over time. It differs from the concept of the life cycle in allowing for many diverse events and roles that do not necessarily proceed in a given sequence but that constitute the sum total of the person's actual experience over time (Elder, 1975). The life course concept also allows for the encoding of historical events and social interaction outside the person as well as the age-related biological and psychological states of the organism. Researchers in the 1960s and 1970s discovered the rigidity of the earlier life cycle concepts and found repeatedly that both changing role patterns and the subjective experience of aging were not predicted by cultural ideals or an invariant developmental sequence. Concerning two concepts in particular, generation and age, a new and more complex understanding developed. What research since 1970 has shown is the relativity of both concepts and the need to supplement each with greater recognition of its multidimensionality.

Generation has in the past stood for many variables that shape the life course but perhaps most especially as the embodiment of age norms in a particular age group regardless of historical period. Newer studies showed, however, that cultural expectations or an internalized life cycle were not sufficient explanations of life pattern; rather, particular historical events and the actual ages of persons had to be taken into account. Thus, for example, Hareven's (1982) *Family Time and Industrial Time* on the textile industry in Manchester, New Hampshire, went beyond the insights of Thomas and Znaniecki (1918-1920/1927), who had assumed an invariant sequence of acculturation among the Polish peasants in America and gave little attention to either period effects or age at time of immigration.

Other generational studies also made clear that "grandparent" generations differed a great deal from each other as well as from "parent" and "grandchild" generations. Hill's (1970) work contrasting a grandparent generation married before 1915 and their children's generation born in the 1920s helped to show the importance of the historical period surrounding the parenting years and to reveal the extent to which the older generation created the intimate social relations surrounding the younger one. On the other hand, Burton and Bengtson (1985), in their study of young black grandmothers, made clear the importance of the specific age at which a person entered the parent or grandparent generation. Giving birth at a very young age resulted in the foreshortening of generations and the possibility that a very young grandmother in her 30s might not be ready to take on the grandparenting role.

  Age, in contrast to generation, has stood for the inevitable physical and mental changes in the individual that come with getting older. New studies of age norms and subjective feelings of age, however, revealed the relativity and complexity of chronological age. Neugarten and Peterson (1957) observed in the Kansas City studies of age that working class people felt older than middle class people of the same age. Neugarten and colleagues (Neugarten, 1979; Neugarten & Datan, 1973; Neugarten & Hagestad, 1976) then developed these ideas into a relativistic theory of age, noting that a woman in her 30s could be a college president and that a man in his 70s could father an infant. Similarly, Giele (1980) reviewed the emerging literature and theory on adulthood and discovered that life after youth was increasingly being thought of as decoupled from a particular age and that age crossovers were leading to a belief in adulthood as the "transcendence of age."

The realization that generation always must be linked to history and age and that subjective age is related to social roles has resulted in a new hybrid. Life course research now looks for cohort effects that are due to the interaction of age and historical period. Thus, Elder's (1974, 1986) studies on the Berkeley, Oakland, and Terman samples showed that the *age* at which children experienced their families' economic deprivation, or the *age* at which young men were drafted or experienced combat, was critical to the types of life adaptation that they would make later on. The Berkeley study children who were 8 years younger than the Oakland study children were more affected by the Depression, and the recruits who were older had their lives disrupted more seriously by their war experiences. Similarly, Giele (1982a) found that the life course patterns of Wellesley College alumnae were related not only to historical period (*year* of graduation) but also to *age* at critical events such as marriage; women who graduated in the 1930s married sooner and were less likely to become launched into careers than were women of either earlier or later cohorts.

The resulting concept of the life course has helped to operationalize the many meanings of timing and age. Sociologists once wrestled with how to distinguish the effects of the three dimensions of age: *period* (the distinctive historical and cultural events experienced by persons of a given age and cohort), *cohort* (the socially shared experience of age peers), and *age* (the biological or developmental time since the births of individuals). They finally gave up because in the case of any specific individual, all of these dimensions are perfectly correlated with each other (Rodgers, 1982). Out of their effort, however, came new insights about how to operationalize these concepts so that data on life experience would be differentiated and precise enough to analyze all three dimensions simultaneously. As was shown in Figure 1.1, these elements are related in the life course paradigm.

Period is related to location in time; cohort is one aspect of linked lives; and age, because it is a marker of individual development, is related to human agency. Finally, the life course perspective introduces a fourth dimension: timing (i.e., the medium for integrating historical, social, and individual activities). Timing can be studied through age records and dates of events in a way that permits more flexible and complex analysis because it assumes the simultaneous and interrelated nature of both socially structured and individually determined life experiences. This four-dimensional concept of life course embraces period, cohort, and age and links all of them with the dimension of timing as the common denominator for collecting data on events and chronology. Thus, the life course approach brings the social sciences to a new frontier in the study and understanding of human lives.

➤ CONCLUSION AND PLAN OF THE BOOK

This volume is the result of a new implicit codification and unification in the field of life course studies. It is now possible to go beyond the foundational elements of historical demography, sociology of age, life history, and longitudinal design to articulate methodological advancements in data collection and analysis that are specific to the life course field. Subsequent chapters take up the key elements of the new methodology and describe lessons learned, best practice, and the current state of the art. Part I outlines the way in which the field of life course research developed and the principal issues that it addresses. Part II focuses on the nature of time-coded data and ways in which to collect them. Part III concerns the various types of analysis that are appropriate at the level of the individual, group, or society.

In a vast body of recent social science scholarship, there has been a convergence over the past 50 years on several key principles for understanding the life course. After World War II, psychologists, sociologists, anthropologists, and historians all sought ways of understanding the nature of interchange between persons and their social and cultural milieux. Most common was a tripartite model in which the individual was seen as combining innate drives with cultural and interpersonal inputs to decide on personal goals and direction. That model has been superseded by a four-part image of an interdependent system of action in which the individual, group, and culture interact but with an added dimension of chronologically ordered events through which all parts of the system are linked in a dynamic way. The restated paradigm now comprises *location* in time and place (history, social structure, and culture), *linked lives* (institutions and groups), *human agency* (individual goals and sense of self), and *timing* (chronologically ordered events that simultaneously encode individual, group, and historical markers).

In describing their own crafts for conducting life studies, our contributors have independently converged on several key principles regarding the way in which to collect data. Whenever possible, life course studies should collect data on historical context (location); relationships in family and work and other social settings (linked lives); health, well-being, and subjective aspects of meaning and satisfaction (human agency); and event histories in major domains of activity (timing). It is noteworthy that the data are most useful when standardized with respect to two dimensions that permit analysis across individuals and social systems; namely, they must be coded chronologically for *time* of incidence and duration of an event, and they must be coded according to functional *domain* of activity such as family, occupation, and residential moves. It also is ideal if the data can be both qualitative (subjective, including the meaning of experience and emotional feelings) and quantitative (objective, including third-party reports and documentary evidence).

Life studies analysts also converge in their suggestions about research design. Absolutely essential is some type of longitudinal framework. Only in this way is it possible to follow the impact of earlier events and feelings on later ones and the lagged effects of interaction with a given social or institutional milieu. Thus, longitudinal design may call for some recasting of data from cross-sectional formats so that data organized by wave are reorganized into life histories for each individual. Life studies researchers also favor a combination of retrospective and prospective designs and techniques. Retrospective studies allow the recapturing of much longer periods of history from a single survey, and they are particularly useful for subjective reporting about meaning and feelings at the time of the surveys. But because of failures of human memory, they are less useful for constructing accurate pictures of surrounding social relations at distant points in time or the feelings associated with them. Prospective studies that survey groups of respondents successively over periods of years solve these problems of accuracy and memory but bring other limitations such as expense and panel attrition. The ideal is some combination of retrospective and prospective strategies.

Finally, our contributors have constructed their analytic models in similar ways. They are concerned with not only how the social context influences the individual but also how persons can change their world. But most of the examples illustrate historical influence on the individual and leave the matter of personal impact on history as theoretically possible but rarely demonstrated. Several chapters hint, however, at the possibilities for tracing the impact of individual lives on the systems of which they are a part. The 19th-century Italian town of Casalecchio was transformed by the out-migration of its inhabitants (Kertzer & Hogan, 1989). The German Life History Study has followed the differential impact of war and reunification on several different age groups but, at the same time, holds the potential for tracing the contributions of these respective groups to the rebuilding of modern Germany. Educated women who formed the backbone of the feminist movement were the product of a particular regional and cultural heritage, but they also shaped a social movement that would change laws and promote equality between women and men. Finally, the anonymous boys and girls who lived through the Depression, fought in World War II or Vietnam, or survived the farm crisis of the 1980s have in their individual ways helped to shape the social and economic eras in which they became responsible adults.

Even though the full potential of the interactive model of life course influence and historical change has not yet been fully realized, the foundation is now in place. The field of life course studies is still young. We view this book as a first step in addressing the craft of life studies. As such, these chapters have begun to codify the work that already has been done. They also map a prospective path toward the destination that life studies should aim for in the future.

Chapter 2

A Life Course Approach

Autobiographical Notes

MATILDA WHITE RILEY

M y husband, in describing our joint sociological lives, often quips, "Our first publications were on contraceptive practices (reporting our 1930s national survey); then on children's mass media behavior; then on adolescent relationships to peers, parents, and grandparents; then Matilda has been working sporadically on middle and old age, while I wrestle with the complex processes of dying." Currently, we are working collaboratively on the full life course and on the surrounding social structures, attempting to piece all ages together (e.g., Riley & Riley, 1994).

In fact, the Rileys' lives have been far less simple, and for the past four and half decades my own studies have moved in fits and starts over age as a component of both the life course and social structures. The editors requested autobiographical notes. But what can be said in a few pages about

AUTHOR'S NOTE: This chapter is a component of the Program on Age and Structural Change, directed by the author at the National Institute on Aging. The following colleagues kindly made comments on earlier versions of this chapter: Duane Alwin, Gilbert Brim, Richard Campbell, John Clausen, Dale Dannefer, Anne Foner, Alex Inkeles, Marilyn Johnson, Arne Kalleberg, David Kertzer, Katrina Johnson, Robert Merton, John Meyer, John Modell, Albert Reiss, Richard Rockwell, Lucinda SanGiovanni, Warner Schaie, Ethel Shanas, Brewster Smith, Gordon Streib, Charles Tilly, Jackson Toby, and my longtime collaborator, John W. Riley, Jr.

the perspectives accumulated in previous decades of my long life (I was born in 1911)? Or about the stimulations gleaned from interaction with numerous colleagues, ranging from our own adolescent children who helped in our studies of other adolescents to the multidisciplinary networks of scholars with whom I have collaborated in many varied activities? In subtle ways, all these experiences have influenced my intellectual life and have, in turn, influenced the intellectual lives of others (cf. Riley, 1990).

Hence, this chapter wanders widely over scattered reminiscences. These selected reminiscences are held loosely together by the central theme of the "aging and society" paradigm that has dominated my work since the late 1960s (Riley, 1994a). The crux of that paradigm is as follows: *Changing lives (aging and the succession of cohorts) are in continuing interplay with changes in society and its structures.* Neither can be understood conceptually without the other. This chapter, however, focuses mainly on one half of the paradigm—on people and their lives (a "life course" approach). It deals only indirectly with the changing social structures that shape, and are shaped by, these lives. The neglect of structure, or its treatment as a mere *contextual characteristic* of people's lives, is rampant in the literature today. I must confess that in my own early zeal for broadening the gerontological approach to cover the full life course, I (despite my own strictures [Riley & Nelson, 1971]) have until recently contributed to the general neglect of structure.

Here I touch on four sets of insights that contributed to the evolution of the paradigm, to its use in designing research on age, and, in particular, to its contribution to the study of people's lives. These autobiographical insights come from (a) an incipient awareness of the *social meanings* of age, (b) studying *phases* of the life course, (c) analysis of *cohort differences* as life course patterns interact with historical change, and (d) combining studies of lives with studies of *social structures* (each as a powerful focus in its own right).

➢ THE SOCIAL MEANINGS OF AGE: SOME PRECURSORS

Back in the 1950s, prior to our systematic focus on age as a component of both lives and structures, the sociological research methods I was teaching to students included studies of human lives. We used case examples that ranged from the diaries and letters of emigres and their families under the impact of industrialization, as analyzed in Thomas and Znaniecki's *Polish Peasant* (1918-1920/1927), to Paul Lazarsfeld's panel studies of changes over time in attitudes of voters variously located in religious, class, and other social structures (Lazarsfeld, Berelson, & Gaudet, 1944). Also at about that time, our team of researchers at Rutgers University, while studying intergenerational relationships, began to take serious note of the power of *age* as a variable.

We were alerted to the complex meanings of age by, as one example, the answers of adolescents to a 1961 survey question as to whether women, in planning their future lives, should have careers. (In the early 1960s, it was assumed that all girls expected to marry.) Our finding? Most adolescent girls, especially those who were college bound, accepted the career norm, but their male peers did not accept it for their future wives.

Prophetic Issues

This early paradox merits revisiting. Not only did the finding cause us to wonder what would happen when such girls came to marry such boys (Riley, Johnson, & Boocock, 1963) (as it turned out, the future lives of members of that particular cohort were, in fact, marked by high divorce rates), but, more important, my collaborators and I were confronted by several questions of interpretation that subsequently led to seminal principles for crafting studies of age. Four come to mind:

1. Would these gender-based norms persist as these adolescents grew older? We could then give only an uninformed answer, but the question foreshadowed the subsequently developed principle: *No single phase of a person's life can be understood apart from its antecedents and consequences* (the "life course principle").

2. Were these girls imitating their mothers as models? The answer was negative because the daughters planning careers far outnumbered the mothers working outside the home. Only much later did we comprehend a second principle: *Because society changes, members of different cohorts (born at different times) grow older in different ways* (the "cohort principle").

3. What were the sources of these marked differences between boys and girls in acceptance of the norm? One startling answer came from interviews with the parents; most wanted their daughters to express themselves in careers yet, at the same time, wanted their sons to marry wives who would stay home and look after the children. This demonstration that "expectations of

the future by significant others"[1] can be a driving force in socialization emphasized a third principle: *Each person's life is intertwined with the lives of other people, influencing and being influenced by social relationships* (the "intersecting lives principle").

4. What was the significance (for girls) of the statistical association between "planning to go to college" and "wanting a career"? This finding, at a time when levels of education were rising rapidly from one cohort to the next, called attention to the then accepted belief that education unlocks lifelong opportunities in work as in other social structures. This association between college and career presaged the central theme of the aging and society paradigm, worthy of repeating because it too often is overlooked today: *Changes in people's lives and changes in social structures are conceptually distinct but interdependent dynamisms (or sets of processes); neither can be understood without the other* (the "two dynamisms principle").

A sociologist of knowledge might inquire why such findings led us to theorize about age rather than gender. (Only much later did we realize that a theory of age must include a theory of gender.) Aware that we were witnessing dramatic changes in gender roles, we were eager to learn how then current adolescent norms derived from the past and where they would lead in the future. We began to ask questions about how these adolescents would progress through their lives and why their generation differed from that of their parents. We came to the realization, all those decades ago, that age is *dynamic*. Beyond that, it was accident of funding that turned our major attention to the need for a *sociology* of age. The grant[2] for continuing our intergenerational research (cf. Riley, 1994a) required, as an "aside," that we summarize existing social science findings on the middle and later years. That aside prompted seven of us to spend 5 years on an "inventory" of those findings (Volume 1 of *Aging and Society* [Riley, Foner, Moore, Hess, & Roth, 1968], with Johnson and Schein).

Emerging Theory of Age

Not until the late 1960s did the four principles (and others) for research on age begin to take shape, initiating our long-term attempt to set out a paradigm, or analytical framework, for designing studies of age and interpreting the findings. This paradigm, which (as John Modell suggests) grew out of the general sociological search for a non-Marxian replacement for functionalism, aims at parsimonious selection, definition, and integration of concepts ("ideal types") as a heuristic model.

The axiomatic sociological bases of the paradigm (i.e., the emphases on *dynamics* and *social systems*) already had been formulated in the crucible of my previous experiences. Among them were experiences in the 1930s in working with Pitirim Sorokin's social and cultural dynamics; experiences in working with Talcott Parsons on people and social structures as systemically interdependent (at both societal and individual levels and including both overt actions and subjective orientations); experiences in finding the common elements in many sociological frameworks, as specified in my textbook on *Sociological Research* (Riley, 1963), for which Robert Merton contributed as many editorial and theoretical comments as there were pages in the manuscript; experiences with Bernard Barber and Alex Inkeles, who encouraged me to write a chapter on "Stability and Change in Social Systems" (Riley & Nelson, 1971) to counter the prevailing notion that social systems are intrinsically static; and other experiences too manifold to be identified here.

Such sociological formulations already were in hand when a group of us, in confronting the mass of empirical findings for the first volume of *Aging and Society*, found no cumulative body of theory to explain the great power of *age* as a variable in research. Attempting to fill this gap, we moved on to the conceptual and methodological Volume 3 of *Aging and Society* (Riley, Johnson, & Foner, 1972a) and began the development, which still is continuing, of the aging and society paradigm. We first called it an "age stratification" paradigm but later abandoned that term as too static, too easily confused with class stratification, and failing to symbolize both people and structures.

Emphasis on Lives

Our Volume 3 included the statement, "Over the life course, individuals enter certain roles but relinquish others, acquire certain capacities and motivations but lose others" (Riley et al., 1972a, p. 10). Thus, a life course approach was specified in this early announcement, although age was identified emphatically there as an element *both* in people's lives and in the surrounding social roles and social structures (e.g., families, firms, communities, friendship groups). Later in the present chapter, this dual identification is brought back to attention as essential to the agenda for future studies of age.

Relevant to the immediate concern of the present book with studying lives, our 1972 collaborative book illustrated methods of research in domains such as the polity (Anne Foner), friendship (Beth Hess), education (Talcott Parsons and Gerald Platt), and science (Harriet Zuckerman and Robert Merton), and it included an entire chapter by John Clausen on "The Life Course of Individuals" (Clausen, 1972). It compared our formulations to the earlier works of Mannheim, Sorokin, Cain, Ryder, Brim, and others and to the innovative models of Warner Schaie, Paul Baltes, and the emerging school of "life-span psychology" (although we abjured their use of "life span" because of its technical meaning in demography).

The focus of the aging and society paradigm on people's lives provided guidelines in the 1970s and 1980s for many of the far-flung examinations of the full life course that were countering the exclusive concern with either gerontology or child development. It set the stage for the influential work of the Social Science Research Council's (SSRC) Life Course Committee (Abeles & Riley, 1977), composed of sociologists, psychologists, and biologists. (Glen Elder, coeditor of the present volume, became a member.) The paradigm led directly to two symposium volumes, published by the American Association for the Advancement of Science, titled *Aging From Birth to Death* (Riley, 1979; Riley, Abeles, & Teitelbaum, 1982), in which we attempted (but failed) to redefine the verb *aging* to refer to the entire life course just as the noun *age* refers to all ages.[3] In these two volumes, scientists discussed many aspects of the full life course from multidisciplinary, historical, futurist, and cross-cultural perspectives. In the decade of the 1980s, the paradigm was translated into an agenda for the Behavioral and Social Research program at the National Institute on Aging (NIA), a program that spurred literally hundreds of researchers from multiple disciplines, with varied persuasions and often using paradigms of their own, to try out new methods and to explore diverse aspects of human lives (Riley & Abeles, 1990).

Probing the Meanings of Age

Looking back over the efforts of these decades from 1950 to 1990 and the developing agenda for the 1990s, what insights from my experiences and those of my collaborators might be useful for "crafting life studies" in the future? What can be learned from our iterative procedures of continually working back and forth between theory and empirical findings? What bits and pieces accrue from our own work in the field? Or from our critical reanalyses of the findings of others (exemplified in that 1968 inventory of literally hundreds of findings)? Or from the advice of critics? How do the early insights accord with the recent massive outpourings of research on the life course? How can they offset the current overemphasis on lives to the detriment of structures? And how can all such insights contribute to the combined future efforts of the social science communities to build a cumulative body of knowledge about age, a worthy goal exemplified in the present book? These questions prompt the necessarily rambling account that follows.

➤ INSIGHTS FROM STUDYING PHASES
OF THE LIFE COURSE

Reminiscences of our practical experiences in studying age in the life course began with selected phases (or stages) of people's lives. Research methods adapted to particular phases were essential to our efforts to apply the full life course principle—that the phases of a person's life are interrelated. Our own research efforts here were stimulated by (as they also stimulated) the works of others. Clausen, the progenitor of the longitudinal approach to the life course, had brought together the existing data sets in the Institute for Human Development at the University of California, Berkeley, and was beginning his long demonstration of the validity of this principle (which was to culminate in his book on *American Lives* [Clausen, 1993]). Elder, who published his classic *Children of the Great Depression* more than 20 years ago (Elder, 1974), had begun his career of research and teaching on the life course. My 1972 detailed exegesis of problems of research on age in the often overlooked appendix to Volume 3 of *Aging and Society* (Riley et al., 1972a, pp. 584-618), although focused primarily on old age, began by setting a broad stage:

> Understanding the place of age in society requires research that is far-flung across time and space. In studies of fruit flies or rats, an investigator can comprehend the processes of aging and cohort succession over a small fraction of his [or her] own lifetime, and under controlled environmental conditions. In studies of human beings, however, the respondent and the

researcher age at the same chronological pace; and environmental conditions—far from being readily controllable—are inseparable from historical and cultural diversity. (p. 584)

Fitting the Approach to Particular Phases

Among our early explorations into the study of the full life course were adaptations of our general research approaches (Riley, 1963, 1990) to the differing characteristics of people at particular ages, notably older people and children.

Old age. The 1972 appendix showed specifically how to apply principles of research design developed over long years of research in other areas, and it quoted liberally from the methodologists of that day (Riley et al., 1972a, pp. 584-618). Not yet dreamed of in 1972 were the "computer-assisted interviews" or the "event history analyses" described in the present volume by Brückner and Mayer (Chapter 7) and others. But many of the problems and solutions described in that appendix still are relevant for applying modern techniques to studies of old age within a life course framework. Among the topics discussed were older people's anachronistic interpretation of the meanings of questions, the frequent need for "proxy interviewers" (citing Shanas, 1968), the vulnerability to sample bias because of high mortality rates at the later ages, and the problems (as Maddox, 1962, put it in describing the groundbreaking Duke Longitudinal Study) of getting elderly respondents back to the clinic for a series of repeated examinations. We also found another widespread problem, unthinkable today, of treating age as if it were an experimental variable; thus, older patients frequently were compared to their youthful doctors with seemingly complete unawareness that the numerous associated factors could not be randomized.

That appendix also included an early discussion of the "age-period-cohort" problem that perennially has tortured dozens of efforts to use just two measures, date and chronological age, to index three different concepts. As one example,

a characteristic—such as income from earnings—may be affected by differences in the value of labor due to age and experience, by increases in the wage levels at which each new cohort starts its work career, and by historical variations in inflationary pressures impinging upon all age strata simultaneously. (Riley et al., 1972a, p. 608)

In deciding which of the three factors are operating, possible procedures based exclusively on age and date were described as requiring additional knowledge or assumptions. (On rereading, the discussions in that appendix were far murkier than those in the "Mathematical Note" by Cohn (1972) in the same volume (pp. 85-88), which has become a classic [see also Blalock, 1967].) More important, the appendix emphasized the still pertinent advice that, instead of statistical manipulation, the most suitable approach is to *specify and measure directly* each of the theoretical variables involved (Riley et al., 1972a, p. 610; for more recent formulations, see Ryder, 1979; Riley, Foner, & Waring, 1988).

Childhood. Although research on child development had antedated the great flood of studies of older people, we were concerned that childhood was only slowly being incorporated into studies of the full life course. I well remember our attempt at Bowdoin College in the 1970s to explore whether children, in parallel with old people, saw little opportunity to be "useful" or "respected" in their families. Obviously, the field procedures suitable for the elderly could not be transferred intact to 5-year-olds. As a consequence, with support from my Russell Sage Foundation colleague, Sarane Boocock, we trained 11-year-olds as interviewers. Each was equipped with a tape recorder (a novelty to the children in those days), and, for safety, we acted as unobtrusive observers. The experiment was a great success. The little children, with no adult to threaten them, expatiated on their lives, reporting in general that they were given scant responsibility or opportunity "to help." And the older children throve in their role as interviewers (for which they were duly paid). Thus, we learned how children can study children.

Our broader understanding of systematic methods of incorporating childhood into life course studies was greatly influenced by the early analysts of the Berkeley data (see also Robins, 1966) and more broadly by Brim and Kagan's (1980) volume, *Constancy and Change in Human Development.* The several chapters in that volume demonstrated both consistency and variability across the life course in wide-ranging domains such as physical growth, health, cognitive development, personality, social attitudes and beliefs, occupational careers, psychoses, and criminal behavior (for more recent examples of cross-age linkages, we note, e.g., Elder, Modell, & Parke, 1993).

Middle age. As a life stage deserving special research techniques, the long years linking childhood with old age have only recently[4] been given the serious attention devoted to childhood and old age. Spearheading the investigation of this link, Bert Brim began writing about "adult socialization" in the 1960s and created an SSRC Committee on Work and Personality in the Middle Years (1972-1979), which influenced much subsequent work (among its members were Janet Giele, Paul Baltes, and myself). The tenor of the varied concerns in this area is reflected, as one example, in my memories of a week-long conference in Aspen, Colorado, that I attended with my husband, Jack, back in 1977. That conference dwelt on the need for analyses of the middle years from psychological, sociological, economic, medical, and biological perspectives. Problems of the middle years, noted by my Russell Sage Foundation colleague, Joan Waring, in her conference report (Waring, 1978), have "their origins in years gone by and will have consequences for the years ahead" (p. 59). Furthermore, her report continued, "by examining middle age from a life course perspective, the conference sought to find crucial linkages between all life stages so that intervention strategies to reduce stress and prevent problems could come into focus" (p. 3). In emphasizing the full life course principle, that conference (like many aspects of my experience at the National Institutes of Health), also provided a cogent reminder to social scientists of the often forgotten point that aging is a biological, as well as a social and psychological, process (the "biopsychosocial principle").

Fitting Lives Together

Quite a different set of reminiscences relate to the intersecting lives principle and our development of sociological methods, unique at that time, for studying *dyadic relationships* as the smallest unit in social structure. In our 1950s collaborative research at Rutgers University, prior to our focus on age, we were concerned with interpersonal relationships—how adolescents responded to conflicting expectations by their parents versus their peers, for example, or to subtle controls by peer groups. Accordingly, we developed methods for studying subjective aspects of relationships between pairs of individuals, or "dyads," and for fitting these dyads together to examine collective orientations among members of the group as a whole (M. Riley, Cohn, Toby, & J. Riley, 1954). In line with the thinking of

Heider, Festinger, and Newcomb, we explored questions such as the following. If A likes B and expects B to like her, then does B reciprocate the friendship? Is this reciprocation especially unlikely if A is accorded less status by the peer group than is B? Unreciprocated expectations, we surmised, were subject to strain and instability.

But this hypothesis of instability brought us up short; it could be tested only through repeated questioning of the same pairs of respondents at future points in time (Riley et al., 1954, p. 720). Our findings were static. Indeed, as late as 1987, Brewster Smith (a member of our SSRC Life Course Committee), in commenting on the perspectives of leading social psychologists assembled by my NIA colleague, Ronald Abeles, noted "a wide gap between life-span research and mainstream social psychology" (Smith, 1987, p. xi). In the meantime, we kept pushing toward a life course approach to intersecting lives that would be dynamic rather than static. We finally succeeded in defining, at least in principle, how panel analyses could be used to study changes in these interpersonal relationships over the lives of the people involved (Riley, 1963, Unit 12). Given the computer inadequacies of those days, we could not implement in practice this principle of changing dyadic relationships, and the principle still seems worthy of reconsideration for the future life course agenda.

More recently, in quite another variant of research on intersecting lives, we have called attention to research on "counterpart transitions"[5] (Riley et al., 1988, p. 253), in which individuals who move from one role to another over the life course produce role transitions for their significant others as well. For example, one person's marriage or divorce alters the lives of others in the family; a husband's retirement affects the timing of his wife's retirement; or, in historical accounts of Western Europe, the death of an older farmer controlled the marriage and the independence of the sons and their families. As we noted back in 1968 (Riley et al., 1968), the finding that "a husband and wife today survive together for a longer period . . . than a husband and wife of an earlier era" raised questions about the transitional middle years as a possible training period for family relationships in the later years (p. 10).

Fitting Phases Together

Apart from dynamic analysis of relationships between lives, we gave much attention to problems of fitting together the phases of single lives through longitudinal (or panel) analysis of the life course as a whole. I do not allude to several issues that concerned us because they are discussed elsewhere in this volume—secondary analysis versus new research (Elder & Pellerin [Chapter 11]), retrospective versus prospective studies (Scott & Alwin [Chapter 5]), and qualitative versus quantitative data (Laub & Sampson [Chapter 9]). Just one insight is worthy of note here because it defines the widely misunderstood relationship of *time* to longitudinal analysis of the full life course.

Lives and time. Two simplistic metaphors, schematized in Figure 2.1, illustrate the point that, although formulated in our 1972 book (Riley et al., 1972a), often remains forgotten. The top panel (a) shows a "ladder" that marks off age-graded roles and social structures at a single period of time (1980 in this instance). But this *vertical* ladder does *not* describe the process of aging (growing up and growing older) over people's lives. A slightly more accurate metaphor for aging is the "escalator" shown in the bottom panel (b). An escalator suggests how, as people age, they move *diagonally* upward with age and *across* time (in this figure of speech, they move through different social scenery). Perhaps this seems obvious. People 45 years old in 1980, for example, were born in 1935 in the aftermath of the Depression and the prelude to World War II; these people will not be 65 years old until the year 2000, when the world predictably will have changed and the surrounding structures will be quite different.

Nevertheless, the full implications of this point are far more complex than Figure 2.1 can suggest, as we later discovered, because, unlike the static floor over which the escalator is moving, the social structures surrounding people's lives—at work, in the home, in the community, and in the society—are themselves continually changing. This difference in the way in which time is built into the diagonal line (the life course) and the vertical line (cross-sectional arrangement of age-related structures) led us to define certain *fallacies* and to introduce the concept of "asynchrony" (as discussed later in this chapter), and it also pointed to special problems of interpreting longitudinal (and panel) data.

Longitudinal and quasi-longitudinal designs. Our own plans for sustained longitudinal follow-up of the Rutgers samples of adolescents and their parents were foiled by lack of funding. But by mid-century, we were examining a few studies in the United States and abroad that demonstrated

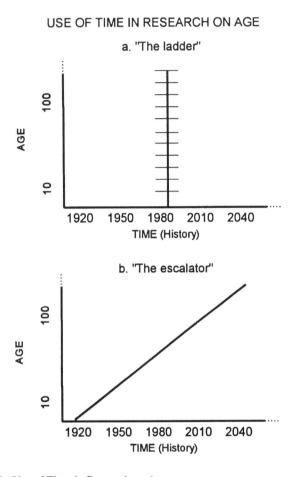

USE OF TIME IN RESEARCH ON AGE

Figure 2.1. Use of Time in Research on Age

the feasibility of tracing the *same* people over large segments of their lives. Such early longitudinal studies included the Framingham Heart Study, which has now followed community residents for more than four decades; the Seattle Longitudinal Study, in which Warner Schaie (cf. Schaie, Willis, & O'Hanlon, 1994) began in 1956 to trace the process of intellectual aging; and Clausen's (1993) *American Lives,* which analyzes influences on the lives of several hundred children born in the 1920s who have now reached old age.

However, aware of many obstacles that beset most attempts to study entire lives longitudinally, as early as 1968 we took note of the need for "devices for offsetting the practical difficulty of the adult researcher who will not himself survive long enough to observe the entire lifetime of even a single cohort" (Riley et al., 1968, p. 10). We examined the use of "synthetic cohorts" or other substitute designs that piece together phases of the lives of a cross section of people who differ in age (see Campbell, 1994). In effect, we saw such quasi-longitudinal studies as applying the ladder design rather than the escalator design. These pieced-together lives cannot be interpreted directly because different people, born at different periods of time, are involved in the several rungs of the ladder. These people belong to different birth cohorts with differing life course experiences. They do not "climb" vertically from one age to the next within a single period of time. Therefore, as we recognized early, special problems of interpretation require outside knowledge or assumptions about how these cohorts have aged "at different times, in different places, and [under] different conditions" (Riley et al., 1968, p. 9). Even recently, Maddox (1993), while complimenting the impressive Berlin Aging Study for its attention to potential cohort differences (as well as age differences), still cautioned that "readers must wait to discover how the issue of cohort differences is taken into account in subsequent reports" as the panel is reinterviewed in the future (p. 476).

➤ INSIGHTS FROM COHORT ANALYSES

Prompted by numerous conflicting interpretations of similar sets of longitudinal data (evident in the inventory), and prior to the awareness generated by the "baby boom cohorts," the need for cohort analysis was brought home to us. Hence, we set out to explore the nature and implications of cohort differences as evidence of the linkage of lives to societal change. As an aid in dispelling the confusion, we recognized that the space in the bottom panel (b) of Figure 2.1 included not only one diagonal but many because in every society cohorts of people are continually being born, aging, dying, and replacing each other. Cohort analysis, then, involves comparing selected diagonals and seeking clues in the course of history to their differences (or similarities). In practice, we learned how to do cohort analysis through collaboration with a medical doctor, Mervyn Susser, who translated from epidemiology many details of this method as needed by social scientists (Susser, 1969). He showed, for example, how mapping the occurrence of particular diseases by age and cohort could provide clues to the nature of etiology and pathogenesis and could point to sources of vulnerability in lifestyles, poisonous environments, and the like. In a somewhat similar vein, the link between lives and historical events has been the "guiding theme" of Elder's influential approach to life course research since the 1960s (see Chapter 11 of this volume).

Evidence of Cohort Differences

By comparing selected cohorts, numerous contemporary cohort differences were identified in the 1980s. For example, members of cohorts then old differ from those who grew old in the past in respect to educational level, family history, work history, diet and exercise, exposure to acute versus chronic diseases, standard of living, number of years in retirement, and (perhaps most significant) number of years they can expect to survive. Moreover, as biologist Huber Warner, my NIA colleague, helped us to make clear, such cohort differences in the ways in which people age "cannot be explained by evolutionary changes in the human genome, which remains much the same from cohort to cohort. . . . [Instead,] they result from the interplay between a relatively unchanging genetic background and a continually changing society" (Riley & Abeles, 1990, p. iii). Our endless harangues finally were successful (the medical profession was especially resistant) in establishing the now accepted cohort principle. It bears repeating here: *Because society changes, members of different cohorts cannot age in precisely the same way.*

Some Fallacies

Use of this cohort principle (and the escalator metaphor) helped us to explode false stereotypes by defining several fallacies (Riley, 1973), which have now become familiar watchwords in research on the life course. One was the *"life course fallacy,"* that is, erroneously interpreting cross-sectional age differences as if they referred to the process of aging. Such misinterpretations were ubiquitous in the 1960s and 1970s, engendering false beliefs and self-fulfilling prophecies (to use Merton's term) about the inevitability of decline with aging. Today, however, this fallacy is generally avoided.

Also identified early was the *"fallacy of cohort-centrism"* (Riley, 1978), that is, erroneously assuming that members of all cohorts will grow older in the same fashion as members of our own cohort. Indicative of the subsequent advances in life course research is the irony that full awareness of cohort-centrism stemmed from the 1972 chapter on "The Life Course of Individuals" by the same Clausen (1972) whose subsequent work has now become the exemplar. In his initial formulation, however, several principles of the life course were abstracted from a single cohort only. (And they were abstracted from the lives of men, not women, in that cohort. That the related "gender differences principle" in the life course still is flouted today is illustrated by the astounding fact that, until recently corrected, most major studies by the NIH were based exclusively on the lives of men.) Today, much life course research still is largely ahistorical, and cohort-centrism remains a threat unless historical and anthropological perspectives are incorporated into the approach, as they are in this book. Tilly (1992) dramatized recognition of the point: "Sociology without history resembles a Hollywood set: great scenes, sometimes brilliantly painted, with nothing and nobody behind them" (p. 1).

➤ INSIGHTS FROM STUDYING LIVES AND STRUCTURES

The cohort differences discussed so far refer to lives of *people* and their link to macro-level societal trends and events (history). Back in 1968, we also had stressed the research need for "disentangling life cycle changes from social change" (Riley et al., 1968, p. 10). Several subsequent developments of our paradigm went still further; they emphasized how lives relate not only to the larger society but also to smaller *groups* within the society. My final set of reminiscences highlights how the surrounding social structures and institutions at all levels—macro, meso, and micro—influence, and are influenced by, people's lives. In particular, the accumulating body of ideas and findings required bringing together the two dynamisms, changing lives and changing structures, and studying the two as not only interdependent but also distinct, as each dynamism follows its own time schedules and its own principles of change.

Impact of Structures on Lives

That people are influenced by structures is, of course, a sociological truism. But how do age and the life course fit in? A dramatic illustration was developed by one of my students, Lucinda SanGiovanni, in her book on *Ex-Nuns* (SanGiovanni, 1978). As teenagers, the women she studied had withdrawn from the usual structures of lay society to enter the special role created by the convent. In this role, they aged differently from their secular peers. Later, when they left the convent as mature women, they were totally unprepared to resume life where they had left off—at 17 years of age. They had to learn, and learn fast, the usual adult roles—consumer, worker, friend, or lover. Without having an adolescence, they had missed the socializing power of the structures in the lay society.

This power of structures over lives has been specified repeatedly by many findings about older people from intervention studies in our program at the NIA (Riley & Abeles, 1990). For example,

- cognitive functioning can be improved *if* . . .
- porous bone mass can be reconstituted *if* . . .
- memory loss can be recovered *if* . . .
- productivity can be increased *if* . . .

In all such instances, the "if" is found in the surrounding social structures— firms, families, friendship groups, nursing homes, and the like. The many findings persistently have demanded answers to the largely neglected structural questions. How do structures change (or remain stable)? And how, in real life outside the laboratory, might such structures *be* altered to enhance health and functioning throughout the life course?

Structures as Mediators

One strategic insight into the study of structural change came from some of our very early work on social systems in another field, mass communications (Riley & Riley, 1959). There we learned the principle of the "two-step flow" of influence (Katz & Lazarsfeld, 1956), a principle that has been confirmed in subsequent studies of people's lives—that macro-level forces exert full influence on individuals as they are screened and reinforced through primary groups. The general significance for the aging and society paradigm can be illustrated, for example, by Elder's allusions to smaller structures as mediating the interplay between societal-level events and individual lives. Thus, Elder (1974) found that the effects of the Depression on the lives of children varied with the degree of economic deprivation of their *families*; or that the repercussions on *family* patterns and resources were more traumatic for children who were younger, rather than older, at the time of the Depression (Elder & Rockwell, 1979); or that a war affects many future lives when military service interrupts *schooling* and *occupational careers* and delays *marriage and parenthood* (Elder, 1986) with reciprocal consequences for the social structures involved. These findings imply an aspect of our dynamism of changing structures that we now want to underscore: that *meso-level structures often mediate* the "intersection of personal and social history" to which this book is addressed. The linkages in our paradigm are not simply between macro and micro "levels" but constitute interdependence among structures and people at all levels of the system.

Impact of Lives on Structures

Such studies of the impact of structures on lives deal with just one direction of the two-way dynamism of changing structures given that changes in the collective patterns of people's lives can, in turn, have reciprocal effects on structures, whether large or small (Riley, 1979, p. 4). One insight into the nature of this process came from a remarkable example (so arresting that we often have repeated it). We uncovered historical data on the work lives of successive cohorts of U.S. women spanning an entire century that reveal a consistent and striking transformation: In *each* more recent cohort, larger and larger proportions of women have spent their adult lives in the labor force. From generation to generation, this wave has mounted until, with the changes in lives, structures also began to change. As women in those early cohorts demonstrated what they could do, more and more work roles opened up for them at every age up to retirement. Gradually, the norms changed as well (we coined a name for this mechanism: "cohort norm formation" [Riley, 1978]). First it became acceptable for women to work. Now it often is expected, even required, that women (at all income levels), even young mothers, *should* work. Clearly, changes in the individual lives of millions of women in successive cohorts (and their employers) have revolutionized both work and family structures.

In such ways, we have shown how behaviors and attitudes that develop in particular cohorts, in response to social change, can become institution- alized as new norms and altered structures. As the alterations pervade all age strata, they will, in turn, affect the lives of everyone. Giele's chapter in this volume (Chapter 10) illustrates and specifies the power of this mecha- nism of cohort norm formation as she brings to bear her early studies of the impact on women's lives of the movements for women's suffrage and temperance (cf. Giele, 1993).

Bringing in Structural Change

In the continuing dialectic between changing lives and changing structures, it is not only lives that change; structures also change. Full understanding of how lives change (as in the life course approach) also requires understanding the processes of change in the surrounding struc- tures. This poses a persistent research problem: how to study the interre- lated changes in *two* research units—both individuals and the surrounding structures. The problem is not new. I once worked out a detailed formula- tion of the problem, with a primitive solution, for a proposed volume by Lazarsfeld on panel analysis. But Lazarsfeld simply could not subsume my formulation in his own thinking; indeed, he said, "Matilda, you are forcing me to call my psychiatrist"—and that book never was published.

One recent insight into the nature of this problem comes from Streib's (1993) research on retirement communities. Streib demonstrated that the characteristics and experiences of residents in these communities depend not only on the residents but also on the "adaptability, vitality, and long- range survival" of the community itself (p. 417). Most studies of retirement communities focus exclusively on the residents, often erroneously portray- ing them as enjoying a largely placid leisure lifestyle. But studies of residents alone can be misleading. They cannot explain how the inner workings of particular communities may result in failure to meet the needs of some residents' leisure or health care facilities, for example. They also ignore the external sources of structural change such as the labor supply, mortgage rates, and shifts in the local population.[6]

Streib (1993) countered with an agenda for complementary studies that use retirement communities as the research unit. Just as residents grow older over time and new cohorts are recruited, structures also move through "stages"—social, economic, and physical. The ways in which particular communities move through these stages depend, for example, on competition with rival housing opportunities for older people. Thus, a community in a "mature" stage may lose its viability if a newer community is organized that attracts younger, more recent retirees. Understanding how communities change can lead, in turn, to deeper insights into the human lives involved.

Models for Linked Analyses

Streib's (1993) example of using samples of communities to explore links between changes in lives and changes in the groups to which these people belong is evocative of newly developing research models made possible by modern computers.[7]

Types of approach. Some of these models can be defined in terms of a rudimentary typology of dynamic research approaches set out in our two-volume textbook on *Sociological Research,* now more than 30 years old (Riley, 1963, pp. 702, 728-730). (We were encouraged at the time by James Coleman and Robert Merton, if not by Lazarsfeld.) Three of the types, when extended longitudinally over time, are relevant for life course research:

- One type (a "constituent" approach[8]) uses the group as the research unit but characterizes groups by properties of the individual members (and by other group-level properties).
- A second type (a "contextual" approach) uses the individual as the research unit but characterizes individuals by properties of the groups to which they belong (and by other individual-level properties).
- A third type (a "social system" approach) uses both groups and individuals as research units and identifies *which* individuals belong to *which* groups. Thus, it combines the advantages of the other two types.

Suggestive examples. This typology has been illustrated in David Kertzer's work on the impact of industrialization over six decades of Italian history (see Karweit & Kertzer's chapter in this volume [Chapter 4]). Karweit and Kertzer's procedure traces the interplay between alterations in *households* and alterations in the lives of their *members* as they grow older, thereby shedding entirely new light on the intricate relationships between individual demographic events and ever-changing household composition.

Karweit and Kertzer's accomplishments derive from innovative use of a remarkable data set. There are separate event history files for each individual and for each household, and the files are cross-linked by identifying (by its own key) every individual and every household. Using these sets of files simultaneously, alternative approaches are then employed for particular analyses. As in our constituent approach, they can focus on the level of groups, examining how individual members are involved in the dynamism of structural change. Alternatively, as in the contextual approach, they can focus on individual lives to see how groups are implicated in the dynamism of individual change. More important for the aging and society paradigm, by putting the two together (our social system approach), they can redirect the analysis back and forth to explore the interplay between the higher level groups and the lower level individuals.

This may be a rare example given that the boundaries of the research area were clearly defined, the groups were small, and few households or individuals were excluded from the sample. Parallel opportunities for full social system analyses may not be impossible, however, as evidenced by the prospective longitudinal study of lives, as related to the changing neighborhoods within the city of Chicago, that is directed by Felton Earls and Albert Reiss. This large-scale multidisciplinary investigation divides Chicago into 80 neighborhoods and, within each neighborhood, samples individual respondents ranging in age from neonatal to 24 years. By tracing the changes (or stabilities) over 8 future years, the investigators can explore the independent and interaction effects of both neighborhood- and individual-level variables (A. Reiss, personal communication, 1992).

In still another example, Kalleberg and Rockwell (1995) designed two alternative plans for combining data on firms and on their employees. Each plan involves two steps, and each has the advantage of bringing the two levels into juxtaposition. When the major research focus is on groups, they begin with data on a sample of firms and then collect information about those workers whose lives are at that time contained within these groups. Alternatively, when the research objective focuses primarily on individuals, they begin with a sample of employees and then survey those firms to which these individuals belong.

Other variants of my early typology also come to attention that provide part, but not all, of the information needed for the social system approach. Most familiar in life course research are *contextual analyses* as used, for example, in studies of workers in the United States and other countries and in the Health and Retirement Study supported by the NIA. Here information is gathered about the firms in which workers are employed and is then treated as a *contextual characteristic of individual employees.* In an early example (although not longitudinal), Lazarsfeld and Thielens (1958, p. 147) classified colleges according to whether faculty attitudes were mainly permissive or conservative and then used this *group*-level variable as a contextual characteristic of *individual* faculty members in relationship to their satisfaction with faculty relations.[9] Useful as they are, however, most contextual analyses do not provide full information about how the firms, colleges, or other structures operate and change or how they interact with changes in individual lives.

At present, such attempts to combine studies of lives with studies of structures are preliminary. High on our continuing aging and society agenda are efforts to encourage wider use of existing approaches, to stimulate development of new methods, and to formulate the research questions that can (and cannot) be addressed by each approach.

Understanding Asynchrony

Perhaps most provocative of the methods that we currently hope to stimulate are those that take into account not only the interplay between the two dynamisms but also their "asynchrony" or paradox of timing; while aging individuals move along the axis of the life course, changes in work, the family, education, and other social structures proceed along their own axis of historical time (Riley et al., 1972a, p. 516). As suggested by filling in the details of Figure 2.1 earlier, the diagonals that mark the lifetimes of successive cohorts of people are continually criss-crossing the vertical arrangements of age structures that move concurrently across history. It is this asynchrony that produces a recurring mismatch or lag of one dynamism behind the other. For example, we have shown how contemporary industrial societies suffer from "structural lag" (Riley, Kahn, & Foner, 1994); lives have been changing rapidly throughout the 20th century, but the social structures are vestigial remains of the 19th century when most people died before their last child had left home. Today, structural arrangements are constraining the life course, allocating most education to the early years of life and reserving most "free time" for the recently added years of later life, while crowding the double burdens of work and family (particularly for women) into the middle years (as noted in Laslett, 1991). Lives cannot be fully understood or intelligently enhanced without deeper understanding of structures.

➢ FOR THE FUTURE AGENDA

As I reflect on these autobiographical notes, one conclusion is obvious: Research on people's lives is far more advanced today than is research on the structural changes as they interact with these lives. The current emphasis on lives, which largely neglects the social structural dynamism, portends a possible *life course reductionism* (cf. Dannefer's [1984] "ontogenetic reductionism"). Unfortunately, our own early efforts toward a life course approach may well have fortified this encroachment on the developing aging and society paradigm, obscuring its transcendent interplay between the two dynamisms. In recent years, most students of age and aging have been caught up in research on people's lives, and age-related structural changes, if heeded at all, have been largely reduced to contextual characteristics of individuals. My colleague, Dale Dannefer, who once studied social systems with me, stated my own convictions when he defined "social context" as not only a powerful organizer of individual developmental patterns but also a set of social system processes that "are themselves organized: self-generating and self-perpetuating in systemic ways" (Dannefer, 1992, pp. 90-91).

The danger of life course reductionism cries out for attention, and already there are signs that the balance is being redressed. The need for complementary studies of changing structures is increasingly recognized by leaders in institutes established under the life course rubric including Phyllis Moen, John Myles, Warner Schaie, and Karl Ulrich Mayer (cf. Mayer & Tuma, 1990, and Mayer & Brückner's chapter in this volume [Chapter 7]). In preparing the later waves of the new Health and Retirement Survey, researchers at the University of Michigan (Thomas Juster) and at the NIA (Richard Suzman) already are contemplating supplementary studies based on firms. My own future agenda in the Program on Age and

Structural Change (PASC) is concentrating heavily on the neglected dynamism. This program (underway at the NIA) involves an international PASC network of scholars who are amplifying the existing conceptual framework and developing related research methods for exploring the structural opportunities and constraints that affect the quality of aging from birth to death (Riley, 1994a).

I end these autobiographical notes with the theme with which I began—by insisting on the dual identification of age with *both* people's lives and the surrounding social structures. Looking toward the next set of experiences, I believe that leaders in the field, members of the PASC network, and books like this one will help transform and enlarge the best features of what we call the aging and society paradigm. I believe they will identify a common approach to *both* changing lives and changing structures.

➢ NOTES

1. For further details of these Rutgers studies, see Johnson (1976) and Rosow (1967).

2. Funding was provided by the Ford Foundation through a grant to Russell Sage Foundation under the direction of Donald Young and Orville G. Brim, Jr.

3. As Marilyn Johnson points out, the truncated definition of "aging" has been deleterious for both sociological analysis and the design of social policy. Issues of allocation of health resources in the United States provide an example in the sociology of knowledge of how concepts of the life course affect policy positions.

4. An example is the current work of Orville G. Brim, Jr., director of the MacArthur Foundation Research Network on Successful Midlife Development.

5. This term was coined by Riley and Waring (1976) during the attempt, contrary to our convictions, to define old age as a "social problem."

6. To be sure, studies based solely on communities also can be misleading. They exclude from the sample those needy nonresidents for whom no suitable retirement community is available or who have been compelled to move because of the institution's financial failure.

7. As reported in my address to the 1993 Biennial Meeting of Official Representatives to the Inter-university Consortium of Political and Social Research at the University of Michigan, Ann Arbor, October.

8. In my early textbook formulation, this type was termed "structural."

9. Compare the analysis of pension and retiree health insurance plans of firms that call for a contextual analysis of retirement behavior of employees in these firms (Clark, Ghent, & Headen, 1994).

Chapter 3

The Craft of Life Course Studies

ANGELA M. O'RAND

Life course research in the 20th century has been driven by the productive tension between traditional humanistic interests in the quality and course of human lives as they are lived, on the one hand, and disciplinary and technical developments in the social sciences that have improved the precision of observation and analysis, on the other. Although the long coexistence of these two concerns in some social sciences occasionally may have developed into rivalries yielding episodes of divisiveness and animosity (e.g., Smith's [1994] recent history of sociology in the 1920s and 1930s), their joint contributions to life course research today are readily identifiable. This chapter examines several contemporary features of the *practice of life course research* that reflect the dual influence of humanistic and technical goals and that contribute to the progressive development of the life course perspective. The emphasis on practice is distinctive in its focus on how some life course researchers have gone about finding and solving problems as opposed to how they should or should not have conducted their research.

The humanistic and technical strands of the development of life course research were illustrated by the first two chapters of this volume. In Chapter 1, Giele and Elder provided an overview of the conceptual and methodological development of the life course perspective over the past three decades. The emergent paradigmatic elements of this perspective—human agency, social relations, sociotemporal location, and timing—integrate several disciplinary heritages to address the questions of how human lives develop in historical context and how human lives, as lived, impel historical change. Psychological, sociological, historical, and demographic concepts and methods are woven into the life course project and constitute both its distinctiveness and its broad scope. Giele and Elder portray the rational strand of this development with efforts toward codification, formalization, and coherent theory. In Chapter 2, Riley presented a scholar's account of a period and of the fruitful conjunction of institutional arrangements, social connections, and individual agency in the construction of the life course perspective. This account of the origins and development of life course research reveals the mutual influence of the rational or codified and the humanistic or noncodified; as such, it is a self-exemplifying case of the life course project.

My assignment for this volume is to reflect on these accounts and on the others presented later in the volume from a sociology of science perspective. I do so by turning first to Merton's observations of the practice of social research and then to other sociologists of science who have studied different scientific contexts from the vantage point of science as craft or work. Building from these sources and the materials available in this volume, this chapter argues that (a) disciplinary heritages and historical conditions experienced by succeeding cohorts of researchers associated with life course perspectives have influenced the problem-finding process, (b) methodological pluralism has led to strategic breakthroughs for theoretical development, and (c) strategic research materials and the application of technical improvements in data retrieval and analysis have brought us closer to understanding people's lives as they are lived by linking lives with historical and "real" time. This new linkage has redirected life course theory.

A Mertonian Checklist and the
Craft of Social Research

In a review of Merton's contributions to sociological methodology, Sørenson (1991) suggested that Merton's contributions to sociological methodology over five decades may be appreciated best as useful representations of the actual research process and the "excitement of confronting ideas with evidence" (p. 519). Their descriptive usefulness may be in their typically eloquent recording of how good social science actually gets done under highly variable conditions of conceptual clarity, technical precision, strategic opportunity, or specified ignorance. As such, their legacy is both technical and personal, granting permission to the researcher to work with the materials at hand, to apply disciplined discretion, to tinker, to follow the data, to doubt preconceptions, and to trust personal experience. They convey both the formal and tacit knowledge bases of the research craft.

The chapters in this volume provide many useful examples of the practice of life course research that correspond to selected aspects of the social research process identified and characterized by Merton over several decades. Many of his characterizations are included in Table 3.1 either as direct quotations or as summaries or paraphrases from five of his essays. Throughout the remaining discussion, his ideas and vocabulary are applied to episodes and practices in life course research.

Although the checklist of items in Table 3.1 is presented in chronological order on the basis of publication date, the items can be reclassified into three general categories of practice applicable to our purposes here. All three categories exclude the textbook trajectory of practice in which theory unilaterally informs method and data. Instead, theory itself is identified as responsive to environmental factors ranging from historical events to immediate research contexts and specific techniques and practices of the craft. The first category represents the *social determinants and contexts* of problem definition in scientific areas. Historical events or conditions provide occasions for the definition of new problems or for the recasting of earlier problems in light of new experiences and perspectives. Included in this category are occasions when multiple perspectives including diverse disciplinary heritages converge on a common problem domain and, through cross-fertilization, cooperation, or even conflict, influence the development of theory and the progress of fact finding. The second includes the *tacit processes of problem definition* that stem from underlying but not easily articulated beliefs or senses (protoconcepts) of a problem or phenomenon. These often inarticulable understandings emerge from working with data and influence the identification of serendipitous findings and the specification of what is not known. The third category pertains to how *strategic data, empirical generalizations, and specific methods and techniques* lead to the establishment of new problem areas, to the recasting of

TABLE 3.1 A Mertonian Checklist for Studying the Practice of
Life-Course Research

Serendipity[1]	When an unanticipated, anomalous, or strategic datum exerts pressure for the initiation of theory.
Recasting of Theory[1]	When new data exert pressure for the elaboration of a conceptual scheme.
Re-Focus of Theoretical Interests[1]	When new methods of empirical research exert pressure for new foci of theoretical interest.
Clarification of Concepts[1]	When empirical research exerts pressure for clear concepts.
Problem-Finding[2]	When a research question is so formulated that the answer to it will confirm, amplify, or revise some part of what is taken as knowledge in the field. The major ingredients of a sociological problem are an originating question, a practical and/or a theoretical rationale, and a provisional specification of the empirical materials (variables, measurements, and analytic methods) for investigation. The latter may be arrived at by accident and/or by design.
Fact-Finding[2]	When the observation of an empirical generalization (social fact) is a frequent prelude to the statement of a genuine sociological problem.
Some Occasions for Problem-Finding[2]	Specialization; corrective emphases (revisions) stemming from previously neglected data or analytic approaches; the recurrence of longstanding problems; inconsistencies and contradictions.

(continued)

theory, and to the refocus of interests in ways relatively unanticipated by
theory.

One sociological model of the sciences is that they are domains of
sociocultural practice that do not depart from other similar spheres of
cultural production including craft activity (Ravetz, 1971). Enculturation
and the transmission of tacit knowledge are as important as, if not occasionally more important than, algorithmic or formal knowledge (Callon,
1995). Styles of research are transmitted by example, and hands-on experience contributes to the development of discretionary resources that defy
explicit categorization. Accordingly, the interaction of practices, instruments, data, and experience produces technical cultures that form proxi-
mate contexts of discovery and justification (Collins, 1974).

TABLE 3.1 Continued

Social Determinants of Sociological Problems[2]	When historical events or conditions generate the definition of new social problems or impinge on the value commitments of sociologists and lead to the selection and specification of new problems.
Theoretical Pluralism[3]	When diverse theoretical orientations overlap in specific fields of study to deal with diverse aspects of sociological problems. This diversity may lead to a division of labor, cross-fertilization, or to theoretical fragmentation and mutual irrelevance.
Protoconcepts[4]	Early, rudimentary, particularized, and largely unexplicated ideas that influence theory because they obscure underlying conceptual similarities of diverse substantive fields by attending to the particularities of each substantive field.
Establishing the Phenomenon[5]	When a phenomenon is shown to exist or occur before one explains why it exists or how it has come to be.
Specified Ignorance[5]	The express recognition of what is not yet known but needs to be known in order to lay the foundation for still more knowledge.
Strategic Research Materials (SRMs)[5]	Research sites, objects or events that exhibit the phenomenon to be explained or interpreted to such advantage and in such accessible form to enable the investigation of previously intractable or new problems.

SOURCE: [1] Merton (1948); [2] Merton (1959); [3] Merton (1981); [4] Merton (1984); [5] Merton (1987).

➢ RESEARCHERS' LIVES AND THE PRACTICE OF LIFE COURSE RESEARCH

Among Merton's contributions to the establishment of the field of the sociology of the sciences is the centrality of the process by which science is normatively defined and historically contingent (e.g., Merton, 1959, 1973). Institutionalized values and norms are transmitted in the practice of research, but, as for all institutional arrangements, historical and situational exigencies create conditions for their reorientation and change. The histories of scientific fields have demonstrated repeatedly how the historical and situational conditions of the lives of researchers have had implications for the simultaneous discoveries, the progress of science, or even the emergence of new fields. A landmark study by Ben-David and Collins (1966) demonstrated the origins of psychology to be related to both intellectual and geographic migrations of physiologists from an overpopulated field.

Mullins' (1972) study of the Cold Spring Harbor phage group led by Max Delbruck similarly depicted the early development of molecular biology from the contact among physicists, biologists, and crystallographers enabled by historical circumstances.

A study of my own on the social sciences in the 1950s revealed how postwar migrations and social-scientific institution-building strategies influenced the patterns by which some social science research groups working in game theory, media research, and group dynamics initially developed and interacted in the United States (O'Rand, 1992). Innumerable other field studies, biographies, and autobiographies have documented the importance of biographical experiences (migration, mentorship, gender discrimination), historical events (war research, social or historical crises), and situational contexts (laboratory accidents, chance encounters, serendipitous results) for the conduct and progress of research (e.g., Edge & Mulkay, 1976; Fleming & Bailyn, 1969; Swedberg, 1990; Urban, 1982). Finally, the most recent findings in the sociology of the sciences indicate emphatically how the actual, as opposed to the idealized or reconstructed, processes of research work consist of the formative interaction of the social, the personal, the situational, and the technical for the construction of knowledge (e.g., Knorr-Cetina, 1982; Latour, 1987).

Life course research has benefited from the post-World War II interests of the private and public sectors in supporting the social sciences. This era frequently is characterized by the growth of "big science" based on the model of the Manhattan Project and its successors. In many respects, it also was the beginning of "big social science" insofar as government and private sector resources were increasingly channeled into large-scale community and national survey projects to promote the understanding of the bases of social opinions and behaviors ranging from political attitudes and voting behavior to family organization and the treatment of the elderly. Research centers such as the Bureau of Applied Social Research at Columbia University, the Institute of Child Welfare at the University of California, Berkeley, and the Center for the Study of Aging and Human Development at Duke University as well as long-term community projects such as the Kansas City Studies of Adult Life became favored sites for the application of scientific methods to the study of social behavior in the decade following the war (Busse & Maddox, 1985; Clausen, 1993; Neugarten, 1987; O'Rand, 1992; Riley, 1988).

The subsequent decades brought the progressive development of the cognitive core of the life course perspective, beginning with early cross-sectional observations of age structure and age-related behaviors and moving toward direct longitudinal examinations of lives spanning several decades of the 20th century. This development is punctuated by the biographical, technical, and intellectual transitions of life course researchers themselves that come into focus with the assistance of Merton's checklist of some of the practices of the social sciences and the sociology of science as cultural practice. The cognitive core of life course research has emerged from this history. The core is grounded in the systematic study of the dynamic interplay of time, structural context, and human agency in the construction of the life course and in the process of social change.

Social Time and the Construction of the Life Course

The multidimensional bases of time in lives and history form the foundation of the life course project. Somewhat serendipitously, Merton's (1984) essay on social time provides a strategic starting point for studying the craft of life course research. Merton returned his attention to the Durkheimian concept of social time that he first encountered as a student of Sorokin in the 1930s and one that Lewis Coser also had considered, although somewhat later. He examined this topic to relate how he and Coser have shared similar interests in the idea of social time and in the process of concept formation in sociology. The essay reports the slow, uneven, and somewhat scattered development of the idea of time as a social category along independent lines ranging from (a) the sociological heritage of Durkheim transmitted through the work on memory and history by Halbwachs and Sorokin to Merton, to (b) Lazarsfeld's research (before coming to the United States) on the impact of unemployment on time orientation, to (c) innumerable other disciplines and domains of social activity with their particular designations denoting an implicit or explicit temporality in social structures and social relations including social phenomena such as the "lame duck" pattern in political systems, tenure and promotional systems in organizations, statutes of limitation, waiting periods of many varieties across contexts, and many others (Merton, 1984).

Merton (1984) identified "socially expected durations" (SEDs) as a protoconcept (see Table 3.1) underlying these disparate phenomena constituting, and simultaneously being constituted by, the tempos of social life. A protoconcept is a rudimentary and largely unrecognized and unexplicated idea underlying quite diverse substantive fields whose respective and particularistic applications of the idea obscure its shared implications. SEDs define socially prescribed or collective expectations about temporal durations constituting various social structures and social relations. Merton argued that they are ubiquitous properties of social structures and social relations and that they can range from the most institutionalized forms (schools, prisons, pension systems) to more ambiguous or indeterminate forms related to aggregate-level temporal expectations (demographic behavior patterns related to fertility decisions, marital duration, geographic mobility, labor force participation) (Merton, 1984). Merton concluded by calling for the systematic rather than sporadic study of SEDs as a significant component of social structure.

Life course research over the past 30 years has both anticipated and responded to his call (see, e.g., Back & Gergen, 1963; Hogan, 1981; O'Rand & Ellis, 1974; and see especially Featherman, 1986; Neugarten, 1968b; Neugarten & Hagestad, 1976). Indeed, a central line of conceptual development has been in identifying, characterizing, and explaining the temporal organization of the life course and its variations across structural and historical contexts. Temporal norms and expectations related to age, life stage, status durations, and the timing and ordering of social transitions have received sustained attention. Importantly, this temporal focus in life course research has steered the practice of life course research in ways and with consequences indicated by Merton's checklist (Table 3.1)—including the social determinants of sociological problems, establishing the phenomenon, fact finding, identifying strategic research materials, applying methods that refocus theoretical interests, and recasting theory (refer to checklist in Table 3.1; Merton, 1948, 1959, 1981, 1987).

Among the earliest investigations to establish the phenomenon of temporal norms in the life course were the Kansas City Studies of Adult Life conducted over 10 years beginning in 1952 (Neugarten, 1987). This longitudinal, community-level project brought together a multidisciplinary group led by R. J. Havighurst, W. E. Henry, and B. L. Neugarten. Longitudinal analyses revealed considerable diversity in patterns of aging that defied explanations following from the prevailing theories of aging of that time (i.e., disengagement and activity theories). Included among the diverse patterns observed were variant life course schedules across social groups, leading some to appear to be "early," "late," or "on- or off-time" in the timing of family and occupational events (Neugarten, Moore, & Lowe, 1965).

Contemporaneously, "simultaneous discoveries" in different disciplines were made of the complex interaction among age, period, and cohort in the determination of patterns of aging (Ryder, 1965; Schaie, 1965; see also Maddox & Wiley, 1976, for a review). These observations revealed the core problematic of life course research, accounting for temporal variations in the aging process as products of individual, social, and historical factors. This discovery raised an immediate challenge to strongly deterministic notions such as life cycle, a concept that has undergone extensive revision in its application over the ensuing period (O'Rand & Krecker, 1990). These studies also anchored the permanent skepticism in the emergent life course perspective that temporal structures (i.e., SEDs) were immutable.

Since these early studies, the ever-changing temporal organization of the life course, especially the timing and sequencing of events associated with the so-called transition to adulthood, with family and work events in midlife, and (lately) with the transition to retirement, has been a persistent phenomenon of interest (Hogan, 1981; Rindfuss, Swicegood, & Rosenfeld, 1987). The apparent normative strength of SEDs in the life course has been reduced in American culture to a level that observed heterogeneity in life pathways and transition trajectories is readily characterized as "disordered" among some populations including the young in their transitions to adulthood (Modell, 1989; Rindfuss et al., 1987) and the middle-aged and aging whose path-dependent lives grow more differentiated over time (Elder & O'Rand, 1995).

Some of these observations are arguably the results of new data and methods that are being applied rather than the results of actual social changes. Over the past decade and a half, the rapid development of demographic methods for dynamic studies, coupled with the accumulating databases that permit the examination of lives over extended periods of time (over many decades in some cases), has clarified concepts, recast theory, and led to new recognitions of what is not known (Merton's "specified ignorance") as well as what is known (Featherman, 1986). Some of these developments are highlighted in this chapter. Other chapters in this volume illustrate all these practices and patterns in exquisite detail.

Riley's contributions to the developing life course perspective demonstrate several of Merton's observations on the practice of social science. She exemplifies the importance of the researcher's own biography for problem finding, fact finding, establishing the phenomenon, and specifying ignorance. A brief review of these contributions follows.

Historical Conditions and Sociotemporal Location

Riley (1988, 1990) produced two revealing documents on the importance of researchers' lives on their work. Through autobiographical accounts of several sociologists including her own, she presented materials that advocate the importance of sociotemporal locations of cohorts of researchers for their substantive and organizational contributions to their fields of study; these contexts occasionally also are identified as obstacles to the recognition of these researchers' contributions. Sociotemporal locations are defined by five historical conditions: wider social and cultural changes extant in the society and four trends of their research areas at the times of their respective (and sometimes numerous) contributions, that is, trends in theory, methods, the organization of research, and ideologies and values.

For our purposes in this volume, Riley's own accounts are specifically relevant. Indeed, her life as lived in association with her husband, John W. Riley, Jr., provides us with a *cameo* of selected origins and critical developmental periods of life course research over five decades:

> My own recollections cannot be separated from those of my husband, Jack. . . . Our joint lives have been intertwined for nearly 60 years of marriage and colleagueship. As he and I often say, our collaboration as sociologists has spanned a large part of the twentieth century and almost our entire life course: we first published empirically based articles on contraception; then sequentially on children, adolescents, and midlife careers; then on old age and death; and now we plan to turn back to leisure, the topic which . . . we had dreamed of being one day "mature" enough to tackle! (Riley, 1990, p. 6)

Riley (1988) identified five areas of potential influence by her that reflect her historical and disciplinary experiences. The first is sociological practice, an area where her efforts were strongly influenced by her early experiences in marketing research in the 1930s and 1940s, when she was exposed to the practical problems of researching social behaviors such as household consumption patterns and contraceptive behaviors and attitudes. She reported that these experiences required the creation and use of multiple methods including classical experimental designs, intensive interviews, national probability sampling and survey design, and personal diaries and logs. Many such innovations were occurring outside academic sociology and would be transported by the Rileys and other figures of the period (e.g., Paul Lazarsfeld of the Bureau of Applied Social Research at Columbia University) into the discipline (O'Rand, 1992).

Gender is the second area identified by Riley (1990). Riley's extraordinary life has informed her sensitivities in defining research problems. Early confrontations with patriarchal definitions of her status (e.g., in the publication of her book on aeronautical gliding and soaring and in her rejection as a teaching assistant at Harvard University), although endured and overcome, did not fit with her personal sense of, and confidence in, women's changing positions. Similarly, the neglect of women as respondents for sociological study would demarcate a broad area of sociological ignorance by the early 1960s. Her research collaborations with students at Rutgers University on women's changing occupational roles serendipitously uncovered an apparent change in adolescent girls' aspirations for both career and family. Riley recalls more about this episode in this volume; her recollection suggests that although the data could not address all their speculations, their specified ignorance, coupled with intellectual and personal experiences, suggested that the implications of their findings were important for understanding both the processes of aging and intergenerational (mother-to-daughter) socialization to aspirations. Her portrayal suggests that a phenomenon related to a change in gender role aspirations had been established and that the specification of the bases for this change required new data to adjudicate between explanations related to age-specific patterns of role definition and a possible social change in gender roles.

Age is the third area identified by Riley and obviously bears considerable gravity for this volume. For many of us in the field, Riley's efforts with her colleagues to recast the status of age as an organizing framework for the study of social change contributed to a watershed period in the emergence of life course perspectives. The sociology of age stratification project represented in Riley, Johnson, and Foner (1972a) was a formidable fact-finding effort that traversed the disciplines of sociology, demography, history, political science, social psychology, economics, and psychology. The fact-finding effort yielded new problem definitions and recast the aging process as a multilevel phenomenon linking individual aging with social change. Age stratification and related concepts such as disordered cohort flow were born in this project; these ideas reoriented the research agenda on age, aging, and gerontology. The age stratification project also revealed the plurality of methods and practices across the social sciences for the study of the historical interplay of changing lives and changing social structures. An organizational byproduct of this effort was the formation of a Social Science Research Council (SSRC) committee in 1977 focusing on the life course and bringing together the proposed age stratification perspective with other related developments (Riley, 1988).

Methods is a fourth area that Riley identified as important in her efforts and potential contributions, although she suspects that this is among her more "invisible" contributions. The attribution of invisibility stems from the incorporation of her work into a two-volume textbook (rather than in journal or monograph form) in which original research was nevertheless critical to the task. Having been exposed to this work myself as a college major in sociology taking methods in the mid-1960s, I can attest to its actual visibility. But I am especially taken by Riley's insight that the conventions of publication and communication followed by researchers may indelibly imprint their place in the history of the discipline. She looks back on textbook writing as a problem in communication. The early to mid-1960s comprised a booming period for sociology with swelling enrollments and majors across the country. Textbooks were a principal socializing force in the discipline; not the least among them was Riley's (1963) *Sociological Research*. Yet, today's conventions more clearly prescribe the communication of primary or original materials by way of other media. This episode reveals how historical conditions impinge on practice.

In this period, survey research and data punched on cards to be read on mainframe computers ascended to methodological prominence in sociology. These specific methods and related techniques came to be primary means of studying lives in time and over time. Riley's textbook materials included these approaches and others.

Finally, Riley's current project, in collaboration with her husband and many others in the life course area, focuses on dynamic social systems. This project is an extension of the age stratification project into a next generation of examinations on structural change. Riley recounts efforts and frustrations from four decades earlier to parameterize group properties and contextual effects (Riley, 1988) to better specify how individual lives and social systems interact reciprocally. Today, new data sources and methods permit the accomplishment of these objectives. The data sources include longitudinal studies sometimes spanning many decades, thus permitting the fine-grained examinations of lives as they are lived in real and historical time. Some of these data are represented in this volume—the Bennington College study follow-up, the Gluecks' data, the Stanford University-Terman studies, the Berkeley Guidance Study, and the Berkeley and Oakland Growth Studies and their follow-ups.

In addition, multilevel modeling and the use of strategic resource materials to link individual lives more closely with social structures and historical events are now in wider use (DiPrete & Forristal, 1994). Micro-level observations can be linked to macro-level observations with the latter measured in at least two different ways: either as context-specific aggregate indexes of micro-level characteristics (means or slopes) or as global variables not expressed in terms of measured individual traits. New methods for handling complicated hierarchical data of this sort have developed rapidly in recent years and are beginning to provide life course researchers with better tools to capture the complex dynamisms of the aging process.

A central task of life course research is to take explicit account of time and context in the study of human lives. Thus, Riley's notion of sociotemporal locations in the lives of researchers is a self-exemplification of the wider life course project. That project defines problems in tracing and characterizing biographies (persons' lives) and linking them systematically with contexts (historical events, structural contexts, environmental conditions). This volume provides a partial view of this problem-finding process and the ongoing practices associated with it.

The Intersection of Biography and History

Elder (1994) recently reflected on the coincidence of biography and history in his own life and practice as a researcher and on the research tradition of life studies that extends back at least as far as the Thomas and Znaniecki (1918-1920/1927) study of the diaries and letters of Polish immigrants to the United States. The central experience he identified was his introduction to, and subsequent analyses of, the data of two samples of "children of the Great Depression" in the United States. In the early 1960s, his appointment as a research assistant with John Clausen at the Institute of Human Development at Berkeley brought him into direct contact with longitudinal data from the Oakland Growth Study based on a panel born between 1920 and 1921 and followed over the 1930s with a significant portion of them followed as far as their seventh decade of life (Clausen, 1993). He recalled his struggle with the data, which did not quite fit conceptual frameworks based on dominant notions of socialization and personality development. The data revealed an anomaly: greater change and volatility than existing concepts permitted.

In many respects, Elder's experience with Mertonian serendipity was unexpectedly and unknowingly shared by Bernice Neugarten working with the Kansas City data:

> The Kansas City data were re-analyzed by Havighurst, Neugarten, and Tobin who, using different measures than those used by Cumming and Henry, found a moderate positive correlation between activity and life satisfaction. . . . More important, they found a diversity of patterns of aging based on combinations of personality type, role activity, and life satisfaction. . . . Further, when the Kansas City measures were used on data sets from several European countries, it was shown that . . . differences in socio-cultural settings produce major variations in patterns of aging. (Neugarten, 1987, p. 373)

The independent discoveries of unexpected heterogeneity both stemmed from the influence of data in redirecting and recasting preconceptions.

Elder reconciled the lack of fit of his data to existing theory by refocusing the individual-level data in light of historical circumstances, which were much like those evident in Thomas and Znaniecki's (1918-1920/1927) earlier examinations of the impact of crises and significant incidents on the lives of Polish immigrants at the turn of the century. The Depression presented a change in the larger environment of ordinary lives that exerted an anomalous influence on individuals' ordinary adaptations and responses. This influence introduced "dramatic changefulness" (Elder, 1994, p. 9) and intracohort variability not readily accounted for by existing theory (Elder, 1974).

Elder's later comparison of the Oakland cohort to a slightly younger one (the Berkeley Guidance Study sample born at the end of the 1920s) added a crucial comparative vantage point that clarified the importance of the linkage of life stage to historical events for the course of individual lives (Elder, 1979). The younger cohort appeared more vulnerable than the older one to the impact of the Depression on later life patterns of achievement and adaptability. These studies uniquely contributed to the watershed in life course research in the 1970s along with Riley's efforts with her colleagues. Elder's contributions linked macroscopic change with the life experiences of children (Corsaro, 1994) and served to lay down some of the basic vocabulary of the life course perspective (Elder, 1975).

Following these studies, Elder and his colleagues have pursued a sequence of projects examining the differential impacts of historical events on strategic samples of individuals. Studies of World War II and Korean War veterans have assessed the effects of combat on midlife emotional health, resilience, and social bonding (Elder & Clipp, 1988, 1989). Recent examinations of the midwestern families trapped in the farm crisis of recent decades have demonstrated the emotional consequences for children living in families undergoing sustained economic stress including the loss of the family farm and geographical migration (Conger & Elder, 1994; Elder, Conger, Foster, & Ardelt, 1992). Ongoing studies of the life course trajectories of the intellectually gifted Stanford-Terman sample followed over 64 years (although not without considerable sample attrition) have revealed the heterogeneous outcomes of lives beginning with similar intellectual promise but following diverse trajectories as a result of differential encounters with major historical events and variable patterns of personal adaptation and control (Elder, Pavalko, & Hastings, 1991).

The latter project has presented its own special problems of measurement associated with the assessment of historical change and its specific relevance for individual lives. The recasting of strategies for these purposes is the subject of Elder and Pellerin's contribution to this volume (Chapter 11). Central to this project is the availability of strategic research materials (the Terman data archive) that impel the refocusing of theoretical interests and the reorientation of analysis in the direction of incorporating history as a formative context for individual development. The specific strategies for codifying wartime experiences and linking them to personal development exemplify the process in which data and method recast theory and concept formation.

➤ METHODOLOGICAL PLURALISM
AND THEORY DEVELOPMENT

The life course perspective is characterized by theoretical pluralism (Merton, 1981). It has emerged since the 1960s as a product of the biographical and intellectual migrations, cross-disciplinary collaborations, fortuitous encounters, and institution building among researchers from several disciplines. Life course publications typically co-cite the works of social historians (e.g., Tamara Hareven, John Modell), demographers (e.g.,

Norman Ryder, Dennis Hogan, Peter Uhlenberg), gerontologists (e.g., Bernice Neugarten, George Maddox, Gordon Streib, Ethel Shanas), sociologists (e.g., Matilda and Jack Riley, Anne Foner, Glen Elder, Vern Bengtson, John Clausen, David Featherman, Martin Kohli, Karl U. Mayer), economists (e.g., Richard Easterlin, Richard Burkhauser, Joseph Quinn), and psychologists (e.g., Paul Baltes, Walter Schaie, Richard Lerner). Cocitation across disciplines (i.e., the recurrent joint citation in a specific publication of works from across disciplines) is a strong indicator of cross-fertilization and theoretical convergence.

The multilevel processes linked by aging, structural location, and living through historical time yield a complex concatenation of cross-level causal relations and temporal-historical contingencies. Riley's cohort-level age stratification theory and Elder's identification of several social-psychological mechanisms linking patterned individual responses to historical changes (including the life stage principle observed in the Oakland-Berkeley studies, among others reported elsewhere [e.g., Elder & Caspi, 1990]) only partially represent the wide-ranging complement of theoretical and conceptual orientations overlapping to constitute this general approach. Other theories/conceptions include life span development theory, role and symbolic interaction theory, adult socialization theory, continuity theory, stress process theory, social support theory, life transition theory, status attainment, gender stratification, family economy theory, family development theory, and state-centered theories of the individualization of the life course, among others (see O'Rand & Krecker, 1990, for a partial review of this theoretical history; see Elder, 1995, for a more general overview).

Theoretical pluralism has resulted from the convergence of multiple research traditions on the common problem of aging in time and place. These traditions have brought together different conceptual schemes, but along with these diverse orientations have come multiple data sources and analytical approaches to this problem domain. Therefore, a major by-product has been methodological pluralism. Accordingly, life history, life review, prospective panel designs, follow-up studies, repeated cross sections, historical demography, event history methods, life table methods, and selected other dynamic measurement and analysis strategies have been applied—occasionally (when permitting) on the same data sources. The SSRC's projects to archive and catalog nearly all of these databases and methods are evident in at least three volumes appearing between 1981 and

1991. (See Young, Savola, & Phelps, 1991, for a history of these projects and for the most exhaustive current inventory of longitudinal studies in the social sciences. As of the publication of the latter, another effort was underway to produce a European equivalent inventory.) Such efforts represent an institutionalization of methodological pluralism.

Alternative methods and creative strategies occasionally are constrained and/or inspired by the limitations of existing data. These situations often have become the occasions for the addition of new data, for the recasting of existing data into new formats, or for the development of new analytic methods to accommodate or compensate for data characteristics. Theoretical development has followed from some of these efforts. Several rich examples are evident in recent life course studies including some conducted by other authors in this volume.

Recasting Theory With Strategic Research Materials

Follow-up studies often combine new data with strategic research materials to develop theory. These data may result from the triangulation or concatenation of archival, census, and survey materials. Or, they may involve the follow-up of samples from data gathered at an earlier time. The strategic value of existing databases usually resides in their historical and/or biographical (life stage) characteristics. The Oakland-Berkeley studies examined by Clausen and Elder over the years historically were grounded in the turbulent decades spanning the Depression, World War II, the Korean War, and the economic recovery of the 1950s. Biographically, the sample permitted the tracking of lives from early adolescence to midlife. As such, lives could be linked to a succession of environments to observe the interaction of personal and historical influences on changing lives and to capture continuities and discontinuities.

The Bennington Studies of Persistence and Change in Attitudes and Values share similar historical and biographical characteristics despite their sample differences (Alwin, Cohen, & Newcomb, 1991). Classes entering Bennington College between 1932 and 1938 participated between 1935 and 1939 in surveys with items examining selected social and political attitudes and personal temperaments. Initial findings indicated that at this liberal institution in a period of social change, attitudes among coeds grew more similar over time. Two follow-up waves in 1960-1961 and 1984 administered many of the same attitude items but also added data on respondents' recollections of their political viewpoints as young women and on the opinions and attitudes of spouses, children, and friends. The follow-up results yield rich materials for understanding the mechanisms of attitude persistence and change. They also presented new problems and generated new insights regarding patterns of recall and memory error and methods for studying families and households.

Dempster-McClain and Moen, in this volume (Chapter 6), provide a very rich set of examples of strategic survey materials with advice on tracking and successful follow-up studies. Their specific experience with the two-generation study of the Cornell Women's Roles and Well-Being Study, initiated by Robin Williams in the mid-1950s, is a first-rate example of the craft of life course research. They recount the creative process of locating respondents both by following well-established protocols (e.g., the Comprehensive Tracking Model developed by Call, Otto, & Spenner, 1982) and by exploiting strategic opportunities (e.g., using eager respondents as "detectives"). The technical and humanistic strands of their efforts are intertwined to provide an account of how strategic research materials can both initiate new research problems and inspire the application of new techniques and approaches.

New Methods Refocus Theoretical Interests

The influence of methods on problem finding and on the reorientation of theory in life course research is well established. Among the most recent sources of change has been the application of life table and event history methods to the analysis of longitudinal data (Campbell & O'Rand, 1988). These methods allow time to be treated explicitly in the analysis to estimate the rates at which persons move from one life state to another and to determine the relative effects of time in state and other variables on life course trajectories. These methods have revealed the temporal complexities of persons' lives leading to the rejection of older views of the life course based on concepts of determinate transition sequences and irreversible life transitions highly correlated with age. New views of the life course are now more sensitive to the temporal and sequential heterogeneity in the organization of lives from the transition to adulthood to the transition to retirement. Even our notions of life phases—adolescence, adulthood, and old age—are being challenged as new data and methods call for their revision.

In this volume, Karweit and Kertzer (Chapter 4) review the practical and substantive implications of organizing life history data as events and durations in the Johns Hopkins Retrospective Life History Survey and in the historical files gathered on a population living in Casalecchio, Italy, sometime during the period 1865-1921. Event history analysis requires event or episode data. In turn, such data files are large and complex. Computer management and storage of these files is now well advanced. According to Karweit and Kertzer, what is now lagging is not the technical facility to use event data and event-based analytical methods but rather the conceptual/theoretical tools to exploit these rich materials in the definition of problems. Prospectively, this account offers us not only the promise that theory can benefit from data and method but also the challenge to bring this to fruition.

The recent reanalyses of the Crime Causation Study of juvenile delinquency conducted between 1940 and 1965 by the Gluecks illustrate a different instance of method influencing both data and theory (Sampson & Laub, 1993). In this case, new data were not added; instead, existing data were recast to fit new methods of longitudinal research capable of exploiting the temporal characteristics of the data to track persons' lives over time. The new analyses revealed how intervening life contexts related to marriage and employment can redirect the earlier behavior patterns of persons. In this volume, Laub and Sampson (Chapter 9) further explicate their multimethod strategies and strongly represent the methodological pluralism characteristic of life course research by integrating qualitative and quantitative techniques on the same data set.

New methods in the acquisition of retrospective, life history, and life review data are active interests of life course research in spite of the well-documented experience with the limitations of these data in the past. The renaissance of this interest is motivated, in large part, by the accumulation of panel and retrospective data sets (e.g., the Bennington study) that have permitted the validity and reliability checks unavailable in cross-section designs. In addition, the same studies have discovered that recollections and reviews may be important life course processes in their own right, representing a distinctive aspect of changing lives.

The impact of methods and data on theory often is reciprocated. New interests focused on tracking lives in real time that have been inspired, in part, by methods and data now make demands, in turn, on new research designs. Along these lines, Brückner and Mayer (Chapter 7), in this volume, review several aspects of the German Life History Study. Their account of the demands of gathering and codifying specific and individualized life histories emphasizes the requirements for preparing highly diverse qualitative materials for quantitative examination. Individualization and standardization are dual demands that, on the surface, appear ironic, if not contradictory. But the life course perspective is now focused on this complex and ironic association. Heterogeneity pervades life course processes. Longitudinal data and dynamic analytic strategies have established this firmly in the research. Now, in turn, data requirements for the fine-grained delineation of events marking individual lives have become more and more stringent. Data, method, and theory have been mutually influential over the past 30 years in the construction and reconstruction of the life course perspective.

New methods also are introducing ways in which to link individual behaviors with larger social units such as families, occupational and industrial categories, and other groups. The properties and temporal organizations of the groups and contexts influencing persons' lives have proven to be difficult to measure and to integrate with individual-level analyses since the late 1950s and early 1960s, when much theoretical concern began to center on structural and contextual effects. However, several strategies have emerged for organizing data and modeling individual and group characteristics. One set of strategies in life course research is fashioning ways in which individual and household data may be linked to measure simultaneous, yet differentiated, individual and group processes. In this volume, Karweit and Kertzer (Chapter 4) share their experiences with confronting this specific concern in the Casalecchio data in which individual and coresidential data are garnered from multiple sources.

Another set of strategies is focusing on analytic techniques using multiple equation systems in which macro-level variables may or may not be expressible as functions of micro-level variables (DiPrete & Forristal, 1994). These quantitative efforts are only beginning to have an impact on the improvement of our theories regarding how social contexts influence individual outcomes.

Finally, multiple-equation approaches have most recently been applied to capture the rich complexity of lives, specifically the simultaneity of multiple trajectories. The life course is lived along several interdependent trajectories. For example, women's lives consist of intertwined processes encompassing event sequences in educational progression, employment/unemployment history, premarital conception, marriage and remarriage, marital fertility, and marital dissolution. Five of these processes recently have been modeled using a multiple-equation system. Upchurch, Lillard, and Panis (1995) directly examined the dynamic simultaneity of multiple processes in the lives of women followed by the National Longitudinal Survey of Youth (they excluded employment/unemployment trajectories from their analysis). By applying hazard and sequential probit models that permit time-dependent and time-varying covariates, they found sequential contingencies among their covariates. The timing of life events within and across trajectories has significant effects on women's lives. But these effects are sufficiently complex and variable to render single-equation models inadequate for the task at hand.

These methods actually come closer than earlier strategies to reflecting the life course processes currently conceptualized in the literature. This set of events carries an ironic implication that is compatible with the Mertonian view of research practice. On the one hand, methodological innovations carry conceptualizations forward and recast theory; on the other, the clarification and progress of conceptual development make new demands on methods. Thus, the multilevel model and multiple-equation approaches are simultaneously related to theory development.

➤ TRACKING LIVES IN "REAL" TIME

Gordon C. Winston, an economist, argued that the proper study of social behavior must be sensitive to the implications of examining lives in terms of both "analytical" and "perspective" time (Winston, 1988). He defined analytical time as the temporal vantage point of the researcher reconstructing events that are abstracted from their experiencing. Perspective time, on the other hand, is the vantage point from which people live their lives. In perspective time, the future is unknowable; in analytical time, there is omniscience. In perspective time, the present is qualitatively different from all other times; in analytical time, each moment is qualitatively equivalent to every other. Finally, in perspective time, we are constrained to the present (the "now"); in analytical time, we may move back and forth in time as we prefer (Winston, 1988, p. 34).

The life course framework has developed over three decades toward an explicit accounting of these two perspectives. The life course studied in analytical time reveals transitions, trajectories, careers, cohorts, and generations. In perspective time, the life course is presented as identities, actions, and choices—as well as recollections and retrospections—constrained by the present. In perspective time, the future and the past are constrained by the immediate historical and structural circumstances of persons as actors. In the present, actors reflect on their past lives and consider the "presently understood past" (Cohler, 1982). Life reviews and retrospectives repeatedly reveal how the developing individual reconsiders and reinterprets the past in light of the vantage point of the present.

In this volume, Scott and Alwin (Chapter 5) and Clausen (Chapter 8) share their discoveries that retrospective accounts of the past (of biography) constitute a fertile ground for new theoretical development of the life course. Vantage points in the present can reconstruct the past. Women in the last Bennington study follow-up reevaluated and (in some cases) revised political attitudes (specifically pertaining to President Richard M. Nixon) that they had held at earlier times in light of the contemporary political climate. Similarly, children of the Depression studied in the Oakland-Berkeley studies initiated 60 years ago reevaluated and reinterpreted the relative importance of transitions as "turning points" in their lives (Clausen, 1993).

Perspective time also is valuable in dealing with innovation in the life course. Giele's contribution to this volume (Chapter 10) examines an understudied, but increasingly vital, aspect of life course research: the emergence of new life patterns at the intersection between biography and history. Heterogeneity and change in the normative life course are readily observable in several demographic trends over recent decades. Women's steady increases in labor force participation, the trends toward early retirement among men, the expanding heterogeneity in midlife transitions, and trajectories across education, work, family, and leisure domains are among the changes in lives as lived in "real" time that have called for more sensitive and dynamic methods of observation and analysis. Human agency is impelling sociological researchers to incorporate time explicitly in research design to capture new transitions and new transition sequences.

Indeed, Riley's (1994a) recent examinations of age and "structural lag" address the issue of the innovative life course head-on; changing lives far outpace social institutions predicated on outdated and erroneous assumptions about age-graded capacities for physical, intellectual, and social activity. Longer and healthier lives punctuated by innovation do not fit well with older constructions of the life course on which much social policy and public prejudice still are based.

I conclude these introductory remarks by concurring with Winston's preference for the balancing of vantage points in the study of people's lives. The practice of life course research appears to have moved as closely as any field of inquiry to a conscientious pursuit of both comprehension and insight. Methodological and theoretical pluralism involving a creative attention to capturing lives as they are lived in historical and real time move us closer to these objectives. The recognition that theory, data, and methods interact in the practices of researchers working in their perspective times also reminds us of the technical and humanistic elements of our efforts.

Part II

Data Collection and Measurement

> ➤ **INTRODUCTION**

Part II of this book focuses on the forms of data and means of data collection that are most useful for life course research. The chapters are arranged in ascending order of generality, beginning with event histories and ending with the collection and analysis of grouped cases in distinct geographical and historical settings. At the first level are *events,* which are formed into trajectories or event histories that together make up the life course of the person. Next up on the hierarchy is the *individual case,* which in life course studies is a person whose life is an integral whole, involving choice of goals, life review, subjective feelings, and prospective planning for change. At the third level are *groups of cases* or *societal subsystems,* which are shaped by members with particular individual attributes. Finally, at the most inclusive level are historical or geographical *systems* comprising subsystems or groups of cases that share common external circumstances such as location, history, and culture. The chapters in Part II are arranged accordingly, beginning with Chapter 4 by Karweit and Kertzer on the format of life events data and continuing with Chapter 5 by Scott and Alwin on construction of individual life histories from retrospective and prospective data and Chapter 6 by Dempster-McClain and Moen on finding respondents in a follow-up study through group memberships and networks. Part II concludes with Chapter 7, Brückner and Mayer's description of a complex data collection effort in Germany that comprises many systems and many individuals.

In Chapter 4 on "Data Organization and Conceptualization," Karweit and Kertzer lay out the principal properties of events and ways in which to record them. The techniques they describe for measurement of life history data constitute a breakthrough in two important respects: standardization of measures and the resulting flexibility of analytic strategies that such interchangeability has made possible. Standardization has occurred on two fronts simultaneously: in time codes and activity domains. Both elements (beginning and ending dates and domain of activity) are essential to the coding of each event, whether it be for a person, a group, or an organization. It is then possible to aggregate the data flexibly by measures of time (e.g., year, age, duration, co-events) and domain of activity (e.g., work, family, residence). Interchangeability across units of analysis provides an important "conceptual bridge" between data on persons and systems. Tagging across events and cases makes it possible to refer to contiguous larger and smaller systems of which the individual is a part. Such capacity to trace the mutual influence of various analytic units facilitates the contextual, constituent, and combined social system types of life course analysis that Riley outlines in Chapter 2. For the great majority of life course researchers, however, the greatest benefits of standardization and interchangeability of life events data are likely to be in the analysis of large panel surveys. Time-coded and domain-specific data permit the handling of varied-length event histories by creation of a relational database for large samples and multiple waves in a longitudinal design. It is then possible to trace the impact of earlier events and co-events on later outcomes not only within the life of a single individual but also among the members of a family or household who also may be part of the study.

By addressing "Retrospective Versus Prospective Measurement" in large social surveys in Chapter 5, Scott and Alwin focus on the individual respondent's event histories, experiences, and beliefs. In their reference to Freedman's life history calendar, they reaffirm Karweit and Kertzer's point that temporal and activity coding of life events are the two essential types of life course information to be gathered. They go beyond Karweit and Kertzer, however, in noting that life history is really more than the sum of events. It also includes cumulative experiences and subjective feelings. Thus, Scott and Alwin focus on data at the *case* level because it is the individual who filters and gives meaning to his or her responses. Their broadened definition of life history as more than the sum of events helps them to evaluate prospective versus retrospective designs. For viewing experiences inward and backward, retrospective surveys seem better; they permit review of a longer period even though they are flawed by potential forgetting and distortion.

Prospective designs are preferable for looking outward and forward to the surrounding social environment and its influences (which involve many complex details that one needs to capture concurrently). In addition to focusing on the case, surveys also describe a *population* of cases. Retrospective designs risk bias through censoring and selection of survivors. Prospective designs are vulnerable to attrition and missing data. A combination probably is best, such as is found in the embedding of retrospective modules within panel surveys. In addition, the best life history studies build on the possibility of a vertical integration of data across cases, households, and larger systems. Retrospective data make possible the richer representation of events, experiences, and meanings for the individual, whereas prospective data are essential for gathering concurrent data on other persons and groups to whom the individual is linked.

Closely related to the choice between retrospective and prospective designs is the "catch-up study" described by Dempster-McClain and Moen in Chapter 6. Although it is cheaper and quicker to do catch-up samples "than to launch a panel study and wait 30 years for the data" (p. 150), it requires special effort to locate respondents who were surveyed many years earlier. In a chapter that especially uses the *linkage* theme of the life course paradigm, Dempster-McClain and Moen describe their own recovery in 1986 of 95.5% of the 417 respondents in the Cornell University project on Women's Roles and Well-Being who were initially interviewed in 1956. Their success depended on leads gathered from the social settings in which the women had lived. The investigators consulted obituaries, city and telephone directories, high school and college alumni records, neighbors, local informants, clubs, and churches. They found it particularly useful to discover *relationships* of the respondents to adult children, former employers, church secretaries, friends, and other contacts who would provide information.

Preventing loss of respondents is important for two reasons: to preserve chronological evidence and to prevent sampling bias. One of the Cornell study's most important findings was that the women who died before 1986 were more likely to have had fewer affiliations and were less well integrated into social networks. To derive such an explanation, it was essential that the authors be able to compare events and experiences at several time points. Only then could they trace changes to previous events and relationships. In addition, they had to be able to account for as many of the members of the original sample as possible to attribute decreases to death rather than to mere loss of contact. If the authors had not found virtually all of the 1956 respondents, then they would not have been able to pursue a life course explanation. Instead, their results would have been clouded by sample attrition or would have been explained by what Stinchcombe (1968) termed the relatively uninteresting "theory of multiple small causes."

Chapter 7 on "The German Life History Study" by Brückner and Mayer extends the elements of life course analysis all the way from the event-history level to comparisons across systems such as between East and West Germany. Thus, their description provides a model of how data must be collected to understand not only the individual life course but also the mutual impact of persons and systems. The German study accomplishes this goal in two ways. First, the project is conceptualized very broadly as describing and explaining life course changes of several key birth cohorts within an entire country. Second, data are collected and coded scrupulously to create an accurate record of the many interlocking events that actually occurred. The goals of the study are ambitious—to understand intergenerational mobility and allocation of socioeconomic status in a way that makes it possible to reconstruct the interaction of family, employment, education, and the influence of the sociohistorical context and, in the process, to identify *causal mechanisms embedded in the life course.* Such an enterprise required a battery of research strategies together with well-trained and motivated interviewers, coders, and analysts to collect the required retrospective data from more than 8,000 individuals in selected birth cohorts in both West and East Germany. Checking for accuracy and consistency of responses to telephone interviews used the interlocking nature of historical events and family, work, and educational systems to good avail. If a reported event was improbable given another event already recorded, then the interviewer pursued the matter further. Thus, the conceptualization of the individual's life course as located in a particular historical period and interacting with others in work and household resulted in detailed and reliable data that could sustain a probing search for the dynamics embedded in both the individual life course and larger social systems.

Chapter 4

Data Organization and Conceptualization

NANCY KARWEIT
DAVID KERTZER

This chapter discusses practical and conceptual issues related to the organization and management of life history data. We describe the evolution of our approach to life course data issues and relate some of the practical issues encountered in working with such data. Illustrations are drawn from the work we have undertaken in two studies: the Johns Hopkins Retrospective Life History Study of American Men (1969) and the Casalecchio Project (1989), a historical study of demographic change in an Italian community in the late 19th and early 20th centuries. These two data sources provide examples of some common, as well as unique, difficulties encountered in the organization and management of life course data. After discussing the issues in these two studies and describing the approaches taken in our work, the final section of this chapter discusses issues encountered in general in the organization and management of life course data.

The topic of data organization in life course studies usually is not addressed as a separate topic in its own right. In many data sets, the data structure already conforms to the structure typically expected by standard statistical packages. Consequently, data organization is not an issue. However, when collecting complex data involving multiple units of analysis and time-varying independent and dependent measures, seldom are all of the

81

data organization requirements met by existing analysis packages. Typically, some sort of ad hoc procedure is used to solve the immediate and specific problems, leading to a proliferation of unique solutions. The two studies we look at here were conducted over a decade apart and involved very different research efforts. The first, the Johns Hopkins Retrospective Life History Study, was directed by two sociologists, James Coleman and Peter Rossi, and was based on U.S. interview data. The second, the Casalecchio Project, was directed by David Kertzer, an anthropologist and historian, in collaboration first with historical demographer Andrea Schiaffino and then social demographer Dennis Hogan. Its database was constructed from historical archival sources in Italy. For both projects, Nancy Karweit directed the construction and refinement of the database systems.

> **THE JOHNS HOPKINS RETROSPECTIVE LIFE HISTORY STUDY: DATA ORGANIZATION ISSUES**

The Retrospective Life History Study collected life history data on a sample of black and white American men, ages 30 to 39 years, in 1969. There were 1,589 men in this sample, and data were collected via interviews on their educational, employment, military, and family histories.

During the interviews, the men recalled the major events in each of these areas from age 14 years until the time of the interviews in 1969. Complete histories in the different areas were taken from age 14 years forward. These data were collected retrospectively by an interviewer who prompted the respondents to recall the major events and dates of change in each domain.

Individuals varied appreciably in the eventfulness of their lives. For example, although the average number of jobs held for the men in this sample was 5, some individuals held as many as 40 different jobs. Similar differences in the average and maximum number occurred for other domains. Table 4.1 enumerates the average number of entries (events) per domain in this study and the maximum number of entries.

This variable nature of the eventfulness of people's lives created appreciable challenges for storing and processing the resultant data. In 1969, when this survey was fielded, the available computing capacity greatly constrained the approach to data organization. The small memory

TABLE 4.1 Average and Maximum Numbers of Events in 15 Life Areas
in the Johns Hopkins Life Circumstances Survey

Variable Number	Maximum Number of Entries in Sample	Average Number of Entries in Sample
1	40	4.97
2	19	1.35
3	14	1.08
4	7	1.23
5	40	8.39
6	13	1.99
7	9	1.35
8	18	3.14
9	7	1.46
10	22	7.69
11	26	2.06
12	18	2.55
13	13	1.17
14	26	7.15
15	21	4.96

of the computer and the linear arrangement of auxiliary storage devices (tapes) meant that the overriding concern was efficient storage and retrieval of the data.

Because the number of jobs, births, and educational changes differed across respondents, a common data format was not feasible. Typically, statistical processing of data required a standard format consisting of a row-by-column (cases-by-variables) format. However, the life history data, due to the variable number of entries, was not in a standard format.

One approach to making the data follow a common format entailed making every person have the same (maximum) number of entries for each variable. For example, if the maximum number of jobs held by anyone in the sample were 40, then each respondent would have 40 job entries even though the majority of these entries would not contain job data but rather "fill." Each respondent's record would be padded out for each domain so that all records in the data file would have the same format—that of the maximum number of entries across the domains in the sample. Unfortunately, if this sample had been converted to such a fixed-format matrix, then the resulting matrix would have been beyond the storage capacity of the existing computing equipment. For this sample, the matrix size for each respondent would have been 481 × 3,557. These dimensions represent the maximum number of months in the sample and the maximum number of entries accumulated across all variables. Therefore, the total sample would have required 2.7 billion words, with each individual requiring 1.7 million words. This was not a feasible arrangement on the computing equipment available at that time.

Looking at the problem in another way, the proportion of usable to "place-holding" data in this constructed matrix was .0007. Clearly, in such cases, the amount of actual data in comparison to the fill needed to position the data in a standard format is extremely small.

Rather than converting this particular data set to a fixed-format matrix, we stored the data for a person in variable-length records and constructed indexes to locate relevant portions of the data record. This entailed storing all data for a given person's record in a list whose length varied for each individual. Because the record format differed for each person, an index to each person's record also was constructed to facilitate locating work histories, residential histories, and the like.

These variable-length lists were efficient ways in which to store the data but created another set of difficulties. First, development of a special program to write and read the index and, in turn, to locate the desired data was required. Second, because different computer systems treated variable-length records in significantly different ways, considerable rewriting of the retrieval program was needed for different operating systems.

A satisfactory approach to the efficient storage of life history data eventually evolved. It maintains the benefits of the fixed-format approach (consistent data format) while avoiding the perils of variable-length records (lack of generality across systems). Rather than storing the data for a person together in one record, we divided the data for each person into separate files. Data pertaining to occupation were stored in one file, data for marital histories in another, and so on. Each file contained data that had the same format for each record and had consistent data definitions within the file. Within a given file, a person could have no entries, one entry, or multiple entries.

Storing data with complex linkages as separate but linkable data files was a strategy developed in several places at about the same time and followed conceptual work in relational database design taking place at this time. In the area of life histories, a paper by Ramsøy and Clausen (1977) described the benefit of using separate files for cleaning/editing Norwegian life history/occupational data. About the same time, Karweit (1973) developed a general system for storing and retrieving life history data based on relational database concepts. Following this approach, data are stored in their reduced form in separate files and are reorganized and reconfigured by a retrieval program. This approach is so common today that the advances realized by the introduction of relational databases may not be entirely appreciated. The relational database concept greatly simplified the work with complex data sets by storing them in their simplest form and using a database management system (DBMS) to retrieve information from them.

In this system, each record contains two types of information: the data itself and the relevant time span over which these values are in effect. For example, in marital histories, the beginning and ending dates of each marital state (e.g., single, married, divorced) would be indicated. Time is an integral part of the data record.

It was assumed that the time in one state (entry) did not overlap with other entries within a domain; that is, it was assumed that within a given domain, the respondent could occupy only one state at a given time. This assumption was made so that the retrieval of a variable at a specific time would result in a unique value. Multiple simultaneous states, such as full-time job holdings, were handled by creating separate data files to separate the overlapping areas (e.g., separate files for primary full-time job and second full-time job). The retrieval function (described later) was used to join together the various job holdings into job histories. Each data file, then, was constructed to ensure nonoverlapping time values so that an unambiguous value could be associated for each domain at any specific time. This does not mean that there could not be multiple job or education entries; rather, it means that the multiple entries were entered in separate files with the retrieval system (discussed later) used to link the data together.

For the Retrospective Life History Study, storing data in their most elemental or reduced form in separate files solved the data storage problem but did require a more sophisticated DBMS to carry out the necessary operations to join the separate domains together into life histories.

The Casalecchio data, however, introduced additional challenges because not only were changes in individual lives over time of interest, the additional complexity of changes in family and household groupings also was of interest. How to organize and manage life course individual-level data with the additional complexity of family/household groupings was the specific challenge posed by the Casalecchio Project. We encountered these issues in attempting to apply a life course perspective to the historical study of family life in Casalecchio, a community in northern Italy near Bologna.

The creation of life course data files for general populations has been one of the major methodological developments in social history over the past two decades, permitting quantitative analysis of historical processes that in the past had been studied only through qualitative (typically anecdotal) treatment. Such longitudinal databases on individuals' lives are difficult or impossible to create in most historical circumstances. However, the existence in Italy (as in a few other countries) of a population register system offered an unusual opportunity. The population register for each community follows members of the local population continuously over time. Individuals must register when they first enter the community; similarly, their departures are noted and dated. In between, all significant demographic events are recorded including births, marriages, and deaths. Separate, cross-referenced individual and household records in the population register provide a continuous view of where and with whom each individual is living.

This source allowed us to create a database that incorporates a record for each person in the community and to follow that person's demographic behavior and coresidential situation over time. By linking population register information for the 19,000 individuals who lived in Casalecchio at some time during the period 1865-1921 with various other types of archival sources (e.g., annual tax registers, periodic manuscript censuses), we were able to capture detailed socioeconomic, demographic, coresidential, and kinship information on the people who lived in this community. Casalecchio in this period was of special interest from a life course perspective because it allowed us to examine the intersection of important historical changes with life course processes. Formerly a traditional sharecropping community in which people typically lived in large, complex family households, in these years the community saw tremendous social, economic, and political changes. Industrialization took hold, urbanization spread, the archaic regime of the papal states gave way to the secular Italian nation, a potent socialist movement swept the area, literacy spread, and death and birth rates declined. Table 4.2 describes how these data were organized at the individual level in the Casalecchio database.[1]

TABLE 4.2 Description of the Individual-Level Data in the Casalecchio Database

File	Description	Records	Characters per Record	Total Data
F01	Description	19,052	54	1,029K
F02	Migration	20,290	52	1,055K
F03	Marriage	2,490	97	242K
F04	Coresidence	22,342	66	1,475K
F06	1861 census	2,372	35	83K
F07	1865 census	2,470	47	116K
F08	1871 census	2,810	37	103K
F09	1881 census	2,860	39	111K
F10	1911 census	4,420	46	203K
F11	1921 census	5,990	47	281K
F12	Legitimation	315	35	11K
F15	Name	32,916	57	1,876K
F17	Household head	3,868	40	154K
F18	Annual tax	18,882	47	887K
F19	Conscription	2,007	30	60K

NOTE: K = thousand.

Moving beyond the analysis of individual transitions to include larger contexts presents both conceptual and methodological challenges. In particular, the problem of defining household units over time has bedeviled both sociologists and historians. The major problem is that the household has no necessary longitudinal continuity. Unlike the case of the individual, who has well-defined birth and death dates, fixing beginning and ending dates for a household often is arbitrary.

Just what constitutes a new household and when an old household should be thought to have gone out of existence are thorny issues. For example, if a wife and her three children leave her husband and move a block away, then which of these two coresidential units should be considered new and on what basis? What if the husband had died? Even when beginning and ending dates are fixed for household units, different individuals move into and out of these units over time, raising questions as to just what we mean in holding that we are dealing with the same households over time.[2] A crucial methodological implication of these considerations is the need to deal with both the individual and the constellation of coresidential relationships among individuals. From a life course vantage point, the emphasis is on coresidence (a dynamic process of relationships among individuals) rather than on households (seen as reified longitudinal units). In the Casalecchio Project, as in the Retrospective Life History Study, the basic data pertaining to individuals are seen as event histories. The Casalecchio data, unlike the Retrospective Life History data, consist of event histories of both individuals and coresidential groupings. The major challenge posed by the Casalecchio data was to extend the unit of analysis to incorporate coresidence and to flexibly link together individual and coresidential histories.

Because of the size of the database, the use of a relatively slow computer system for system development (IBM 286 or equivalent) and the need to flexibly retrieve the data according to quite different definitions, how we stored and accessed the data were critical concerns. For issues that focused primarily on retrieval of individual event histories, the strategies developed for the Retrospective Life History Study were entirely satisfactory. Coresidential histories also were thought of as event histories. Within either the individual or coresidential level, the procedures that we developed earlier were adequate. The challenge was to link together the individual and coresidential event histories over time.

➢ DATA MANAGEMENT ISSUES

Although efficient storage of the data is nicely handled by the separation of the life histories into separate domain files, actual analysis of the data requires linking these separate areas back together into life histories. One important set of research issues for the Retrospective Life History Study, for instance, was the relationship between events across domains. Therefore, the ability to flexibly join together the various domain files is essential. For example, to examine the relationship between the timing of the birth of one's first child and the timing of job changes requires several steps. First, the time of the event "birth of first child" needs to be determined; next, this date must be used to locate the relevant entry in the occupational data. Table 4.3 shows the occupational and birth histories for hypothetical respondents and indicates the relevant dates for birth of the first child and then the occupational record that would be linked to this event.

TABLE 4.3 Linking Two Domain Files: Occupational Status at Date of Birth of First Child

(a) Birth Histories

Person	Data	Date
1	Male	**October 1977**
1	Female	December 1978
3	Male	**April 1980**
3	Female	April 1980
4	Female	**September 1977**
4	Female	November 1978
4	Female	November 1980
4	Male	July 1984

(b) Occupational Histories

Person	Data	Date
1	Waitress	October 1974 to June 1975
1	**Hairdresser**	**July 1975 to July 1979**
1	Waitress	October 1979 to December 1985
2	Computer programmer	October 1976 to January 1982
2	Area manager	February 1982 to December 1985
3	**Grocery store clerk**	**June 1975 to October 1980**
3	Grocery store clerk	October 1983 to December 1985
4	**Writer**	**December 1975 to December 1985**

NOTE: Bold entries show dates of first births and occupations held at dates of first births.

As was the case with the development of approaches to storing the data, we have developed numerous approaches to the data management task since 1969. These different versions in part reflect developments in computer software and hardware but also stem from our changing understandings of the requirements for a flexible data management system for life course data.

One important understanding that has remained throughout the development of different implementations is the view of the data as event histories. Event histories record the changes over time in the value of a variable. Each entry records not only the value of the variable but also the date or span of time when that value is in effect. The format of each entry is the same, containing the individual's identification code, the value of the variable, and the relevant dates. The basic requirement for the retrieval system is the need to link together records for individuals using time as the delimiter. Time may be age, date, or when another event took place. In the following, we provide some specific examples of time-contingent retrievals that were possible with a program designed for the Retrospective Life History Study:

    a. Retrieve the occupation held in January 1960.
    b. Retrieve the occupation held at age 20 years.
    c. Retrieve the occupation held at the date of first marriage.
    d. Retrieve the occupation held 1 year after the first divorce.
    e. Retrieve the occupation held at the birth of the second child.
    f. Retrieve the age at date of marriage.
    g. Retrieve the age at first job.
    h. Retrieve the age at which had first child.
    i. Retrieve the age at which occupational prestige was the highest.

The explicit incorporation of time (e.g., age, date) and event time (e.g., date when an event occurs for the first time) as a part of the retrieval language was conceptually very important. All accesses of the database specify a time clause. The time clauses just mentioned include specific dates (e.g., January 1960), ages (e.g., 20 years), and events (e.g., date of first marriage, 1 year after first divorce, age at first job). The time clause indicates which of the multiple entries in the event files are to be considered.

These examples entail determining a unique entry for retrieval. Other types of retrieval may accumulate frequencies or durations across events. Determining the frequency of the number of births between ages 20 and 30 years is one example of this type of retrieval. The duration of unemployment from first entering the labor market until age 45 years is another example.

For many analyses, the unit of analysis is clearly understood to be simply the individuals for whom data were collected. Typically in such cases, each row in a matrix represents the individual's data and each column contains the values of the variables for that individual.

In analyzing life event data, however, other units of analysis may be relevant. In some analyses, the unit of interest may be the spells themselves (e.g., length of time remaining in a job). In others, it may be transitions between states (e.g., leaving school). This need to focus on different units of analysis is an important aspect of research in life events. It suggests the importance of being able to define the unit of analysis flexibly as an attribute not of the data themselves but rather of how the user will look at the data. In other words, the data may be stored in whatever way is convenient and economical, and the task of the DBMS is to create working files that will mirror the particular view required by the analysis.

The need to create files from the same database that are physically structured in very different ways typically is treated on an ad hoc basis. One simply writes a "little program" to create data pertaining to spells or transitions.

The ability to easily restructure the data to pertain to transitions or persons has been a feature of the various versions of the retrieval system we have created. This proved to be very useful. For example, in the Retrospective Life History data, we could create an output file that pertained to all (or selected) individuals in the sample or one that pertained to transitions in particular domains (e.g., job changes). The output when the transition was the unit of analysis would contain two adjacent jobs. Another useful feature allowed tagging or associating other variables in the database to the job change record. For example, we might create a job history file and associate counts of the number of children born accumulated from the date of marriage to the beginning of each job held.

The flexible definition of the unit of analysis is an important requirement for work with life history data. Its significance and some of the associated difficulties came to be more fully understood in our work with the Casalecchio data, which involved not just individuals and their transitions but also individuals and their coresidential situations (and these also changed over time). The Casalecchio Project appreciably extended the data organization and management problem by requiring units of analysis other than those derived strictly from the individual level.

We addressed this problem in a relatively straightforward manner by providing linking files at the individual and coresidential levels that allowed us to locate the coresidents for a given individual and the individuals within a household at any specific point in time. The virtues of this approach were the ease of maintaining the data file and its ease of use. To improve efficiency, we assigned identification codes for the individuals and the households in such a way that the record in the database that provided this linkage information was directly accessible from the identification code itself. This direct access of the data from the identification code greatly decreased data access time, an important consideration given the size of the database and the complexities of the retrievals.

To illustrate this point, we briefly give two specific examples of the flexibility that is possible with this type of approach. First, assume that we are interested in the age/sex composition of households (coresidential situations) in Casalecchio on June 15, 1873. This type of statistic is readily obtainable with this system as a retrieval that asks for the household as unit of analysis. Mechanically, the management system first locates all coresidential situations that were in existence on that date in 1873 and then uses the individual identifiers located in the household-to-person file to locate the sex and calculate the ages of all the people living in that particular household on that date.

Another related example starts at the individual level to document the age and gender composition of the household into which people move when they enter Casalecchio. This analysis specifies individuals as the unit of analysis and links attributes of their coresidential situation to their individual data.

These two examples entail different access paths through the data and provide, in the former case, estimates for all households in 1873 and, in the latter case, estimates for all individuals as they moved into Casalecchio. These two examples illustrate the capacity of the retrieval system to flexibly view data according to the analytical question at hand.

➢ THE NATURE OF LIFE HISTORY DATA

Our work with the Retrospective Life History database and the Casalecchio Project began with the pragmatic task of locating workable schemes for efficiently handling complex data structures. As we worked with these data and with other data sets that focused on life histories, several key elements that were common to them became apparent.

Three key features of life histories have framed our development of computer methods for their organization and management. First, life histories are viewed as a collection of interconnected histories in various domains such as education, occupation, and family formation. Second, these domains are conceptualized as event histories. As such, the basic measurements include the state of the variable (i.e., its value) and the time when changes in the variable occur. Third, there are multiple units of analytical interest associated with the study of life histories. It is useful to separate these units into different levels of *case* and *temporal* aggregation. Case aggregation indicates whether the unit of analysis refers to persons, households, or other groupings of which individuals may be members. Temporal aggregation indicates the time frame of the case aggregation. For instance, time may be specified as at a particular point or on a particular date, between two dates, or across all events. Specification of the unit of analysis involves indicating both the case and temporal view of the data.

➤ DOMAINS, EVENT HISTORIES, AND UNITS OF ANALYSIS

The view of life histories as a collection of interconnected event histories in separate domains served as a useful practical and conceptual starting point. Domains or life areas such as education, occupation, and family formation clearly are interconnected, but analytically it is extremely useful to consider them as separate areas for measurement and data organization purposes. Separating lives into domains that share the same data structures was a fortuitous insight that greatly simplified data storage. It also forced some unexpected conceptual clarifications such as what is meant by "job held" when a person simultaneously holds more than one job.

Let us take the occupational domain to illustrate our approach. The individual's occupational history is thought of as a collection of job or occupational spells, each indicating relevant features of the job as well as the beginning (T1) and ending (T2) date of the job. The events within a domain are nonoverlapping; that is, the T1's and T2's within a domain do not overlap. When events do overlap, the data are redefined until the conflict in time is eliminated. For example, if a person holds two full-time jobs simultaneously, then these two jobs would be stored in separate files and treated as separate domains such as primary and secondary job.

The T1 and T2 may be years, months, days, minutes, seconds, or whatever unit of time is analytically sensible. Because the basic data are thought of as a collection of event histories in which changes in status, not complete accounting across time, are recorded, the choice of time metric does not affect the data representation.

An entry (record) in a particular domain file always contains a measure of each variable in the domain and the beginning and ending time for the entry. A new entry is recorded when there is a change in the variable of interest such as a change in status (e.g., unmarried to married, married to divorced). This raises the question of the appropriateness of "events" as a data type in the study of life histories. For many changes that take place in the life course, it may not be possible to determine the onset or exact time of occurrence of the change. In fact, the transitions from one state to another may be gradual, not abrupt, more of a process than an event. Thus, the requirement that a beginning and ending time be attached to each change may be problematic. The event history approach is more appropriate for studies that focus on changes in areas such as births, deaths, marriages, divorces, and migration rather than on questions such as changes in a person's emotional status, cognitive abilities, and worldview.

The most difficult database issue in both the Retrospective Life History Study and Casalecchio Project is the need to flexibly restructure the data for different units of analytical interest. As already discussed, the unit of analysis specification includes both case (i.e., the level of aggregation such as individual, household, or kinship grouping) and time. Time includes alternatives such as looking at all events as of a specific date, accumulating counts or durations of events between specific dates, or looking at all events that are recorded for a given level of case aggregation.

In the Retrospective Life History Study, there is only one level of aggregation for cases: the 1,589 men who were interviewed. Therefore, the unit of analysis issue in this study involves only the temporal views of the data.

In the Casalecchio database, both case and time specifications are needed. The levels of aggregation for case could be individual, households, or kinship relations. The level of aggregation for time also is needed to provide the specification of unit of analysis.

The data structure that most nearly approximates these types of complex time and case specifications is a network in which the nodes indicate the case level of aggregation and the linkages between the nodes indicate the time over which the link is active as well as the nature of the link (e.g., has a specified kin tie or lives in the same household).

We handled the problem of dealing with the coresidential unit by creating two cross-referenced sets of data files: individual level and household level. The household-level files employed the numbering system used by the officials of Casalecchio themselves in distinguishing household units in their population register. Using these records, we created, for example, one file that provides dates of beginning and ending of each period of household headship, along with the identification number of the head, as recognized by the town officials. Other household-level records, such as the annual household tax records, likewise constitute separate files, the data pertaining to the household unit.

For each individual, on the other hand, we created a file that consisted of a series of dated records indicating the sequence of households in which the individual lived. The household identification number in the individual's record permits us to determine, for any date, exactly who lived together.

The DBMS that has evolved from the Casalecchio work incorporates the view outlined here of the unit of analysis as the specification of case and time. Building in specific views of the data (essentially all Case × Time combinations) provides a convenient manner of working with these complex data structures. In the next section, we briefly describe the basic elements of this system.

➤ BASIC ELEMENTS OF A DATABASE SYSTEM FOR STUDYING LIFE EVENTS IN SOCIAL CONTEXTS

Here we suggest some general requirements for a database system designed to facilitate the study of life events in social context. Karweit recently incorporated many of these features into a PC-based program. It is useful to see the basic task as that of defining *what* is to be retrieved, *for whom* it is to be retrieved, and *when* (i.e., the time contingencies that are in effect). For example, if we want to determine the occupational status of all the men in the Retrospective Life History Study at age 25 years, then this amounts to a retrieval statement that specifies *what* (the value of occupational status), *for whom* (the unit of analysis, in this case individuals), and *when* (at age 25 years). The *for whom* and *when* specify the case and time aspects of the unit of analysis. More complex retrievals, such as finding the average age of the members of a household in which one resided at age 30 years, also can be specified in terms of *what, for whom,* and *when* clauses. In this case, the *what* is average age, the *for whom* is the individual's coresidents, and the *when* is the date when the individual respondent was age 30 years. The *when* part of this specification is straightforward and entails stipulating either an age, a date, or a co-occurrence of an event to determine which events are to be considered. The flexible definition of time as age, date, or when an event occurs is critical for working with life events. The first part of the retrieval statement specifies *what* is to be retrieved. This might simply be the value of the variable (e.g., occupation). In addition, the *what* statement of the retrieval may ask for the duration of a state (e.g., length of time spent in first marriage) or the count across a span of time of the occurrence of a variable (e.g., number of times married between ages 15 and 45 years). When the unit of analysis (the *for whom*) pertains to coresidents or other aggregates, the *what* specification also can be statistical means and percentages.

The *when* part of the retrieval sentence qualifies which events will be included in the retrieval. The specification of time may be in terms of age, calendar time, or the occurrence of another event. Examples include requesting the marital status of all respondents at age 50 years or at the dates they took their first jobs or when they last attended school.

➤ DISCUSSION

At the time we began developing computer methods for handling life course data, relational database systems and personal computers did not exist. Because such systems are now commonplace, it is reasonable to ask whether there is need for future work in this area and, if so, in what direction it might proceed. Storage problems that plagued us when working with the 16,000-word IBM 1401 in the 1960s clearly are not an issue today in the world of personal computers that measures disk space in gigabytes. The retrieval problems that haunted us when working on mainframes without benefit of a DBMS also are not much of an issue given the availability of numerous relational database systems.

So, in contrast to what usually is argued in the ending sections of a chapter about the need for better methods, this chapter argues that the methods probably are already there. What is lacking is a conceptual bridge to those methods.

It is ironic that our work, which has involved a good deal of effort in the development of computer methods for life course studies, may, in the end, be more useful in providing this conceptual bridge than in providing the actual methods themselves. Two particular conceptualizations that have emerged from our work and that may help in building this bridge are the view of life course data as event histories and the formulation of the units of analysis problem in terms of case and temporal levels of aggregation. These understandings, coupled with powerful relational database systems, may provide a conceptual and practical base for studies of complex and dynamic processes in future life course research.

➤ NOTES

1. For more information on the data sources used in the Casalecchio study and the record system, see Kertzer and Hogan (1989, pp. 189-208). Some of the results of the life course analysis of these materials, using the database described in this chapter, may be found in the previously mentioned work along with Kertzer and Hogan (1985, 1986, 1990), Hogan and Kertzer (1985a, 1985b), Kertzer and Karweit (1991, 1994), and Kertzer, Hogan, and Karweit (1992). For an excellent discussion of the value of using life course data and adopting a life course approach to historical family study, see Alter (1988).

2. We discuss these issues at greater length in Karweit and Kertzer (1986). On the problems of dealing with households as longitudinal units, see also Kertzer and Schiaffino (1983) and Kertzer (1986).

Chapter 5

Retrospective Versus Prospective Measurement of Life Histories in Longitudinal Research

JACQUELINE SCOTT
DUANE ALWIN

To link earlier and later events within individual lives or show the evolving structure of the life course, we need valid and reliable reports about people's life histories. Obtaining accurate and complete information about the past is not easy. The focus of this chapter is on two distinct, but related, methods for collecting life history data in formats that are amenable to life course analysis. One method involves collecting data prospectively by a series of current reports on present circumstances. In this design, the same individuals are reinterviewed at different points in time to build up a series of measures that can be used to study the unfolding changes in people's lives. The alternative method is to collect data retrospectively and rely on people's present recollections about the past (Schwarz & Sudman,

AUTHORS' NOTE: During the preparation of this chapter, Jacqueline Scott was Director of Research at the Economic and Social Research Council's Research Centre on Micro-Social Change at the University of Essex, the support of which is gratefully acknowledged. Duane Alwin was supported by grants from the National Institute on Aging (AG04743 and AG09747). The authors thank Paul Thompson, Glen Elder, and Janet Giele for helpful comments on previous drafts.

1994). One of our aims in this chapter is to assess the conditions under which one approach or the other is more useful. In particular, we weigh the advantages and disadvantages of the different methods for collecting data over the life span, whether by looking backward, by a series of current reports on present circumstances, or by a combination of these two approaches.

This chapter provides a framework for discussing these different methodological approaches and provides illustrative examples of life history data collection methods from existing studies. We focus primarily on the opportunities and limitations of large-scale survey data, but many of the same issues would apply to smaller scale qualitative studies. We draw on different types of longitudinal studies from Europe and the United States that have used both retrospective and prospective methods for collecting life history information on issues as diverse as marriage and fertility, employment, income and standards of living, collective memories of national historical events and changes, intergenerational mobility, psychosocial well-being and personality, psychiatric symptoms, and political attitudes. We then evaluate the use of retrospective and prospective approaches according to standard practical and methodological criteria, specifically cost and the quality of measurement.

> MEASUREMENT OF
> LIFE HISTORIES

One of the key insights of the life course perspective is that people's lives are uniquely shaped by the timing and sequencing of life events (Elder & O'Rand, 1995). This emphasis points to the wider sociohistorical influences on people's lives and to the interconnection of the various strands of individual life trajectories such as those concerning schooling, employment, military service, marriage, family, wealth, and health. Thus, Elder, Shanahan, and Clipp (1994) could argue that the point in a man's life cycle when he was called into active military duty during World War II had lifelong implications for employment, schooling, and many other aspects of life.

To understand how earlier events influence the present (and future), or to understand the processes by which various life changes occur, it is essential to have accurate information about both the past and the present.

There is wide agreement that it is preferable to collect data that relate to current circumstances. Nevertheless, this is not always possible, and, due to failed opportunities, lack of resources, or poor planning, researchers often find it necessary to get people to reconstruct the course of their past lives. We subscribe to the view that, all other things equal, it is clearly better to collect information from individuals and households prospectively, that is, to gather data on people's lives as they are living them. Yet, that often is not possible. Moreover, longitudinal research designs can be both time-consuming and expensive. Thus, the question becomes one of trade-offs because *all other things* rarely are equal.

Life History Data

The discussion of longitudinal measurement can be clarified by stating more precisely what we take to be the subject of measurement, that is, what it is about life histories that we wish to know. According to Elder (1992), a life history is "a lifetime chronology of events and activities that typically and variably combine data records on education, work life, family, and residence" (p. 1122). He gave examples of the use of life history calendars (as in the Freedman, Thornton, Camburn, Alwin, & Young-DeMarco [1988] study) and what has come to be called "event history data," which record the precise timing of transitions in and out of various states (Teachman, 1982). Yet, the scope of quantifiable life history information could be broadened to include subjective states as well as the more common demographic, organizational, positional, and structural states. As Thomas (1966) pointed out, subjective states have tangible consequences, and attitudes, values, expectations, and morale are useful subject matters of life course analysis and are, therefore, a legitimate form of life history data; for example, Kessler, Mroczek, and Belli (1994) discussed the importance of knowing childhood psychopathology in epidemiological studies of mental illness. Prospective data on this topic are essentially unavailable, and the main approach has been retrospective. But either way, the point is that things such as past levels of psychological well-being should be viewed as relevant pieces of life history.

To capture this broader view of life history data, but also to simplify our discussion, we suggest that the object of measurement in the study of life histories includes variables that fall into three categories: (a) event histories, (b) the cumulation of experiences, and (c) the evaluation or interpretation of experiences. These three categories are given, along with examples, in Table 5.1. The first category refers to the collection of past events, their timing, their duration, and their sequences. A complete event history would cover multiple domains and would, within a particular substantive focus, cover the interconnections of different events. Also, within a given domain, an event history would include all transitions from one state to another (e.g., from being unmarried, to married, to marital termination, to remarriage). It should be clear that any design that simply records the "state" a person is in at a distinct time in his or her life, without recording the entire history of events and transitions, falls short of measuring an event history. This category also includes, as part of an event history, the current occupancy of given states (e.g., never married, married, separated, divorced, widowed), but, by definition, durations and transitions out of current states are censored.[1]

The second category shown in Table 5.1 refers to what probably is the main focus of most survey measurement, namely *where people are* at a particular point. It refers to the cumulation of experiences that result directly from people's event histories (but are attained via many different types of biographical sequences) and to the cumulation of experiences resulting indirectly from a life's events; for example, amount of schooling, years of labor force experience, and number of children are examples of cumulative experiences that result directly from event histories, and it is clear that individuals can arrive at having a given "trait" (e.g., a college degree) via many different routes. Other cumulative experiences are less directly tied to events and transitions and result more from what happens within a given "state." Characteristics such as job skills, academic abilities, knowledge, commitment to parenting, and mental illness reflect both ontological factors and the environment to which individuals are exposed through their histories of development and life experiences. As the examples in Table 5.1 show, it is conceivable to measure the cumulation of experiences both in the past (e.g., aspects of family background) and in the present, and it also is possible to gather expectations of future experiences. In all cases, measurement of variables in this second category assesses an individual's past, present, or future status without regard as to how he or she got there (or how he or she feels about it). Thus, social surveys that measure current attitudes, beliefs, values, abilities, and other individual traits or characteristics are focusing mainly on the "factual" cumulation of experiences in the present.

TABLE 5.1 Types of Life History Data

1. Event histories
   a. Past events: Domain-specific events, their timing, duration, and sequences

      Examples: Residential, marital, fertility, employment, job/occupation, and schooling histories

   b. Present statuses: Current domain-specific statuses, the duration of which are right-censored

      Examples: Current residence, marital status, parity, employment, job/occupation, and school attendance

   c. Future expectations

      Examples: Fertility intentions, mobility expectations concerning residence or job

2. Cumulation of experiences
   a. Past experiences

      Examples: Parental statuses, schooling, labor force experience, achievements, skills, past interests, past attitudes, values, and so on

   b. Present experiences

      Examples: Schooling, work, abilities, skills, interests, attitudes, and values

   c. Expectations of future experiences

      Examples: Longer term aspirations concerning careers and life plans

3. Evaluations/interpretations of events and experiences
   a. Past evaluations

      Examples: Evaluation of past circumstances in contrast to present conditions to determine direction of change

   b. Present evaluations

      Examples: Income, job and marital satisfaction, assessment of quality of life

   c. Evaluations of future expected events and experiences

      Examples: Evaluations of future in contrast to past and present, optimism, and beliefs in efficacy of planning

Our third category of life history measurement objectives refers to the evaluation of life's experiences, in either the present or the past or as anticipated in the future. Such evaluations are essentially subjective, and, in a broad sense, the interpretations of events and experiences are the meaning an individual places on variables in the first two categories. To some, because of the inherent confounding of the role of informant and the autobiographical content, much of the life history data in which we are interested never can be excluded from this category (Back, 1994). This view would force us to blur the distinctions among *events, experiences,* and *meanings* as our classification scheme, but we do find in ourselves some sympathy for the philosophical stance that communication of "truth" in surveys is nigh impossible and that all survey data are essentially "interpretational." Of relevance here is an interesting review by Pearson, Ross, and Dawes (1992) that showed how responses about one's past are influenced by personal beliefs about individual stability and change (see also Ross, 1988). In certain circumstances, people are likely to assume that their attitudes have remained the same even though reinterview data show clear change; in other circumstances in which change was expected, the past is recalled as different from the present despite evidence to the contrary. Of course, "true change" is confounded with measurement error in such types of data, and without some correction for measurement errors, it may not be possible to draw any clear inferences about what has changed (Alwin, 1994).

Regardless of philosophical equivocation, we hope that this simple classification scheme will assist us in examining the trade-offs between the two basic approaches to measurement we review here—retrospective and prospective measurement. We do not intend to suggest that such a scheme captures the complexity of what is of interest to life course analysts; rather, we suggest that some classification is useful in evaluating the various longitudinal designs. For example, one conclusion might be reached about the quality of retrospective measurement, when the focus is on cumulation of experiences, but quite another might be reached when the focus is on gathering event histories. Or, one might conclude that specific types of retrospective information can be collected given that certain practical procedures are followed to ensure its relative quality. We turn now to an examination of these issues.

Retrospective and Prospective Life History Data

The life course perspective explicitly emphasizes the need to consider individual lives from the point of view of trajectories of events and experiences. This implies the need to collect longitudinal data. Yet, as Featherman (1980) suggested, it is important to distinguish between longitudinal *data* of the types reviewed heretofore and longitudinal *designs* for measuring such variables. From a design point of view, life history data can be collected prospectively (working forward in time) and/or retrospectively (working backward in time). The two approaches usually are contrasted, but ultimately both are needed. The advocation of longitudinal data does not imply any particular longitudinal design. Therefore, it is necessary to define precisely what we mean by prospective and retrospective *data* as opposed to prospective and retrospective *designs*. In so doing, we would note that in the survey methodology literature, the term "retrospective data" often is used as if it is a synonym for collecting information about past events and experiences. Yet, this fails to capture the distinctive meaning of the term "retrospection" in that it also involves reviewing things past and reporting present reactions. Merton (1956) made this distinctive meaning clear in his discussion of the *focused interview* in which he defines retrospection as asking people to think back to their responses to an event at the time it was happening. In the most trivial instance, one would want to know whether the person remembers a particular event (Schuman, Reiger, & Gaidys, 1994).

Merton (1956) drew a clear line between retrospection in this sense (recollections of past experiences and earlier responses) and retrospection (referred to by Merton as "introspection"), which is aimed at a review and reconsideration of the past and reporting present reactions. This type of data belong to the realm of "life review," that is, accounts of past states that are filtered through current mind-sets. These have been used extensively in life course research; for example, Elder (1974) drew on these in his early research on the Depression, and Clausen (1993) made use of such data in his *American Lives* volume.

Thus, the term "retrospective" may mean looking back on or thinking about things past or reviewing/contemplating the past rather than simply recalling or remembering things. In this sense, retrospections are not longitudinal at all; they are "current" or rooted in the present. Memoirs, autobiographies, biographies, and the like all are viewed as current "looking back" and, as such, are assumed to be affected not only by past experiences but also by present conditions. Used in this way, the term "retrospective" captures the nuances of what often is meant when one collects data on subjective interpretations of past events (Line 3a of Table 5.1). Such interpretations of the past draw on things that have happened more recently and explain past happenings in the context of the present.

This type of retrospective data differs from factual recollection or recall of previous events or happenings and their timing, durations, or sequences. The problem is how to disentangle the two types of retrospections because, as Bartlett demonstrated in the 1930s, *remembering is a reconstructive process, and memory inevitably is open to a range of distortions and reinterpretations in the light of subsequent knowledge and experience.* We return to this issue in our later discussion of problems in obtaining information about past events and experiences retrospectively, but we emphasize it here because it is one of the most critical issues to be confronted in obtaining retrospective data of high quality.

We also must note that, in addition to the ambiguities in the meaning of the term "retrospective," the term "prospective" also is potentially ambiguous. The term literally means "looking to the future." In a prospective panel study, the measurement design is forward looking, although the data collected usually are about the present and the past. In this sense, a panel design is prospective in that the plan is to interview a person/ household members at some later point in time, but "prospective data" would refer to expectations or aspirations about the future (see examples in Table 5.1).

Retrospective and Prospective Designs

When is it appropriate to use a retrospective or prospective design? Clearly, the research question at issue often points the design in a particular direction. For some issues, the central question concerns why particular events happen to people in the sense of being able to predict or explain why some people enter into a particular state or leave another (e.g., marriage or divorce, leaving the parental home, attending college). This is the type of question that can be addressed with *event history analysis* (Tuma & Hannan, 1984). For other issues, the key questions involve the consequences to the individual of either entering into or leaving a particular state; for example, what happens to the political attitudes of women as they leave the liberal college that was so influential in forming their views (Alwin, Cohen, & Newcomb, 1991)? This research question suggests that one would start with a sample of women who attended a liberal college and follow them through their lives, attempting to measure the factors that were likely to reinforce or undermine their earlier political leanings. Conversely, a retrospective issue might be concerned with how a person's present perceptions are influenced by the events or changes that occurred in the formative years of his or her adolescence. We return to this example later. Although people's recollections of the past are likely to be influenced by present circumstances and current conditions, for many purposes people's own perceptions of their past histories are precisely the information that researchers require. Moreover, one of the basic justifications for the survey method is that asking people questions is a remarkably efficient way of finding out about their lives—and this does include their past and present lives.

Of course, many research questions could be answered with both prospective and retrospective designs. Take, for example, the issue of how a woman's career advancement is affected by her taking time out of the labor force to have children. Retrospective event history data may provide quite reasonable information concerning the timing of women's transitions in and out of employment statuses, which could be used to analyze the impact of time out of the labor market on subsequent career advances. But if the analyst wished to include women's career aspirations and commitment to work in the analysis, then there would be little hope of collecting such information retrospectively without substantial bias. Rationalization, denial, and all the other convenient psychological mechanisms for reconciling people with their fates are likely to influence people's perceptions of their past hopes. There also is the psychologically important function of forgetting, and an immense amount of once familiar detail becomes irretrievable with the passage of time (Brewer, 1994). Even measuring objective data such as household income is all but impossible to collect with high reliability at a much later point in time, although concurrently it can be measured quite reliably (Duncan, 1992).

It is important, however, not to make too rigid a division between retrospective and prospective designs because, in practice, nearly all social surveys elicit some information about the distant past, for example, questions about the respondent's place of birth or the socioeconomic status of his or her family of origin. Moreover, prospective studies are almost invariably in the business of collecting retrospective data, albeit over a shorter recall period. Even measures about current occupation usually refer to the week preceding the survey, measures of current educational attainment often refer to qualifications that were obtained many years earlier, and most annual panels attempt to identify critical transitions that have occurred in the intervening year to build up continuous measures of change.

So, what does differentiate prospective designs from retrospective ones? Retrospective designs can, on their face, cover a longer time span than usually is practical with prospective designs. However, prospectively collected data are generally considered to be more reliable than recall data because of the limitations and biases of the human memory. In addition, prospective designs can increase the validity of the data because they can tap a far wider range of information on other life events or changes that might relate to the topic at issue but are not memorable at a later point in time. Prospective studies, however, have some important disadvantages, as we shall see, in that they tend to be very expensive, and panel attrition and missing observations due to nonresponse can present serious problems when using such data for life course analysis. In short, the main differences between these two measurement strategies involve elements that have both practical consequences and implications for the quality of data.

➢ LONGITUDINAL DESIGNS AND MEASUREMENT

Longitudinal designs incorporating measurements over time usually are depicted as superior to "cross-sectional" studies in which respondents are interviewed at one time only. Longitudinal studies sometimes are misleadingly equated with those that gather longitudinal data via prospective designs, whereas, as we have noted, longitudinal designs in fact often do use retrospective methods; for example, longitudinal or dynamic data on fertility and occupational histories can be collected quite reliably retrospectively. However, other information is more difficult to recollect accurately; for example, people's memories of their past plans and expectations are likely to be influenced by subsequent outcomes and present circumstances.

Another drawback of retrospective studies is that they can result in substantial selection biases because only survivors can be interviewed. This can be a serious problem for some life history studies in which the surviving members of older cohorts are likely to be less representative than survivors of younger ones (Featherman, 1980). But for many types of life history analysis, this is not a problem; for example, differential mortality has only a very limited impact on the analysis of individual work histories because survival chances of working age men and women are high. However, if the analysis relates in some way to household formation and dissolution, then differential survival can be a very serious problem indeed (Scott, 1995). This means that prospective panel studies have a considerable advantage over retrospective designs if we wish to understand how household changes affect individual lives.

Thus, different research issues in the intersection of personal and social histories require different types of longitudinal design and measurement methods. Here we concentrate on three types of design: prospective panel designs, cross-sectional retrospective studies, and studies that combine the two. In the following subsection, we draw on examples of longitudinal studies in Europe and the United States to illustrate some of the unique features of data associated with each design type.

Prospective Panel Designs

The sine qua non of prospective panel designs is that many of the causal antecedents of later behavior or events in people's lives can only be measured concurrently—at the time they occur (Featherman, 1980). This is particularly relevant for the life course perspective, which emphasizes the importance of the conditioning influences of prior life experiences and seeks to track various individual and family trajectories and transitions across time. One of the prime sources of prospective panel data on income is the Panel Study of Income Dynamics (PSID), which began in 1968 as a poverty study. New respondents are added to the PSID as the result of life course events that alter household composition, and the PSID has, over time, collected data on more than 37,000 people. Because the PSID follows the same people for a long period of time, and because it follows individuals who leave the original family to form new households, this panel provides invaluable information for studying the dynamics of life histories and particularly life histories as embedded in the family context.

One major finding of this prospective study is that the whole concept of the family must be rethought when placed in a longitudinal context. The family context clearly is of critical importance for understanding individual life histories, but this context is subject to a great deal of change over time. Nearly one quarter of the PSID's families experience at least some type of change in the typical year, and only about 1 in 20 households remained completely unchanged for the first 18 years of the study (Hill, 1992). Some of these life-cycle changes are routine and relatively straightforward; for example, couples divorce, spouses die, children grow up and leave home, and new children enter families at birth or adoption. Yet, many other family changes involve rather fuzzy concepts and, therefore, are subject to considerable measurement error; for example, children leave home and then "return to the nest," and couples separate and then reunite. One of the advantages of a prospective design is that it is able to monitor the complex and intricate sequence of family compositional changes by asking about the state at the time of interview and about recent "joiners" and "leavers." This reduces the definitional problems that would occur in any retrospective attempt to measure household change. Moreover, prospective panel designs allow research into the many interesting and important dynamics of individual lives that are associated with family compositional changes.

As a source of life history data, however, the PSID is not without its drawbacks. The study is primarily economic in focus and has very little psychological data. Moreover, it gathers information about the household on the basis of an interview with only one adult, usually the male "head of household," which means that there is no possibility for unpacking the complexity of internal family dynamics. This is a very serious limitation because family realities are likely to be very different for men and women or for the young and the old. Some of these limitations have been rectified in other panel studies in both Europe and the United States such as the British Household Panel Study (BHPS) (Buck, Gershuny, Rose, & Scott, 1994), the German Socio-Economic Panel (Brückner & Mayer's chapter in this volume [Chapter 7]), and the Study of American Families (SAF) (Freedman et al., 1988). Inevitably, different panel studies will have different strengths for life course analysis depending on their major foci and objectives. Ten examples of major prospective panel surveys are shown in Table 5.2, illustrating the range of topics and the different types of design (see also Young, Savola, & Phelps, 1991).

One of the simplest analytic uses of panel data is the description of gross change (Kessler & Greenberg, 1981). Repeated cross-sectional surveys can measure the aggregate level change only in the phenomenon of interest, whether it be poverty, unemployment, or whatever. However, panel data allow the analyst to measure the gross flows in and out of a state. This is useful, for example, in accounting for America's shrinking middle class (Duncan, Smeeding, & Rodgers, 1993). Using a cutoff level that left about 20% of adults as having low income, 10% as having high income, and 70% as being somewhere in the middle, it was possible to compare the transitions into and out of the middle class before and after 1980. On the

TABLE 5.2 Panel Studies in the United States and Europe

Study	Country	Type	Longevity	Main Focus
Panel Study of Income Dynamics	United States	Household	Annual 1968-	Income
National Longitudinal Study	United States	Cohort	Annual 1966-	Employment
National Longitudinal Youth Study	United States	Cohort	Varies 1971-	Employment
Wisconsin Longitudinal Study	United States	Cohort	Varies 1957-	Social mobility
National Child Development Study	Great Britain	Cohort	5 years 1958-	Child development
Survey of Income and Program Participation	United States	Household	4 months 1984-	Income support
Study of American Families	United States	Mothers and children	Varies 1961-	Attitudes and lifestyle
Bennington Study	United States	College attenders	Varies 1938-	Political attitudes
German Socio-Economic Panel	Germany	Household	Annual 1984-	Socioeconomic
British Household Panel Study	Great Britain	Household	Annual 1991-	Socioeconomic

positive side, more middle income American adults became more affluent in the 1980s than before. But on the downside, more Americans fell from middle-income to low-income status, and it became more difficult for low-income families to climb into the middle class. To measure such transitions in economic levels, prospective data are essential because it would be almost impossible to obtain accurate continuous income measures retrospectively.

One of the great advantages of the prospective panel design is that if the study survives and the representativeness of its sample can be maintained, then the potential for the analysis of change over the life course expands enormously. The PSID, for example, is now of sufficient longevity to be interviewing the grown-up children of the original sample households. This means that extensive intergenerational information is available with measures on the family circumstances of individuals when they were children as well as measures collected directly about their adult lives. Such data allow for research that traces continuity and changes in life choices and constraints across the generations and opens up new research possibilities on the interconnectedness of the life circumstances and trajectories of different generations.

Cross-Sectional Retrospective Designs

It requires a panel study of considerable longevity to study intergenerational change prospectively, whereas in a cross-sectional retrospective design such data can be collected relatively instantaneously. One of the most common retrospective questions used in cross-sectional designs is to ask the respondent for information about his or her father's occupation. Indeed, a whole industry of mobility research has been built on such retrospective reporting about the family of origin; for example, retrospective reports have been used to assess education's role in achieving social equality and the extent of intra- and intercohort occupational and class mobility (Blau & Duncan, 1967; Erikson & Goldthorpe, 1992; Featherman & Hauser, 1978).

A recent edited volume by Schwarz and Sudman (1994) concentrates on the use of retrospective measurement in the collection of autobiographical data. The volume reflects an endorsement of the need to consider the collection of retrospective data within the framework of a coherent conceptualization of the underlying cognitive processes that permits the identification of variables that determine the nature of the data. Their volume contains many useful chapters on the problems with collection of retrospective data including topics as diverse as reports of cigarette smoking, the experience of physical pain, dietary histories, reports of child support payments, the nature of past relationships, adolescent experiences, and the memory of historical events.

As illustrated by these examples, one great advantage of retrospective designs is that they can cover a very long time span. For example, in a study exploring how collective memories result from the intersection of personal and national histories, Schuman and Scott (1989) asked people to think back over the past 50 years and report what national and world events and changes they regarded as most important. People's choices clearly were structured by cohort, with people's memories referring back disproportionately to events that occurred in adolescence and early adulthood (see also Schuman & Rieger, 1992; Scott & Zac, 1993). Moreover, the qualitative retrospections indicate that the meanings people gave to particular events were heavily influenced by their own experiences during the impressionable years of youth. Of course, whether such retrospections depict the meanings of past events as they existed in the past or whether people's memories are inextricably linked to the present is difficult to determine without additional data. To assess the reliability of such retrospective accounts, it would be desirable to have measures that were collected contemporaneously with the event in question because, ideally, retrospective data should not be the sole basis for information on the past (Alwin et al., 1991; Henry, Moffitt, Caspi, Langley, & Silva, 1994).

Retrospective Measurement Within Prospective Panels

In most prospective panel studies, the use of retrospective measurement is an essential feature, especially for event histories, which are, by definition, about things that happened in the past. Virtually all prospective panel studies that gather data on event histories ask respondents to report events and experiences retrospectively over the past few months (e.g., Survey of Income and Program Participation [SIPP]), the past year (e.g., PSID, BHPS), or over several years (e.g., SAF, Wisconsin Longitudinal Study). Given that there are limitations to the accuracy of retrospective information, one key question, for which there is no easy answer, concerns the length of time over which events can be recalled with some reliability. The optimal design for gathering life history data is likely to be one that combines the best features of both prospective and retrospective measurements. One approach that embeds periodic retrospective measurement within the prospective panel design is the life history calendar (LHC).

A variety of forms of LHCs have been used in a number of prospective panel studies. One example, reported by Freedman et al. (1988), collected monthly data on the incidence and timing of event histories within a set of interrelated domains in a sample of 900 23-year-olds who had been interviewed once before. The sample was drawn from a population of the July 1961 birth records of first-, second-, and fourth-born white children in the metropolitan area of Detroit, Michigan (Wayne, Oakland, and Macomb counties), and the mothers of this sample had been studied prospectively from the times of births of their children. The database for this sample of women and their children includes eight waves of personal interviews with the mothers between 1962 and 1993. In 1980, the first personal interviews with the children born in 1961 were conducted, and these respondents were reinterviewed in 1985 and 1993. The rows of the LHC were the life domains and the categories of events covered by the study. The columns were monthly measurement intervals, beginning with the 15th birthday through to the occasion of the interview in December 1985. A recent study by Axinn and Thornton (1992) reported an additional application of this technique for the time lapsing between 1985 and 1993.

The application of the LHC in this study is important for several reasons. First, it provides a good example of how retrospective measurement methods can be embedded in what is otherwise a prospective panel study assessing the cumulation of experiences. Second, as Freedman et al. (1988) pointed out, the use of the LHC to link events and transitions over time improves the quality of the data. It is important to note in this regard that some events (e.g., marriages, births) are more easily remembered and provide important reference points for the timing of other events (e.g., geographic mobility, living arrangements, schooling, employment status) (Auriat, 1993). Third, Freedman et al. (1988) argued that the types of monthly detail their analysis required would have been very cumbersome to deal with in a conventional questionnaire; for example, the recording of monthly changes in living arrangements for a young population, who frequently change residences and patterns of living, would have been quite complicated in a standard sequence of survey questions. Finally, for most events, data can be collected quite accurately using this approach.

One of the flaws of the Freedman et al. (1988) study (although not related to their retrospective measurement of event histories) is that, except for characteristics of the mothers obtained from the earlier interviews, no data were collected on the lives and development of their sample prior to 18 years of age. This is somewhat at odds with the life course perspective, which usually would require the measurement of individual differences in developmental trajectories, or differences in personality or personal dispositions, at an earlier stage. Such earlier measures are important to understand the ways in which individual development and social change interact to affect outcomes (Elder & Caspi, 1990).

One example of a study that sought to relate adult development to aspects of individual differences at an earlier time is the classic study by Theodore Newcomb demonstrating how women students who were exposed to the rather liberal climate of Bennington College in the 1930s and

1940s shifted their social and political attitudes in the more liberal direction (Newcomb, 1943). Newcomb's original study spanned the women's 4-year stay at the college, but then the same women were reinterviewed some 25 years later in 1960-1961, revealing that, in general, the more liberal attitudes were retained into middle age (Newcomb, Koenig, Flacks, & Warwick, 1967). In 1984, Alwin, Cohen, and Newcomb (1991) conducted a nearly 50-year follow-up that gave support to a theory of political attitude development, the generational and attitude persistence model, which suggests that people are most vulnerable to historical and generational influences when they are young and that generally, after some period of formative years, people tend to grow more rigid in their viewpoints (Alwin, 1994; Alwin et al., 1991; Alwin & Krosnick, 1991a; Sears, 1983).

The Bennington study actually is an example of a combination of a prospective attitude measurement design and a retrospective assessment of the nature of the social processes affecting the development and maintenance of attitudes over the life span. This example is particularly instructive for assessing the reliability of retrospective life history data because (a) it covers a very long span of time, (b) it deals with attitudes, and (c) its special value is to be able to look at what happened *objectively* to these women, as indicated by the contemporaneous attitudinal measurements, within the context of their recollections about how and why their views had changed.

In 1984, the women were asked to give retrospective quantitative assessments of their attitudes at various stages in the life course, and these retrospective reports provide confirmation of the developmental processes that the prospective data revealed, that is, that the women's attitudes had shifted markedly in the liberal direction as a result of their college experiences and that these liberal leanings persisted over time. Thus, it appears that, at least on issues of real import and salience, retrospective attitudinal data can be quite reliable, contrary to assumptions commonly made. Kessler et al. (1994) reinforced this notion in their review of studies seeking valid retrospective indications of childhood psychopathology. They suggested that it might be possible to recover long-term memories of salient aspects of childhood psychiatric disorders with active memory search but that less salient memories might be difficult to recover because of either low salience or active processes of repression.

The Bennington study is somewhat unique in that in addition to having three waves of quantitative data collected over a nearly 50-year period in the biographies of the 335 women studied, the 1984 study also included qualitative interviews with 29 of these women. The qualitative data cast an interesting light on the women's own perceptions of why their attitudes had changed. One respondent who had changed from "leaning toward liberal" in 1960 to "very liberal" in 1972, stressed the important role played by her children, saying "My children radicalized me. All three of them became involved in causes, marches, and other worthwhile activities." Another respondent said, "With two sons and with the war in Vietnam . . . I had to deal with their feelings and with my feelings. I gradually lost faith in the government. I began disagreeing with many things I hadn't before—or [had] not thought about." It seems that not only were the children part of the supportive environment for the maintenance of their mothers' liberal views, but they also were an active socializing influence, stimulating further shifts in liberal orientations. Yet, despite the fact that women often recognized how their views had become more liberal, there still was a tendency to understate their earlier, more conservative leanings. Such systematic bias in retrospective reports is something we examine in more detail later in this chapter.

> ➤ EVALUATING RETROSPECTIVE
> AND PROSPECTIVE DATA

As we already have indicated, we reject the implied polarization between retrospective and prospective methods. Nevertheless, the terminology can be useful to our discussion of the validity and reliability of life history data. A major difference between these two methods undoubtedly is the practical one in that prospective longitudinal research requires considerable patience on the part of both the user and the funding agency, whereas the retrospective method has the appeal of providing relatively instant longitudinal data (Janson, 1990).

In discussing the different types of longitudinal designs, we already have touched on the main advantages and disadvantages of retrospective and prospective approaches. Yet, it is worth summarizing these briefly because it is important to consider such factors in not only the design but also the analysis of life history data. Practical considerations of time and money obviously weigh heavily (e.g., what type of data, and how much data, can be gathered for the money?), but they cannot be considered in isolation; they interact with substantive concerns (e.g., is the present reconstruction of the past an obstacle or a help to the research objectives?) and with issues of measurement quality (e.g., are more reliable contemporaneous measures more important than potential bias due to attrition?). There are no general answers to such questions, and researchers have to be guided by their particular research objectives.

Advantages and Disadvantages

In weighing such issues, the practical advantages and potential biases of retrospective designs have to be placed against the major cost and efficiency drawbacks of prospective designs and the real concerns raised by panel attrition and conditioning. However, first we consider several potential advantages of prospective data. The first is that prospective designs allow for data to be collected concurrently with the events in question; for example, parent-child interactions in early life may have important ramifications for child development but are impossible to collect retrospectively without substantial bias. A second and related advantage of prospective studies is that they allow for the continuous measurement of events and changes (whether they be detailed employment status changes or changes in subjective experiences such as mood changes in the menstrual cycle [Rossi & Rossi, 1977]) that would be far too burdensome in retrospective studies. In addition, prospective designs allow for the use of bounded recall techniques in which information about the status at the time of last interview can be used to anchor and, hopefully, improve respondents' memories concerning the timing of subsequent changes (Bailar, 1989).

Third, in prospective designs, it is far easier for researchers to impose theoretically driven definitions of life events that are ambiguous in practice; for example, it often is unclear when children leave the parental home because "leaving home" is a rather fuzzy concept (Buck & Scott, 1993). Similar considerations can apply to unemployment, marital separations, retirement, and other life or work history events and transitions. Fourth, prospective designs provide an opportunity to collect prospectively oriented data concerning individual aspirations and expectations and to compare these to actual outcomes at later points in time. Life course analysts, however, may well feel that individual histories and prospects are too limiting, and the fifth advantage of prospective designs is that they can provide data on the interaction of individual life trajectories within the household or family context. Retrospective designs would be limited to only those households that survive intact.

Prospective panels are not, however, without their drawbacks. First, there is the very real statistical problems that accrue because of attrition or nonresponse. In cross-sectional surveys, an original response rate of 70% might be regarded as acceptable. If, however, we assume that nonresponse is independent from one wave to the next, then by the third wave a panel study would have retained only 34% of the original sample. Because it is well known that panel attrition is not random (Kessler & Greenberg, 1981; Lillard, 1989), this may seriously undermine the representativeness of the panel across time.

Second, there is the issue of whether interviewing the same people over time affects the essence and quality of respondents' answers. This concern with panel conditioning is somewhat similar to what is known as the "Hawthorne effect," whereby the very act of making people subjects of a social investigation affects their subsequent behavior and thus makes them less "typical." There is some evidence of this phenomenon from election study panels in which panel participation appears to heighten people's political awareness and may even affect their likelihood to vote (Anderson, Silver, & Abramson, 1988). Such effects also have been observed in studies of marital satisfaction in which interviews can unintentionally trigger new perspectives in respondents and subsequently change their views or actions (Veroff, Hatchett, & Douvan, 1992). Panel conditioning also may affect the quality of the data reported; for example, there is evidence from the U.S. Current Population Survey that the longer people participate in the panel, the less likely they are to report current unemployment (Featherman, 1980). Yet, on the positive side, panel participation actually may improve the quality of data because, over time, respondents can be "trained" to keep records and documents that will help them report past events and changes with more accuracy.

Another drawback of prospective designs is the real problem of obtaining comparable measures across time. Even when a measure is repeated exactly, this is no guarantee that its meaning will remain unchanged. There is considerable support in the methodological literature for what Lykken (1968) called "literal replications" in studies over time (see also Duncan, 1975; Presser, 1982). At the same time, there are strong arguments in favor of "conceptual replications," especially for measures where what was appropriate and valid at one point in time would seem irrelevant or archaic at another point in time (Alwin et al., 1991, p. 76). This is an important concern because changes in either the content or meaning of repeated measures undermine much of the strength of prospective designs for investigating how the sociohistorical context of the life course has changed over time.

Retrospective designs have two major disadvantages over prospective designs. First, with retrospective designs, it is only possible to interview survivors. As we have seen, this is a real problem if the research relates in some way to household formation and dissolution because to study only households that survive intact would be highly biased. The second problem of retrospective designs is concerned with the reliability of recall data (Dex, 1995). In some cases, measures of past occurrences are unavailable both because of memory lapse and because the information is only available at the time. This applies to many psychological traits and developmental indicators; for example, it is hard to see how cognitive sophistication could be measured retrospectively. Even where retrospective data can be obtained, as in employment histories, people can misclassify episodes or events or recall them inaccurately. Moreover, individuals might give inaccurate information about their statuses at particular times in the past, usually because of errors in their recollections of the timing or dating of events. In general, the longer the recall period, the greater the concerns about the reliability of retrospective data, although there are important differences by subject matter and salience. Nonetheless, prospective designs seem likely to yield more reliable datings of life transitions and changes because the length of recall between waves usually is relatively short. Perhaps the most serious problem of retrospective data, as we have already noted, is that recent experiences and events may bias the recollections people make about their earlier experiences, making inferences about trends or causation somewhat circular (Dex, 1991).

Cost and Efficiency

Among the most significant realities that face those who carry out research on the life course are the cost and efficiency of gathering life history data. As we have suggested, longitudinal studies are very costly, not only in terms of the high level of funding required but also in terms of the labor needed to bring these studies to full term. Even so, the cost-benefit analysis is not entirely straightforward in that there are some major administrative advantages to maintaining a panel over many waves compared to studying cross sections of a population repeatedly, not the least of which can be a savings in financial costs (Duncan & Kalton, 1987). Nevertheless, retrospective cross-sectional designs have the considerable advantage that not only can they cover a far longer time span than is realistic for most panel surveys, but also retrospectively generated longitudinal data are relatively instant to produce. The degree of patience required for prospective designs, on the part of funders and researchers alike, is likely to be forthcoming only if the quality of the longitudinal data produced is significantly higher in terms of its validity and reliability. Yet, despite the fundamental concerns about the reliability of recall data, there are surprisingly few studies that have systematically compared the quality of retrospective and prospective longitudinal data (some notable exceptions include Markus, 1986, and Peters, 1988; for a review of the literature, see Dex, 1995).

Data Quality

One of the central concerns in any comparison of prospective and retrospective methods is the comparable quality of the data gathered from either approach. It ordinarily is assumed that data collected about the present is of higher quality than those collected about the past. The validity of quantitative retrospective survey data can leave much to be desired, as Thompson (1978) pointed out, citing one of the most pivotal studies in American sociology: Blau and Duncan's (1967) *American Occupational Structure*. The tales of imperfection in measuring father's occupational status related by Blau and Duncan (1967, pp. 14-15) are indeed somewhat disturbing. In brief, when they compared respondents' reports of their fathers' occupations to matched census records, they found only 70% agreement (out of 173 cases). They made the singularly *unreassuring* argument that although 30% disagreement may appear high, assessments of reports of current occupations to the census are not much better. Thus, whereas retrospective data may be poor, so are contemporaneous self-reports. On the face of it, that retrospective reports of parental occupation are as accurate as self-reports seems highly surprising. Yet, this conclusion has been borne out in more recent research reported by Bielby, Hauser, and Featherman (1977) and Hauser, Tsai, and Sewell (1983).

One method, discussed earlier, intended to improve the reliability of people's retrospective memories is the use of an LHC. The aim is to improve recall by placing the measurement of timing and duration of events in several domains (e.g., living arrangements, marriage, fertility, schooling, work) simultaneously within the same time frame. Thus, inconsistencies in the timings of events and sequences are made apparent by the calendar itself, and efforts can be taken to remove them. To our knowledge, little information about the reliability of LHCs exists because its assessment requires panel data. Freedman et al. (1988) gave several examples of reliability assessment in their use of the LHC including their report on employment status, which was measured on a three-category scale (full-time, part-time, no attendance/employment).

When reinterviewed in 1985, respondents appeared to have a noticeable bias in reporting that they had worked in 1980, whereas they had indicated otherwise in the 1980 interviews. Data presented by Freedman et al (1988, p. 64) showed that of the respondents who said in 1980 that they were not working, one third reported in 1985 that they had worked in 1980. But of the respondents who reported in 1980 that they were working either full- or part-time, only 7% or 8% reported in 1985 that they had not worked. In this example, respondents were only 23 years old in 1980, and the period of recall was not very long. The real test is to know how well people can recall their employment statuses over the life course. As part of a reliability assessment of retrospective work history data in a British study on social change and economic life, 400 Scottish couples were reinterviewed in 1986 after having originally been interviewed some 22 years earlier in 1964 (Elias, 1991). Thus, it was possible to compare their recollections of their occupational statuses to what they actually had said at the time. For both men and women, the agreement between their reported and recollected employment statuses was more than 60%. However, there were major discrepancies with regard to whether people were working or not for 20% of women and 27% of men. More recent research with other retrospective data sources has revealed the severity of recall problems, particularly for women and for older workers generally (Elias, 1996).

Perhaps our focus on employment status has given an unduly pessimistic picture of the reliability of retrospective data because of the ambiguities in this oversimplified categorical variable. Indeed, Freedman et al. (1988) drew attention to the fact that employment status is measured with far less reliability than reports of school attendance. Estimated reliabilities for school attendance and employment status are .90 and .62, respectively (calculated by the present authors from data presented by Freedman et al., 1988). Even more reliable was the recall of births and marriage, although, because respondents were only in their early 20s, there were relatively few such incidents. Nonetheless, enough comparison was possible to establish that the reliability of retrospective reports in these domains is extremely high.

We suggested earlier that even retrospective attitudinal data can be quite reliable if the attitudes concerned are highly salient. Yet, the Bennington study revealed some interesting divergences between retrospective data and attitudes measured at the time that indicate certain consistent biases in recollections. Alwin et al. (1991, p. 133) reported that among the most striking of the divergences in current and retrospective reports was the later denial of favoring Richard Nixon in the 1960 election. Of those who favored Democrats in the 1960 election, 93% had a consistent recollection in 1960. By contrast, 45% of those reporting in 1960 that they had preferred Nixon denied that report in 1984 and claimed they had supported the Democrat candidate. It seems reasonable to assume that the 1960 report, which essentially involved no retrospection, is the more reliable and that the distortion is in the liberal direction. Whether the distortion is to make political orientations appear more consistent over time, or whether it merely reflects a disavowal of the disgraced president, or both, is unclear.

In the Bennington example, the explanation of bias is likely to reside in a real attitudinal change. But often bias can result as an artifact of the survey design. For example, in many prospective studies, "seam effects" are observed in which reported transitions tend to concentrate either at the end or the beginning of a reference period (Hill, 1987). In the SIPP, for example, a "seam week" has been found to be by far the most important predictor of transitions from unemployment (Hill & Hill, 1986). This suggests that people's memories, in terms of the dating of transitions, are influenced by the reference period of the measurement instrument. Prospectively generated longitudinal data also can underestimate change, even for something as fundamental as marital histories. In an interesting comparison of retrospective and panel marital histories, Lillard and Waite (1989) found that there were a substantial number of marital disruptions that the panel history missed because they were short-lived and occurred between the times of interviews. This poses a real problem for the design of household panels. Establishing that there were no household changes between interviews could be very time-consuming, but a sequence of "snapshots" can miss important interim changes in household composition. One solution is to shorten the time between interviews, but that, of course, has negative implications for respondent burden and financial costs.

Unfortunately, costs are incurred in most strategies for improving the quality of the data. For example, the use of diaries may well improve the quality of retrospective data for a whole range of life history information such as daily hassles, consumption, travel, time use, and sexual behavior, but such diary methods place a considerable burden on respondents and require substantial investment in coding and processing the often nonstandardized data.

One final way in which the quality of life history data can be improved, although still at additional cost, is by using both self- and proxy reports. In general, self-reports are likely to be more reliable than information that can be provided secondhand by a proxy informant. Proxy information, however, can be used to gain some insight into the reliability of self-reports. As we have noted, for life history studies that wish to make use of respondents' own assessments of the impact of past events on their current states, there is a problem of circular causality. It is impossible to disentangle the effect that present states and emotions have on people's reconstruction of the past from the effect that previous experiences exert on current behavior. This problem was partially addressed in an interesting study of stamina in later life (Colerick, 1985) by comparing how the proxy reports of confidants matched the respondents' own reports of their current functioning (Clipp & Elder, 1987). People may not see themselves as others do, and the quality of life history data can be enhanced if more than one source of information is used.

How Should We Assess Data Quality?

The quality of retrospective data, however, is not easy to assess, especially if people revise their recollections of the past in the light of subsequent outcomes and present experiences. Of course, the present construction of past events can be interesting in its own right, but researchers are getting into fairly murky waters when they attempt to gauge how respondents' past lives were influenced by particular events on the basis of their later recollections. Some have even discounted retrospective data as "perhaps as much the products of the informants and instruments as they are of the phenomenon being investigated" (Yarrow, Campbell, & Burton, 1970, p. 36), and "cautionary tales" of the use of retrospective data are plentiful (see Alwin et al., 1991; Henry et al., 1994; Markus, 1986). On the other hand, retrospective accounts can be presented in a more positive light as the "most internally consistent interpretation of the presently understood past" (Cohler, 1982, p. 207), with the respondents' own interpretations of past events viewed as an essential aspect of life history data. Regardless of whether such data are obtained prospectively or retrospectively, or whether researchers employ qualitative or quantitative techniques of measurement and analysis, it is important to establish some guidelines regarding the assessment of the validity and reliability of the data on which our growing understanding of life history processes is based.

The term "reliability" is one that often is used to describe data quality, although there are many different ways in which it is used. It sometimes is used very generally to refer to the overall stability or dependability of survey results including sampling error, nonresponse bias, and reporting accuracy. Most usages of the term are somewhat more narrow, focusing specifically on the accuracy or reliability of measurement. Even then, there are at least two different conceptions of error. The psychometric definition of reliability, as applied to survey data, refers to the absence of random error. This conceptualization of error is far too narrow for most survey research purposes in which reliability is better understood as the more general absence of measurement error (Alwin, 1989).

Some of the confusion is reduced if we introduce the concept of "validity" as distinct from "reliability." Whereas on the one hand, reliability often can be gauged by reference to the consistency of measurement (net of actual changes and flaws of memory) over multiple attempts to measure the same thing using the same methods, validity, on the other, is concerned with assessing whether what actually is being measured corresponds to some external reality. Or, to put it simply, validity refers to the extent to which we are measuring what we think we are measuring. When issues of both reliability and validity are considered in relation to retrospective reports, it is little wonder that the two concepts often are confused because they are, in fact, confounded in most empirical data. Suppose, for example, that we consider how well a person reports his or her father's occupation or mother's employment. If the same measure is administered at Time 1 and Time 2 and the respondent's report is judged to be perfectly reliable, then this tells us nothing about the real issue in this case—whether the respondent's retrospective account of father's occupation or mother's employment corresponds with what his or her parents actually did. The latter refers to the validity of the report, the former to the reliability. Both are relevant to the assessment of data quality because even if one were able to measure both the parental status and the child's retrospective report of it, as an indication of validity of retrospective reports, each measure also would be affected by reliability. The issues obviously are confounded. Thus, the pessimistic account we gave earlier of the failings of social mobility researchers in being able to recover accurate reports of father's occupations would have to be revised if we clarified the role of unreliability of measurement in affecting each variable.

To quantitatively oriented researchers, it may be highly desirable not only to understand the sources of error (both unreliability and invalidity) in life history data but also to pursue them with the motivation to uncover their sources, reveal and reduce them, and ultimately purge them from our inferences, if not from the data. But to some qualitative life history researchers, this is silly. As Plummer (1983) put it, "To purge research of all these 'sources of bias' is to purge research of human life. It presumes 'real' truth may be obtained once all these biases have been removed" (pp. 103-104). Certainly, it may not be appropriate, even if it were possible, to simply export the concepts and techniques of analyzing the reliability of quantitative survey data and apply them to the more narrative forms of life history data.

In the end, it is very difficult to get a clear picture of the quality of retrospective data, in part because of the problems just mentioned but also because there are very little systematically interpretable data on this topic. Moreover, given the effects of design factors in data quality assessments (Alwin, 1989), it is difficult to draw comparisons across studies. Rather than try to review an entire literature and draw some type of conclusion from a meta-analysis of the results, it seems more useful to rely on the conclusions of the best available research. One recent study (Henry et al., 1994) reported the extent of agreement between retrospective and prospective measures of variables across several content domains in a large sample ($N = 1,008$) of 18-year-olds who had been studied prospectively since birth. Two types of comparisons were made: (a) comparisons of retrospective reports at age 18 years of childhood and adolescent events and experiences with the same variables measured at an earlier time and (b) comparisons of retrospective reports at age 18 years with archival records. As one would expect, their findings revealed that psychological variables (e.g., reports of psychosocial well-being or aspects of family functioning) revealed the lowest amount of consistency in reporting, whereas objective measures (e.g., physical height and weight) revealed much higher degrees of convergence. The authors warned, however, that even when retrospective reports correlated strongly with prospectively gathered data, the absolute level of agreement was quite poor. They concluded, "The use of retrospective reports about psychological variables should be approached with caution" (p. 100). Before one endorses this conclusion, however, it would prove a valuable lesson if the assessment of data quality in such types of "retrospective-prospective" comparisons could take into account the distinction referred to previously concerning the difference between validity and reliability of measurement, especially given the need to take developmental change into account in evaluating correlations of the same trait over time (Alwin, 1989, 1994).

> ➤ SUMMARY AND CONCLUSIONS

In *Alice Through the Looking Glass* (Carroll, 1952), the White Queen remarked to Alice that "it is a poor memory that only works backwards" (p. 229). She was right; if only people could remember the future, then we would not need to invest so much time and money on prospective research and, at the same time, we could dispense with the need to rely on retrospections. Unfortunately, like Alice, most people have imperfect memories of their past lives, and thus it seems unwise to rely on retrospective data as the sole basis for information on the past. Respondents are not disinterested observers of their own lives, and people have very limited insight into the sources of their own attitudes and behavior and are subject to denial, distortion, and lack of self-knowledge. Thus, although it is true that retrospective questions are a very efficient tool for social research, it is unwise to assume that answers will be entirely accurate.

In this chapter, we have tried to present a balanced view of the possibilities and limitations of both retrospective and prospective designs for gathering life history data. We made it clear that both approaches have disadvantages, which at times can be severe. We assessed the general advantages and disadvantages of each approach and the conditions under which each often is more useful. We made it clear that although it is generally preferable to collect data on people's lives as they are living them, that is not always possible. Retrospective designs often are essential, and, if gathered properly, data from such type of measurement can be very valuable. Indeed, when weighed against the costs of conducting prospective panel studies, both the monetary costs and the potentially severely biasing problems of nonresponse and panel conditioning, the advantages of retrospective measurement may seem to loom large. At the same time, retrospective designs simply cannot compensate for prospectively collected detailed life histories. Retrospective data also can be very misleading, especially when the individual's efforts to present a coherent, socially acceptable self get in the way.

If both prospective and retrospective data have merits, then the ideal may point to a middle ground solution. There is no denying the great benefits of prospective panel studies, but few can afford such a vehicle for primary data collection and many of the existing panels have limited foci that restrict their potential for secondary analysis. Therefore, retrospective measurement is, for most social researchers, an indispensable tool. But to rely on retrospective measurement alone seems ill-fated, especially when one recognizes the great risks of recall bias that exist. As noted earlier, it probably is unwise to base one's conclusions about the past and its influence on retrospective data alone.

The challenge to those designing the optimal longitudinal measurement design, given considerations of cost and data quality, is to find the acceptable limits for gathering data retrospectively. Unfortunately, we do not know enough at this point to offer any firm conclusions about a reasonable remeasurement interval for gathering essential data retrospectively. Perhaps the optimal design for most applications of longitudinal measurement of life histories, then, is one that attempts to combine the best features of both—one that embeds periodic retrospective measurement within the prospective panel design. In particular, the gathering of event histories, by definition, requires retrospective dating and interlinking of events across domains. Even panel studies that gather data on a subannual cycle, as in the SIPP, require respondents to report events retrospectively over the past few months. Certainly, panel studies such as the PSID and the BHPS gather much event history data over the past year.

Finally, we note that the quality of retrospective data is an issue that is relevant to all social scientists interested in life course analysis. As

Maines (1992) observed, "All social science data are made up of human interpretations, and nearly all such data are reconstructions or representations of past events and experiences" (p. 1137). Thus, concerns about the reliability and validity of retrospective data span the qualitative and quantitative divide, with data quality an important issue for both camps (Scott & Alwin, 1993). It is clear that both quantitative "event historians" and the more qualitative "oral historians" are united in their reliance on the use of the retrospective design, with both regarding any serious defects in the quality of recall as problematic. A mutual interest in the trustworthiness of evidence about the past could be the grounds for future common dialogue that, hopefully, might help advance our understanding of "best practice" and optimal designs for collecting life histories.

➤ NOTE

1. Persons in a particular state at the time of the interview are "right-censored" because the data cannot reveal when a transition will be made out of that state. Persons in a particular state at the beginning of a study (without any retrospective measurement) are "left-censored" because the data do not record when the persons entered the state. These imperfections are inherent in event history data and, in most cases, can be dealt with in the approach to analysis (Allison, 1984; Teachman, 1983; Tuma & Hannan, 1984).

Chapter 6

Finding Respondents
in a Follow-Up Study

DONNA DEMPSTER-MCCLAIN
PHYLLIS MOEN

Two influences, refinement of the life course perspective (Elder, 1994) and development of methodologies for analyzing the changing structure of lives (Mayer & Tuma, 1990), have encouraged social scientists to look for ways in which to use data collected by earlier generations of scholars. Longitudinal studies, based on archives that collected data on children and adolescents in the 1920s (e.g., the Berkeley and Oakland Growth Studies) and then reinterviewed respondents as they moved into adulthood (Elder, 1974), serve as shining examples of the benefits of following people over time. It is clear that there is a connection between person finding and linked lives in a life course paradigm.

Change is a key theme in social research, and panel data are optimal for the study of change. As early as the 1930s, Lazarsfeld encouraged sociologists to study change and causation through the use of panel data

AUTHORS' NOTE: Funds for the the preparation of this chapter were provided by research grants from the National Institute on Aging (R01-AG05450 to Phyllis Moen and Robin Williams [1986], "Women's Roles and Well-Being: A Two-Generation Study"; IT50-AG11711 to Karl Pillemer and Phyllis Moen [1993], "Cornell Applied Gerontology Research Institute: A Roybal Center for Research on Applied Gerontology"), the Bronfenbrenner Life Course Center, and the College of Human Ecology at Cornell University.

(Lazarsfeld, 1948; Lazarsfeld & Fiske, 1938). Yet, most research remains cross-sectional in design, ending after a few articles are published. Typically, authors save the data and the list of respondents for a few years but then discard everything to make way for new projects.

Launching a panel study is expensive. It also is time-consuming; one has to wait years to observe the transitions and trajectories of interest. An alternative strategy is what Kessler and Greenberg (1981) called a "catch-up" study, locating and reinterviewing respondents surveyed years earlier. Researchers in the 1950s and 1960s held onto their computer cards and yellowing address lists, perhaps hoping to follow up on their initial surveys at some future time. Some of these materials have been discovered and used years later by others who then embarked on the long process of relocating and reinterviewing.

This chapter focuses on one of the key issues in conducting such a catch-up study: finding respondents who originally were part of a cross-sectional study. We first describe our "Women's Roles and Well-Being" project and the specific techniques we used to locate women who had participated in a 1956 study. The second section of the chapter focuses on other projects that also began with an old yellowed list of names. We conclude with a brief summary of selected tracking resources.

➤ CORNELL WOMEN'S ROLES AND WELL-BEING: A TWO-GENERATION STUDY

The second wave of the Women's Roles and Well-Being project began in 1979 over a discussion of the historical changes in sex role inventories. Robin M. Williams, Jr. shared with us the "feminine independence scale" that he and co-investigator John Dean developed for their 1956 National Institute of Mental Health (NIMH)-funded project titled "Women's Roles" (Dean & Williams, 1956). A comparison of these inventories led to the discovery that Williams possessed a gold mine—IBM double-punched cards, initial data analysis tables, original proposal, progress reports, and a list of the names, addresses, and telephone numbers of the 521 women interviewed in 1956.

This gold mine represented for Williams the only project he had let slip through his fingers. As an established sociologist at Cornell University since the late 1940s, Williams was involved in several projects. The most well known from this era are his textbook, *American Society: A Socio-logical Interpretation* (Williams, 1970) and his research on minority group relations that led to the classic *Strangers Next Door* (Williams & Suchman, 1964). This devotion to intergroup relations sparked his interest, in the 1950s, in the changing roles of women. He and John Dean developed insightful questions, created precise Guttman scales, and carried out a first-rate research project, collecting interview data on women in their 20s to 50s in a mid-sized community in upstate New York. However, due to several untimely events, the data languished in a file drawer, used only by a few students for master's and Ph.D. theses in the early 1960s.

Williams gambled on a graduate student (Dempster-McClain) and an assistant professor (Moen). Giving the data to them seemed like a good idea; perhaps they would reanalyze the sex role scales and compare the responses to more recent data. Realizing the potential of this data set took several years. The first plan was for the graduate student to locate and interview 50 of the women for her dissertation. Location efforts commenced in 1980, but we decided it would be better to locate a larger subsample and, accordingly, sought funding to launch a major study on women's changing roles. Our goal was to locate the women first interviewed in 1956 to trace out their life pathways through the time of revolutionary change in women's roles in society at large and also to interview their (now adult) daughters.

Tracking Activities Before Major Funding

Before beginning to dream of conducting a follow-up study with respondents who had not been contacted for more than 25 years, we had to determine the likelihood of locating enough women to make the adventure worthwhile. During this early phase (1982-1983), we used the local telephone directory, Historical Society obituary records, city directories, local informants, and visits to neighborhoods.[1]

Telephone directory. Surprisingly, the current telephone directory of the original medium-sized community in upstate New York sampled by Williams and Dean was used to locate more than one fourth of the original respondents. In half of the cases, the exact names were found; in the other half, the surnames were located with between 1 and 50 different first names.

Historical Society obituary records. The local Historical Society has an alphabetical file of death notices as they appear in the local newspapers. These are organized, in file cabinets, with one and sometimes two decades in one cabinet. We began with the 1950s and 1960s and discovered, as expected, that some of the women had died. We were confident that a thorough search of these files would provide a good count of our survivors. In addition, information from the death notices of relatives proved to be very useful. If respondents' husbands or parents had died, then we used the list of living relatives to help locate the original women.

City directories. Since the 19th century, specialized publishers have conducted door-to-door or telephone surveys of cities, small towns, and rural areas producing city directories (King, 1992, p. 11). The Historical Society and the public library have excellent collections of such city directories. These vary somewhat by publisher, but in general they contain two helpful lists: an alphabetical list of all residents contacted by the publishing company and a street list that enabled us to find the respondents' former and present neighbors. These lists also contain telephone numbers, home ownership/rental information, occupation of head of household, number and names of other people in the household, and duration at the current address. Searching the 1955, 1956, 1980, and 1982 directories, we realized that it would be possible to trace individual families as they moved around or into and out of town but that poring over the yearly directories would be a time-consuming task. These directories proved to be our most valuable resource once we had the funding to use them properly.

Local informants. During the initial phases of our search, we hired Dikkie Schoggen, a senior research associate, to help with our detective work. Schoggen and Dempster-McClain spent many cold winter afternoons at the Historical Society, which occupied three rooms in a beautiful old building near the center of town. The staff was very helpful, friendly, and curious. As we searched the obituary records and city directories, other visitors began asking about our project. One inquirer, Janet Howell, who was studying cemetery headstones, proved to be our most important community contact.

Visits to neighborhoods. The original sampling in 1956 occurred in three different neighborhoods, with respondents at every third house being selected. Locating these neighborhoods on the map, analyzing the changes that had taken place (a cross-town highway destroyed the edge of one neighborhood), and driving by to determine whether the houses still existed gave us much needed preliminary information.

These four "passive" tracking techniques—using telephone directories, city directories, obituary records, and neighborhood visits—and discussions with informants took approximately 72 hours and resulted in positive identification of 280 respondents who still lived in the community, 24 who had died, and 217 not yet located (for a total of 521).

Other Pre-Funding Activities
Related to Tracking

To become more systematic about our tracking efforts, we undertook a literature search on techniques related to finding respondents. Reviewing this tracking literature led to four invaluable resources. We drew on the theoretical and methodological insights in the literature both to begin locating our respondents and to strengthen our second grant proposal, submitted to the National Institute on Aging (NIA) (Moen & Williams, 1986). (An earlier proposal, submitted to the National Science Foundation in 1985, had been rejected. Reviewers felt that it would be impossible to find a sufficient number of original respondents.)

Tracking Respondents (Call, Otto, & Spenner, 1982) introduced us to the theoretical and methodological analysis of tracking. The authors' Comprehensive Tracking Model views tracking as a process that integrates a logic for why people respond with a method for organizing tracking techniques. They evaluated the existing methodological literature, stating that it "continues to be scarce, technique oriented, non-cumulative, and largely inaccessible" (p. 1) for three main reasons. First, researchers may develop hypotheses about the effectiveness of various tracking techniques, but very few are willing to carry out experimental studies on tracking. The length of time needed to locate some respondents and an unwillingness to risk losing panel members discourage studies that compare techniques. Second, details of tracking efforts seldom are reported in journal articles. The procedures used and an evaluation of their effectiveness usually are part of the project director's memory and never appear on paper. Third, interested scholars have concentrated on the techniques or "bag of tricks" used by others. This "craft" approach tends to overlook the reasons why certain techniques work.

Call et al. (1982) detailed the theoretical rationale for why people participate in panel studies and integrated this rationale into a design for tracking strategies that reduces panel attrition. They reviewed previous experiences with the three major approaches (mail, telephone, and community visits) and introduced a strategy for sequencing the sources of information to increase tracking efficiency. In addition, the authors provided an excellent case example of their Career Development Study, a follow-up of 6,729 Washington State high school students who were first interviewed in 1965-1966 and were relocated 13 years later with a 98.2% recovery rate (Otto, Call, & Spenner, 1981).

Booth and Johnson (1985) reported on tracking strategies used with 2,032 married respondents who were first selected by random digit dialing (RDD). They concluded that attrition using RDD was similar to that in studies using personal interviews. They recommended frequent (at least annual) tracking using a combination of mail and telephone follow-ups. Suggestions such as checking the telephone number for transposed numbers and, in cases where the number had been reassigned, asking the current holder about the respondent's whereabouts were helpful.

Earlier work by Crider and associates (Crider & Willits, 1973; Crider, Willits, & Bealer, 1971, 1973) at Pennsylvania State University assessed the utility of various tracking methods (mail, long-distance telephone calls, community visits, and public records) for locating respondents after a lapse of years. In 1966, they reactivated a project that began in 1947 when the attitudes and aspirations of 2,810 sophomores in a rural high school were assessed. Fully 83% (2,344 respondents) of this cohort were relocated and interviewed in 1957. Using a subsample of 320 from the group interviewed in 1957, they conducted a comparative study of various tracking methods. They were able to locate 100% of this subsample and concluded that "the widely held belief that many cases are certain to be lost in longitudinal research is false. Most cases apparently can be retrieved if the investigator is willing to spend the necessary time and effort" (Crider et al., 1971, p. 620). We were encouraged by their optimism and decided that our goal also would be to find *all* of our respondents.

McAllister, Butler, and Goe (1973) reviewed research strategies for ensuring successful follow-up of respondents and recommended that all new surveys be designed as though they were to be longitudinal even if no such plans exist in the minds of the researchers. They provided detailed suggestions about the type of information that should be collected for every respondent. Thanks to their suggestions, we feel confident that we will be able to relocate our respondents if we ever decide to conduct a third wave of our study.

Post-Funding Refinement of Tracking Strategy

Our second proposal, complete with a detailed discussion of how we had thus far located 212 of the original 427 respondents who were wives and mothers in 1956 and our plans for tracking others, received funding from the NIA in May 1986. We were so eager to find our remaining respondents that all thoughts of conducting an experimental study of tracking techniques vanished. We planned to begin interviewing in September. How many additional respondents could we locate in 4 months?

As Call et al. (1982) suggested, a successful tracking strategy must involve an understanding of respondents' willingness to help, an integration of the four basic parameters (resources, time, panel characteristics, and respondent characteristics), and an appreciation of the three principles (simplicity, diversity, and persistence) that govern the organizing of tracking efforts.

We felt confident that the original respondents would be more willing to participate if they knew the project was sponsored by Cornell, was funded by the NIA, and would lead to not only scholarly articles but also practical suggestions for living. We prepared a short article for the local newspaper, which was published in September 1986, stating the purpose of the study and our goal of locating women first interviewed in the 1950s. We found that few of the women actually remembered being interviewed but that once recontacted, their first impressions were shaped by our positive and exciting news article (which we sent to them).

The four basic parameters of a tracking strategy, as applied to our study, can be summarized as follows.

Resources. Our NIA funding (Moen & Williams, 1986) provided support for personnel, equipment, and facilities to keep track of the information we collected on each individual. All our tracking efforts were supervised by the project director (Dempster-McClain) and a graduate student (Melody Miller), neither of whom had any formal training or experience in tracking.

Time. As the amount of time between panel observations increases, tracking becomes more difficult (Call et al., 1982). By the time our study was funded, we faced a 30-year hiatus since the first interviews in 1956. From our previous efforts, we knew we could find a sizable number of original respondents, but these were the "easy" cases. Could we find the remaining, more elusive respondents? Time allowed for completing of the tracking efforts also influences the types of approaches one can use. Because our sample consisted of older women who were (literally) in danger of dying off, we desperately wanted to complete the interviews as soon as possible. We decided to devote the summer to locating all the remaining women.

Panel characteristics. Panel size and panel dispersion influence both the time required for tracking and the amount of record-keeping procedures that must be implemented. In the grant proposal, we opted for following those interviewed in 1956 who were married and had children at the time ($n = 427$). This original sample lived in three neighborhoods in a medium-sized upstate New York community. We assumed that a moderate amount of dispersion had occurred due to the closure of numerous factories and large businesses in the late 1970s. We managed record keeping on the original respondents and tracking efforts to locate them with a software package called *Notebook*. Once all the names of the original respondents were entered into the computer, we could sort, produce mailing labels, and keep ongoing records of our tracking attempts.

Respondent characteristics. Several respondent characteristics are thought to affect ease of tracking. Rural residents are easier to locate than are those in urban areas, whites are easier to track than are nonwhites, and those of lower socioeconomic status are harder to find than are higher status individuals. Participation in formal organizations also makes respondents easier to locate. Particularly difficult to locate are military personnel. Families with children are easier to locate (Call et al., 1982, pp. 17-19). Our sample of 427 married mothers was selected because the greatest transformation in women's roles has occurred among this group, and it would offer the greatest analytic potential. We drew on the 1956 data to identify selected characteristics of the respondents (religious affiliations, ages of children, social class, and organizational involvement) that would provide clues to their social connections.

Implementation of our tracking strategy followed three principles: simplicity, diversity, and persistence (Call et al., 1982). Simplicity means that the tracking team should focus its time and energy on locating respondents and not try to start the interviews at the same time. Luckily, Miller, the graduate student assistant, focused her time solely on tracking efforts. Dempster-McClain was able to provide adequate supervision but was preoccupied with the care of her infant daughter. Moen provided guidance and encouragement. Diversity means the more tracking approaches that are applied, the greater the probability of locating all panel members. These approaches are discussed in the next subsection. Persistence is extremely important to tracking success. This involves a sense of adventure, a desire to follow every lead, a compulsion to check and recheck every piece of information, and a "sociological imagination" (Mills, 1959). Moen continued to emphasize the goal of locating all members of the original sample of wives and mothers, even in the face of no leads. A quote from Miller showed the pervasiveness of this goal: "I started this, and I'm obsessed enough to try anything to locate the remaining 24 women."

Tracking Techniques

By May 1986, our tracking activities had resulted in locating approximately 50% of the original sample of 427. The following activities, carried out over a 4-month period of time, resulted in finding 95.6% of the 427 married women with children (including those who had died).

Obituary records. We returned to the Historical Society to analyze both the alphabetical collection of obituary notices from the newspapers and the gravestone files provided by the major cemeteries in the community. We thought that caretakers at the cemeteries might be helpful in locating records that were missing from the Historical Society's files, but we obtained no additional information.

Respondents as detectives. Early in the tracking process, we located a respondent in an adjacent community who, after hearing about the study, asked whether she could help in any way. Violet was confined to a wheelchair and had been doing "telephone work" for more than 18 years. She proved to be a very valuable detective. Her knowledge of the community, local businesses, and community organizations made it possible for us to follow up on leads that only made sense to an "insider." We hired Violet, giving her the difficult cases—those respondents who could not be traced through the telephone directory, city directory, or local informants. Violet introduced us to the crisscross directories, in particular the "street directory." Unlike the city directories that are based on survey information, crisscross directories are rearrangements of the phone directory (King, 1992, p. 12). Violet used these to call respondents' neighbors, looking for people who remembered our respondents and could provide leads about their new addresses, friends or family still in the area, occupational or organizational affiliations of any persons in their households, and so on.

City directories. We returned to the city directories to check the most recent edition. This confirmed the information we had collected previously and provided a few new leads. Following individuals from 1956 until the dates they no longer were listed allowed us to pinpoint major transitions. We could then use those dates to begin the search for neighborhood informants and so on. The city directory also allows for tracing job changes, marriage breakups and remarriages, and deaths. In addition, for the hard-to-locate individuals, we returned to the 1956 edition to make note of husbands' names, occupations, and homeowner statuses. Many of the occupational listings proved to be helpful. For example, if a husband worked in a nearby larger community in 1956, then we checked whether the family had moved there to eliminate the long commute.

Telephone directory. Because many of the respondents had relatively uncommon ethnic last names, we used the telephone directory and called anyone living in the community with the same last names. These calls often produced valuable information—names of relatives and identification of others in the phone book who might be able to help. This technique helped locate our 42 "snowbirds"—individuals who had moved to the southern and southwestern states. (These 42 respondents represent 13.5% of 313, the total number we interviewed.)

High schools. Two of the four area high schools had excellent alumni records. These were used to trace the children of respondents. We found a few by contacting the individuals in charge of class reunions. At one of the high schools, a secretary was more helpful than the alumni list. She knew some of the families and remembered details about their lives that led to several successful contacts. A local informant loaned us her high school yearbooks from 1952 to 1956. Using the computerized 1956 data, we were able to select all the "unfound" women who had children in high school during that time. Using the same techniques, we were able to find several of the adult children, which resulted in locating their mothers.

College records. The local college was very cooperative. We provided a list of our unfound women along with their husbands' names and 1956 addresses. The alumni director then searched the records and located eight respondents. The college also was helpful when we occasionally would drop in to check the name of a son or daughter who was listed as a student in the city directory.

Former employers. Although some employers had long since gone out of business and some kept no records, others were able to provide information about why the respondents or their husbands had left the companies and where they had relocated. This began the task of following leads, often resulting in recovered respondents. Some employers would not give out any information about their former employees but did put us in touch with coworkers and friends who provided the needed information.

Visits to neighborhoods. Safety of the neighborhood is a major consideration when using this strategy. We limited our visits to safe locations, and (luckily) most of the people were friendly and willing to help. A neighborhood visit involved three strategies. First, we looked for an "old-timer"—the family or person who had lived in the neighborhood for the longest period of time. When that family or person was found, we could either ask directly about our unfound respondent or pass the name on to Violet, who would continue the search over the telephone. Second, going door-to-door helped us reach many of the people who had unlisted telephone numbers. Third, while walking through one neighborhood on a hot summer day, we rediscovered Janet Howell, the local informant who previously had helped at the Historical Society. She renewed her offer to help. We hired her as our interview coordinator. She conducted more than 85 of the interviews, oversaw the six local interviewers, and eventually convinced 60% of potential refusals to participate.

Local informants. Three groups were especially helpful: original interviewers, several respondents from the 1956 survey, and other townspeople. Our yellowed list of names of respondents also contained the last names of the 1956 interviewers. We had lunch with two of these women, who provided information that facilitated the location of a few respondents. We organized all of the unfound women into small neighborhoods and identified "found" respondents who could tell us about the missing women or provide names of relatives, friends, and the like. Other townspeople (e.g., old-timers, local officials, members of specific organizations, friends, cemetery caretakers) suggested additional ways in which to search for our respondents. For example, one woman suggested searching high school yearbooks for the children, and another let us check our unfound list against the past records of a major professional organization. While obtaining data on the causes of death for our first article from this project (Moen, Dempster-McClain, & Williams, 1989), the caretaker at a local cemetery, who was an avid baseball fan, identified the spouse of one of our missing women as a former member of a local farm team. This clue provided enough information to locate our missing respondent.

Clubs, organizations, and churches. Clubs and organizations in the community provided assistance in identifying individuals by linking us with members who were active in the 1950s. Visits to churches, especially the smaller religious groups, provided some helpful clues.

Military. Four of the unfound women were wives of military recruiters. A call to the Department of Defense provided us with the address of the locator office for each branch of the service. However, we were unsuccessful in our attempts because the husbands of these respondents had left the service years ago.

Table 6.1 illustrates the success of our efforts at various points in time. By pursuing all leads, diversifying our techniques, and following our imagination, we eventually located 408 (95.5%) of the 427 original respondents we were seeking. Of these women, 82 (19.2%) were deceased and

TABLE 6.1 Success of Tracking Techniques: Women's Roles and Well-Being Project (1982-1986)

	Found	Deceased	Not Found	Total
Pre-funding "passive" efforts (1982-1983)				
Original sample of 521	280 (53.7)	24 (4.6)	217 (41.7)	521
Our sample of 427 married women with children	212 (49.7)	13 (3)	202 (47.3)	427
Post-funding "active" initial efforts (summer 1986)	324 (75.9)	79 (18.5)	24 (5.6)	427
Final follow-up efforts (late 1986)	326[a] (76.3)	82 (19.2)	19 (4.4)	427

NOTE: Percentages are in parentheses.
a. Of the 326 subjects found, 313 (96%) were interviewed and 13 (4%) refused.

326 (76.3%) were contacted for interviews. We were left with only 19 (4.4%) who could not be found.

➢ OTHER FOLLOW-UP STUDIES

Interviews with the researchers responsible for relocating respondents in other studies have provided us with valuable information about techniques used at different times and in different geographical locations. In this section, we focus on two studies that originally were intended to be cross-sectional and two well-known longitudinal studies that have attempted to "resurrect" nonresponse families or individuals. Generalizations about techniques for relocating respondents are difficult to make because each study starts with different basic information and takes place in different historical and geographical contexts.

Clausen's Mental Health Study

The Mental Health Study, initiated by John Clausen and funded by the NIMH (Clausen, 1984, 1986), originally was a cross-sectional project aimed to assess the impact of mental illness on the family. The first interviews were conducted between 1952 and 1958 with 63 married males and females who lived in the Washington, D.C., area and were hospitalized for the first time with mental illness. The locating information collected at that time included the respondent's name and address, spouse's name, children's names, hospital name and address, and respondent's employer. In 1972, approximately 20 years after the original cross-sectional study was started, Clausen and Carol Huffine decided to relocate and reinterview their original respondents plus 17 additional women who had been part of Sampson, Messinger, and Towne's (1964) study of schizophrenic women. They used the following techniques to locate all but a few of the 80 respondents.

Hospital records. In 1972, Huffine, the person responsible for relocating the respondents in the Washington area, had full and free access to the hospital record rooms. She started with the hospitals at which the respondents were first admitted but also traced their entries and exits at other hospitals in the area.

Telephone, crisscross, and city directories. These were used to locate individuals at their 1972 addresses or to follow their moves throughout the city. If a person could not be located, then a neighborhood informant was identified.

Death certificates. These obviously were very helpful if the respondents had died. If their spouses had died, then the researchers used the information given in the obituary notices to trace relatives and eventually locate the respondents.

Other techniques. Contacts with the individuals' employers were used as a last resort. Driver's licenses and automobile registrations were searched but did not yield any helpful information. The researchers did not try to search the divorce or marital records.

The main recommendation from this study: *Find out where the respondent's family of origin lives. Get the addresses of parents, siblings, and good friends.*

Bengston's Longitudinal Study of Three Generations

Another important mail survey is that of Vern Bengston and Margaret Gatz at the University of Southern California. Their study, originally funded by NIMH, aimed to study family relationships and psychological well-being across three generations (Bengston, 1975). In 1971-1972, grand-fathers who were members of a large metropolitan health maintenance organization were recruited to participate in the study. Data were collected from 516 grandparents, 701 parents, and 827 grandchildren ($N = 2,044$) (Young, Savola, & Phelps, 1991, pp. 45-46). The original study was not designed as a longitudinal or panel study. It became a panel study following the fortuitous discovery in 1982 of the list of approximately 3,000 names and addresses of the original (1971-1972) respondents. The purpose of the follow-up panel study, funded by NIA, was to investigate changes and continuity in family relationships, especially intergenerational social sup-port and their consequences for physical and mental health.

The relocation efforts were aimed at maximizing the lineages, recov-ering as many parent-child dyads and grandparent-parent-grandchild triads as possible. The 1985 eligible sample consisted of 2,452 individuals (including some nonresponse individuals from the first wave) (Campbell & Richards, 1985). Because each of the original respondents had two other family members in the study, the researchers often located an entire line through one cooperative individual. This unique feature of the study also was a liability; an entire lineage of 3 to 18 people could be lost.

Sample recovery techniques began by sending a computer tape of the names, addresses, and birth dates of the entire sample to the California Department of Motor Vehicles to obtain computer-matched address up-dates (25% were identified). The second step was a check for deceased respondents through the Computer Automated Mortality Linkage System in the Department of Epidemiology at the University of California, San Francisco, a subcontractor for the California State Department of Vital Statistics (it was expensive and resulted in only 96 names). In addition to these computerized checks, location efforts included searches through the local telephone directories. These three techniques resulted in approxi-mately 1,000 confirmed addresses prior to the first letters being sent (Campbell & Richards, 1985).

Both computer and card files for each individual and each family group were created from the original data. These family files provided much needed information used for tracing/locating missing family members. The first letters (July 1984) were sent with an address correction request. Once processed, questionnaires were sent to all respondents with confirmed addresses. These included requests for information about all family members who may have died and the addresses and names of additional living relatives. Telephone tracking proved to be very useful in locating the remaining respondents. In Southern California, two requests can be made at a time using multiple area codes and variants on the spelling of the last name.

As reported in Young et al. (1991), 1,341 respondents were located for the 1985-1986 wave and 1,481 for the 1988-1989 wave. These numbers include not only the original 1972 respondents but also some formerly eligible persons who did not respond in 1972 as well as new respondents (spouses of the youngest generation) who were added for the latest wave.

Once the research team completed the first follow-up, the next goal was to maintain contact (M. Preston, personal communication, May 1993). A project newsletter, sent out in January and July of each year (deliberately avoiding December), keeps the sample informed about study results, but the main purpose is to update any address changes. Additional contact is made by sending sympathy cards to the spouses of deceased participants. Preston reported, "We follow up on any reason to make a personal contact by either telephoning or sending an informally written note. These contacts might be in answer to a question about the study or some remarkable event in the respondent's life" (personal communication, January 1994).

The staff of interviewers, mostly middle-aged women hired for their "people skills," try to call the respondents in the early evening. Leaving messages on answering machines and asking for return calls has proved to be an ineffective strategy in reaching participants. The interviewers keep a handwritten file on each call, noting the family members with the "fattest address books"—the "kin keepers."

At this point, only 10 of the eligible participants are "lost." The sample tracking and maintenance staff will continue to try to locate them through the kin keepers. Additional techniques include calling people with the same last names, hoping that they might have received mail for the persons in question and remember their addresses. The staff members also are using computerized databases that contain the names and addresses of all U.S. citizens. These software packages, developed by the market research industry, are available on CD-ROM in any university library. In addition, they have followed some of the recommendations made by professional trackers such as Dennis King. King's (1992) book is discussed later.

Institute of Human Development

Between 1928 and 1931, three remarkable studies were started by a diverse group of researchers at the University of California, Berkeley. These three studies "probably offer the richest collection of data ever assembled on human beings over a long period" (Yahraes, 1969). They initially were supported for 5 years by the Laura Spellman Fund. Since that time, the University of California has maintained basic support through facilities and some salaries. Additional funds have been provided by more than seven different private and federal sources (Eichorn, 1981a).

The Oakland Growth Study, carried out by Clausen, Harold and Mary Jones, and Herbert Stoltz, focused on the physical, physiological, and personal-social development of 212 adolescents who were fifth- and sixth-graders in 1931 and followed continuously until age 18 years. Three adult follow-ups have been conducted with data on offspring of the original sample collected in 1970-1971. Adult assessments focused on social relationships and satisfaction within familial, employment, and community settings; personality characteristics; and physical and emotional health (Young et al., 1991, pp. 92-93). The Berkeley Growth Study, under the direction of Dorothy Eichorn, Nancy Baley, and Lotte V. Wolff, started in 1928 analyzing the mental, motor, and physical growth of 61 white, full-term, healthy infants in middle class Protestant families. Data were collected continuously from birth until age 18 years (1941) (Young et al., 1991, pp. 131-133). The Berkeley Guidance Study, conducted by Huffine, Marjorie Honzik, and Jean W. MacFarlane, initially was designed as a study of the effect of parental counseling on the incidence of behavioral problems among preschool children. They began in 1928 with 248 infants (3 months old); by age 18 years, 150 study members still were being seen. This study developed into an examination of interactions of psychological, social, and biological factors in personality development, with the mothers, children, and spouses of the respondents being included (Young et al., 1991, pp. 230-232).

The Berkeley and Oakland studies obtained the full names and addresses of the parents of all the children as well as the names of all the siblings. Because the original goal of all three studies was to follow the respondents until age 18 years, they had a distinct advantage in that frequent contact developed into a commitment on the part of both respondents and researchers. However, after the data were collected on the 18-year-old respondents (1941 for Oakland, 1946 for both Berkeley studies), the researchers thought that they were done. The first follow-ups occurred 20 years later. Details about the sample size and dates of reinterviews are provided in Young et al.'s (1991) *Inventory of Longitudinal Studies in Social Sciences* and in Eichorn's (1981b) "Sample and Procedures."

Tracking the students from the Oakland Growth Study was facilitated by their junior high school affiliations. The students had maintained friendships and were able to provide researchers with essential information for locating those who had moved from the area. Another advantage for all these studies was that they had parents' and siblings' names and addresses, which were used extensively to locate "missing" respondents.

After the first follow-up, in the early 1960s, institute staff members developed numerous systematic means of maintaining continuous contact. They sent twice-a-year mailings to every individual—a Christmas letter in early December and an annual report in June. Marking these materials "Do Not Forward—Address Correction Requested" enabled the researchers to track their respondents. In 1982-1983, the respondents were paid, and as a result the researchers now have social security numbers for everyone. This "essential" identifier can now be used to find any lost individuals. (For details on how to use the Social Security Administration Letter Forwarding Service, see King, 1992, p. 65.) The institute staff members also read the obituary notices and send letters of condolences when individuals connected with the study die. This technique has been facilitated by the commitment of the research staff; during the past 15 years, no one connected with the study has left (C. Huffine, personal communication, May 1993).

At the present time, the samples have been merged together. Huffine and colleagues are in touch with more than 300 respondents (C. Huffine, personal communication, May 1993). Their major recommendation is "Do not let them get lost." Keeping in contact with the respondents via letters, cards, reports, and publications develops a commitment, and in response the researchers must be willing to provide information when the respondents ask for help. Huffine related that they have been asked to write letters of recommendation for jobs and colleges, provide referrals for professional services, and so on (personal communication, May 1993).

Panel Study of Income Dynamics

The Panel Study of Income Dynamics (PSID), originally funded by the (then) Department of Health, Education, and Welfare, began in 1968 with the goal of generating data on individuals and families related to poverty and changes in economic well-being. The annual interviews began with all (coresident) members of 4,802 families; the total number of participants grew from roughly 16,000 in 1968 to more than 38,000 in 1993. Following encouragement in 1992 from the (current) principal funder, the National Science Foundation, the PSID staff began trying to locate siblings, children, or parents of currently responding family members who had, at an earlier point in time, refused to be interviewed. The goal is to become the premier data set for intra- and intergenerational studies of U.S. families. "Its power lies in tracking parents and their *full* set of children throughout large segments of the life course, interviewing each independently if and when the children establish separate households" (G. Duncan & M. Hill, personal communication, February 28, 1992). With the exception of the 2,000 Latino families added in 1990, all families that are part of the PSID sample have descended from the original 5,000 families. Each interviewer is assigned a set of "descendant" families and is asked to interview all households that contain members of these families. The interviewer is provided with a list of all "attriters" (those who refused to be interviewed or could not be contacted at any time since 1968) from a given descendant family. Thus, whenever an interviewer establishes telephone contact with anyone in his or her descendant family, the interviewer can inquire about the full set of missing individuals.

The PSID staff would like to add back into the study the 3,000 households containing 4,075 attrited parents and grown children. (This number represents between two thirds and three quarters of the total group of attriters.) This group of 4,075 has been lost due to a PSID tracking rule that was designed to save money: for each new wave, interviews were attempted only with households successfully interviewed in the prior wave (omitting anyone who attrited in the prior wave or any wave before that). The staff members are confident that this group of individuals could be interviewed successfully if interviews were attempted with them (G. Duncan & M. Hill, personal communication, February 28, 1992). As a first step, they are working on several subpopulations with varying degrees of success. For example, they have located approximately 42% of a group of randomly selected families from 1975 with ex-spouses who had moved out. They have recontacted about 25% of the nonresponse (refused and lost) individuals from the 1991 wave. Of the 600 to 700 Latino families that did not respond following their 1990 inclusion in the study, approximately 40% have been located. Once an address is obtained from a still participating family member, the attriter is sent a "persuasion letter." If this is returned, then the search techniques include contacting schools, asking telephone operators for new phone numbers, and returning to the family for more information. The in-the-field trained interviewers also are called on to search former neighborhoods for informants, friends, and other contacts (P. Hildebrandt & T. Loup, personal communication, May 1993).

The PSID interview always has asked respondents to provide the names and telephone numbers of contact persons who will know their whereabouts each year. This has proved to be very valuable. In addition, the staff members send a series of letters and reports to respondents each year. If any of these are returned, then they resend the letters to the respective contact persons. They also ask the respondents to inform the PSID staff of any name or address changes.

The PSID staff members who are responsible for "keeping in touch" have developed very effective "detective" skills (P. Hildebrandt & T. Loup, personal communication, May 1993). As more funding is obtained, they will continue to search for the attriters and hopefully reach the goal of finding *all* relatives of the original 5,000 families.

Additional Studies

In the *Inventory of Longitudinal Studies in the Social Sciences,* Young et al. (1991) outlined more than 200 research projects, providing details about the original sample size and the attrition at each successive wave. Information about techniques used to track the respondents is not provided, but personal correspondence with the investigators could yield additional suggestions.

Among the many other studies that could be summarized, two more are mentioned here. Clarridge, Sheehy, and Hauser (1978) reported on their successful efforts to track a very large sample (more than 10,000 persons) who, after 18 years, were geographically dispersed. This study, which began in 1957 with high school seniors in Wisconsin, successfully located 97.4% in 1975. The researchers attributed their success to extensive use of the telephone, an organized tracking operation, persistence in trying to locate difficult cases, adequate information about the respondents from the first interviews (mainly parents' names and addresses), and sufficient resources. Cairns, Neckerman, Flinchum, and Cairns (1992) reported on their techniques for finding children who are "lost" during the course of a longitudinal study. Their project began with 695 elementary school children in 1981. Over the 10-year period, they lost up to 13% of the sample but were able to recover all but 1% by the end of the study. Each year, the respondents provided their social security numbers along with the names, locations, and telephone numbers of two persons who were likely to know where they could be located. The researchers' article, titled "Lost and Found," spells out their 13 techniques along with common failures. Cairns and colleagues drew on Bronfenbrenner's (1979) social ecology and provided insightful comments on the importance of the social network as a primary determinant of initial and continued participation in a longitudinal project. "The research task of tracking individuals cannot be divorced from the social setting in which it occurs and the network of relationships that are formed and attitudes that are engendered" (Cairns et al., 1992, p. 6).

➢ ADDITIONAL TRACKING RESOURCES

EQUIFAX Government and Special Systems, Inc. (8180 Greensboro Drive, Suite 302, McLean, VA 22102; phone: (703) 749-9707) provides epidemiological support services tailored to the specific needs of individual clients. Founded in 1899, the company currently employs thousands of information specialists working from more than 942 offices strategically located throughout North America. Tracing and locating missing respondents is one of its main services. EQUIFAX employs a sequential approach in its location efforts, ranging from a simple file check to a full-scale street investigation. The file check uses a multiplicity of databases drawn from consumer transactions, insurance applications, benefits, mortgages, and public records searchers. If a respondent is not found in these files, then EQUIFAX's field personnel use the following sources: last known addresses, employers, schools, local union offices, clubs, associations, hobbies, religious affiliations, public utilities, postal service, Department of Motor Vehicles, and other public records (e.g., marriage, voter registration, tax records, licenses, criminal, traffic, birth, death, mortgage). If all these techniques fail, then they will conduct a full-scale street investigation. Location projects are quoted on a case-by-case basis, and the company welcomes both small and large studies.

A book by King (1992), *Get the Facts on Anyone,* provides excellent descriptions of the basic tools and resources (everything from crisscross and city directories to computer databases) and an exhaustive list of the basic techniques and procedures used to locate anyone. Chapter 4 of King's book focuses on "Finding 'Missing' People" and describes all the techniques reported by the studies we have summarized as well as procedures such as electronic yellow pages, subscription lists, licensing agencies and certification boards, abandoned property lists, trailer rental and moving companies, and local government records. King's book even provides detailed suggestions about how to use biographical, newspaper, and periodical searches to find background information about an individual. Locating a person's social security number and using credit-reporting agencies and databases also are discussed.

Another important resource is a book by a former Federal Bureau of Investigation agent turned private investigator, Ted L. Gunderson, titled *How to Locate Anyone Anywhere Without Leaving Home* (Gunderson, 1989). The book charts a pragmatic, step-by-step process for locating missing persons. His description of the basic tools—the U.S. Postal Service, *Haines Crisscross Directory,* telephone directories, and public libraries—is clear and informative. The book provides an exhaustive introduction to more than 1,500 city, county, state, and federal sources of information on individuals that can be accessed through the use of the postal system and telephone. The nine appendixes give addresses, fees, and other information essential to a successful search. For example, addresses and techniques for locating military personnel in each branch of the services are provided. State-by-state information regarding birth, death, marriage, and divorce records along with addresses for state driver's license transcripts (must have full name and date of birth) will make social scientists' job of locating respondents a lot easier. Chapter 8 of Gunderson's book, "Computers, Credit, and Consumers," describes nine sophisticated search centers: Friendfinders International (FFI) (Seattle, WA), Finder of Missing Persons (Santa Monica, CA), Information Resource Service Company (Fullerton, CA), National Data Research Center (Miami, FL), Information on Demand (Berkeley, CA, and Elmsford, NY), Database, Inc. (Sacramento, CA), Infosearch, Inc. (Sacramento, CA), TRW Consumer

Relations (Orange, CA), and Executive Search Corporation (Phoenix, AZ). FFI is unique in that it offers only "friendly" assistance. Simply call and provide information on your respondent. A search will be made of the tens of thousands of names in the FFI data bank. Privacy is safeguarded. The searcher is not notified; instead, the respondent is told who is looking for them and where he or she can reach the searcher—if the respondent so chooses. The remaining eight companies and agencies are more business-like and charge a fee. Gunderson (1989, p. 74) suggests writing to each one to obtain a catalog of its capabilities and service costs. In addition, Gunderson discusses when and how to use private investigators and professional searchers such as accredited genealogists.

Gunderson (1989) highlights the importance of obtaining three vital search statistics for each person involved in a study: first, middle, and last name; date and place of birth; and social security number.[2] Social scientists designing studies would be wise to follow this advice.

➤ SUMMARY AND CONCLUSIONS

Our own experiences in locating respondents, the Comprehensive Tracking Model (Call et al., 1982), the books by King (1992) and Gunderson (1989), and the lessons learned from the social science literature on tracking and successful follow-up studies have convinced us that "most panel members can be located and interviewed in an efficient and cost-effective manner" (Call et al., 1982, p. 118). Several key points are worth reiterating:

➤ Any search should be systematic and focused. Creating profiles of the respondents, identifying the most logical and hopeful search channels, and systematically following each lead will enhance the likelihood of finding all the respondents.

➤ Persistence, persistence, and persistence!

➤ It is cheaper and quicker to do catch-up samples than to launch a panel study and wait 30 years for the data. Investigators should spend time analyzing existing data archives such as those at the Murray Research Center at Radcliffe College and the Institute for Social Research at the University of Michigan.

➤ Search the news media for recent developments that change the advice given in this chapter and in the books we have described. For example, as of November 1993, the New York telephone directory assistance has provided the zip code in addition to a person's telephone number and street address (cost: 45 cents). The U.S. Postal Service announced in January 1994 that it would stop giving address change information to the public in an effort to protect people who move for their safety. This was to end the practice of providing address changes to anyone with the old address and a $3 fee, but information on change-of-address cards still will be available to 25 companies licensed to update mailing lists including direct mail advertisers and credit bureaus. Developments such as these will continue to surface and have an impact on the search procedures used by social scientists.

➢ Check the ever growing number of www resources: Data Base America—People Finder, Switchboard—Find a Person, Infospace—The Ultimate Directory, and so on.

➢ Anyone you encounter during the search may turn out to be an informant. Be ready with your questions.

We found tracking respondents from what originally was a cross-sectional study to be extremely beneficial in producing an invaluable panel data archive for life course research and in demonstrating the connection between person finding and linked lives (Bradburn, Moen, & Demspter-McClain, 1995; Esterberg, Moen, & Dempster-McClain, 1994; Forest, Moen, & Dempster-McClain, 1995, 1996; Miller, Moen, & Dempster-McClain, 1991; Moen & Dempster-McClain, 1990; Moen, Dempster-McClain, & Williams, 1989, 1992; Moen & Erickson, 1995; Moen, Erickson, & Dempster-McClain, 1997; Moen, Robison, & Dempster-McClain, 1995; Moen, Robison, & Fields, 1994; Robison, Moen, & Dempster-McClain, 1995). But the process of doing so also was a very positive experience. Not only did we get to be detectives, but we also obtained important, and frequently very moving, insights on the twists and turns of individual lives.

➢ **NOTES**

1. Some funds for these early tracking efforts were provided through a Hatch grant (321-6408-408) to Phyllis Moen.
2. Consult the Social Security Administration and other privacy forums for the latest advice on using SS#s to locate respondents. In late 1996, a major on-line service (P-Track—a Lexis-Nexis product) removed SS#, mother's maiden name, and medical and credit information from their 300-million-person database as a result of widespread criticism.

Chapter 7

Collecting Life History Data

Experiences From the German Life History Study

ERIKA BRÜCKNER
KARL ULRICH MAYER

The life course is an important topic of research in the social sciences. Autobiographical material and numerous qualitative studies provide a wealth of data not only for psychologists and sociologists but also for historians and scholars in other disciplines. The German Life History Study (GLHS) described here differs from such qualitative studies in several important aspects. Most important, it deals primarily with numerical or quantitative information such as the timing of events and characteristics of activities as opposed to narratives about lives. Events are not treated in isolation but rather are treated as elements in continuous sequences; for example, a given job is merely one element in a sequence of jobs making up an individual's employment history. Furthermore, the study is based on representative samples of defined birth cohorts drawn from the entire population as opposed to only small and local groups or particular individuals.

Whereas much attention has been devoted to methods of collecting data for qualitative biographical studies (Fuchs, 1984; Voges, 1987), relatively little has been written on methods and techniques of collecting data for quantitative life course studies. Most of it has remained tacit knowledge of the researchers involved, and very little is accessible in the literature (Brückner, 1993). This chapter attempts to remedy this situation by describing the general characteristics of life course data and corresponding strategies for the collection of such data. Special emphasis also is placed on how the collection of this type of information differs from that of cross-sectional data.

➢ THE GERMAN LIFE HISTORY STUDY: ORIGINS AND GOALS

We discuss a number of methodological problems and their solutions using the GLHS as our reference. Therefore, we want to start with some observations on the initial purposes and contexts as well as the further life history of the GLHS. The plans for such a survey were developed within a prior project on intergenerational social mobility conducted by Karl Ulrich Mayer, Walter Müller, and Johannes Handl at the University of Mannheim and based on individual-level microcensus data collected in 1971 (Handl, 1988; Mayer, 1977; Müller, 1978). There were five main motives for initiating the GLHS. First, we wanted to fill the black box of intergenerational transition matrices and reconstruct the generating processes and mechanisms of allocation in the class structure. Second, we wanted to go beyond traditional mobility research by also focusing on interrelationships between the family domain and the employment and education domains. Third, we wanted to provide longitudinal data for purposes of social policy analysis. Fourth, we had learned from the half million cases of a 1% microcensus study that there were large differences between specific birth cohorts resulting from the many discontinuities of German history; therefore, we wanted to reconstruct the sociohistorical and generational contexts of social inequalities. Fifth, we wanted to conduct a replication study to investigate changes in mobility processes. Only involuntarily did we have to collect our own data because the Federal Statistical Office started to deny access to individual-level data and stopped collecting the type of detailed data we had analyzed before. In the initial project proposal, the goals of exploring causal mechanisms embedded in the life course and developing appropriate methods of data collection and analysis were added as further objectives.

The study commenced in 1979 with Mayer as the principal investigator. The first West German component of the GLHS, collected in the years 1981-1983, constructed representative samples of three different groups of birth cohorts: 1929-1931, 1939-1941, and 1949-1951 (Mayer & Brückner, 1989). In the years 1985-1987, when the research team had moved to the Max Planck Institute for Human Development and Education in Berlin, the birth cohort of 1919-1921 was added (Brückner, 1993), and in 1988-1989 data for the cohorts born 1954-1956 and 1959-1961 were collected (Brückner & Mayer, 1995). Why this extension in regard to birth cohorts? It became clear very soon that by focusing on the cohorts born between 1930 and 1950, a very particular "success story" of continuous collective advancement would have to be written, whereas we had good reasons to assume that the 1930 cohort was much worse off than the cohorts born before and that a similar reversal was argued for the cohorts born after 1950. Also, we found it very desirable to include the earlier cohort because we could trace its members up to retirement age and look at the impact of their war experiences. For the two younger cohorts, we knew that their demographic behaviors had changed radically, and we wanted to pursue explanations for these changes (Huinink & Mayer, 1995).

Finally, when the Berlin Wall fell, we seized the opportunity to extend the study to East Germany and its transformation because it seemed to us an exemplary case for studying the life course under the conditions of extreme societal discontinuities. Data on four cohort groups were collected in East Germany in the years 1991-1992: 1929-1931, 1939-1941, 1951-1953, and 1959-1961 (Huinink et al., 1995). We went back to our East German respondents with a written questionnaire in 1993 and interviewed them again in 1996-1997 to cover the entire transformation process and explain its outcome in a life course framework. In conjunction with this recent panel study, we also collected complete life histories of East German men and women born in 1971.

At the present time, we are preparing a new survey on the cohorts born in 1964 and 1971 in West Germany. This survey will focus in particular on employment biographies in the context of severe labor market conditions.

We also should mention that we included an only somewhat simplified life history component (Mayer & Wagner, 1996) in the Berlin Aging Study (Mayer & Baltes, 1996). Here we collected, among other varied data on aging outcomes, retrospective life history data for a stratified, representative sample of men and women in West Berlin born between 1887 and 1922.

Altogether within the GLHS, more than 8,000 life histories covering more than 100 years of German history (Figure 7.1) have now been collected. The GLHS has lived its own complex life history that is slowly drawing to a close, at least for us. However, the data is in the public domain and we hope that it will find many users. It is obvious that the GLHS is the work of many individuals, and the appendix acknowledges the convoy of researchers and staff in the study.

It also should have become apparent that during its own life history, the GLHS has accumulated and broadened its substantive problem areas. Although issues of the production and distribution of socioeconomic inequalities, changes in class structure and in educational and occupational careers, and inequities between cohorts still are at the heart of the project (Blossfeld, 1990; Henz, 1996; Mayer, 1995; Mayer & Carroll, 1987; Mayer & Solga, 1994; Solga, 1995), we also have directed our attention to migration (Wagner, 1989), family formation (Huinink, 1994; Huinink & Mayer, 1995), women's employment and family commitment (Mayer, Allmendinger, & Huinink, 1991; Sørensen & Trappe, 1994; Trappe, 1995), and the relationships between social policies and the life course (Allmendinger, 1994; Allmendinger, H. Brückner, & E. Brückner, 1991, 1993; Mayer & Müller, 1986).

How was the GLHS organized and financed? The first three birth cohorts were surveyed within the framework of a so-called Special Research Unit of the German National Science Foundation that allows projects to be funded for up to 12 to 15 years (with interim evaluations every 3 years). This context was very important because the cooperation with economists and social policy specialists markedly sharpened both our substantive and methodological skills. The start of the GLHS also benefited enormously from the fact that the principal investigator was, from 1979 to 1983, director of the German National Survey Research Centre (ZUMA) in Mannheim, where the best competencies with regard to sampling, survey fieldwork, and data processing were assembled (Mayer & Brückner, 1989). Most of the other surveys within the GLHS, and almost all of the data analyses, were organized and financed by the Max Planck Institute of Human Development and Education in Berlin (Center for Sociology and the Study of the Life Course), and the study was moved there in 1983 when the principal investigator became one of the institute's directors. The

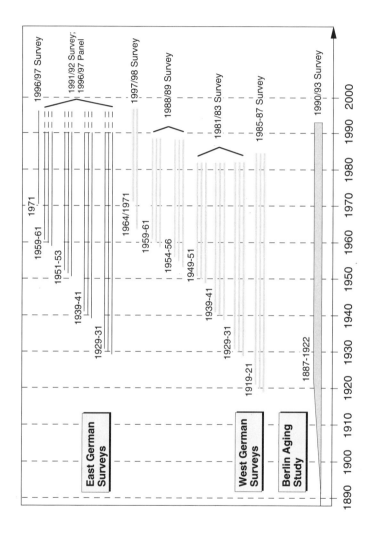

Figure 7.1. The German Life History Study: Retrospective Surveys and Birth Cohorts

NOTE: The horizontal cohort lines indicate the time span for which the life span has been reconstructed. The historical years on the right-hand side indicate the time of interviewing for the respective surveys.

excellent resources and intellectual environment of the Max Planck Society, as well as its commitment to basic research, were of crucial importance to the success of the GLHS. Finally, we cannot appreciate enough the commitment, enthusiasm for innovation, and financial risk taking of the opinion research firms GETAS (which conducted about 2,500 personal interviews), INFRATEST (which developed and administered more than 3,000 computer-assisted telephone interviews [CATI]), and INFAS (which was responsible for the East German Study), with whom we contracted the fieldwork.

The following section is based primarily on the West German component of the GLHS. The other surveys (East German Study and Berlin Aging Study) would warrant special treatment. The West German component included four different surveys or rounds of interviewing. The fieldwork was conducted in the years 1981-1983, 1985-1987, 1988, and 1989. A total of 5,591 interviews were conducted (not including pretests and pilot studies).

The third section deals with the general development of the instruments and presents the questionnaire contents and structure along with various data collection techniques (face-to-face and CATI). The fourth section deals with problems specifically associated with life course surveys, in particular with problems encountered during fieldwork. The fifth section contains a brief discussion of how to store, edit, and check the quality of the data collected. The final section deals with ethical, scientific, and practical issues in conducting retrospective life history studies.

> ➤ SURVEY DESIGN AND METHODS
>   OF DATA COLLECTION

There are only a few examples of quantitative life course studies using large samples. Moreover, the approaches used and results obtained in these studies are not always comparable. Balán, Browning, Jelin, and Litzler (1969) investigated the employment histories of men in selected areas around Monterrey, Mexico, in the mid-1960s. A representative survey of the male population known as the Johns Hopkins Study was carried out by James Coleman and Peter Rossi in the United States in 1968, and a similar survey, the Norwegian Life History Study, was carried out in Norway in 1971 (Ramsøy, 1984). There also are life history components in some earlier studies of social mobility such as the Irish Study (Hout, 1989), the

Hungarian Study from 1970 (Andorka, 1971), and the Polish Study (Mach, Mayer, & Pohoski, 1994). Noteworthy studies influenced by the GLHS are the British Social Change and Economic Life Initiative Study (Gallie, Marsh, & Vogler, 1994), the Swedish Life History Study (Tåhlin, 1991), the Dutch Study (Graaf, 1987), the studies conducted by Treiman and Szelenyi on the transformation of Eastern European societies, and, most recently, the Italian Life History Study conducted by Antonio Schizzerotto and Gøsta Esping-Andersen.

The West German component of the GLHS followed, in part, the lead of these prior attempts and, thus, can be used in conjunction with them as the basis for international comparisons (Allmendinger, 1989; Featherman, Selbee, & Mayer, 1989; Mach et al., 1994). However, it differs from the aforementioned studies in two important aspects. First, it is more representative, including women and a broader range of birth cohorts. Second, it is more comprehensive with regard to life domains, including education and employment history along with medical history, full residential history (not only of locations but also of apartments), family history, and a number of other important thematic areas of the life course such as parents and children. The goal of the questionnaire construction was to represent the "natural history" of individuals to the greatest extent to which it could be rendered in a fashion strictly comparable intersubjectively and be made quantifiable. Thus, we first reviewed life domains—family of origin and one's own family history; education and training; residence and household; employment, income, and consumption; social, religious, and political participation; friends and informal networks; and disabilities and medical history. For all of these life domains, we first tried to convert them into continuous event/state histories and constructed measurement instruments. We started with the idea that there is a more formal, institutionalized, and legitimate path as well as a more informal, marginal, and less institutionalized path. Thus, besides natural parents, we asked for foster and stepparents. We also asked for formal schooling and training for further education, for marginal employment, and for unmarried partners. Limitations of the already excessive interviewing time, as well as measurement problems, led us to cut down the life domains that finally were included. For instance, we did not use an instrument for diachronic associational membership or for friends across the life course. Also, we economized on the household composition history by attaching a shortened version to the residential history. We also dropped a good and tested instrument for consumption history, namely, a history of bought cars and their properties.

Although data collection in a retrospective life course study has a cross-sectional character (i.e., a population sample is interviewed only once at a given time), the content of the data themselves correspond, in principle, to that of a sufficiently long prospective panel study including information on the entirety of the respondents' lives. The caveat "in principle" relates to prior selectivity (emigration or true mortality) in retrospective studies and to panel mortality in prospective studies.

The use of retrospective data collected in a "one-shot" survey offers a plausible alternative to prospective data collection, especially in the case of life course studies (Featherman, 1980). Moreover, objections raised against retrospective data, in particular regarding the accuracy and precision of people's memory (Balán et al., 1969), apply to all types of biographical data. Even cross-sectional studies often contain questions of retrospective character, usually dealing either with the frequency or duration of certain events such as medical treatment or with the time at which a given event took place (e.g., age at marriage or divorce, birth dates of children, employment dates). Such retrospective questions in cross-sectional studies usually are of a much more ad hoc nature than when they are in the context of event sequences; therefore, they should be more prone to recall biases. Also, most prospective panel studies do collect some retrospective information that covers either events or changes between the points of data collection (e.g., once a year) or information on the respondent prior to the beginning of the panel survey. It also is worth mentioning that major prospective panel studies, such as the U.S. Panel Study of Income Dynamics and the German Socio-Economic Panel, do not actually allow construction of continuous event histories.

If one compares and cross-checks retrospective data and autobiographical data from external data sources such as school or firm records, then inconsistencies frequently show up. This appears to suggest that retrospectively collected data cannot be trusted uncritically; one well-known source of error is the "telescoping effect" (Rubin & Baddeley, 1989). However, once sources of error are known, one can take them into account while designing the instrument and thus attempt to eliminate or compensate for them. In contrast to individual events that have to be recalled ad hoc (at most, questions might be introduced by a phrase such as "Think back to the time when . . ."), a life course survey is based on the conceptual foundation of a complete, systematic reconstruction of the life course. Individual events are embedded in both a diachronic and synchronic life context.

Our decision to use birth cohorts as population units instead of the entire population was primarily motivated by prior work about cohort differences in Germany (Handl, 1988; Mayer, 1977; Müller, 1978) based on census data. Financial restrictions ruled out obtaining a sample covering the full population and, at the same time, gaining a sufficient number of people in single birth cohorts or narrow birth cohort groups. Therefore, specific cohort groups were selected. Our prior work with census data provided the criteria for these cohort selections. For instance, the 1939-1941 cohort was chosen because it was one of the baby booms of the century. The 1929-1931 cohort was chosen because we already knew that this was the cohort most affected by World War II and the breakdown after the war. The 1954-1956 (West Germany) and 1951-1953 (East Germany) cohorts were chosen due to their pivotal role in demographic changes (on the selection of cohort, see Mayer & Huinink, 1990).

There are important reasons to rely on cohorts rather than cross sections in longitudinal surveys (Featherman, 1980; Mayer, 1980), but there are even more cogent reasons not to rely on one single cohort in either retrospective or prospective studies (on cohort sequential studies, see Baltes, 1968; Schaie, 1965).

Questionnaire Design

First, the following factors had to be taken into account while designing the questionnaire:

a. the degree of complexity of the questionnaire, which had to record a great deal of information and also do justice to the interindividual, group-specific, and cohort-specific variance of life courses;

b. the historical conditions under which structurally equivalent life events took place in different historical periods;

c. the recording of time (frequencies, durations, and absolute and relative points in time) both as a simple measurement (dimension) and as a way of structuring the life course;

    d. the "sensitive" topics in the respondent's life and the sociodemographic
       data and life events of the respondent's relatives (parents, siblings, spouse,
       children, and grandchildren);
    e. the adaptation of the questionnaire to the size and field conditions of a
       representative national survey (i.e., the quality of the interviewers); and
    f. the specifically retrospective character of the data collected.

Time obviously is the most important dimension in the collection of continuous sequences of events such as the schools an individual attended, the residences in which he or she lived, and the jobs he or she held. Thus, these events can be depicted by plotting them along a continuous time axis. Such a representation shows both the individual events and how they relate to one another chronologically.

Moreover, a life course can be divided into various thematic areas such as educational history, residential history, and employment history. The events from each of these areas can then be plotted along a time axis devoted exclusively to the given area. By arranging the time axes devoted to the various thematic areas parallel to one another, one produces a two-dimensional illustration of the life course containing two axes: a continuous time axis and a discrete thematic area axis. Using this so-called life history matrix, one can collect data systematically merely by following the chronological order of the events.

This format for depicting events provides the maximum amount of data transparency and ease of consistency checking. However, although it was used in other life course studies (Blum, Karweit, & Sørensen, 1969; Freedman, Thornton, Camburn, Alwin, & Young-DeMarco, 1988) and in one of our pilot studies (Papastefanou, 1980), it was not incorporated into the questionnaire used for the larger representative study. Instead, the various thematic areas were dealt with separately by using an individual time axis for each of them.

There were two main reasons for this, both of which involved practical physical constraints on the questionnaire. First, a great amount of data was recorded for each of the thematic areas. For instance, the employment history was not characterized merely by the number of jobs and their starting and ending dates; instead, every single job was characterized by a wealth of information (e.g., starting and ending dates, starting and ending salaries, hours worked per week, detailed job description). A single life history matrix capable of recording that much data either would have been of enormous physical proportions or would have used exceedingly fine print. In either case, it would have been essentially impossible to work with such a life history matrix. Moreover, it would have lost the data transparency that is one of its main advantages. Second, for the same reasons, it would have been difficult to record the answers to open-ended questions, which often were relatively long texts.

In contrast to other questionnaires that use explicit dates as stimuli (e.g., "What were you doing in 1956?") and order events into prestructured intervals, the questionnaire used in the GLHS does not use explicit dates as stimuli. Instead, explicit dates are reconstructed on the basis of event sequences. The latter method seemed to be more conducive to aiding respondents' memories than did the former.

Dividing the life course in various thematic areas naturally entailed asking respondents about chronological progressions throughout their lives more than once. This initially caused worries especially among the interviewers. They were concerned that the respondents would lose patience or become annoyed. However, these worries proved to be unfounded.

Question Modules on Family Background

Except for special investigations of networks or family structures, most studies collect data solely on the respondent and include only a few statistics about other persons in his or her household. By contrast, the West German component of the GLHS collected extensive data on the respondent's family of origin and own family. These were among the most sensitive topics contained in the survey. Moreover, they have possible legal ramifications for the study given that West German data confidentiality laws restrict the amount and type of information that an interviewer can obtain from a respondent about a third person.

In accordance with the chronological principle of order used throughout the survey, questions about the family of origin were asked at the beginning of the interview, whereas questions about the respondent's own family were asked later. Figure 7.2 presents a schematic overview of the questions dealing with family development that were used in the survey conducted in 1988 (dealing with the 1919-1921 birth cohort).

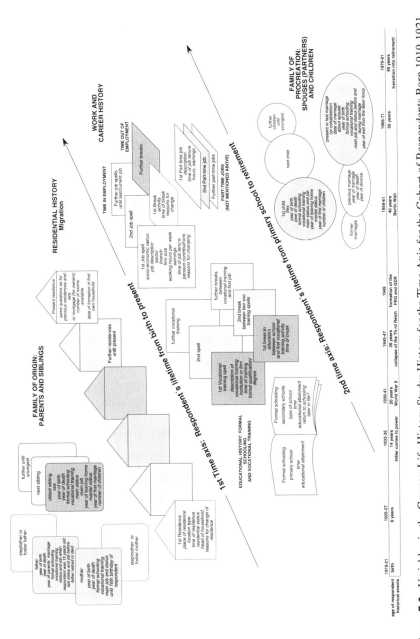

Figure 7.2. Variables in the German Life History Study: History for the Time Axis for the Cohort of Respondents Born 1919-1921

163

Screening

Due to the high interindividual variance of life courses, screening presents one of the main problems during the questionnaire design and data collection process. Screening is necessary for a large number of individual questions or thematic areas, especially in the form of preliminary questions that establish the relevance of further questions on a given topic. For instance, questions about a respondent's spouse are relevant only if the respondent is married. The screening process used in the first questionnaire was quite detailed, but the interviewers were nevertheless not entirely relieved of their own judgments. These problems were eliminated by the introduction of a CATI system. For example, we asked some screening questions that controlled the path through the individual interview. Figure 7.3 gives an example for the control of one spell of working history.

Cohort-Specific Questionnaires

In one sense, cohort-specific questionnaires are merely a specialized case of screening; that is, if the respondent belongs to this cohort, then ask the following set of questions. However, they go beyond mere screening in that the actual content of the questionnaires is changed. German institutions and society as a whole have undergone a great many changes in the past 100 years, and people growing up in different historical periods have encountered widely varying historical conditions. To name just one obvious example, the older cohorts experienced World War II and its immediate aftermath, whereas the younger ones did not. Similarly, the national socialist educational system in which the oldest cohort received its schooling differs considerably from the West German educational system after the war, which also has undergone several fundamental changes over the past 40 years.

These differences had to be taken into account in the questionnaire. Thus, the phrasing of certain questions, as well as the meanings or values of certain variables, depended on the cohorts that they described. Although this approach usually limits the extent to which different cohorts can be compared, this deliberately was ignored in favor of a more accurate reflection of historical reality.

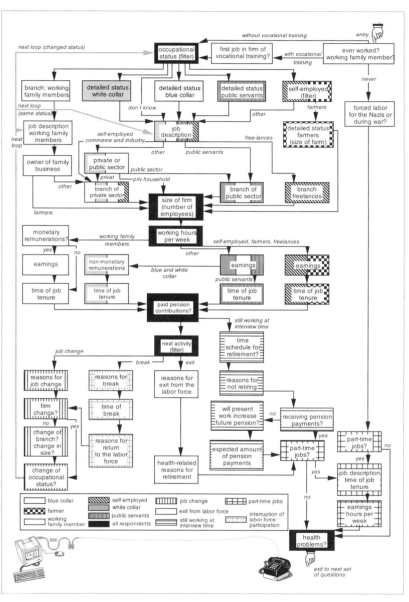

Figure 7.3. Flow Chart of Screening Procedures in the Computer-Assisted Telephone Interview System for Job Spells: German Life History Study Cohort of Respondents Born 1919-1921

Use of Computer-Assisted Telephone Interviews

The first two surveys were conducted using the classical personal or face-to-face interview method. This method was accompanied by several difficulties, some of which are discussed later. Due to these difficulties, the decision was made to conduct further surveys via telephone. Once this decision was made, it was but a small step to replace the previously used paper questionnaire with a computerized questionnaire, in other words, to make use of CATI. This proved to be an extremely beneficial decision. One of the most important advantages of using CATI was the ability to automate the screening process. The interviewer no longer had to leaf through a long questionnaire filled with little arrows and boxes with screening instructions. Instead, the computer would automatically screen questions and display the next question to be asked on a CRT screen. This freed the interviewer to concentrate exclusively on conducting the interview and recording the data as precisely and accurately as possible.

Moreover, an unlimited number of data validity and consistency checks could be automated. If erroneous or inconsistent data were entered, then the interviewer would immediately receive a message asking for a correction or confirmation of the data. Data validity was checked merely by comparing the data entered to previously established valid values or ranges. For instance, the year of birth for the oldest cohort had to fall within the 1919-1921 range. If a year outside this range were entered, then an appropriate message would be displayed (e.g., "Try again. Year must be between 1919-21").

Data consistency was checked by comparing the data entered both with previously entered data and with previously established plausible (not necessarily exclusively valid) values or ranges. For instance, it might be assumed that a woman has her first child between the ages of 18 and 30 years. By comparing a woman's year of birth to that of her first child, her age at the child's birth could be determined. If it fell outside the previously established range of plausible ages, then a message asking for confirmation would be displayed (e.g., "Was your mother really 14 years old when she had her first child?"). Thus, a major source of errors could be eliminated; that is, corrections could be shifted from the later process of data editing and high-cost rechecking with the respondent to the initial interview.

In addition, questions could incorporate information gained from previously asked questions and could, thus, be made very precise and specific (e.g., "Until when did you work as a file clerk in the bookkeeping department of Company X?"). Besides the fact that such questions vastly reduce the odds that the interviewer or respondent will confuse one event with another, such questions also give the respondent the impression that the interviewer is an intelligent person paying attention to what he or she is being told.

One of the few disadvantages of using CATI was the loss of transparency offered by a large matrix on a single sheet of paper. Due to the physical constraints of a computer system (i.e., only a given amount of information can be displayed on a screen at one given time), it was necessary to split the matrices into smaller templates (i.e., sets of questions that could fit onto one screen). However, the loss of transparency was more than compensated for by the automated consistency checks already described. Furthermore, it was possible to maintain an overview of the data by switching between displays of information at different levels, for instance, one display showing a list of all the jobs an individual had held and another display showing detailed information for only one of those jobs. However, we did observe that telephone interviewers sometimes took notes on paper to keep track of interdomain consistency. Technically, these problems could easily be remedied by larger and split-screen monitors.

➤ FIELDWORK

Problems with conducting the interviews were expected from the outset for several reasons. To begin with, the format of the questionnaire appeared unusual and unfamiliar to the interviewers. It was unknown to what extent the respondents would cooperate given that they would be asked so many questions of a personal nature. Moreover, the institutes entrusted with conducting the interviews had to deal with many tasks that were much more demanding than those they routinely encountered.

In general, the difficulties encountered during fieldwork are attributed to a lack of cooperation on the part of the informants. However, this did not prove true for the study described here. On the contrary, with few exceptions, the respondents exhibited almost astonishingly positive reactions to the interviews. It was, in fact, the interviewers who presented the most difficulties throughout the entire data collection process (even after the introduction of CATI), although a great deal of effort was made to supervise and support them.

Cohort Samples

The sample design required selecting people born in specific years. In contrast to representative, cross-sectional samples of a population, the cohort-centered selection of samples (with a sufficient number of people in each cohort) requires special procedures. (An exact description of these procedures is contained in Kirschner & Wiedenbeck, 1989; a general theoretical and methodological discussion of these procedures is contained in Mayer, 1989.)

This subsection, in particular, deals with the practical consequences of using a cohort-centered approach in a nationwide face-to-face and telephone survey. Arriving at a representative sample made up of different adjacent and nonadjacent birth cohorts requires extensive preparatory work. Because the sample is limited to only these cohorts, it had to be selected out of the entire corresponding population. Two different methods were used to accomplish this. For the face-to-face surveys (1981-1983 and 1985), a household list based on the Association of German Market Research Institutions master sample was created to identify the target population (GETAS, Bremen). On the basis of these 13,974 private households, a sample on the individual level was chosen (ZUMA, Mannheim).

The telephone surveys were based on a representative sample of households with telephones (Infrascope [Heyde, 1988]), out of which the informants for the second survey of older cohorts and the two samples for the younger cohorts were selected (Infratest-Sozialforschung, Munich). The various procedures used are described here only in terms of their influence on the way in which the surveys were conducted.

Special strategies were necessary to compensate for specific regional losses, which affected primarily major cities or urban centers in the first field survey and primarily the points lying in rural areas in the second. In both these (face-to-face) surveys, it was necessary to make repeated follow-up trips to interview informants who were difficult to reach geographically or who were indecisive about participating in the surveys. Besides the geographical dispersion of the informants, another probable reason for the slow tempo at which data were collected was the strict procedure used to select the informants (no substitutions could be made on either the household or individual level). Response rates of around 60% may raise doubts about whether the results obtained in laborious field surveys were worth the effort required to obtain them. However, these response rates are close to the ones for the usual cross-sectional surveys in Germany despite the fact that our demands on the respondents' time were much higher.

Switching to collecting data by telephone made a more centralized field operation possible and, likewise, appeared to present a viable solution in identifying samples of specific cohorts.

The rate of those not at home could be reduced from nearly 4.0% to 1.5%. The "direct line" to the respondents further made it possible to split up the long interviews into several telephone conversations. This proved to be a big help especially for the oldest cohort, whose interviews sometimes were extremely long (one third of all interviews in the survey of the oldest cohort were conducted in two or three calls). In view of the mobility of the two youngest cohorts, the up-to-dateness of the telephone sample, as well as the ease of repeated contacts, proved to be an advantage in the process of data collection.

Interviewer Quality

Due to the complex questionnaire used in this study, interviewers were selected on the basis of their levels of education and previous experience in conducting relatively complex interviews. Interviewer training concentrated on the special features of the study. In the first study, the training consisted solely of written instructions that were quite long and complex. Afterward, a trial interview was staged as a dry run. The interviewers' reactions to these instructions were not checked directly, but an indirect indication was the dropout rate among them. Of 428 selected interviewers, 72 dropped out.

The second (face-to-face) survey was carried out by a significantly smaller team of interviewers consisting of about 60 highly motivated and supported interviewers. This, however, resulted in increased travel costs. Besides economic considerations, there also are methodological arguments for using a large team of interviewers, for instance, the reduction of interviewer bias by distributing these errors.

Despite such counterarguments, the unusual strategy of using a small team was chosen because it permitted more intensive training and support for the interviewers.

In the pilot study for the second survey (Brückner, 1993), analysis of the tapes of interviews revealed a high level of interviewer error. The quality of the interviewers who had received only written training was significantly lower than that of the interviewers who had received oral training. Day-long seminars for small groups and a specially designed training program (with practice interviews and their subsequent analysis) were introduced. As an anonymous interviewer survey showed, these interviewers felt more confident and well informed due to their having had better knowledge of the study's research goals and historical context. They also were more interested in their work than was the large group of interviewers used in the first nationwide survey who never had a chance to meet the researchers involved in this study.

The second survey investigated an older and, for fieldwork purposes, more problematic group of people. The efforts of the small team did not, however, result in a significantly higher response rate than that of the first survey. The broad geographical distribution of the respondents made it necessary to deal with some cases via telephone (e.g., persons who initially refused to participate), which helped to increase the response rate.

In the first survey, also in the round of personal interviews collected in the second survey, about 20% of the respondents were telephoned back to check and clear data errors. This initially showed the suitability of using the telephone to collect data on the life course. During the planning phase, this decision appeared risky, if not altogether foolish. Telephone interviews were then regarded—and perhaps still are—by German social scientists as inappropriate for demanding interviews, particularly those with sensitive questions, that take a long time to conduct, or that deal with elderly persons (Groves et al., 1988; Herzog & Rodgers, 1988; Körmendi, Esgsmose, & Noordhoek, 1986). Because all these characteristics are true to an even higher degree for life course surveys, from the very outset telephone interviews might have been seen as an unsuitable method. However, in the meantime, there is a wealth of actual experience in dealing with long telephone conversations and psychologically sensitive topics (Hormuth, 1990; Hormuth & Brückner, 1985; Hormuth & Lalli, 1988).

The telephone offers many favorable solutions to the problems of, and with, interviewers. Some of the advantages of using a CATI system already have been discussed here. Another advantage proved to be the continuous and individual support for, and supervision of, interviewers made possible by such a system. Interviewers could easily ask for help, for instance, when it became difficult to apply given codes. Furthermore, this method of centralized fieldwork and direct data entry allowed the researchers to have a continuous, real-time record of interview results, thus enabling them to communicate with the interviewers while the fieldwork was still being conducted. There is no doubt that this also created a completely new working environment for the interviewers (Brückner, 1995).

Reaction of Respondents

Willingness to Participate

Ethical considerations alone require that the respondents be told as clearly and completely as possible the research goals and the methods used to carry out the research. Moreover, given the content and methods of a life course study, pragmatic considerations also require that the informants know as much as possible about the research to win their cooperation. In contrast to qualitative studies, which usually can make do with only a few volunteers who are particularly interested in participating, a representative study depends on the cooperation of every one of the randomly chosen respondents. Accordingly, all the respondents in this study were sent detailed letters in advance describing the selection and interviewing process (face-to-face or via telephone), the main topics of the interview, and the research goals of the study. The reactions of the respondents were quite diverse.

On the basis of everyday experience, one can imagine two contradictory reactions to the content of the survey. On the one hand, describing one's own life history—usually in some bureaucratic format such as a résumé—is not something that most people like to do. However, on the other hand, most people do like to talk informally about themselves and their lives.

Similar contradictory arguments could be made for or against the validity of data acquired in the context of an interview. On the one hand, there is the hypothesis that it is exceedingly easy for people to provide valid information. After all, they are describing important events in their own lives, and they either still remember the basic facts or can easily reconstruct them by using personal documents such as diplomas. On the other hand, the hypothesis that nobody is able to recall such events spontaneously, systematically, and without any gaps is at least as plausible as the previous one.

These sorts of "common sense" hypotheses illustrate the problems of the investigation from the respondents' points of view and, thus, are worth mentioning at this point. The respondents themselves did, in fact, use such arguments either to refuse to participate in the study (because it appeared to them to be "infeasible" or "making unreasonable demands") or to accept all too quickly (because they thought the interviews would somehow give them the opportunity to present themselves in a favorable light), which created a danger of disappointed expectations.

In addition to arguments typically used by people refusing to participate in interviews (e.g., no interest, no time), more specific arguments were offered in our life course interview. These included statements such as "My life is my own business" and "That's a private matter" but also rationalizing objections such as that the study was "useless" and "a waste of money." Refusals also could have been the result of shame for having had what were perceived as lives devoid of any significant events or, in the case of older or seriously disadvantaged persons, fear of painful memories.

Besides the preceding objections to content, other factors certainly also played a role. The unusual length of the interview was mentioned both in the letter of introduction and in the conversations. Furthermore, the interviewers either consciously or unconsciously got across to the respondents the importance of reconstructing events and, thus, also an impression of the degree of difficulty of the task ahead of them.

The different, but generally high, rates of refusal probably were due to the unusual demands of the survey and its related interviews. In addition, however, the rate of refusal clearly depended on the age and sex of the respondents. There was a higher rate of refusal among women, and this rate increased with age. Young men had the lowest rate of refusal (in the face-to-face interviews). Similar tendencies, although not quite so pronounced, were found in the telephone interviews. Problems with getting older people to participate have been described in other studies (e.g., Bungard, 1979). Many people in the oldest cohort, who were almost 70 years old at the time of the interviews, could not be easily persuaded to participate in the study. Despite repeated attempts to persuade the approximately 100 individuals who had "weakly" refused altogether, almost 30% of the older respondents could not be persuaded to participate in the face-to-face survey. In the telephone survey, a response rate of 73.1% was achieved for the oldest cohort. Compared to that of the two youngest cohorts, who were born between 1954 and 1961 and had a response rate of more than 80%, this result is somewhat worse; however, considering the general problems involved with the participation of older persons, it is astonishingly good.

Cooperation During the Interview

In contrast to those people who refused their cooperation, the respondents who did cooperate usually declared their willingness to do so quickly, and almost all of them were exceptionally motivated. Some spared no pains in using photographs and documents as sources of information or proof of the veracity of their statements, even though this was not required. The respondents' patience and stamina were astonishing despite the length, monotony, and difficulty of the interviews. The length of the interview tended to depend on the individual in question, although the respondent's age was an obvious factor. In some cases, the length of the interview exceeded 6 hours, but the average length of the face-to-face interviews was just under 80 minutes for the middle cohorts (those born between 1929 and 1951) and just over 2 hours for the oldest cohort (1919-1921).

The questionnaire for the oldest cohort had to be shortened for the telephone survey. Nonetheless, the average length of the interview could be reduced to only about 90 minutes. That only this much time was needed for an interview consisting of several telephone conversations requires an explanation, especially because when comparing survey methods in the scientific literature, one often can read that the face-to-face method is the only viable (or at least the best) method for conducting long interviews. Having carried out more than 3,000 successful telephone interviews, we cannot support this thesis, although collecting life course data does require an unusual sort of interview.

As already has been discussed in detail, the technical possibilities offered by CATI offer optimal solutions to the problems of questionnaire design (i.e., dealing with structures related in terms of sequence or content). A computerized questionnaire and the use of the telephone seem to offer an ideal setting for the specific communication problems involved in reconstructing a life course. The greater anonymity of the two people communicating, between whom a close rapport exists nonetheless ("dyads" [Brückner, 1985]), turns the situation into a sort of "confessional" that can prove helpful for somebody attempting to concentrate on and recall events in his or her own life. The distanced conversational setting without any sort of visual contact along with confidence-building measures, which has been interpreted by many researchers as a deficit of telephone communication, seemed to have had a positive influence on the process of "specifically stimulated anamnesis." Distractions caused by handling the many interview aids (e.g., questionnaire, charts, tables) that are important or even indispensable in face-to-face interviews may annoy the respondents and make them lose their trains of thought.

The questionnaire described heretofore might sound like a résumé or other bureaucratic form on a vast scale and might more likely be intimidating or monotonous rather than stimulating. Apart from relatively few open-ended questions with subjective content, the only things about which the respondents actually are asked are facts (numbers and other dry pieces of information). There seems to be a mismatch between what kind of information the researchers want and the comprehensive stories the respondents want to tell. The latter do not perceive events in the form of numbers (dates) and other individual pieces of information; rather, they perceive them as complex experiences that are connected to other experiences. Although the respondents almost always were able to go from somewhat hazy memories of events in general to specific details of individual events, almost all of them (not just the older ones) also often started telling stories instead of answering specific questions about points in time or details of certain events. Stories or anecdotes used up valuable time during the interviews and distracted the interviewers, who were using a complicated questionnaire that was designed to be strictly sequential, used complex filtering, and was not intended to allow any digressions. The argument initially used by interviewers to interrupt any such stories and get the respondents back on track (i.e., that "the precise details" were not really necessary) tended to result in gaps in the data. Therefore, conducting the interviews was something of a balancing act because, on the one hand, the rigid format of the questionnaire had to be accepted and adhered to and, on the other, it was equally necessary to create a flexible conversational situation.

The amount of discipline required by the questionnaire provoked surprisingly few negative reactions. The respondents showed remarkable patience in answering the same or similar questions during the course of the interviews. Apparently, the structure of the questionnaire not only appealed to and aided the respondents in terms of content but also corresponded to the organization of the desired (retrospective) retrieval processes.

The Risk of Catharsis:
A Benefit or Danger?

Many researchers of the psychology of memory (Rubin, 1986; Rubin & Baddeley, 1989) have emphasized that the autobiographical reconstruction of one's past is a central function of one's "self." The significance of retrospection at an advanced age is undisputed, a fact that can be made use of in therapeutic settings (Molinari & Reichlin, 1984-1985). The meticulous structure of the questionnaire strengthened or induced the need to recall events as precisely and completely as possible. The chance that something would have been deliberately left out or suppressed was relatively small in this process because the respondents were systematically led through their lives. They hardly had sufficient time to make up fictitious life histories. Giving the respondents too many details of the questionnaire's content in advance may lead to suppression or distortion of information and is, in terms of the data collection process, psychologically problematic. However, having confronted the respondents with their own pasts, without any advance preparation made, led to unpleasant or painful memories, which both the respondents and the interviewers had to work to overcome.

Especially among the oldest cohort, who as young adults had gone through the war and its immediate aftermath, questions could provoke emotional (and sometimes also physical) reactions. Such reactions were only rarely observed during face-to-face interviews. On the other hand, respondents were less prone to self-control during telephone interviews because they were either alone or in a relatively private setting. In fact, the greater anonymity of telephone interviews seems almost to encourage such reactions (the "confessional effect"). Therefore, the interviewers had to be trained to notice and deal with signs of emotional or physical exhaustion.

Although specifically trained interviewers and, in the case of telephone interviews conducted from a central office, supervisors were able to catch such situations and keep them under control, the problem of provoking emotional reactions during telephone interviews remains a topic worthy of discussion in terms of its ethical implications for further research in this area.

Finally, some of the respondents, apart from any personal emotions they might have experienced, perceived the interviews and the reconstruction of their life histories as a (technical) challenge and had feelings of accomplishment on completion of the tasks. Signs of fatigue were measured on a rating scale at the end of each interview. The results showed that the interviewers felt more tired than did the respondents.

➢ STORING, EDITING, AND VALIDATING DATA

Storing Data

The first survey of the West German component of the GLHS made use of conventional code sheets and punch cards for data entry, although the data were then transferred into a computerized scientific information retrieval (SIR) data bank. The second survey made use of a special data input system developed at the Max Planck Institute for Human Development and Education that, on the basis of SIR forms software, enabled data to be directly input, encoded, and checked for validity and consistency (Brückner, 1993, pp. 81-94). The last two surveys made use of CATI, so these steps could be completed, for the most part, during the interview itself. However, the software used for the CATI system (PLUTO, developed for internal use by Infratest, Munich) was not SIR compatible, so the raw data collected had to be reformatted before they could be processed further. Needless to say, a CATI system requires a good deal of advance planning and preparation, hardware with a large memory capacity, and constant technical support and supervision during the fieldwork. Furthermore, the data collected still are not ready for analysis by any means; it would be very much a mistake to assume that using a CATI system makes subsequent detailed editing and validating of the data superfluous.

As already mentioned, a computer can carry out any number of data validity and consistency checks, and it can do so faster and more reliably than can humans. Nonetheless, one cannot do entirely without human checking. Individual life courses vary so much that it is virtually impossible to predict all the possible forms they can take. In addition, broader historical, institutional, and geographical information can explain apparently spurious or erroneous pieces of individual data of the life course. Therefore, individual life course data must be examined and checked in their entirety within this broader framework.

Editing Data

Editing plays an extremely important role in the processing of life course data. Linear, chronological events and numerous events linked to one another in terms of content have to be combined into a single, individual life history free of inconsistencies. Completeness and plausibility are important criteria both on the individual and interindividual levels (for a detailed description of the process, see Brückner, 1993; Brückner, Hoffmeyer-Zlotnik, & Tölke, 1983; Tölke, 1989). Consistency and plausibility, as well as continuity of sequential events, can be checked in detail by using the intrinsic logic of the events and their relation to one another as well as to institutional and historical contexts. In this respect, editing serves as a sort of internal validation. Like questionnaires, editing methods have to be adapted to the specific historical context of each cohort.

The treatment of missing values was a particular problem. Completeness is an important prerequisite for the analysis of sets of event data. Gaps in the data had to be filled somehow, even when additional checks, which included going back to documents or respondents, could not produce exact information to fill them.

Dates were reconstructed by using so-called artificial months, for instance, 21 for January = beginning of year, 26 or 27 for June/July = middle of year. Landmarks, which usually are major historical events used to set relative dates for personal events, also played a role in the editing. These relative dates (e.g., "It took place in the same month as the assassination attempt on Hitler") occasionally misled the interviewers into entering false dates despite the fact that they were provided with a chronological list of historical events. Using history books and similar reference material, the editors were later able to reconstruct the actual dates on the basis of the respondents' relative dates, which usually were authentic and very accurate (they are referred to as "flashbulb" phenomena in psychology). Residential and employment histories were compared to check for data validity and consistency and also to enhance or clean the data in difficult cases.

An ever increasing number of data validity and consistency checks were computerized during the course of the study, but computers still could neither completely eliminate nor even significantly reduce the task of editing the data by hand. All in all, the amount of time needed for the data to be edited was about the same as that needed for the interviews themselves (for a comprehensive study on the quality of our retrospective survey, see Brückner, 1995).

➢ CONCLUDING REMARKS

A chapter such as this cannot hope to give an exhaustive description of all the methodological problems associated with a life course study, let alone to offer a "cookbook" of techniques for conducting such a study. The problems described—those of instrument design, fieldwork, and data editing and validation—should nonetheless focus the attention of those doing research in this area or, in general, survey methodology on the particulars of life course studies. Further discussion should deal with the problems of collecting process-oriented, retrospective data and of further analyzing it. In contrast to typical questionnaires, a questionnaire for a life course study must be structured according to the temporal order in various life domains. Moreover, it must be capable of representing linkages between states and events across domains.

The apparently simple process of answering specific questions about simple facts of one's own life should not obscure the fact that biographical reconstruction during a standardized interview is a very demanding task. Such investigations are prone to error both while being conceived and also while being conducted. It is all too easy to attribute erroneous or incomplete data to memory gaps or a lack of motivation on the part of the respondents. Empirically checking whether this actually is the case is no easy task. In a certain sense, the numerous surveys and different methodological approaches described in this chapter present a sort of reality check. It has been shown that a continual and complete reconstruction of individual life courses is possible. In general, the respondents exhibited a high degree of motivation and cooperation, even when asked to recall the details of numerous events, some of which had taken place in the distant past over the course of long lifetimes. Although the extraordinarily productive and, in general, very efficient cooperation of the randomly chosen respondents probably could be attributed to the special content of the survey, the studies show that demanding questionnaires and long interviews (also by telephone) can be used successfully.

The very intensive checks required in such an investigation gave indications that the interviewers were overburdened and spotlighted weaknesses in their performance more so than with typical surveys. Replacing the very complicated paper questionnaire with a computerized questionnaire solved some of the problems of data collection. Automating the interviewing process eased the task of the interviewers and guaranteed better data quality, if for no other reason than that numerous automated data validity and data consistency checks provided the interviewers with the chance to immediately detect and correct input errors. Another advantage of this system is that raw data are available for analysis even while the interviews still are taking place. Given the highly diverse nature and numerous chronological and thematic links within a life course, a computerized questionnaire seems almost ideal, especially in terms of the resources it offers for data checking. However, this undeniable improvement of the data collection process does not eliminate the task of editing each individual protocol in detail. This is due to the demands that subsequent analyzing procedures place on the data; they must be free of missing values (i.e., continuous and chronologically consistent).

The GLHS can be described as a quantitative or standardized survey more in terms of the methods used to conduct it than of its content (which includes open-ended questions). The unusual demands of using these methods obviously influence the amount of time and money needed to carry out such a survey, especially if there are large numbers of cases to be investigated. Accurately recording and depicting the heterogeneity of individual and cohort-specific life events is virtually impossible without a considerable amount of effort. Both quantitative and qualitative methods must be used but, at the same time, must be viewed critically. This is the (admittedly high) price of creating a database capable of serving as the basis for analyses of societal changes both as a whole and in specific cohorts and subgroups.

Appendix

Convoys in the Life Course of the German Life History Study: Research Associates, Staff Persons, Doctoral Students, Postdoctoral Fellows, and Collaborators (1979-1997)

Principal investigator:
> Karl Ulrich Mayer (1979-)

Research associates:
> Hans-Peter Blossfeld (1984-1990)
> Erika Brückner (1985-1994)
> Martin Diewald (1991-)
> Johannes Huinink (1986-1994)
> Ineke Maas (1991-)
> Georgios Papastefanou (1979-1988)
> Götz Rohwer (1996-1997)
> Heike Solga (1995-)
> Annemette Sørensen (1992-1994)
> Angelika Tölke (1979-1987)
> Heike Trappe (1997-)
> Michael Wagner (1988-)

Staff persons:
> Monika Albin (1992-)
> Wolfgang Bach (1979-1981)
> Hannah Brückner (1989-1991)
> Doris Hess (1985-1988)
> Sonja Menning (1996-)
> Birgit Jesske-Müller (1988-1989)
> Maria Martin (1993-1994)
> Renate Minas (1990-1992)
> Jürgen Moka (1989-1991)
> Reinhard Nuthmann (1988-1990)
> Karen Visser (1997)
> Joachim Wackerow (1985-1989)
> Sigrid Wehner (1988-)

Doctoral students:
> Rolf Becker
> Anne Goedicke
> Ursula Henz

Dirk Konietzka
Wolfgang Lauterbach
Britta Matthes
Klaus Schömann
Heike Solga
Heike Trappe
Sylvia Zühlke

Postdoctoral fellows:
Karen Aschaffenburg
Tak Wing Chan
Nan Dirk de Graaf
Paul de Graaf
Ineke Maas
Wilfred Uunk

Collaborators:
Erika Brückner (ZUMA) (1979-1983)
Barbara von Harder (GETAS) (1980-1983, 1985-1987)
Doris Hess (INFAS) (1990-1997)
Jürgen Hoffmeyer-Zlotnik (ZUMA) (1979-1983)
Klaus Kortmann (Infratest) (1987-1989)

Part III

Strategies for Analysis

➢ **INTRODUCTION**

Part III of this book focuses on the analysis and interpretation of life course data. To derive meaningful interpretations of why life course patterns vary or change from one period to another, it is necessary to engage in comparisons that will isolate determining factors. Three major strategies for analysis are included in Part III. They differ by whether they focus on differences in events and trajectories *within* individuals, *among* individuals sharing a common personal characteristic, or *across groups* of individuals who have experienced a common historical or economic environment. As in Part II on data collection and measurement, we have arranged the chapters of Part III in an ascending order of generality beginning with Clausen's chapter on the life review, continuing with Laub and Sampson's focus on the lives of delinquents as they move into adulthood, then Giele's use of cohort comparison to track innovation in men's and women's lives, and ending with Elder and Pellerin's review of ways in which to analyze the effects for different groups of sharing dramatic historical experiences such as depression and war.

In Chapter 8, "Life Reviews and Life Stories," Clausen compares events and periods *within the life* of a single individual and focuses on the intra-individual organization of personal events and trajectories. The person looks backward or forward at his or her life and constructs an identity and a direction. The means for eliciting life stories range from psychoanalysis and biography to spontaneous and structured interviews, letters, and diaries. The data elements on which life stories are based are the same as in the life course paradigm: time-marked events; the person's roles and experiences; relationships in work, family, and community; and location in a particular historical and cultural context. What is distinctive about Clausen's chapter is his analytic focus on identity and the self. He writes, "I repeatedly found myself coming back to the concept of identity" (p. 202). Identity makes sense out of continuities and discontinuities, ups and downs in life satisfaction, and turning points. Identity is especially related to the concept of human agency, and Clausen finds that positive life satisfaction is associated with a greater sense of confidence and control, whereas dissatisfaction is associated with a sense of inadequacy. The larger significance of Clausen's work for this book is his focus on the dynamics of self-integration, a dimension that the life course paradigm suggests but does not fully capture in the concept of human agency. What Clausen does is place the individual in the driver's seat, so to speak, as *the* appropriate focus for life course analysis. It is the person, after all, who is integrating events and experiences and giving them meaning. Culture, yes, and climate of the times have some influence, but these are faceless factors. What gives the life course its *life* is the sentient individual going through vital changes, encountering new relationships and circumstances, and, in the end, deciding whether to hold or change course.

In Chapter 9, "Integrating Quantitative and Qualitative Data," Laub and Sampson use a "person-centered" approach rather than a "variable-centered" approach. By "quantitative" they mean objective data (e.g., court records, school reports, military service), and by "qualitative" they mean subjective accounts by self and others of the feelings and meanings associated with particular events and experiences. Their project is by nature retrospective and, thus, makes possible the review of a whole life. A key analytic focus is the concept of "turning points" and the role of human agency and the self in determining why certain persons become delinquent in the first place and why some of these then go straight. Laub and Sampson go beyond case studies to consider a whole class of individuals who are similar in background and social milieu but whose lives take different paths. The Gluecks' data archive on 500 delinquent and 500 nondelinquent men from underprivileged Boston neighborhoods is nearly ideal for the reanalysis that they undertake. The respondents were first surveyed in 1940 and then again in 1949-1965 to gather rich and valid subjective and objective data. Thus, the present authors can search for systematic patterns that explain continuity or cessation of delinquency. The data they find relevant correspond to the now familiar elements of the life course paradigm—a combination of life *events* (timing) such as school completion, military service, and marriage; *relationships* (linked lives) with family, schools, and employers; and the *historical era* (location) of wartime and a postwar boom in which these events occurred. It is the *turning points* (human agency) that provide the conceptual armature around which the other elements adhere. Deriving a positive learning experience from being in the army, finding and keeping a steady job, and forming a lasting marriage all are positively associated with, but cannot alone explain, the abandoning of a delinquent life path.

In Chapter 10 on "Innovation in the Typical Life Course," Giele poses a true challenge to a bidirectional model of the life course: How should we study those instances in which not only are individuals' lives shaped by the surrounding context but they, in turn, forge new patterns that add up to a changing norm? In men's lives, a classic case is the dramatic change in typical retirement age since 1900. In women's lives, it is the growth of multiple roles in midlife that result from the massive entry of women into the paid labor force after 1940 and their continued presence there even as they married and had children. In both instances, three types of research questions are possible that identify (a) which persons are the first to adopt a new pattern within any given age group, (b) which cohorts are most likely to be the originators of a given change, and (c) how the innovation is variously adopted in different nations. Giele provides answers from her own studies of women's changing life course patterns.

To discover the innovators in a given age group, Giele examines temperance and suffrage leaders whose different life histories prefigured the types of reform they chose. The temperance women who wanted to protect their homes were more likely to have suffered family losses, whereas the suffragists who sought a role in public life had been denied professional or educational advancement because they were women. To discover which cohorts were the innovators of the multiple-role pattern, she compares several generations of college alumnae and their timing of major events and finds that the largest group of pioneers were born in the 1930s and 1940s. Finally, using the U.S. National Longitudinal Surveys and the German Socio-Economic Panel Studies, she probes the adoption of multiple roles cross-nationally and discovers that the innovative cohorts were born in the 1930s and 1940s in Germany as well as in the United States. Given these three levels of analysis, Giele has begun to flesh out the "combined social system" approach that Riley calls for in Chapter 2 by attending not only to the characteristics of innovators who are constituents of a given age group but also to the historical context (period and cohort) and place (country) in which innovation is found. In addition, she shows how to cast biographical accounts, retrospective reports on life events, and longitudinal survey data to accomplish this end.

In Chapter 11, "Linking History and Human Lives," Elder and Pellerin review analytic strategies that represent the most encompassing form of life course analysis—tracking the effects of macrohistorical change on individual lives. Data are collected and organized around a chronological record of retrospective accounts, letters, and other documents as well as prospective reports. The elements to be described are the familiar parts of the life course paradigm: the historical phenomenon itself, social relationships, individual events and roles, and individuals' subjective feelings. In their reanalysis of the Terman data, the investigators recast the available information to assess the impact of combat experience on later lives. By linking family financial situation to the Oakland and Berkeley longitudinal data on child development, they are able to trace the impact of the Depression on adult roles.

From these projects, Elder and Pellerin derive several important lessons. To use data archives, one must first make an inventory of all available information, array it alongside the study goals, and, where possible, recast it in the form of individual life records arranged chronologically. The "holes" in the data will likely suggest some new types of analysis and use of available facts that previously had been overlooked. New projects should begin by defining the historical event of interest and then gather reports and records of life events; relationships in family, work, and community; and respondents' subjective feelings about these experiences. The ultimate purpose of the analysis is to discover the *interaction* between history and individual lives. Children of the Depression, having surmounted hardship, helped to produce a family-oriented culture and the economic success of the 1950s. In the Iowa farm crisis of the 1980s, couples in strong marriages and fathers who were good decision makers enabled their children and families to survive successfully. Thus, not only does history influence individuals, but persons also make social history.

Chapter 8

Life Reviews and Life Stories

John A. Clausen

In this chapter, I consider some of the issues in securing people's accounts of their lives or of important segments or episodes of their lives. What are the strengths and weaknesses of life reviews as research data? How are such subjective reports to be conceptualized and interpreted? Under what circumstances and to what degree should the researcher provide a structure for life reviews as opposed to letting the respondent roam freely to tell his or her unique story? Life reviews and life stories can be used to serve many purposes, and it is critically important to attend explicitly to the type of codification of data that will be required in any particular instance. In this chapter, I draw primarily on my own experience in working with data on the lives of mental patients and their families and with the archives and study members of the Berkeley longitudinal studies.

In 1938, as a beginning graduate student at the University of Chicago, I served as a research assistant to Clifford Shaw and Henry McKay at the Illinois Institute for Juvenile Research. My assignment was to marshal data on the subsequent criminal activities of delinquents who had been seen in the juvenile court 10 to 15 years earlier. I worked on a table in one corner of a large room. At other tables around the room, young and not-so-young men were writing the stories of their lives, explaining how they got started in delinquency and crime. All had served time in reformatories or prisons. Some had been murderers, some had been car thieves, and a few were disparagingly referred to as "hamburger hoodlums" because the crimes they had committed had so little payoff. The oldest and most revered by the others had been a successful safecracker until he was shot in the hand and thereby disabled.

I would have much preferred to analyze the men's life stories than to tally arrest records, but I hardly had the background for the task. These men were involved in life reviews focusing on how they had experienced their early years and had become delinquents and criminals, reviews intended for others to interpret. Their reviews often were superficial and self-serving but at the same time revealing of the perspectives of the writers. Their life reviews were then highly subjective retrospective accounts prepared for a particular purpose. They were edited and published with commentary based partly on material from court records, psychological evaluations, and other materials gathered by Shaw and his colleagues in a memorable series of books (Shaw, 1930, 1931; Shaw, McKay, & McDonald, 1938).

In 1938, the term "life review" had not yet come to have the special meaning it has acquired in recent years. That special meaning derives largely from an influential article by Robert Butler (1963) titled, "The Life Review: An Interpretation of Reminiscence in the Aged." Butler built on Erik Erikson's (1950) description of the last of eight postulated life crises to be confronted, namely, through a review of one's past, the acceptance of one's life, leading to a sense of integrity or, failing that, a sense of despair. Butler (1963) wrote, "I conceive of the life review as a naturally occurring, universal mental process, characterized by the progressive return to consciousness of past experiences and particularly the resurgence of unresolved conflicts; simultaneously and normally, these revived experiences can be surveyed and reintegrated" (p. 66). Much of the subsequent literature on the life review has described therapeutic endeavors aimed at helping the aged achieve a sense of integrity through reminiscence (for reviews of this literature, see Merriam, 1980; Wallace, 1992). However, where Butler spoke of a "naturally occurring universal mental process," subsequent articles have, to a very large extent, talked about reviews that were elicited as part of a therapeutic program.

This chapter is primarily concerned not with life reviews of the aged but rather with life reviews that occur at any time along the life course. However, I deal with the differences that are likely to occur between life stories that are spontaneously told and those that are elicited by the researcher. We may consider these to be polar types, the one told or written with no guidance from others (but aimed at communicating to some particular audience, sometimes the self, for some particular purpose) and the other a construction built on a framework of guidelines and queries to get at the researcher's objectives, whether to understand how a person experiences his or her life, the effects of a particular event or circumstance in the course of life, or some particular social process as it impinges on people's lives. In their ideal forms, both types of life stories provide knowledge of how the person sees his or her past and present life and the influences that helped to shape it. Both entail a person's presentation of self and, potentially, may reveal how that self developed over time, especially if the accounts have a longitudinal perspective. There is, indeed, no better way to get at the elements that have become most firmly integrated into a person's sense of identity than a thoughtful account, whether spontaneous or elicited by prolonged, empathic interviewing. I am primarily concerned with elicited life stories and combinations of spontaneous accounts and explorations with an interviewer. Supplementation of either type of account by securing the views of others can also enrich the records. Here, however, I go beyond life stories or reviews to full life histories.

Historical Background

The use of personal accounts of life experiences as basic social science data goes back at least to the beginning of this century, when Willliam James (1906) drew on just such accounts to illustrate and illuminate *The Varieties of Religious Experience.* Less than two decades later, Thomas and Znaniecki (1918-1920/1927) drew on letters from immigrants and the life story of a Polish peasant to depict life in Poland and the United States and the immigrant experience. They wrote,

> We are safe in saying that personal life-records, as complete as possible, constitute the *perfect* type of sociological material, and that if social science has to use other materials at all it is because of the practical difficulty of obtaining at the moment a sufficient number of such records . . . and of the enormous amount of work demanded for an adequate analysis. (pp. 1832-1833, emphasis in original)

This statement, and the material presented to back it up, eventually led to a series of books sponsored by the Social Science Research Council on the use of personal documents and life histories in psychology, sociology, anthropology, and history (Allport, 1942; Blumer, 1939; Dollard, 1935; Gottschalk, Kluckhohn, & Angell, 1945). A good overview of the social science literature is contained in Denzin (1970), and a more philosophically oriented treatment is found in Denzin (1989). Anyone planning serious use of personal documents for the construction of life histories will want to dip into some of these earlier works, most of which relate to materials produced prior to the present researcher's entry on the scene. Here I am somewhat more concerned with how one collects or generates such data.

Life reviews tend to be fragmentary. Except as a person endeavors to describe chronologically the story of his or her life in an autobiography, it is doubtful that anyone attempts a full life review. Like a continent viewed from an airplane, the distant past tends to be a patchwork largely obscured by clouds that represent dimmed memories, but it is illuminated and brought into focus here and there by shafts of sunlight through breaks in the clouds, where events or special circumstances have left indelible imprints. It seems impossible to trace a continuous developmental thread through the intervening shadows unless one has maintained a diary or log of the life journey. By "life review," I refer to a person's efforts to reenvision episodes or long sequences from the past. I follow Bertaux (1981, p. 9) in preferring the term "life story" to "life history" when we deal exclusively with the person's subjective, retrospective report of past experiences and their meaning to that person. A full life history most often incorporates both the person's own reports and other sources of data. This is a topic to which I return later.

> ➢ **SPONTANEOUS LIFE REVIEWS**

Erikson wrote of "integrity vs. despair" as the last of the polarities to be resolved in the course of life, chiefly as we face the realization of our mortality. At many points along the life course, however, our sense of integrity (of being what we claim to be) or our sense of direction (where we are headed) may be subject to challenge. We may not be reduced to despair, but we are either forced to make some adjustments to our self-images or forced to try to explain (often to explain away) behaviors that do not go with the images we had of ourselves. Learning how such demands come about, are interpreted, and are responded to requires the person's own story.

Psychoanalysis is one way to try to come to terms with such dilemmas and feelings of perplexity about them, and psychoanalysis itself can either lead toward integrity or (occasionally) induce despair. Cohler (1982) suggested that psychoanalysis is the ideal way to reveal the life story. In psychoanalysis, one reviews spontaneously, and most often with minimal interruption or guidance, what is "on one's mind." That means reporting on present relationships and emotions, but inevitably one is led to review past relationships and emotions. An ever changing picture emerges over the course of several years of psychoanalysis. It is never a complete picture. It is not a story that has a clear beginning, a plot, and a clear end, and I disagree with those students of what has come to be known as "narrative psychology" who claim that most life stories do have the quality of novels or short stories in this respect (e.g., K. Gergen & M. Gergen, 1987). Episodes in the life course do, of course, have beginnings, plots, and endings, but the life course itself is an incomplete collection of such narratives. Jung (1963), in reviewing his own life, wrote,

> The story of a life begins somewhere, at some particular point we happen to remember; and even then it was already highly complex. We do not know how life is going to turn out. Therefore the story has no beginning, and the end can be only vaguely hinted at. (p. 4)

Very few, if any, full accounts of a psychoanalysis exist; few analysts or patients are willing to tape-record their interchanges, and the transcription of a typical analysis might well run more than 10,000 pages. An eminent psychoanalyst, Robert Cohen, who for many years was director of clinical research at the National Institute of Mental Health, noted in a personal communication that even a fully reported psychoanalysis probably would not resolve issues of either content or interpretation:

> In my view, if such a complete record of a completed therapy were available, different reviewers would come to different conclusions about the data as a whole, although there would be many areas of agreement about the nature of the patient-therapist interactions at specific times. I also believe that treatment by different analysts of equal ability would lead to significantly different life accounts.

Apart from psychoanalysis and other forms of psychotherapy, life reviews may occur from time to time, depending on the individual's life circumstances and openness to looking within, backward, and forward. There is general agreement that in the later years, most people increasingly look within—what Neugarten (1968a) called "interiority." The approach of death appears to increase the tendency to review one's life. In the months before a death foretold, a life review may be inevitable, but it is not always comforting.

The recognition of one's mortality and of the limited time remaining available may be triggered by many circumstances in addition to old age. We often become aware of our mortality through brushes with accidental death, serious illness, the deaths of loved ones, or catastrophes (Lowenthal, Thurnher, & Chiriboga, 1975; Marshall, 1975). Spontaneous reviews of the past are also likely to be evoked by a feeling that one has come to a dead end in a role or relationship, by the termination of a role or relationship, or by an encounter that brings one face to face with his or her past. At reunions with old friends, we look back together, amplifying our memories by relying on what Halbwachs (1925) called "the social frameworks of memory." Wendell Bell (1979) dramatically illustrated the impact of historical events and circumstances in a life review triggered by a high school reunion. Reminiscences not elicited by focused questions can tell us what was uniquely important to the person.

A spontaneous life review at any given time is not a factual account but rather a construction influenced by the circumstances that triggered the review, the quality of the person's relationships at the time, and the accuracy of memories of past events. The narrative of such a review is subject to even more influences. Nevertheless, it becomes a basis for inferences as to how that person has constructed the self that is revealed, whether intentionally or not. Indeed, there is no other way we can assess the construction of a self than by seeking to understand how relationships, circumstances, and events have been interpreted and incorporated by the individual himself or herself. One may assess life events and weight them as to average impact, but an event generally scored as negative in impact may have primarily positive effects for some persons and vice versa. We must know how situations were defined, and here we must look to our respondent. Over time, interpretations may be changed, but we often find that the self has itself been transformed.

➢ WRITTEN LIFE REVIEWS

Autobiographies would appear to be the quintessential expression of a life review, and sometimes they are. How much they reveal of the person's times and the person's own development, however, depends largely on the writer's purpose. People much in the public eye may write (or participate in the writing of) their life stories because they have a message they want to convey or because books on popular or notorious persons tend to sell. An autobiography may be highly personal without being deeply revealing if written primarily to entertain the reader. On the other hand, a memoir written to deal primarily with one's life as a public official or professional may give a great deal of insight into institutional structures and historical events but very little insight into personal development. Most novelists draw on their own experiences and relationships in their works, and occasionally a gifted writer will feel impelled to exorcise a ghost by writing his or her own story (e.g., *A Hole in the World* [Rhodes, 1990]).

Solicited autobiographical accounts are a highly efficient means of securing life reviews where some degree of focus in content is suggested but where the writers determine what is most important in telling their own stories. Respondents must, of course, be motivated. Shaw's delinquents, writing their life stories in the Depression years, were paid with public relief funds. The rewards were less than they might have obtained by committing additional crimes, but many of the young men felt a certain pride in being asked to give their accounts. Oral history interviews to elicit an autobiographical account also may bring a reward, that of having an attentive listener (and recorder) to one's account of what was important in one's experience.

One can always follow up a spontaneously written account with questions to get at particular aspects of the person's experience that were not dealt with in the story told. They may have been omitted because they seemed unimportant, because they simply did not come to mind even though they were significant, or because one resisted dealing with difficult issues. When such questioning is done, we move into the area of more systematic focus on particular aspects of the life course, whether on career lines, on the process of achieving a self-definition, or on any one of the myriad topics that can be explored through the use of life stories.

Where the investigator wishes to mobilize data systematically on some particular issue or transition, it becomes necessary to provide a structure that will elicit the needed information. The structuring may come after an open-ended reminiscence or may be presented in very broad outlines. In either case, the researcher must keep in mind the essential nature of the life course and conceptualize those facets or issues that are of primary concern.

➢ SECURING LIFE REVIEWS

The life course is a developmental process in which the individual moves from helpless organism to more or less autonomous person and which (a) takes place in a changing cultural, social structural, and historical setting; (b) increasingly involves individual choices as to the direction taken; and (c) almost always entails both continuities and discontinuities. Although the term "trajectory" is employed frequently to refer to the course of a life, the connotations of the term are misleading; a person is not launched into a free trajectory but rather follows a path whose twists and turns are a result of complex interactions between a "minded self" and an environment. When our focus is on developmental processes, it is the path itself that we wish to describe along with the influences that shape it—constitutional, interactional, social structural, cultural, and historical.

From studies of memory and accounts of longitudinal research, we know that the past tends to be reviewed in terms that make it congruent with present circumstances (Vaillant, 1977; Yarrow, Campbell, & Burton, 1970). Relationships and events are cast in changing light. Traumatic events may leave scars at one period and yet later leave a feeling expressed by "I wouldn't have wanted to miss that for the world." Thus, a life review at any given time reflects how the person views particular aspects of the past now, not necessarily how the past was seen previously or how an observer might have interpreted its effects. This is well illustrated by the discrepancy between the later life reports of (minimal) effects of the Depression on people's lives (Clausen, 1993, pp. 504-505) and assessment from longitudinal data, permitting classification of economic deprivation, of actual substantial effects in the adolescent and early adult years (Elder, 1974). This in no way invalidates the scientific value of personal accounts when we are interested in developmental issues. Persons change in many ways over the life course, and their changes are reflected in modified memories and modified senses of identity even though they may themselves be unaware of the degree of change.

Interviewing Approaches

To learn how a person sees the meaning of his or her life at any given time, it is necessary to secure a broad sampling of the person's current views of self in various roles and relationships at that time and in the past. This requires either intensive repeated interviewing or autobiographical efforts guided by instructions that will induce consideration of the major critical events experienced, commitments made, and salient roles occupied, the crux of the sense of identity and the ambivalences that are inevitable in complex relationships. Autobiographical efforts are likely to require discussion and elaboration. The final product as a narrative statement is then a joint construction (Mishler, 1986, Chapter 3).

For the past decade, I have carried out analyses of continuities and discontinuities in the lives of members of the Berkeley longitudinal studies and compiled representative life histories that illustrate how some of the statistical relationships seem to have come about. Periodically, we have secured both clinical interviews (to assess personality tendencies and secure relatively spontaneous reports of past and present relationships) and structured interviews (to focus more sharply on experiences in particular roles over the preceding years). Both approaches can help one get at sources of major life satisfaction and dissatisfaction, the tenor of relationships in the family and the community, the way in which problematic situations have been defined and dealt with, and the beliefs, activities, and relationships to which the person is most committed. The two types tend to reinforce each other and give a more complete picture of the person's development.

By having longitudinal data over a 50-year period and knowing what our study members were like as children and adolescents, we do not have to rely solely on retrospective reports to reconstruct the life course. In the Berkeley studies, we have observations, inventories, physical examinations, intelligence tests, family data, and school records to put beside the person's own report. These became very valuable assets in attempting to delineate the influences that shaped the individual's life course. However, they were not drawn on as we interviewed the study members in their adult years. Except for the final "life history interview," in which we focus on adolescent aims, adult development, and how the person characterizes his or her self and hopes to be remembered, the interviewers at any given period were not informed about past history so as not to have preconceived notions as to what the person was like. Interviewers might point out discrepancies between what was said at one point in an interview and what was said subsequently in that interview or interview sequence, but the respondent never was confronted with the material derived from the early years until the life history had been sketched out. Only when the life history was compiled would we then discuss some of the discrepancies between what our early record showed and the respondent's current recollections.

Clinical Interviews

It may be useful to describe in some detail the clinical interview used in our last major follow-up of the Berkeley respondents. The clinical interview users had a general guide to the areas that should be covered, but they had permission to proceed in whatever way was most comfortable for themselves and for their respondents. Here is a summary of a transcript illustrating how one of the skilled clinical interviewers developed her approach with a highly verbal respondent.

> I find that the best way to learn about your life is to start from the beginning. I want to focus on the significant relationships in your life but also the things that have influenced those relationships. So, let's start back with your parents and what they were like and what life was like when you were a kid.

The respondent replied, "Well, I had an unusual childhood." The interviewer said, "You did?" Then came a long description of that unusual childhood.

This interviewer interrupted primarily to ask for a clarification or more details or to express interest and understanding. When the topic of parents had been thoroughly covered, she asked about siblings, bringing relationships with each up to date. The family had moved around a good deal, and some 29 pages of typescript were devoted to parents and siblings. Then she asked, "Let's go back a bit and talk about school. You must have had quite a broken-up school life, then, didn't you?" The answer was "yes" but that it was not a problem because the siblings had each other and had no difficulty in making friends and the honor roll wherever they went to school. With this respondent, all that one needed was a good listener who could move the interview along. School and college covered another 15 typescript pages with discussions of feelings, performance, relationships, problems of financing college, jobs while in college, dating, and so on. Then on to work, war service in the WAVES, meeting her future husband, courtship, marriage, family life and parenting, relations with grown children, friendships, death of her husband, health, aging, and so on. The progression was chronological, with occasional backtracking to get at multiple roles and other ongoing activities.

In two hours, this clinical interview resulted in 68 typescript pages that give a clearly defined picture of a 62-year-old woman in command of her life, enjoying warm relationships within the family and the community, intellectually involved, able to look back with pleasure and satisfaction, and able to look ahead with confidence. Her identity is clearly limned, and we see how it was achieved, but we get some surprises as to sources of motivation (e.g., the determination to live life to the fullest after being diagnosed with breast cancer).

Clinical interviews, very loosely structured to allow the respondent to reveal whatever seems most important to her or him and encourage the discussion of feelings, are evocative of a person and very often reveal the respondent's sense of identity to the readers. But one cannot count on a respondent to sustain the interview line so readily, and much judicious probing may be required. Even when the respondent does sustain the interview line, there remain many questions that have to be posed to pin down sequences and influences. Here a more focused interview is called for, one that probes systematically to secure needed information. For construction of a life history, one needs to know the social status and values of the parents, the types of responsibilities given to the respondent as a child, early images of goals for the adult years, the impact of major social and cultural changes, and transitions into new roles and relationships. Not all of these may be obtained in the clinical interview. The interview guide must serve one's research objectives, but in the clinical interview they never can be constricting.

Structured Interviews

What one asks about in more focused or structured interviews will, of course, depend on having adequately specified the data needed to attain one's research objective. If the objective is to ascertain the effect of wartime military service on a man's career and family relationships as Glen Elder has done, for example, then one focus will be on matters such as preservice educational and occupational attainment, family ties, age and timing of entering the service, in-service training, relationships in the service, duration of service, combat experience, possible disabilities, and timing of release from the service (Elder, 1986; Elder & Clipp, 1989; Elder, Shanahan, & Clipp, 1994). Another focus will be on postservice experience such as flashbacks and other signs of posttraumatic syndrome, subsequent occupational and marital experiences, and ties to wartime comrades.

Any phase of life experience that is to be examined will require a thorough preliminary analysis of what are likely to be the critical issues, drawing on theoretical formulations derived from previous research on the topic and pretest interviews to learn how best to get at a review of the past. Because individual experiences and their meanings to the person vary so enormously, the questioning must be extremely broad to assess them. For periods long past, there must be an opportunity for the respondent to try to recapture that past and the feelings experienced then (Merton, Fiske, & Kendall, 1990, Chapter 2). When the investigation is focused on a particular role or facet of the life course (e.g., education, military service, marriage, career), there will be considerable variation among respondents in the salience of that role or facet, but that is precisely what is to be learned along with such regularities as exist. I want to stress that both clinical and structural interviews in the service of life reviews can, and indeed must, be aimed at the subjective assessment of events and life circumstances.

Use of a Life Chart

An adequate review of some past period of a person's life will require an opportunity for the person to think about that period in some depth and to consider the historical and personal contexts that preceded the period as well as those that characterized it. A number of investigators have found that one helpful approach is to ask the person to prepare a life chart, plotting life satisfaction at each age or period (Back & Bourque, 1970; Clausen, 1972). The form we have used (Figure 8.1) is a simple grid, extending from early childhood to the present or beyond (for expected life satisfaction in the future), with satisfaction rated on a scale of 0 to 10. Most respondents can do this on a year-to-year basis into the early middle years and for somewhat less precisely specified ages subsequently.

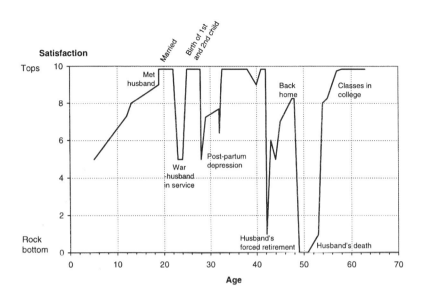

Figure 8.1. Life Satisfaction Chart for Mary Wylie
SOURCE: *American Lives: Looking Back at the Children of the Great Depression* by John A. Clausen (p. 137). Copyright (c) 1993 by John A. Clausen. Reprinted with permission of The Free Press, a Division of Simon & Schuster.

The life chart can be sent to the prospective respondent prior to interviewing or requesting autobiographical efforts, or it can be completed at the time of the initial or a later interview. Not all respondents are willing to share the stories of their lives, but those who are usually complete life charts. In our use of the life chart, we have asked respondents to label briefly their high and low points (e.g., "married," "promoted," "entered army"). Respondents occasionally will draw flat lines across their charts, indicating that each year was very much like any other. Such persons may resist exploring the sources of extreme disappointments. They may acknowledge highs and lows within any given year but deny that any particular year was more satisfying or more problematic than another. Interviews, exploring each major transition along the way, and the person's relationships, will almost always reveal considerable variation. If one is seeking a full life history, then a series of interviews definitely will be needed and, indeed, more than a single interview is likely to be required for any thorough review of a single period or a single facet of a person's past life.

The life chart in itself can be helpful in revealing turning points and peak and nadir experiences (e.g., life crises), discontinuities, and the major sources of satisfaction and dissatisfaction. It also can give clues to the extent to which historical events and circumstances have impinged on the person's consciousness. Subsequent questioning, with the life chart in view, can probe into such issues and the reasons underlying major fluctuations. Thus, a degree of structure is afforded by the respondent's own lifeline.

➢ CONCEPTUALIZING LIFE REVIEWS

In my own work with the Berkeley data, I wanted to know how people whose development we had been studying—and whose personalities, social backgrounds, and careers we had classified over the past 50 years—saw their own lives. What did they see as the dominant influences on their own development? What had been the major turning points or decision points? What had been, and were currently, their major sources of satisfaction and dissatisfaction? How did they view their careers and their marriages? Both the clinical interviews and structured interviews bore on those issues. I repeatedly found myself coming back to the concept of identity. I listed the various components that are somehow more or less integrated when we envision identity. I combed the literature for formulations. I never have been content with any one listing because identities differ so much in complexity. But when we can examine how people saw their lives in terms of some of these questions, we have one approach to getting at identity.

Turning Points

A turning point may be defined as a time or event when one took a different direction from that in which one had been traveling. It is in this sense that the term was used in a popular movie and in several books written subsequently, and it is in this sense that many social scientists have used the concept. Thus, Hareven and Masaoka (1988) defined a turning point as "a process involving the alteration of life path, a 'course correction.' " This was precisely what I had in mind when, in 1982, I posed the interview question, "As you look [your life chart] over, can you pick out any point or points along your life course that you would call turning points—where your life really took a different direction?" Respondents were then asked about the turning points, the changes that occurred, and what caused them, starting with the most important turning point. Elsewhere, I have discussed some of the problems that arose because of the inadequate probing by the interviewers occasioned by time pressures (Clausen, 1995). The point I want to make here is that more than half of the so-called turning points reported were not so much changes in direction as role transitions, and of these, more than two thirds were expected transitions such as entering an occupation, marrying, or becoming a parent. These transitions entailed some reorientation of priorities and activities but no substantial change from the direction in which one had been heading. From the standpoint of many respondents, marriage was a turning point in the sense that life after marriage was very different from what it had been before. The same thing could be said about entering a career for which one had prepared; it was a turning point in that it constituted a new set of experiences and satisfactions, not a change in direction.

Every major role transition can quite reasonably be considered as potentially constituting a turning point. In addition, we are constantly shifting our perspectives as we encounter obstacles that force us to make at least minor adjustments or as we find opportunities that open up new vistas to us. Thus, every life is filled with little turning points, but, of course, what we are primarily interested in is the identification of major turning points along the way. These frequently can be recognized only as one looks back long after the events or circumstances that produced the turning points. Hareven and Masaoka (1988) characterized turning points as "perceptual road marks along the life course, representing the individual's subjective assessment of continuities and discontinuities in their lives." They are road marks that often cannot be placed until long after the route has been traversed. Thus, they are not at all the same as "life events" that are objectively defined.

In some instances, turning points were indeed points in time—the time of a death, of an incapacitation, or of a job loss—although their consequences obviously were long term. In other instances, reported turning points represented circumstances or decisions that led in time to new opportunities or events that would influence their lives such as going to the college at which one would meet one's future spouse. Sometimes the "point" would be imperceptible, as in the long drift downward from a happy marriage to a miserable one.

The Classification of Turning Points

How should one classify and attempt to code the data elicited in interviews on turning points? The variety and scope of turning points reported make this a somewhat daunting task. I am by no means satisfied with the classification scheme I have developed thus far, but the following may be a helpful point of departure for other work:

1. *The major role or roles affected (e.g., educational, occupational, marital, parental) or the relationships, activities, aspects of life most affected.* How pervasive was the effect?

2. *The source or cause of the turning point.* Was it an expected transition, purposive change as a consequence of perceived obstacles or opportunities, a conversion experience, the recognition of role failure, or a crisis due to the illness or death of loved ones or to economic conditions, war, natural catastrophes, and the like?

3. *The timing of the turning point.* At what age and life phase did it occur?

4. *The ultimate consequences as viewed by the respondent.* Here one will need to classify positive and negative effects for a substantial series of potential consequences because these are perceived in retrospect, dealing with changed activities, relationships, self-confidence, life satisfaction, and the like.

The meaning of turning points, even in the same segment of life such as career, marriage, or a death in the family, can vary enormously. In general, the death of a loved one will be evidenced by a sharp drop in life satisfaction on the life chart. Sometimes, however, a death can be a release, as it is when a person had been attending to a spouse or parent suffering from Alzheimer's disease.

Many of the events or circumstances mentioned as turning points in our research led persons (most often women) to have more confidence in themselves, to see themselves in a different light. Leaving home and being on one's own sometimes was mentioned in connection with starting one's occupational career, sometimes in terms of going off to college, sometimes in terms of simply moving out of the parental home, but always with the emphasis on having become a more or less autonomous person for the first time. The same feeling of having gained strength and autonomy might come from dealing with a difficult family situation. A woman whose husband developed a mental illness in late middle age commented, "It strengthened my faith, which I always had. It gave me an opportunity to see that I could handle something really serious." Incidentally, I found in my study of the impact of mental illness on husbands and wives (Clausen, 1983, p. 200) that a husband's mental illness frequently was seen, 15 to 20 years after his initial hospitalization, as having led to his wife's first realization of her own competence. Conversely, a wife's mental illness, viewed at the same point by her husband, far more often was reported to have led to his realizing inadequacies in himself.

It is clear, then, that even when one asks about turning points in which one's life took a different course from the way it had been going, respondents often answer in terms of changing attitudes and feelings or personal development rather than in terms of redirecting their lives. This suggests that one might focus on the acquisition of a changed perspective on self, or events and circumstances in the life course that led to such a changed perspective, rather than on talking about turning points as such.

I believe that it will be especially fruitful to focus on sequential decisions in a given realm of life experience or the vagaries of a major role if we wish to secure data that can be brought to bear in comparative analyses. What are the turning points in an occupational career, starting with orientations at the initial termination of formal education? I specify *initial* because returning for further education to pursue another career is becoming an increasingly important turning point. Marital careers also increasingly tend to have multiple turning points. If we want to understand occupational or marital careers better, then we need to examine those turning points. In most instances, we will be dealing not with points in time but rather with increasing tensions in an occupied role and/or increasing attractions of other possibilities. A good illustration of this approach and of the processual nature of turning points is Diane Vaughan's (1986) *Uncoupling*.

Another example of the fruitfulness of focusing on a single role or area of life experience is given in Matilda Riley's (1988) second presidential volume, *Sociological Lives.* Here eight sociologists were asked to prepare brief autobiographies describing their intellectual development within changing social structures. They described the development of their careers—how they found their ways into sociology, influences that led them to shift or maintain directions, and the changing nature of sociology itself.

Sometimes it was an exciting undergraduate course, sometimes disappointment in an earlier chosen field, sometimes the offer of an assistantship, and sometimes a gradual shifting of interests that enticed them into sociology. Once in the field, commitment to particular problems and methods tended to occur but at the same time to be responsive to social issues and social climates in the larger society. The documents so created illuminate both individual development and the development of modern sociology in America.

Life Satisfaction

Some lives entail a great deal of misery and some a great deal of joy, but most lives have their ups and downs, as life charts make abundantly clear. The sources of satisfaction and dissatisfaction and the means of coping with the latter afford an important perspective for examining the life course. They can tell, to some degree, what types of experiences in a given period most enhance a sense that life is good and how extremes of satisfaction or dissatisfaction in one role or another in the past appear to have influenced the person's efforts and choices subsequently.

Retrospective accounts of earlier satisfactions and dissatisfactions are likely to differ from reports that might have been given at that earlier period. New perspectives may have put a more positive gloss on events, activities, and relationships in the past or may have rendered them less acceptable. Particularly when major social changes such as those brought about by the Vietnam War or the women's movement have occurred, they are likely to impinge on remembered satisfactions from before these changes and to affect satisfactions now.

One needs to explore sources of variation in satisfaction with relationships (especially in the family), with activities, and with sense of accomplishment, whether in work or in other major investments of effort. Moreover, a life review can be extended into the future. Does the person anticipate receiving the social support needed and having the resources needed in later years?

We sought reported sources of both satisfaction and dissatisfaction decade by decade in our structured interviews in 1982. Here we wanted comparative data on the relative importance of particular relationships and activities, so we presented a list from which the respondent could select the most important source (or two sources): spouse, children, job, social activities, leisure activities, health, or something else. Marked shifts occurred with aging of respondent and children and with social changes, although, of course, we could not distinguish causes with such a highly structured question. But from clinical interviews and probing, one could get a sense of the reasons for the waxing and waning of dissatisfactions in jobs, in marriage, and in parenting. Gender differences become very clear in such data.

Basic to general life satisfaction is satisfaction in major roles. As with turning points, one wants to secure the sequences of role performance. When was a marriage at its best and at its worst? What considerations led to the choices made of marital partner and of career? How does a career look in retrospect? Was it the career one would choose again (the source of a solid sense of accomplishment), was it reasonably satisfying, or was it just something to put up with? What were the most trying times? How do marriage, family, and occupation compare in their contributions to a man's or woman's sense of who and what he or she is? These are broader issues than satisfaction; they are the stuff of which identity is shaped.

Perceived Influences

How does one best get an indication of a person's sense of identity and its perceived sources? In several structured interviews over the years, our respondents were asked to describe themselves, their strengths, and their weaknesses. By and large, the questions led to a rather hackneyed set of responses, seldom leading to significant characterizations. One learned far more from accounts of their friendships (or the lack thereof), the things in which they were interested, and above all, the people to whom they were attached as well as the activities to which they were committed. How did they handle conflicts within the family? What are they most proud about in talking of their children?

In the life history interview conducted with a subsample of our study members in their 60s, I asked about adolescent goals and orientations, paralleling questions asked nearly 30 years earlier. Most now had only vague ideas, much less consonant with records from adolescence than what they had reported when they were in their 30s. Nevertheless, certain patterns were very clear: Men most often said they were thinking about their future occupations but gave almost no thought to the qualities they wanted in a wife, and women most often gave considerable thought to the qualities they wanted in a husband but very little to the work they would do before marriage. Identities were being shaped by the climate of the times, and those orientations tended to remain dominant until well along in the middle years. We asked about awareness of options in the adolescent years, about respondents' sense as to when they became intellectually and emotionally mature and what the term "mature person" meant to them. We asked about their own sense of whether they had "remained pretty much the same person[s] [they] were in early adulthood, excepting for becoming more mature" or whether they felt they had "changed in some significant way." We asked, "When you think of your life as a whole and the difference it has made, how would you most like to be remembered?" Finally, we asked for their own theories as to how their lives had been shaped. Adequate coverage of all these topics requires a series of relaxed interviews. When the respondent is encouraged to expand on brief answers and to reminisce, one secures the most revealing life reviews.

Study members whose histories are reported in *American Lives* (Clausen, 1993) received draft copies of the histories as a basis for further discussion. Those reviews almost always entailed further reminiscences that added to an understanding of their lives and the influences on them.

Use of Supplementary Materials

Written comments at the end of questionnaires that are supplementary to interviews and letters sent by respondents after interviews can often add to the richness of data secured previously. These often are completely spontaneous expressions, some elicited by further thinking about responses to a questionnaire and some by crises or the surmounting of crises in the recent past. Such expressions sometimes approximate the free associations of psychoanalysis except that inhibitions more strongly enter into what is reported. A man whose wife left him when their oldest child was reaching adolescence and whose children (deeply disturbed) want nothing to do with him now that they are adults, feeling desperately unhappy, wonders, "Where did I go wrong?" He writes,

> I spent a lot of time agonizing over how I should respond to your questionnaire. Obviously, I had two choices. One was to say that, in retrospect, in spite of all the usual hard times which all of us have had, I

feel that my life was basically self-fulfilling. The other was to express my feelings honestly. Perhaps I should have answered the former because I'm sure others and even I would prefer to believe it. Still, I finally decided that I should tell the truth about how I really felt.

Lest anyone think that my current evaluation is simply a product of my current miseries, I assure you that I have felt, however irrationally, the same all through my life. I cannot explain why, or really understand it, but it is a fact.

He reviews his past, but he can neither understand nor undo it, and that is the source of much pain. More often, the spontaneous letters tell of having weathered hard times, of sources of support and strength.

There is another very important use of letters, diaries, or any other records that a respondent may have from earlier times. Although we want to know how a person sees his or her past life *now*, it is desirable that he or she be able to have a reasonably clear idea of the sequence of past events. Any material that will enable a respondent to correct faulty memories and to incorporate the correction into his or her account will be useful.

I recently have been reading letters exchanged with my wife-to-be some 55 years ago. I have been amazed to learn that I had transposed decision sequences in my memory and that I already had been thinking about problems that I would have attributed to developments in recent decades. Such materials permit one to reconstruct one's story in ways still congruent with one's sense of identity but more faithful to the course that was actually followed. Diaries or even themes written in school relating to current events or personal experiences and saved can also be drawn on if they exist. Undoubtedly, such resources are less often venerated in the era of electronic communication, but sometimes they can be found.

➢ QUANTIFYING LIFE REVIEWS

There has been a great increase in interest in narrative accounts on the part of linguists, ethnographers, historians, and other behavioral scientists. The focus of this interest is, variously, on subtleties in the use of language, the effects of context on the construction of meaning, the criteria by which narratives may be assessed, and myriad content areas such as becoming a drug user or an alcoholic, coping with mental illness in the family, and entering various occupations. The great bulk of research is qualitative in nature, illustrating through individual histories how certain patterns of behavior or understanding have come about.

Detailed narrative accounts are costly to obtain, and one seldom can secure a large sample of respondents, but I want to argue for the value of obtaining such accounts systematically so that one has the possibility of quantifying one's findings, at least roughly. Such efforts entail developing rather elaborate coding schemes that can be applied to the analysis of sequences that entail classification of contexts, relationships, problematic situations, interpretations, and actions taken. Perhaps an example from an earlier study of a spouse's recognition and response to the initial manifestations of mental disorder (Clausen, 1983; Clausen & Yarrow, 1955) will be useful.

Mental illness is manifest in a variety of behaviors, many of which may nevertheless be seen as essentially normal. In classifying how the person's problem is defined and dealt with, we first must get a description of what was perceived by significant others. Then we move to the interpretation of the problematic behavior. Here the general context, situational demands, usual personality of the troubled person, and state of relationships between actors all come into play. The actions taken depend on still other circumstances and contingencies. They can have long-term consequences for the life story of the patient and the stories of other family members.

To get a first-person report of the initial and subsequent behaviors and moods manifest, the sequence of interpretations made, and the actions taken requires that one try to get the respondent to recapture aspects that he or she may not have recognized at the time. The interviewer provides guidelines for the respondent's review but must allow the respondent to express concerns and explore feelings as to what was most salient in the critical interactions.

Here is a highly individual, qualitative type of inquiry, yielding rich information about the unique circumstances of each person's entry into patient status and the consequences of actions taken for each participant's own self-feelings. At the same time, one can learn to code such data along a series of interrelated dimensions, categorizing symptoms and signs, initial interpretations, effects on relationships, feelings engendered, and other facets.

This type of limited life story, secured by interviewer inquiry, seeks to reconstruct the mental state of the actor as well as his or her actions. It must allow the respondent to voice his or her concerns and perplexities. It must be seen as a means of helping the respondent to understand what happened, not as the grilling of a witness. In general, we saw the husbands and wives of patients over a sequence of from 4 to 12 or more interviews, producing case histories. Once a score or so of such histories had been accumulated, code building could be undertaken and then applied to a larger sample. We categorized the major varieties of responses at each step of the definitional process. By so doing, it was possible to quantify our life review data and to generalize findings much more adequately than if we had only individual case histories. For example, we could demonstrate substantial gender differences in the definitional sequence (Clausen, 1983).

Even if one does not seek to quantify life review data, the construction of individual life histories for a subsample of a population studied quantitatively can yield substantial dividends. One can get a much clearer notion of the dynamics through which central tendencies have come about. This is what I tried to do in *American Lives* (Clausen, 1993). One also can examine deviant cases in which the central tendency was not realized, as Sampson and Laub (1993) did and as Laub and Sampson document in the present volume (Chapter 9).

As men and women review episodes in their lives such as the mental illness of a family member, we find them discovering things about themselves that they had not known. We also learn what resources in the community were helpful and how often the formal institutional structures failed to meet or even perceive their needs. Perhaps nothing is more important in this type of interviewing than the ability to be a good listener who can express sympathetic understanding but offer little more. By giving great leeway to the interviewer and seeking first to establish a relationship, one can learn about facets of a life that might never emerge with highly structured interviewing. Ultimately, however, the interviewer must be able to guide the respondent so that relevant data are secured for coding all applicable dimensions.

➢ CONCLUSION

In any attempt to elicit a life review or a life story that goes beyond a single interview, the researcher has to consider what type of claim for the respondent's time can reasonably be made and what type of potential reward can be offered. For persons faced with a threatening problem such as mental illness in the family, just having a sympathetic interviewer, especially one whose questions help to focus on issues to be dealt with and who can listen attentively, may prove rewarding enough to ensure participation over many months. For those who lead highly pressured lives and over whom no claim exists, eliciting a major life review will be a more difficult task. Sometimes one can intrigue such a potential respondent with a research question that has implications for that respondent so as to secure an interview or an autobiographical fragment relating to a segment of the life course. To be of real value as social science data, however, the period, role, or other aspect of the life course of particular interest must be reviewed in sufficient depth to understand how that particular segment fits into other segments and sequences as well as how social currents and historical events are reflected. We all occupy multiple roles, but individuals differ greatly in the priorities allocated to different roles.

There obviously are many different ways in which one can try to elicit life reviews that will serve as valuable data for understanding a person, a life transition, or the impact of institutional structures and life events on people. Too little attention has been given to the methods of eliciting life narratives despite the increasing popularity of the narrative approach in psychology (e.g., Sarbin, 1986). Among those who have provided helpful guidance in this respect, McAdams (1985) spelled out in some detail how he has secured life stories from students and adults. Mishler (1986) provided an impressive analysis of issues in interviewing and interpretation. Consummate skill in interviewing—listening and probing as needed— seems to me the most critically important condition for securing good life reviews. For detailed treatment of the type of interviewing required, I would strongly recommend both Mishler (1986) and Weiss (1994).

The narrative approach to the study of personality or society requires an investment of patience and persistence on the part of the investigator and of time and effort on the part of the person whose life story is being built up. It may be possible to secure a brief life review in a single interview, but the inferences that may legitimately be drawn from such a narrative are decidedly limited. As persons think back over their lives, only limited segments can be reviewed. Early experiences are hard to recapture in the later years, although myths often will have been created. Those myths become incorporated in the person's concept of self. We may wish to confront subjective reviews at one period with those at another period, or with the observations of other persons or records from the past, but the person's own account, if freely given, will give us the best point of departure for our analysis of his or her life experience.

Chapter 9

Integrating Quantitative
and Qualitative Data

JOHN H. LAUB
ROBERT J. SAMPSON

In this chapter, we recount our efforts to integrate quantitative and qualitative data in addressing a series of research questions regarding continuity and change in human behavior over the life course. Our work on this issue stems from a long-term research project using a unique data archive, the Unraveling Juvenile Delinquency (UJD) study, and subsequent follow-ups conducted by Sheldon and Eleanor Glueck of the Harvard Law School. In 1986, we uncovered 60 cartons of case files in the basement of the Harvard Law School Library. These boxes contained the original case records from the classic longitudinal study of 500 delinquents and 500 nondelinquents initiated by the Gluecks in 1940 (S. Glueck & E. Glueck, 1950, 1968). The UJD data and data from three other studies were given to the Harvard Law School Library by the Gluecks in 1972. The UJD data eventually were fully cataloged and stored at the Murray Research Center at Radcliffe College, a national repository for data on the study of lives.

AUTHORS' NOTE: A version of this chapter was presented at the annual meeting of the American Sociological Association, Miami, Florida, August 1993. The data are derived from the Sheldon and Eleanor Glueck archives of the Harvard Law School Library, currently on long-term loan to the Murray Research Center at Radcliffe College. We thank Anne Colby, Glen Elder, and Janet Giele for their helpful comments on an earlier draft.

Our energies initially were devoted to coding, recoding, validating, and computerizing the Gluecks' complete longitudinal data set for a study of individual lives over time. Once the data were "recast" to fit our needs (Elder, Pavalko, & Clipp, 1993), our attention shifted to a substantive focus on criminal careers including the onset of criminal offending and persistence and desistance in criminal activity over time. Most criminological research has been cross-sectional in design; thus, the longitudinal nature of the Gluecks' data, in addition to their explicit focus on serious and persistent offenders, offered numerous possibilities for further analysis. However, as we worked with these data, we were increasingly amazed at their richness and depth. For instance, the Gluecks collected data on a variety of dimensions of juvenile and adult development including major life events (e.g., schooling, work, marriage, parenthood). By contrast, many longitudinal studies in criminology have been limited to structural and demographic variables such as poverty and race. Coupled with shifting intellectual interests on our part, we broadened our theoretical focus and integrated our interests in crime and delinquency with theory and research on the life course. This strategy eventually led us to develop an age-graded theory of informal social control to explain crime and deviance over the life span. We then tested this theory using the longitudinal data we reconstructed from the Gluecks' study. The results of this effort are reported in our book, *Crime in the Making* (Sampson & Laub, 1993).

This chapter describes the quantitative and qualitative data in the Gluecks' study and discusses our methodological strategy for integrating these two types of data.[1] We believe that merging quantitative and qualitative data analyses provides important clues for explaining the processes of continuity and change in human behavior over the life course. We illustrate the insight and understanding produced by this merger by drawing on examples from our work with the Gluecks' data archive. As Clausen (1993) pointed out, both case history and statistical data are required "if we are to understand the influences on the lives of persons who have lived through a particular slice of American history" (p. 43). We agree wholeheartedly with this assertion. We conclude the chapter with a description of our current research, which involves collecting new follow-up data from the original respondents in the Gluecks' study to extend the Gluecks' archive along more constructive avenues.

➤ THE GLUECKS' UNRAVELING
JUVENILE DELINQUENCY DATA

The Gluecks' prospective study of the formation and development of criminal careers was initiated in 1940 and involved a sample of 500 delinquents and 500 nondelinquents. The delinquent sample contained persistent delinquents recently committed to one of two correctional schools in Massachusetts: the Lyman School for Boys in Westboro and the Industrial School for Boys in Shirley. The nondelinquent sample was drawn from the public schools in the city of Boston. Nondelinquency status was determined by criminal record checks and through a series of interviews with key informants (e.g., parents, teachers). The Gluecks' sampling procedure was designed to maximize differences in delinquency, an objective that, by all accounts, succeeded (S. Glueck & E. Glueck, 1950, pp. 27-29). For example, approximately 30% of the delinquent group had juvenile court convictions at age 10 years or younger, and the average number of convictions for all delinquent boys was 3.5 (p. 293).

A unique aspect of the UJD study was the matching design whereby the 500 officially defined delinquents and 500 nondelinquents were matched case by case on age, race/ethnicity, intelligence, and neighborhood socioeconomic status. The average age of the delinquents was 14 years, 8 months and of the nondelinquents was 14 years, 6 months when the study began. As to ethnicity, 25% of both groups were of English background; another one fourth were Italian; one fifth were Irish; less than one tenth were American, Slavic, or French; and the remainder were Greek, Spanish, Scandinavian, German, or Jewish.[2] As measured by the Wechsler-Bellevue Test, the average IQ of the delinquents was 92 and of the nondelinquents was 94. The matching on neighborhood ensured that both delinquents and nondelinquents grew up in "underprivileged neighborhoods"—slums and tenement areas—in central Boston. Given the similarity in neighborhood conditions, the areas were, in essence, matched on delinquency rate along with poverty. Overall, then, the 1,000 male respondents in the UJD study were matched on key criminological variables thought to influence both delinquent behavior and official reactions by the police and courts. Thus, that 500 of the boys were persistent delinquents and 500 avoided delinquency in childhood and adolescence cannot be attributed to residence in urban slum areas, age differences, ethnicity, or IQ.

The original sample was followed up at two different points in time: at age 25 years and again at age 32 years (S. Glueck & E. Glueck, 1968). This data collection effort took place from 1949 to 1965. Extensive data are available for analysis relating to family life, schooling, employment history, military experience, recreational activity, and criminal history for the matched respondents in the age ranges of 11 to 16, 17 to 25, and 26 to 32 years. More important, data are available for 438 of the original 500 delinquents (87.6%) and 442 of the original 500 nondelinquents (88.4%) at all three interview waves. When adjusted for mortality, the follow-up success rate is approximately 92%, relatively high by current standards (see, e.g., Wolfgang, Thornberry, & Figlio, 1987). The low attrition rate is testimony to the Gluecks' rigorous research strategy but also to lower residential mobility and interstate migration rates in the 1940s and 1950s compared to those today. It should be noted, however, that the follow-up of criminal histories and official records covered 37 states, the most common involving California, New York, New Hampshire, Florida, and Illinois (S. Glueck & E. Glueck, 1968, p. xix).

> ➢ **ARCHIVAL LIFE RECORDS**

A wealth of data on social, psychological, and biological characteristics; family life; school performance; work experiences; and other life events were collected on the delinquents and nondelinquent controls in the period from 1940 to 1965. These data were collected through an elaborate investigation process that was developed by the Gluecks and employed with great success in their earlier research studies (S. Glueck & E. Glueck, 1930, 1934a, 1934b). The data-gathering process used by the Gluecks' research team in the UJD study included interviews with the respondents themselves and their families as well as with key informants such as social workers, settlement house workers, clergymen, schoolteachers, neighbors, employers, and criminal justice and social welfare officials (S. Glueck & E. Glueck, 1950, pp. 41-53). An important component of this process is what the Gluecks called the "home investigation." This consisted of an interview with family members and offered an opportunity for the investigator to observe the home and family life.

These interview data were supplemented by field investigations that meticulously culled information from the records of both public and private agencies that had any involvement with the individual respondent or the family as a whole. These data verified and amplified the case materials gathered during the home investigation. For example, a principal source of record data was the Social Service Index in Boston, a clearinghouse for every contact between a family and every welfare or social agency in the Boston area. Similar indexes from other cities and states were used where necessary. For information on criminal activity, the Gluecks collected data from the Massachusetts Board of Probation, which has maintained a central file of all court records from Boston courts since 1916 and for Massachusetts as a whole since 1924. These records were compared and supplemented with records from the Boys' Parole Division in Massachusetts. Out-of-state arrests, court appearances, and correctional experiences were gathered through correspondence with equivalent state depositories and federal agencies such as the Federal Bureau of Investigation.

Therefore, the Gluecks' strategy of data collection focused on multiple sources of information that were independently derived from several points of view and at separate times. The Gluecks' data represent the comparison, reconciliation, and integration of these multiple sources of data (S. Glueck & E. Glueck, 1950, pp. 70-72; Vaillant, 1983, pp. 243-247). It should be noted that the level of detail and the range of information sources found in the UJD study will likely never be repeated given contemporary research standards on the protection of human respondents. The Gluecks' data also are different in kind from contemporary data. As Robins and her colleagues (1985) pointed out regarding earlier social science studies such as that of the Gluecks, "In conformity with the precomputer era of data analysis, the coding was less atomized than it would have been today. Consequently, we have only the coders' overall assessment based on a variety of individual items" (p. 30). Because of this, accessing the Gluecks' raw data for purposes of recoding became a crucial component of our data reconstruction efforts.

The case records from the Gluecks' study also contained a wealth of "richly descriptive qualitative details" (Riley, 1994b, p. 2). Kidder and Fine (1987) distinguished two types of qualitative data. The first, referred to as "big Q," includes fieldwork, participant observation, and/or ethnography. The chief characteristic of big Q is that "it consists of a continually changing set of questions without a structured design" (Kidder & Fine, 1987, p. 59). The second type of qualitative data is "small q," which "consists of open-ended questions embedded in a survey or experiment that has a structure or design" (p. 59). The Gluecks' qualitative data are of the second variety. For each respondent in the Gluecks' study, qualitative data can be found in several parts of the case file including the following:

  a. detailed handwritten interviews with the respondents and their families conducted by the Gluecks' research team;

  b. interviewer narratives that were produced for each respondent at each interview including detailed information on tracing and locating each respondent;

  c. interviews conducted with key informants including teachers, criminal justice officials, and employers; and

  d. volumes of miscellaneous notes and correspondence relating to family and school experiences, employment histories, military service, and the like.

> ## RECONSTRUCTING AND RECASTING
> ## THE GLUECKS' DATA

   Our strategy of reconstructing the Gluecks' data for a longitudinal study of individual lives had two components. During the early stages of the project, we discovered several boxes of computer cards derived from the Gluecks' study in the basement of the Harvard Law School. Although the cards were very old and contained multiple punches in a majority of columns (most modern card readers cannot read multiple-punched cards successfully), we investigated whether the cards could be used to build a computerized data set. With the assistance of staff at the Murray Research Center, more than 15,000 computer cards were read and reconfigured.

   Thus, one component of our strategy was to build a data set using the Gluecks' original coding schemes. This allowed us to secure a wide range of data (more than 2,500 variables) in a relatively short time frame (9 months). However, there was a concern regarding the validity of the coded data. In several cases, we had coded variables but no codebook. Therefore, to assess the utility of the data, we developed a validation scheme that contained a number of steps. First, we checked (whenever possible) frequencies for the coded variables to the frequencies found in published sources of the Gluecks' data. Second, we examined the logic of the coding schemes across several variables. Third, we generated a 10% random sample of cases and compared the values for each variable to the values found in the raw interview files. We completed this validation procedure for the delinquent group and found an extremely high level of agreement between the raw data and the coded data (generally > 98% for the 2,600 variables we examined). This extremely high level of agreement increased our confidence in the quality of the preserved files and the overall feasibility of our data reconstruction project.

In addition to our technical validation scheme, we examined the substantive validity of the Gluecks' coded data in two areas. First, we examined several family variables and found that parental supervision, attachment, and disciplinary practices were important correlates of juvenile delinquency (Laub & Sampson, 1988). The fact that our results are supported by the Gluecks' own findings and contemporary research (see, e.g., Loeber & Stouthamer-Loeber, 1986) added to our confidence in the quality of the Gluecks' data. Second, we analyzed reports of delinquent behavior and other misconduct for juveniles in the sample that were collected by the Gluecks' research team from parents, teachers, and the sample respondents themselves. Overall, we found the degree of overlap among these reporters to be substantial (Laub, Sampson, & Kiger, 1990). More important, we found a substantial degree of overlap between the unofficial crime-specific measures and the unofficial composite measure as well as our official measure of delinquency. Moreover, our total self, parent, and teacher measures were strongly related. Thus, both the official and unofficial measures of delinquency and other misconduct found in the Gluecks' data appeared to be valid (Laub et al., 1990).

Unfortunately, there were aspects of the Gluecks' coded data that prohibited analyses of interest. This was particularly the case regarding our primary area of interest—the criminal histories (careers) of the Gluecks' respondents. Although the Gluecks used a longitudinal research design, their data collection procedures and subsequent analyses often were cross-sectional in nature. For instance, the Gluecks did not code the number of arrests by specific crime types across all three time periods; instead, they provided only summary arrest measures and artificially truncated the upper end of arrest history distribution. More important, they did not code any dates of arrests or dates of dispositions (e.g., the dates of incarceration). Thus, contrary to our interests in the life course, information was not available on the sequence of events in an individual's criminal history, and it was not possible to precisely estimate "time free" when calculating individual rates of offending. At the same time, there was no way in which

to examine the effects of criminal justice sanctions because specific dispositions were not linked to specific arrests.

Because this information was available in the original case records, the
second component of our research strategy aimed to recode the raw data
into a more useful format (Elder, Pavalko, & Clipp, 1993). In other words,
we developed a new coding scheme that recast the Gluecks' data to fit into
our dynamic longitudinal framework as derived from current research on
criminal careers (Blumstein, Cohen, Roth, & Visher, 1986). Specifically,
over a 15-month period, we reconstructed a complete criminal history for
each respondent in the study from first arrest to age 32 years. During this
time period, the Gluecks' men respondents generated more than 6,000
arrests. For each arrest event, we coded the date, the specific type of charge
or charges, the exact sequence of arrests, and the dates and types of all
criminal justice interventions including the actual dates of incarceration (if
any). Such a scheme captures all the richness of the Gluecks' longitudinal
data (for more details, see Sampson & Laub, 1993).

➤ A STRATEGY FOR INTEGRATING QUANTITATIVE AND QUALITATIVE DATA

In the analyses for our book, *Crime in the Making* (Sampson & Laub,
1993), we followed a twofold strategy for explaining continuity and change
in criminal behavior over the life course. The first involved quantitative
analysis of the longitudinal data from the Gluecks' study. These quantitative analyses covered a range of statistical techniques including event
history analysis, maximum likelihood covariance structure models, and
generalized least squares random effects models that take into account
unobserved heterogeneity. Our goal was to portray, in statistical terms, the
major predictors of desistance from criminal careers over time. Drawing
on a theoretical model of turning points through the life course, we found
that job stability and marital attachment in adulthood had significant
negative effects on later crime independent of early childhood experiences
(Sampson & Laub, 1993).

The second component of our strategy entailed an intensive qualitative
analysis of the life history records for a subset of cases from the Gluecks'
study (see Sampson & Laub, 1993, Chapter 9). We used these qualitative

data to build on a strong tradition in criminology of using life histories of offenders as a data source about crime and criminality (see Bennett, 1981, for a historical overview). Classic works in criminology such as Shaw's (1930) *The Jack-Roller* and Sutherland's (1937) *The Professional Thief* illustrate the power of life history data to illuminate the complex processes of criminal offending (see also Katz, 1988). Our analysis of the life histories of the Gluecks' respondents pursues the same goal. A major difference from these earlier works, however, is that we merge quantitative and qualitative analyses to provide a more complete portrait of criminal offending over the life course.

In contrast to the traditional "variables-oriented" approach dominant in criminology and the social sciences at large (Abbott, 1992; Katz, 1988), we adopted a "person-oriented" strategy that allowed us to explore "patterns or configurations of relevant personal characteristics in a developmental perspective" (Magnusson & Bergman, 1990, p. 101). This approach enables one to investigate person-environment interactions, sequences of action, and individual change over time (Abbott, 1992; Cairns, 1986; Magnusson & Bergman, 1988, p. 47). Overall, our plan was to combine data on variables and on persons. This follows Cook's (1985) call for "multiplism" in social science research "by establishing correspondences across many different, but conceptually related, ways of posing a question" (p. 46). Our approach contrasts sharply with the Gluecks' analytical strategy, which tended to be static and variable oriented; that is, the Gluecks emphasized behavioral continuity in the men respondents' lives and did not identify major sources of change over the life course.

Given the large size of the Gluecks' sample, we developed a "sampling" plan for the analysis of life histories. This plan entailed the identification of a random subset of cases for intensive qualitative analysis defined by cross-classification of key social dimensions (e.g., employment, marriage, crime). Consistent with the goal of merging quantitative and qualitative methods, we used the results from our quantitative analyses as a means of identifying these cases (persons) for in-depth qualitative analysis. To illustrate, our quantitative analysis showed that job stability was an important mechanism fostering desistance from crime. Based on this finding, we selected cases that displayed *high* job stability (e.g., upper 10%-15% of the frequency distribution) in combination with no arrest experiences as adults. Similarly, we selected cases exhibiting *low* job stability (e.g., bottom quartile of the frequency distribution) and arrest experiences as adults. We followed the same procedures for the marital attachment variable.

We also targeted cases that were clearly *inconsistent* with our quantitative findings. For example, using the frequency distribution on job stability plus information from the criminal histories of the Gluecks' respondents, we selected those who had low job stability yet desisted from crime. At the other end of the spectrum, we selected cases in which job stability was high yet recurring criminal activity as adults was evident. Again, we followed a similar strategy for marital attachment in selecting "off-diagonal" cases.

We were able to analyze qualitative data for at least eight unique cases within each cell of interest. When there was a sufficient number of cases in a cell (usually on the diagonal), they were randomly selected for in-depth analysis (e.g., strong marital attachment and no offending in adulthood). In other instances, we were forced to use all available cases for our qualitative analysis (e.g., strong job stability and persistent offending in adulthood). In total, we reconstructed and then examined in detail 70 life histories from the Gluecks' delinquent sample (Sampson & Laub, 1993, Chapter 9).

This strategy has two distinct methodological benefits. First, the quantitative findings are enhanced by the analysis of qualitative data, resulting in more illumination of the complex processes underlying persistence and desistance from crime (Cairns, 1986; Jick, 1979; Kidder & Fine, 1987; Magnusson & Bergman, 1990). For example, integrating divergent sources of life history data (e.g., narratives, interviews), our qualitative analysis was consistent with the hypothesis that the major turning points in the life course for men who refrained from crime and deviance in adulthood were stable employment and good marriages. At the same time, we found that persistence in criminal behavior in adulthood often was the result of a developmental process of "cumulative disadvantage" in which the negative influences of structural disadvantages (e.g., dropping out of school, having a criminal record or a dishonorable discharge from the military) persist throughout adult development (see also Sampson & Laub, 1997).

Second, by examining residual cases that do not fit with empirical results, the analytical model under inspection is expanded and becomes enriched to account for previously unidentified pathways into and out of crime (Giordano, 1989). This strategy often is referred to as "negative case analysis" (p. 261). As Jick (1979) argued, "In fact, divergence can often turn out to be an opportunity for enriching the explanation" (p. 607). For instance, in our qualitative analyses, we found that alcohol abuse can counteract the expected positive effects of strong marital attachment or strong job stability on later criminal offending (Sampson & Laub, 1993, Chapter 9).

➤ USING LIFE HISTORY DATA TO STUDY TURNING POINTS THROUGH LIFE

We recently extended the life history, person-based approach to uncovering turning points and processes of change over the life course (Laub & Sampson, 1993). Specifically, we selected cases (persons) for qualitative analyses that demonstrated a *change* in social bonds as measured by our quantitative indicators of job stability and marital attachment in adulthood. The cases we selected revealed evidence of both incremental and abrupt change. For instance, incremental change usually occurred over a period of time in the context of an ongoing relationship or institutional affiliation (e.g., marriage). For instance, one respondent with an erratic work history up until his marriage stated that "home responsibilities forced him to be a stable and regular worker." In another case, the incremental processes of change consisted of several circumstances including leaving Boston, becoming a parent, and finding a steady job. In his interview, the respondent remarked,

> Well, for one thing, I got out of Boston. I began to work steadily, and now I have a family—a son whom I always wanted. My father helped me to get back on the road to respectability, and he has lived with us since we moved here. My wife always wanted me to do the right thing, and I try to follow her advice. I got away from the old gang and the bookie racket which my uncle runs in the city. In a small town such as this, you have to go straight.

Our analysis of qualitative life history data also provided important clues relating to the investment processes that are involved in the development of strong marital ties. Marital investment is a reciprocal process between husbands and wives that, if successful, encourages desistance from crime because of the strength of the social relations that are built up in the family. The life history of the respondent we call "Tony" illustrates these investment processes.

Tony had five arrests during the ages 17 to 25 years period including arrests for serious crimes such as armed robbery and burglary. He also served considerable time in penal institutions—32 months from ages 20 to 25 years. Tony's marital situation at ages 17 to 25 years also was rocky. At the time of his marriage, Tony was 22 and his wife was 17 years old. His wife was in high school when she became pregnant, an event that precipitated their marriage. Shortly after the marriage, the couple separated on and off. They continued to experience poor conjugal relations throughout the early period of their marriage. Despite marital discord and a record of crime as a young adult, Tony had no criminal activity (official or unofficial) during the ages 26 to 32 years period. What accounted for this change in behavior? Inspection of the life history material reveals a distinct change in the marital relationship. At Tony's interview at age 32 years, his family situation had changed dramatically to the point where the couple's conjugal relations were cohesive. Tony was described as a rather dependent type who clung to his wife. She was portrayed as a strong, sensible person whose interests were in the home and in her family. The couple had two sons, and overall there was a strong "we feeling" in the household.

According to Tony, his reasons for reformation include (a) "I have steady work," (b) "I have family responsibilities now," and (c) "I have learned my lesson" (he feared returning to prison). According to detailed interviewer notes and additional narratives, the strong influence of Tony's wife was the most important reason for his reform. Indeed, in what appears to be a form of informal social control, the interviewer wrote that Tony's wife "gives him good counsel, and she sees to it that the respondent follows her advice."

In other cases, we found evidence of abrupt change, and this often was linked to a single event such as entering the military. Several of the respondents reported that serving in the military removed them from their familiar environments and exposed them to unique situations and different perspectives. In fact, the cases we examined pointed to the military as a "settling influence" or turning point in the life course (see also Elder, 1986). According to narrative data, one respondent, who had joined the navy while on parole from reform school and remained there for 13 years, stated that his enlistment in the military changed his outlook on life. "In the navy, I was thrown in with guys from all over the country; some of them were well educated and had good backgrounds. I began to see that my thinking was way out of line and that I was probably wrong. I began to do things their way, and things have gone well ever since."

Given the available information in the Gluecks' case files, it is hard to uncover exactly what it was about the military experience that facilitated a change in behavior. In addition, our finding of a positive influence is somewhat surprising given our results on the continuity of antisocial behavior from adolescence into adult domains including misconduct in the military (Sampson & Laub, 1993, Chapter 6). However, it is not inconsistent that the military can function to turn some men's lives around even as it disrupts other men's lives (Elder, 1986) or provides yet another setting for some men to continue their criminal and deviant behaviors (Gottfredson & Hirschi, 1990, p. 165).

We also examined the life histories for a subset of men who experienced a significant *decline* in social bonding from ages 26 to 32 years. In these cases, it was difficult to detect clear turning points, but certain patterns did emerge. For some men, a decline in job stability was due to changes in the labor market. Not surprisingly, layoffs, seasonal work, and factory closings all contributed to the weakening of ties to work. For one respondent, his troubles in adulthood started when the company for which he was working "folded." All employees were let go, and his "good job" was simply gone. Macro-level transformations of the economy clearly bear on individual lives.

In several other cases, the following scenario emerged. The respondent married young, and often the marriage was forced due to pregnancy. Although prior to marriage there was some evidence of excessive drinking by the respondent, the respondent's wife claimed that the respondent had matured into his familial responsibilities and initially the couple got along well. Work typically was of a seasonal nature (e.g., construction work) and was weather dependent. But as the man became older and we normally would expect an increasing "conformity" or settling down, ties to marriage and work unraveled. There were separations, followed by reconciliations, followed by further separations. There often was evidence of physical abuse and nonsupport of children. The respondent's wife objected to the respondent's drinking and was not pleased by the financial uncertainty of seasonal work. The respondent resented what he perceived to be "overprotectiveness" on the part of his wife and claimed that she "nagged" him. The respondent's drinking often continued to be a problem, exacerbated in part by the fact that in certain jobs drinking seemed to be tolerated or even encouraged so long as one did not drink on the job (Vaillant, 1983, pp. 96-97). As a result, crime and deviance became more pronounced over time due to the severing of social ties to work and family.

➤ EXTENDING THE GLUECKS' DATA

Although our integration of the quantitative and qualitative data in the Gluecks' data provided a more detailed picture of stability and change in criminal behavior than either data source alone would have yielded, we were increasingly frustrated by the fact that the Gluecks' study was not designed to investigate turning points throughout the life course. Indeed, as mentioned earlier, the Gluecks emphasized behavioral continuity in their research; as a result, the Gluecks' data, especially the qualitative data, are limited in their utility for assessing and understanding behavioral change in the lives of the Gluecks' respondents.

Therefore, we are launching a new follow-up study to extend the Gluecks' archive. Specifically, we are planning to conduct life history interviews with a subset of the original respondents of the Gluecks' study. The delinquent respondents were born between 1924 and 1934; thus, in 1996, the oldest respondent was 72 and the youngest was 62 years old. Clausen (1990) contended that the idea of a turning point is an important concept for those interested in the study of lives. In our previous work (Laub & Sampson, 1993; Sampson & Laub, 1993), some key turning points in the life course were marriage, meaningful work, and serving in the military. The idea of a turning point is closely linked to role transitions, and, conceptually, turning points are helpful in understanding stability and change in human behavior over the life course. Adapting this perspective here leads us to ask the following: What are the turning points in the lives of juvenile delinquents? What led some of the Gluecks' delinquents away from continued involvement in crime as adults? And, conversely, what are the turning points (or lack of turning points) that facilitated continued involvement in crime?

Using criminal record data, we plan to select delinquent respondents for life history interviews based on different trajectories of criminal behavior over the life span. A trajectory is a pathway or line of development over the life span such as work life, parenthood, and criminal behavior. Trajectories refer to long-term patterns of behavior and are marked by a sequence of transitions. Following Cline (1980), we have identified eight distinct behavioral trajectories across three stages of the life course (juvenile < age 17 years, young adult ages 17-32 years, and middle/later adulthood ages 33-65 years).

The first set of trajectories we will examine consists of four different life course patterns for those individuals who were violent as juveniles. The four groupings are (a) Individuals who were violent as juveniles, young adults, and older adults; (b) individuals who were violent as juveniles and in later adulthood but not between the ages of 17 and 32 years; (c) individuals who were violent as juveniles and young adults but not between the ages of 33 and 65 years; and (d) individuals who were violent as juveniles but not as adults. We propose to interview *five* individuals in each of these four groupings for a total of 20 interviews.

The next set of trajectories consists of four different patterns for those individuals who were not violent as juveniles. The four groupings in this category are (a) individuals who were nonviolent as juveniles, young adults, and older adults; (b) Individuals who were not violent as juveniles or in later adulthood but were violent between the ages of 17 and 32 years; (c) individuals who were not violent as juveniles or young adults but were violent between the ages of 33 and 65 years; and (d) individuals who were not violent as juveniles but were violent as adults. We propose to interview *five* individuals in each of these four groupings for a total of 20 interviews.

Overall, then, we plan to conduct detailed life history interviews with 40 of the Gluecks' men respondents as they are about to reach the age of 70 years. These life history interviews will focus on retrospective views of one's own life course (Clausen, 1993). We recently completed a pilot study that involved locating and interviewing two respondents from the Gluecks' original study. For this pilot work, we developed an interview schedule accompanied by a modified life history calendar (Freedman, Thornton, Camburn, Alwin, & Young-DeMarco, 1988) to help respondents place major life events (e.g., marriage, divorce, retirement) in time. Based on our earlier work (Sampson & Laub, 1993), we asked the men about their educational and work experiences, military service, family relationships, living arrangements, neighborhood characteristics, and social activities including both official and unofficial involvement in crime and violence and alcohol/drug use. Of special interest is the self-evaluation of turning points in one's life course and their relationship to the cessation of criminal activity. At the age of 69 years, one respondent recounted,

> I'd say the turning point was, number one, the army. You get into an outfit, you had a sense of belonging, you made your friends. I think I became a pretty good judge of character. In the army, you met some good ones, you met some foul balls. Then I met the wife. I'd say probably that would be the turning point. Got married, then naturally, kids come. So now you got to get a better job, you got to make more money. And that's how I got to the navy yard and tried to improve myself.

Another respondent (age 67 years) told us that a major turning point was moving out of the house he shared with his girlfriend and her son some 14 years earlier and establishing his own residence in a different town.

Although the life history approach has clear limitations (Janson, 1990; Moffitt, Caspi, Henry, Langley, & Silva, 1992), narrative or qualitative interviews provide a unique perspective often lacking in criminological research (Becker, 1930/1966; Katz, 1988). In particular, our hope is to portray "the inner logic of lives" as told in their own words for a group of men who engaged in crime and violence (Modell, 1994, p. 1391). Following Clausen (1993) and Vaillant (1993), we expect that these life histories will provide important clues on the unfolding of adult development that cannot be obtained from statistical tables. Furthermore, by focusing on several offender subgroups, we will begin to unravel the developmental trajectories of continuity and change in criminal behavior over the life course. Of course, these interviews will not provide full life reviews, but they will provide a rich supplement to the quantitative data we have collected and the existing information we have extracted from the original files in the Gluecks' study.

➢ CONCLUDING REMARKS

By uniting quantitative and qualitative data, our goal has been to shed light on the dynamic processes of human development and criminal behavior over the life course. As shown in this chapter, qualitative data appear especially helpful in uncovering the underlying processes of continuity and change in criminal behavior over time. For example, with respect to change, qualitative data expose human agency in the processes leading to individual change and, thus, redirect our attention on how individual lives, macro-level events (e.g., war), and life course transitions (e.g., marriage, work, neighborhood) intersect and reshape life course trajectories. At the same time, qualitative data can help uncover the developmental sequences under-lying patterns of continuity found in quantitative data. Thus, without qualitative data, discussions of continuity often mask complex and rich developmental processes (Sampson & Laub, 1997).

Another important issue in life course research is the historical context of the study itself. This is especially true in the study of crime and crime control (Schlossman & Cairns, 1993). We believe that both quantitative and qualitative data are essential for understanding the role of historical context in individual development through time (Laub & Sampson, 1995). For instance, the Gluecks collected data on 1,000 respondents (white males) who grew up during the 1930s and early 1940s in Boston. These men reached adulthood in the late 1940s and 1950s. This is a fascinating time period in which to study crime and deviance as well as more general developmental patterns over the life course (e.g., the adolescence-to-adult-hood transition). For example, drugs such as "crack" cocaine were not even known in this time period, and the level of criminal violence, especially gun use, was below what we see presently. Also, the role of alcohol abuse coupled with the virtual absence of other drug use (e.g., cocaine) suggests a strong period effect. With respect to developmental trajectories, the likelihood of military service coupled with the expanding employment opportunities and the normative expectations surrounding early marriage make this a distinguishable and important context to study. Individual development can be understood only in the specific historical context in which it occurs. Therefore, quantitative and qualitative data on individual lives and social structures must be integrated to fully understand stability and change in behavior over time (Riley, 1994b).

➢ NOTES

1. The material presented in this chapter draws in part on our previously published work on the integration of quantitative and qualitative data (e.g., Laub & Sampson, 1993; Sampson & Laub, 1993, Chapter 9). However, we extend our earlier work here by focusing on the assembly of quantitative and qualitative data for a life course analysis. In describing the details of this process, we reveal how secondary analyses that involve both quantitative and qualitative

data on the life course can take full advantage of the strengths of the data set while appropriately recognizing their weaknesses.

2. Previous analyses suggest that crime in the Gluecks' era was not all that different from that today in terms of its structural origins and underlying nature (Sampson & Laub, 1993). Therefore, we contend that the fact that sample members in the UJD study were drawn from settings of social and economic disadvantage yet all were white provides an important comparative base in which to assess current concerns of race, crime, and the underclass (Kotlowitz, 1991).

Chapter 10

Innovation in the
Typical Life Course

JANET Z. GIELE

Two major examples of life course innovation in modern times are the change in men's retirement age after 1900 and the massive entry of women into the paid labor force after 1950. Although many recognize these changes as having far-reaching significance, the phenomena themselves rarely have been studied as anything more than demographic shifts in the way in which people lead their lives. Yet, each of these trends has been accompanied by a major change in the norms and ideals of how life should be lived. The new life patterns have become the basis for new social institutions that persist beyond the lives of the pioneers.

My mission in this chapter is to examine the process of innovation in the life course. Recognition of innovation is important because it helps society distinguish master patterns that have yet to be institutionalized from deviance that is to be punished and cultural variation that is to be accommodated with special programs. In the case of women's changing roles, for example, the pioneer women who developed dual work and family careers in the 1960s and 1970s were treated as deviants and subjected to resistance and discrimination. By the 1990s, however, it was widely recognized that women's new life patterns were here to stay and that major social policies should take these shifts into account. Welfare rules began to require that indigent mothers eventually return to work rather than stay at home, and the Family and Medical Leave act of 1993 asked employers to provide temporary leave and job protection for workers who wished to take time off for family caregiving.

One of the first questions about innovation in the typical life course is how to recognize it when it occurs. How do the new life course patterns come about? How do wars, depressions, or longer life expectancy set the stage for innovation? How do myriad small changes in the lives of individuals suddenly add up to a sea change? Recognition of innovation can guide individuals as they chart new paths to adulthood, midlife, or old age. In addition, understanding that innovation has occurred can potentially illuminate some of the most pressing policy issues of our day such as how to live through old age happily or how to help dual-earner families fulfill their parenting responsibilities. By studying social change and life pattern innovation quite deliberately, life course scientists can clarify which innovations are likely to become the norm and then document the changes in other institutions that will be required.

True innovation in the life course, according to Kohli (1986), comes about when the temporal ordering of life events or the sum total of an individual's roles not only depart from tradition but also prefigure the institutionalization of that way of life so that it becomes the standard. The type of life course innovation considered in this chapter is distinguished from the biography of a pioneering individual by its eventual widespread adoption. A normative change in life course pattern is evident when the new pattern becomes institutionalized so that it is reproduced through the socialization process and cultural expectations. In the lives of women, such major changes have been rather few and far between. Beginning around 1840, the ideal of true womanhood gained importance among middle class women who gradually withdrew from economic production on farms and in the new regional towns to lead the lives of "ladies" (Welter, 1976). For nearly a century, most middle class women preferred not to be employed or involved in public life but rather to manage their households, care for children, and represent their families in the community through volunteer work. After 1950, however, the spread of a service economy, longer lives, and lower fertility introduced millions of women to what Antler (1981) termed "feminism as life process," the independence and potential for recognition made possible by expanded education, smaller families, and the promise of careers.

The question for life course scientists is how such momentous and long-lasting changes came about. What made it possible for isolated individuals to depart from the cultural script and chart a new path without knowing exactly where it would lead? And how did it happen that so many individuals made the change independently without knowing that they were part of a wider trend?

In recent years, the life course field has made new advances in recording massive changes in individual and family life and their connections to particular economic and political circumstances. But the findings have yet to be codified in ways that illuminate how innovation occurs. This chapter identifies methodological strategies for identifying and describing innovation as well as some of the main theories that have been offered to explain it.

➢ HISTORY OF THE QUESTION

It is first necessary to describe the background and significance of studying life course innovation—what the major issues have been and how they currently are understood in relation to historical change and human development. Two of the best-known examples of change in the normative life course are retirement age among males and rising labor force participation among females. Studies on age of retirement have made clear a continuing and profound interaction between institutional change and life course change.

The Lower Retirement Age of Men

As Kohli (1986) showed, the institution of age 70 years for pension eligibility in Germany in the 1880s and of age 65 years in the United States (with the institution of social security in 1935) has reshaped the typical life course of men over this century. The decrease in older men's labor force participation has been dramatic, dropping in Germany from 47% of men age 70 years or over in 1895 to only 5% in 1980. In the United States, the pattern was similar, with a drop in the employment rate of men over age 65 years from 68% in 1890 to only 19% in 1980. Moreover, the numbers of men ages 60 to 64 years who still were employed also fell; between 1970 and 1988, the rate dropped from 80% to 55% in the United States and fell even more sharply in France, Germany, and the Netherlands (Kohli, Rein, Guillemard, & Van Gunsteren, 1991).

Employers who currently want to downsize their companies and move older people out of the workforce use the workers' own internalized expectations about retirement age and the pension and social security systems to accomplish their ends. Life has become compartmentalized into what Riley (1978) termed "three boxes"—the first one at the beginning of life for preparation and training, the second in midlife for work and family, and the third at the end of life for leisure. Together, these changes have solidified not only what Kohli (1987) termed a "work society" but also a "tripartite" life course. In other words, the macro-structural rules of pension eligibility have induced changes in life planning while at the same time longer life, improvements in health, and job insecurity have reshaped the use of the pension system (Mayer & Müller, 1986). Thus, the new institutionalized life course represents two sides of the same coin.

This work on men's retirement patterns is instructive for suggesting how to codify knowledge about women's changing life course. A first step is to identify the key changes that have occurred and then to describe and explain them.

Emergence of Women's "Multiple Roles"

Up until the end of World War II, change in women's lives was conceived primarily as winning the vote. Although woman suffrage had been proposed as early as the "Declaration of Sentiments" at Seneca Falls, New York, in 1848, it was not until 1920 with the passage of the 20th Amendment that women could vote in every state. A variety of factors produced the change—women's higher education, women's reform work, the need to represent the interests of families and children, and recognition of women's patriotism and contributions during World War I (Giele, 1995).

Nevertheless, despite women's having won the vote, the ideal economic role of the woman as a lady and homemaker had not deviated very much from the rule enunciated by Mill (1869/1909) that it was "not . . . a desirable custom that the wife should contribute by her labour to the income of a family" (p. 75). Mill reasoned that children were better off and the management of the household was superior when a mother did not have to divide her effort between gaining bread and providing for the comfort of her family.

Beginning in the 1940s, however, the picture changed markedly. Although in 1948 only 35% of women ages 25 to 54 years were in the labor force, this proportion had almost doubled in a mere 25 years to 67% in 1983. The trends were even more dramatic for married women (whose participation rose from 21% to 52%) and for mothers of children under 6 years of age (whose participation increased from 11% to 50% during the same period) (Giele, 1988, p. 300). By 1988, more than half of all mothers with children under 1 year of age were employed at least part-time or for part of a year (Moen, 1992, p. 15). Komarovsky (1982), comparing the results from two studies of freshmen at Barnard College, found that four times as many women expected to have careers in 1979 as did in 1943 (48% vs. 12%); of those, all but 2% expected to be married, and all but 14% expected to be mothers.

Working class women and black women had, of course, long had "multiple roles" in the sense of combining paid work with family responsibilities (Bell, 1974; Jones, 1985). What was different for the white middle class majority after World War II was a new legitimacy for paid work that allied it as much or more with women's satisfaction and self-fulfillment as with economic necessity. Among black women too, work histories began to change. Gilfus and I found in our 1982 survey of three colleges that even though more graduates of the black women's college had mothers who had been domestic workers, more of them had gained postgraduate educations and held jobs at high professional ranks than did their age peers at another women's college and a coeducational college (Giele & Gilfus, 1990).

Corresponding with the changing employment rates and career expectations of women with family responsibilities was a changing age profile in women's labor force participation. The profile was gradually changing its shape from that of an M-shaped curve (indicating women's early departure from employment and later reentry at midlife) to that of an inverted U-shaped curve similar to men's (indicating more continuous employment through the middle years).

To pinpoint this change and to capture the fact that the change was not just a matter of rising employment but of *combining women's work and family roles,* researchers and commentators began to speak of a rise in women's multiple roles. Women also were continuing their educations beyond their late teens and early 20s. Davis and Bumpass (1976) found in the 1970 National Fertility Survey that more than one fifth of all women had attended high school or college since marriage, and the proportion was higher among younger women. Felmlee (1988) reported that the number of women over age 22 years who were enrolled in college had more than doubled between 1972 and 1982. In 1980, at least one third of all women college students were over age 25 years (Rossi, 1980).

After 1980, the description and explanation of these rising multiple roles became the main device for tracing change in the typical life course of women across historical periods, different age groups, and even different societies. Myrdal and Klein (1956), as early as the 1950s, wrote of *Women's Two Roles* and the tension of combining responsibilities to home and work. Likewise, using the two-role rubric, Moen (1992) updated the analysis in light of all the changes that had taken place from the 1960s to the 1980s. A focus on multiple roles made it possible to link the impact of changing economic and family structures to women's changing life patterns. One also could observe that the trend toward combining work and family roles created a demand for displaced homemaker legislation in the 1970s and more extensive provision of child care outside the home in the 1970s and 1980s (Burstein, Bricher, & Einwohner, 1995). Tough new work requirements for welfare mothers surfaced in the Family Support Act of 1988, and supports for parental leaves received legislative endorsement in the Family and Medical Leave Act of 1993 (Wexler, 1997).

The Problem of Role Conflict

At first, in the 1950s and 1960s, these massive changes in women's roles were analyzed primarily as social problems that created *role conflict and role strain* for the women who were trying to combine "male" and "female" roles. The best view of the role conflict perspective was provided by its critics. In *The Feminine Mystique,* Friedan (1963) roundly criticized the psychoanalysts and psychologists who assumed women's innate need to look after families and to be subservient in the world of politics and economics. She ridiculed the "functionalist freeze" of the anthropologists like Mead (1949) and sociologists like Parsons and Bales (1955) who saw the division of labor between male and female roles as needed by society and, therefore, unlikely to change.

By the late 1970s, however, several scholars were beginning to see role combination in positive terms. Marks (1977), Sieber (1974), and Thoits (1983) began a theoretical revolution that identified the advantages of holding several roles simultaneously. Multiple roles could protect a role incumbent by preventing women from putting all their emotional eggs in one basket. The presence of alternative roles also could increase a sense of choice and satisfaction. Rather than being torn between the two roles of work and family, both women and men might actually benefit from being able to limit their commitments to "greedy roles." As Kanter (1977) argued in *Work and Family in the United States,* the experiences gained in the world of the family were useful to the world of work and vice versa. This reorientation among theorists then led to women's simultaneous work and family involvements being recast as beneficial. In a major analysis of policy directions for women's roles that was done for the Ford Foundation, I showed that a new paradigm of greater role crossover and flexibility was beginning to permeate American society (Giele, 1978). Women were gaining access to achievements and leadership that once had been reserved for men, and men were being encouraged to take on some of the affiliative and caregiving functions that traditionally had been the province of women. Baruch, Barnett, and Rivers (1983) studied a sample of Boston-area women and discovered that women who were able to satisfy both their need for a sense of competence through work and a need for pleasure through family ties were better off psychologically (less depressed and feeling a greater sense of personal control) than were those women who were limited to only work or family roles.

The Issue of Adult Development

By the early 1980s, the attention given to the dramatic changes in women's lives came under a new rubric of "adult development" and "the middle years." The new focus was needed because human development theories (like that of Kohlberg, 1969, on moral development) tended to stop with adolescence and leave unspecified what happened in adulthood. No one could really say whether the rapid and unprecedented changes in women's roles were healthy or not. Levinson (1978) elaborated Erikson's (1950) "eight stages of man," and Sheehy (1976) popularized his work and produced several generalizations about the "midlife crisis"—that it could be provoked by the loss of a parent, the loss of health and vigor, or a sudden feeling that life was finite and must be lived more intensely with perhaps a new marriage or a career change before it was gone.

Efforts to apply these insights to women revealed the limitations of stage theories and of the middle years as a conceptual category. The Social

Science Research Council, under the auspices of its Committee on Work and Personality in the Middle Years, sponsored a scholarly year-long seminar in 1977-1978 of experts on women's lives at Brandeis University.[1] One of the clear conclusions of the seminar was that stage theories were inadequate to the task of mapping all the changes in women's lives and their consequences for society, families, and women themselves. The chief problem was that women's changing roles were not only tasks given by the self as a project for adult development but also were being driven by a tremendous economic demand for women's work, by the growth of higher education for women, and by increasing divorce and uncertainty about future family life (Giele, 1982a).

Demographers and sociologists began to suggest that a preoccupation with the middle years was "cohort-centric" in the sense that it concentrated on the problems of a particular generation born in the 1920s who happened to reach middle age in the 1970s. If the scheme was truly generalizable, then why had midlife not been raised as a problem by earlier generations, and would it disappear for younger groups who were coming along? There was a distinct possibility that the midlife crisis was a transitional phenomenon that had come to that cohort of persons who were living through midlife in a society that was different from the one they had expected (Rossi, 1980).

Insights From a Life Course Perspective

With the eclipse of role conflict and midlife stage theories, the foundation was laid for the ascendance of a new conceptual framework, the *life course perspective*. By the mid-1980s, changes in women's lives had begun to take on a new meaning. They seemed to be a massive adaptation by women to profound trends in the larger society—the rise of a service economy, increased numbers of female-headed families, and women's own need to be ready in case the traditional age-gender system did not work for them. Coinciding with these actual social changes were developments within the field of psychology. The new life-span development psychology focused on positive adaptation to the aging process (Baltes, 1993). Thus, the pioneers of women's changing roles could be understood to have hit on new, more adaptive patterns for their particular circumstances.

A reinterpretation of age-related patterns also was occurring within demography and sociology. Historical period, social experiences of a birth cohort, and chronological age of the individual at the time of a significant life event all were seen as highly correlated but distinguishable dimensions that helped to explain changing social roles. The new sociology of age stratification suggested that novel women's roles would be found among particular age groups who were located in distinctive social and historical environments and who had adapted to their situations by developing more effective or satisfying life patterns (Elder, 1975; Riley, 1978; Ryder, 1965; Swidler, 1986; Uhlenberg, 1979).

This new life course perspective was able to illuminate a much more complex dynamic of change in women's lives than had been suggested either by role conflict or adult development theories. The emergence of women's multiple roles could now be seen as the product of changes in demography, economy, and family as well as individual life history.

Oppenheimer (1970, 1979, 1982) demonstrated the interconnection between historical period and cohort size in the conditions favoring innovation. Women flooded into the labor market in the 1950s because of rising demand in the female-labeled occupations of teaching, nursing, clerical work, and other service occupations. Yet, the traditional supply of young unmarried women with the requisite education was unusually small due to the low birthrate of the 1930s. The upshot was a redefinition of who could be hired that included older married women who might reenter the labor force.

But within the eligible age groups to be hired, there were some who were ready and interested and others who were not. The difference had partly to do with their individual life experiences prior to adulthood. Elder's (1974) work on *Children of the Great Depression* illuminated some of the relevant family dynamics that connected historical events and chronological age of the innovators. Those women who had grown up in the most economically deprived families, where their mothers had worked and they had to do many of the household chores as teenagers in the 1930s, were more likely to become full-time homemakers than were the women whose families had not been deprived and whose mothers had not worked. Age at time of the Depression also was crucial; girls born several years later whose families also experienced economic deprivation did not show such marked effects in their career choices (Bennett & Elder, 1979).

Still, there were women who married after World War II or who graduated from college during the 1950s who, as young adults, expected to follow the traditional homemaker path. But even these women had revised their life course by the time they had reached their 50s in the mid-1980s. An unexpected divorce, a change in goals as a result of further education, and/or the desire to have other interests in addition to one's family brought many women back into the labor force or back to school and caused them independently to create their own idiosyncratic dual career patterns (Gerson, 1985). In a meta-analysis of 15 longitudinal studies of college graduates collected by Hulbert and Schuster (1993) and of work histories of less well educated women in the U.S. National Longitudinal Surveys, I found that multiple roles had become a new norm, especially among those cohorts of women who were born in the 1930s and 1940s and who had together experienced the economic expansion, higher educational levels, and family insecurity of the intervening years (Giele, 1993). As shown in Figure 10.1, this interpretation traced the ways in which the three dimensions of age were interwoven. The table designates historical period by the different study waves in the columns, birth cohorts in the rows, and respondents of similar age at time of the studies in the shaded cells along the diagonal. Goldin (1995), using the National Longitudinal Surveys, came to similar (although less detailed) conclusions about the increasing readiness of younger cohorts to enter the labor market.

Of course, one may wonder whether these trends toward multiple careers can be reversed. Although Easterlin (1978) hypothesized that "the good news about 1984" would be women's return to the home in a burgeoning economy that made their employment less necessary, no turnaround has yet appeared. Since 1985, women's employment has continued to rise to *nearly 70% in 1995 and to more than 80%* among college-educated women ages 25 to 54 years. Thus, women's multiple roles appear to be truly an innovation in the normative life course of women.

➢ METHODS FOR STUDYING INNOVATION IN THE LIFE COURSE

How, then, should innovation be studied? To identify innovation requires solving three different methodological problems. First, one has to know innovation when one sees it. This requires a *research design* that compares successive age cohorts so that one can observe the start of an innovation and then trace its growth into a trend. Second, one has to collect *comparable data* from different age groups. This is more of a challenge than meets the eye because it is more difficult to get the same type of facts about life at age 35 years from a 65-year-old than from a 35-year-old. Having compared age groups and collected comparable data, the third step is to look for *patterns* in the life course. These patterns are diverse and complex, and the nature of major trends is not always self-evident. Although there still are relatively few studies of life course innovation, it is nevertheless possible to articulate some general principles of research design, data collection, and pattern identification in the study of women's changing lives.

Research Design and Cohort Analysis

Locating innovation in the life course usually requires some sort of comparison by age groups. Because change is the result of a tension between the programming by society of the life course and the individual's own biography that expresses choice and agency (Kohli, 1986), one way in which to understand the connections between micro-level aging over the life course and macro-level institutional change is to observe the changing life patterns of successive cohorts. The study of cohort differences provides clues as to why change is occurring (Riley, 1987). As Ryder (1992) remarked, "Cohort analysis is peculiarly appropriate for the study of long-term normative change, whether in reproductive institutions [the family] or elsewhere in the social structure. . . . Each new cohort is simultaneously a threat to social stability and an opportunity for social transformation" (p. 230). *Inter*cohort comparisons permit one to contrast life events across age groups and to identify the nature and extent of innovation. *Intra*cohort comparisons make possible the analysis of why certain individuals in an age group become pioneers of change while others do not. These insights can then be extended to understanding why some age groups, more than others, are the originators of change.

Comparisons across age groups. Hogan's (1981) study of U.S. men born between 1907 and 1952 compared how men of different class backgrounds and ages experienced depression and war. The World War II soldier generation from blue-collar and rural backgrounds tended to follow new patterns of getting married before getting a job or finishing their education. Featherman and Sørensen (1983) found a similar pattern of growing complexity in the major life events of young Norwegian men born in 1921, 1931, and 1941. The younger men, by combining more different

Birth Cohort	Survey Wave					
	1930s-1940s	*1950s*	*1960s*	*1970s*	*1980s*	*1989-1990*
1900-1909 born 1907-1913		Vassar (40-48)	Vassar (46-54)			Vassar (76-84)
1910-1919 born 1902-1920	Terman (16-34) (25-43)	Terman (31-49)	Terman (44-58) Bennington (43-47)	Terman (52-70) (57-75)	Bennington (61-72)	
born 1912-1923						
1920-1929 born 1906-1930 (midpoint 1923)			Columbia (35-40)	Columbia (46-51)		
1930-1939 born 1935-1936		Vassar (22-23) Mills (22) UCLA (18)	Vassar (27-28) Mills (25-28)	Vassar (43-44)	Mills (43-45) UCLA (46)	Vassar (54-55) Mills (51-53) UCLA (51)
born 1936-1938						
born 1938-1939						

Figure 10.1. Studies of Educated Women by Birth Cohort, Survey Wave, and Age at Time of Study

Birth Cohort				
1940-1949 born 1943 born 1945 born 1946 born 1947	Radcliffe 1964 (18) U. of Michigan (22, 25) Carnegie-Mellon (18-22) Radcliffe 1969 (22)	Radcliffe 1964 (31, 33) Radcliffe 1969 (32)	Radcliffe 1964 (37, 43) U. of Michigan (36)	Carnegie-Mellon (44) Radcliffe 1969 (43)
1950-1959 born 1953 born 1953-1955 born 1952-1959		Riverside (17, 26) New England Colleges (18-21) U. of Michigan Inteflex (18, 25)	Riverside (34) New England Colleges (29-31) U. of Michigan Inteflex (34-37)	
1960-1969 born 1960-1964 born 1963			U. of Michigan Inteflex (18, 25) Illinois Valedictorians (18, 21, 22, 25)	U. of Michigan Inteflex (34-37) Illinois Valedictorians (28)

SOURCE: Reprinted with permission from Kathleen D. Hulbert and Diane T. Schuster (Eds.), *Women's Lives Through Time: Educated American Women in the Twentieth Century* (pp. 34-35). Copyright (c) 1993. Jossey-Bass Inc., Publishers.

NOTE: Ages at times of studies are in parentheses (in years). Shading in the cells along the diagonal highlights respondents who were in their thirties at the time they were surveyed.

roles simultaneously, were adapting to the complex demands of a modern society. The comparison of different cohorts of women college graduates provides an analogous survey of changes in women's lives. Among Wellesley College alumnae who graduated between 1911 and 1960, I observed that the rise of a multiple role pattern began with the classes of the 1930s. They were the first group who, at the time of the alumnae census in 1962, had combined marriage, motherhood, employment, and some postgraduate education over their life course. By contrast, the most common life pattern among the classes of 1911 to 1915 was remaining single. Fully 25% of these early graduates did not marry but gained postgraduate educations and pursued careers as compared to only 20% who had been employed (if only briefly), gained further education, married, and had children, as shown in Figure 10.2 (Giele, 1982a; Perun & Giele, 1982).

The 1962 cross-sectional survey did not, however, make it possible to pinpoint when innovation occurred in the organization of the adult years because one could not analyze event histories by age and year of event. Event history analysis did not become possible until the Life Pattern Study of 1982. A mailed survey asked 3,000 women alumnae from three colleges who graduated between 1934 and 1979 to report retrospective life histories of major events. Comparison across age cohorts revealed that a *simultaneous combination* of marriage, motherhood, and employment at age 35 years, together with having gained some postgraduate education, only began to accelerate with the graduation classes of the 1950s (born in the 1930s).[2] The timing of their marriages, childbearing, and postgraduate educational events was well *ahead* of the peak of the new women's movement in 1970, suggesting that the innovations of this age group may have actually helped to spawn the revival of feminism. Only 6% of the class of 1934 had a multiple role pattern at age 35 years , but this proportion had risen to 36% among graduates of the class of 1969 (Giele, 1987; Giele & Gilfus, 1990).

Life course comparison within age groups. Age cohort comparisons do not, however, explain the precise mechanisms that link history with individual development or change (Elder & O'Rand, 1995). For that, we have to turn to within-cohort studies. With biographies or other life history materials, it is possible to compare women's lives so that the connections between family background and subsequent life paths become apparent.

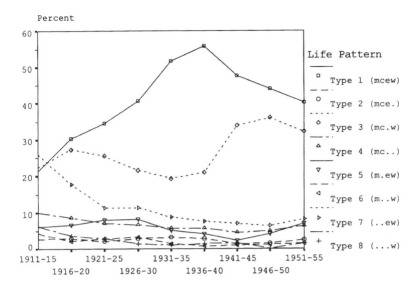

Figure 10.2. Distribution of Major Life Patterns, Wellesley College Alumnae, Class Groups of 1911-1955 in 1962

SOURCE: Giele (1982a). Reprinted by permission.

NOTE: Role histories up to 1962. For example, Type 1 (mcew) = ever married, had children, further education, ever worked.

Using archival materials in a comparison of 49 temperance and 49 suffrage leaders who were active between the 1840s and the 1920s, I described in *Two Paths to Women's Equality* how the two pioneer groups were different from the norms for their day as well as from each other. All the women were leaders and thus shared background characteristics such as coming from secure middle class roots and having advanced education. But differences in their personal tragedies and frustrations helped to explain why they chose different reforms, with the temperance leaders more often having experienced family losses and the suffrage leaders more often having experienced denial of professional opportunities (Giele, 1995).

Among investigations on contemporary women, a prime example of an intracohort study of pioneer and traditional behaviors is the qualitative analysis by Gerson (1985) in *Hard Choices*. Gerson interviewed 63 women ages 35 to 44 years who revealed the factors in their choices between homemaking careers and paid work. Significantly, Gerson did not use a cohort comparison to identify innovation. Instead, having identified growth in married women's employment as a key trend, she held cohort, age, and historical period constant by choosing women of similar age and focused on events in their own personal histories that gave them reason to follow domestic or nondomestic careers.

Comparative and cross-national research. Just as intracohort comparisons can illuminate the individual differences that help to account for a particular life pattern, cross-national comparisons of similar age groups can illuminate the macroeconomic, social, and cultural conditions that foster or retard a particular innovation. Kohli and colleagues (1991) used this methodology to compare advanced industrial societies in average age of men's retirement. Women's labor force participation and multiple roles can similarly be compared across countries to discover which social institutions and cultural factors facilitate women's multiple roles.

The principal challenge to such comparative work is to find data sources on women's lives that are set up in such a way that it is possible to compare changes in life patterns across similar cohorts. Fortunately, several national longitudinal panel studies can accommodate this need. For example, the German Socio-Economic Panel (GSOEP) Study that began in 1984 provides biographical information on all respondents up to 1983 or the last year before they began to take part in the survey. When these data are arrayed to compare successive age cohorts in their frequency of occupying multiple or single roles at ages 25, 30, 35, 40 years, and so on, the results are very similar to the American alumnae results and National Longitudinal Surveys in the United States. As shown in Figure 10.3, older birth cohorts were more likely to occupy single roles (marriage *or* motherhood *or* school attendance *or* employment), whereas younger cohorts were more likely to combine roles across the public-private divide (working and/or education *with* marriage and/or motherhood) (Giele & Pischner, 1994).

When contemporary women's life patterns are compared in Germany and the United States using the GSOEP Study for 1984-1990 and the U.S. Panel Study of Income Dynamics for 1983-1989, it becomes apparent that the "static" factors in individual women's employment patterns work in similar ways in each country. The employed women in both places are likely to have more education, fewer children, and lower initial incomes

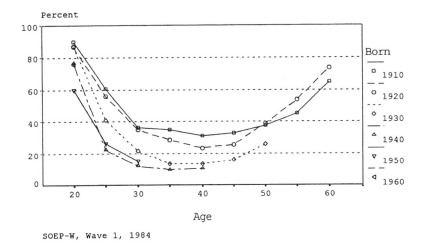

SOEP-W, Wave 1, 1984

Figure 10.3a. Single-Dimension Roles by Age: West German Women Born 1910-1960

SOURCE: Giele and Pischner (1994). Reprinted by permission.

NOTE: *Single-dimension roles* refers to being in only one of any of the following roles: work, education, marriage, or parenting.

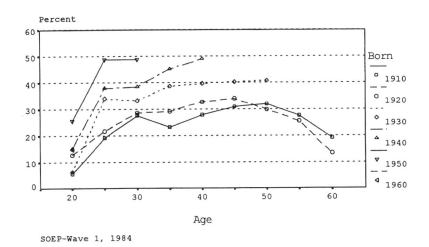

SOEP-Wave 1, 1984

Figure 10.3b. Public-Private Role Combination by Age: West German Women Born 1910-1960

SOURCE: Giele and Pischner (1994). Reprinted by permission.

NOTE: *Public-private role combination* refers to combining at least one "public" role (work, education) with at least one "private" role (marriage, parenting).

than are the nonemployed women. But the fact that the German women have a 10% to 15% lower labor force participation rate than the American women leads to a search for the dynamic factors that push the American women's work rate upward. Analysis of differences at the macro level between societies reveals that German women's lower employment may be due partly to more conservative gender roles in Germany as a whole. In 1989-1990, only 11% of employed women in Germany had more than one child in their households compared to 28% in the United States. In addition, the Germans appear to have a broader safety net, as revealed by the fact that as many as 67% received some sort of government benefit in 1987 (e.g., pensions, housing subsidies) compared to only about 16% of Americans in 1986 (Giele & Holst, 1997).

Collection and Analysis of Life History Data

Having developed a research design that brings out period, cohort, and cultural differences, the next key challenge to the longitudinal study of pioneering behavior is the question of how to collect relevant data and how to organize the analysis so that some pattern is revealed. As shown earlier in this volume by Karweit and Kertzer (Chapter 4), life course research treats *life events* as the basic building blocks for descriptive and explanatory analyses. Calendar dates and the person's age are the markers attached to each event that help researchers piece together connections between biographical threads and the historical landscape. Individual life processes can then be dynamically linked to social structure and changes in the social order. To study innovation, then, life history data always should include major life events, timing markers, and a construction of career paths or life histories that pieces together these discrete observations.

Nature of events. In study after study of women's lives, the types of events that are coded turn out to coincide with certain key *role domains:* (a) education, (b) employment, (c) marriage, and (d) parenting (Elder, 1974; Marini, 1984; Otto & Call, 1990; Young, 1978). A fifth domain that might be called public service takes different forms according to gender. In the case of men, it is military service; in the case of women, it is volunteer work and community service. Another dimension of these role activities is level of achievement or role *attainment* such as number of years of education, number of children, or occupational status. In addition to the person's role activities, a record of major life events includes changes in household composition (Kertzer, 1986) and a place for unexpected events such as accidents or illness. Various devices can be used to record these events. A good example is Freedman's Life History Calendar (Freedman, Thornton, Camburn, Alwin, & Young-DeMarco, 1988), which is referred to in Scott and Alwin's chapter in this volume (Chapter 5). The 1982 Life Patterns Study of women alumnae of three colleges used the retrospective Life Events Chart shown in Figure 10.4.

Timing markers. Chapter 1 of this book showed how timing of events is the common medium for linking human agency, social relationships, and geographical and historical locations to account for the shape of the individual life course. Thus, along with events and role transitions, the life history record must capture the timing of role entries and exits as expressed in two ways—*person's age* and *calendar month or year* at the time of beginning or ending an event; entry into the event is coded as T1 and exit as T2. With these data points, one can reconstruct not only the sequence and duration of the events but also the amount of role concurrence or simultaneity in the numbers of roles or events being combined at any one time.

Constructing career paths and life histories. Once the events data with timing markers have been collected, the next step is to construct career paths for an individual in each of the principal role domains and then to assemble these into a life history for each person. Because individuals of different ages are likely to have differing numbers of educational, employment, or other events, data management using the conventional rectangular form with the same numbers of rows and columns for each respondent is an inefficient use of storage space. To respond to this problem, two major types of data reduction technique have been proposed recently that take the form of either a "matrix" or a "chain." Together, these recent developments represent a welcome ferment in the search for usable data reduction strategies that go well beyond the coding techniques and conceptual frameworks reported by Dex (1984). It still is too soon, however, to summarize their strengths and limitations.

The *matrix form* of life history is well suited to following a number of roles at once. Karweit and Kertzer (1986) used their Casalecchio database system to handle variable-length files in each major role domain such as

Age (individual development in chronological time as marker or referent)	Year	Age	Education	Family Events	Paid Work	Moves	Other
	1972	20					
	1973	21		Cohort (age group as marker) graduation cohort of 1973 Birth cohort of 1952		Boston to Chicago	
	1974	22					
	1975	23	Began M.S.W.				
	1976	24		marriage			
	1977	25	Received M.S.W.		Social Worker (PT)		
	1978	26					Mother died
Period (historical era--specific date as marker)	1979	27		Son Born			
	1980	28			Began Own Prac. (FT)		
	1981	29					
	1982	30		Divorced	Moved Practice (FT)	Presque Isle, ME	

EDUCATION

1. Year you entered post-college program and type of study (e.g., social work, business, etc.)
2. Year you received degree, if any, and type of degree
3. If no degree, year you left program

Co-event (contemporaneous transition or life event as referent or marker)

FAMILY EVENTS

1. Year of first marriage
2. Year of subsequent divorce, widowhood, remarriage, if any
3. Years children born (and GENDER), or years that children came into your home
4. Years of other major household changes, if any (e.g., relative or friend came to live)

PAID WORK

1. Year you took first job
   a. Job title
   b. Part-time (PT) or full-time (FT)
2. Year you left job
3. Same information for later jobs

MOVES (GEOGRAPHICAL)

1. Years of move. (Don't count change of address in same city.)
   a. Town or city
   b. State
   c. Country (if outside the U.S.)
2. Same information for later moves

OTHER

1. Years of other significant events in your life
      (e.g., major illness, death of close friend, special recognition or honor, etc.)
   a. Type of event

Figure 10.4. Age, Period, and Cohort Operationalized on the Life Events Chart
SOURCE: Adapted from *Life Patterns Study Questionnaire*, 1982 (Giele, 1987; Giele & Gilfus, 1990).

employment, education, childbearing, or coresidence. One can then construct a "sample path" of events for each person in each major role domain

and examine co-events and antecedents and consequences. Otto and Call (1990) developed a special algorithm that constructs a unique number in each year for different combinations of multiple roles. Elder, Pavalko, and Clipp (1993), using examples from the Berkeley Growth and Guidance Studies and the Terman data, demonstrated how to construct life paths in parents' fortunes, health, work, and other role domains and then to link these event histories to each other.

The *chain form* of data reduction focuses on the chronological ordering of events to emerge with several major alternative pathways. Abbott and Hrycak (1990) developed techniques for "optimal matching" of careers of 18th-century German musicians to several major types of sequences in career events. Blair-Loy (1996) used these techniques to construct five major career sequences for women who have reached senior executive positions in finance. Using data from the Wisconsin Longitudinal Study, Carr, Ryff, Singer, and Magee (1995) used Boolean sets to characterize the different chronological representations of life course histories that are associated with depressed, healthy, vulnerable, and resilient mental health outcomes.

Locating Innovative Patterns

The third methodological challenge in studying innovation is to identify it when it has occurred. The patterns seen by any given researcher probably are related to his or her particular analytic questions and investigative techniques. A researcher who traces interlocking events across many domains of a person's life probably will be interested in how innovation is expressed as a different combination of roles. The researcher who codes for sequence is likely to be looking for new sequential patterns.

Modernity and multiple roles. Thomas and Znaniecki (1918-1920/1927), the authors of some of the earliest attempts to write modern life history, focused on the changes in life experienced by the peasant who left rural Poland and was thrust into a modern urban society. They found a man named Wladek, on whom they focused a whole volume of description. In his life, they identified a number of thematic trends that ranged from individualization and a search for efficiency to less traditional and fatalist ways of relating to his occupation, women, social class, and the larger neighborhood and community. Bauer, Inkeles, and Kluckhohn (1956), in

their study of changing life patterns within the Soviet Union, and Inkeles and Smith (1974), in a study of modernity in several developing countries, noted a new set of experiences and attitudes among the more modern: They were more likely to read newspapers; participate in egalitarian relationships with women; communicate with a larger world than the local community; and believe in flexibility, self-direction, and choice.

The comparable theme in women's lives is less acceptance of the traditional sex role system and an interest in equality and "feminism" that plays out in assuming part of the breadwinner role. Thus, modernity in women's roles has largely been studied through the adoption of multiple roles, meaning the combination of employment with marriage and motherhood. "Modern" women usually will have limited their fertility, gained further education, and delayed marriage as well as pursued employment beyond early adulthood. Adoption of multiple roles in this sense has been copiously documented on an aggregate level for the United States by Oppenheimer (1970), Smith (1979), and Spain and Bianchi (1996). Cross-national studies show broad similarities in the impact of modernization on women's lives—greater longevity, fewer children, more education, and more paid employment (Giele & Smock, 1977; Kahne & Giele, 1992). Studies of college alumnae pinpoint the pioneer cohorts. Rather than focus on the coming of modern attitudes and personal traits, this research takes the adoption of multiple roles as the mark of innovation in the life course patterns of 20th-century women (Gerson, 1985; Giele 1993; Giele & Pischner, 1994; Goldin, 1995).

New sequential patterns. Use of sequence to identify innovative patterns has been less prominent than efforts to link deviance from the normative life course to unfavorable outcomes (Hogan, 1978), but a decade of work suggests that the negative impact of a disordered life sequence is not at all clear (Marini, Shin, & Raymond, 1989). If anything, the normative trend may be toward a less clearly ordered sequence of life events overall. Modell, Furstenberg, and Hershberg (1976), in their study of Philadelphia youths in the 19th century, discovered that a typical sequence of finishing education, gaining employment, and then getting married became less common in younger groups. Hogan (1981) found that such sequencing also became less common among veterans of World War II, especially among those from rural and blue-collar origins, because they delayed employment and gained further education after having married. On the other hand,

Blair-Loy (1996), in her research on American women financial executives, discovered that pathways to success became more rigidly ordered among younger age cohorts; it is now extremely rare for senior women to have worked part-time or to have spent time outside the labor force.

➢ EXPLANATIONS FOR INNOVATION IN THE LIFE COURSE

Whatever the patterns of innovation that are uncovered, the theoretical challenge is to explain why they occurred in one period rather than another and in some groups and not others. The explanations proposed generally fall into three classes that relate to the basic paradigm of the life course presented in Chapter 1. The first type of explanation focuses on *human agency* and the motivations that characterize the pioneers. A second type notes the *social linkages* between a person's intimate world and his or her distinctive life course adaptation. A third interpretation uncovers an association between *cultural and temporal location* and its impact on the life course. Life course patterns are seen as adaptations to circumstances, or what Thomas and Znaniecki (1918-1920/1927) termed "the solution of a situation," in which the person reacted to objective conditions with preexisting attitudes and defined the situation accordingly. Or, in the words of Clausen (1991), "The life course is shaped by the interaction of cultural and social structural features with physical and psychological attitudes of the individual and by the commitments and purposive efforts of the individual" (p. 805). Elder (1985) summed up the process as one of *adaptation:* "Crises may arise when claims are elevated well beyond control of outcomes. Novel adaptations to crisis situations are ways of dealing with resources and options in order to achieve control over the environment" (p. 42). Such efforts to regain control are prompted not only by the individual's inability to produce life outcomes that are in line with expectations but also by large-scale historical events and processes such as depression, war, and migration.

Human Agency: Motivations of the Innovators

At least four types of motivation are commonly given as explanations for why pioneers invent new life patterns: (a) a change in moral outlook or consciousness, (b) an attempt to meet economic needs and new threats to survival, (c) a conscious or unconscious search for improvement in quality of life, and (d) a need to cope with uncertainty. All of these factors interact and feed back on each other to reinforce traditional roles or stimulate new ones.

Changing moral outlook and consciousness. Beliefs usually are the most prominent reason given for why reformers mount their social movements. In the case of the women's movement of the past century, the largest single contingent were the temperance women who were drawn to a cause that would protect men and families from the ravages of alcohol. Women's temperance leaders were shaped by the moral outlook of small midwestern towns and the frontier Methodist, Baptist, and Presbyterian churches and reported more experience of personal family losses such as the early deaths of children or husbands. Suffrage leaders, on the other hand, were more likely to be from eastern urban centers or the West and from established Congregational, Unitarian, or Episcopal churches or the Quakers, and they more often reported educational or career frustration. These differences were consistent with the ideologies and organizational structures and strategies of the two movements (Giele, 1995).

In research on contemporary women's life course innovation, an egalitarian sex role ideology (believing that wives can have careers and that mothers can work) appears to be an important foundation for a woman herself to be positively oriented toward a career (Bielby, 1978). Women's greater numbers in the labor force have been explained as a grassroots movement that began "in the hearts and minds of women" (Uchitelle, 1994) and that "broke the feminine mystique" (Nasar, 1992). In Heilbrun's (1988) eloquent terms, writing about women poets, "Only in the last third of the twentieth century have women broken through to a realization of the narratives that have been controlling their lives. Women poets of one generation—those born between 1923 and 1932—can now be seen to have transformed the autobiographies of women's lives, to have expressed, and suffered for expressing, what women had not earlier been allowed to say" (p. 60).

Economic and survival needs. Probably the most prevalent reason given for women's life course innovation is the economic necessity of work. Women of the 1850s-1870s sought women's right to control their own earnings in the face of irresponsible husbands or fathers who might squander their wages. During the Depression of the 1930s, women went into the labor force not only to supplement their incomes but also to meet heightened standards of consumption; it was much more legitimate for them to work than for their children to work (Wandersee, 1988). Today, women work for many types of economic reasons—as a result of divorce, to put children through college, or to reach a higher standard of living (Oppenheimer, 1979).

Economists since the 1960s have understood women's rising employment as the product of rising demand in women's occupations and women's increased education and higher wages whereby women's leisure became more costly and they chose paid employment instead. Women were more likely to be employed if they had more education, less family responsibilities, and less household incomes. Conversely, they were more likely to be out of the labor force if they had less than 12 years of education, were married, had more than one child, and had incomes above the mean (Cain, 1966; Mincer, 1962). Recent analyses have elaborated a dynamic dimension to the understanding of women's employment decisions. Change in marital status, taxes, and transfers result in a complex interaction of internal and contextual factors in the employment decision. Women who already are working are surprisingly insensitive to changes in the wage rate, suggesting that women work not only for income but also for important intrinsic and nonpecuniary reasons (Mroz, 1987; Van der Klaauw, 1996).

Well-being, satisfaction, and personal control. An increasingly common explanation for women's dual careers is the search for a better quality of life, by which is meant a greater sense of well-being, satisfaction, freedom from depression, and personal control. These motivations crop up repeatedly in the accounts of those women who have adopted multiple roles. Helson and Picano (1990) found that the Mills College graduates with multiple roles had better health and greater satisfaction. In a study of the college class of 1961 surveyed by the National Opinion Research Center at graduation and 7 years later in 1968, when the respondents were roughly 28 years old, Baker and Sween (1982) discovered that the young women were deciding about how to coordinate families with careers. Their actions were based not only on earlier family/career choices but also on the extent to which their career activities had been rewarding. Because these changes in women's life patterns were occurring *before* the new women's movement peaked in 1970, they suggest that a search for more satisfying life patterns may be part of the reason why women have gravitated toward the new multiple roles.

Numerous studies have documented links among multiple roles, greater sense of personal control, and better mental health. Barnett and Rivers (1996) found that the happiest women feel both mastery and pleasure. A sense of mastery is reinforced by competence and autonomy at work, whereas pleasure is reinforced by strong emotional ties to family. Barnett, Kibria, Baruch, and Pleck (1991) concluded that multiple role involvement nourishes women's subjective well-being because each role provides an independent source of positive experience, the benefit of which accrues regardless of the nature or quality of the other roles a woman occupies. In their follow-up of women studied in 1956 and 1986, Moen, Dempster-McClain, and Williams (1992) also found that occupying multiple roles and doing volunteer work was positively related to health and social integration. Heilbrun (1988), in her study of women writers, touched on the issue of multiple roles in noting the traditional ideal of selflessness but also importance of activities in both the public and private domains: "The hardest part of all for women to admit and to defend is that woman's selfhood, the right to her own story, depends upon her ability to act in the public domain" (p. 17).

Coping with uncertainty. The newest explanation for life course innovation in contemporary society is adaptation to the need for contingency planning and uncertainty itself. The trend away from traditional patterns is apparent on many different fronts—education, work, marriage, and childbearing. In the United States, even rather traditional husbands encourage their wives and daughters to get educations and have professions as "insurance policies" in the event that something unforeseen happens to the principal breadwinners. Women themselves can compare their situation and the society around them to the lives of their own mothers and see that conditions have changed drastically. Less time is needed to perform necessary household tasks. Nor can household production produce much cash income if there is no market worker in the family. Moreover, numbers of children have declined and the amount of time requiring a mother in the home has shrunk just as women's life expectancy has increased. In addition, it is becoming increasingly evident that time out of the labor force worsens chances for later reentry. These trends suggest that the multiple role pattern represents a positive *adaptation* to longer life expectancy and economic uncertainty and not just the "need for two incomes." Thoits (1987) observed that uncertainty in the form of uncontrollable or involuntary events such as natural catastrophes, family crises, or plant shutdowns are likely facilitators of role bargaining because they destabilize established patterns and sometimes alter power relationships, thus making room for renegotiation and innovation. These new behaviors, when routinized, then begin to take on a normative power of their own. But the possibilities for role negotiation and innovation are more limited among those who lack financial power, educations, and complex social networks.

Ott (1992) theorized that uncertain conditions make household partners avoid a very high degree of specialization by gender because it is risky if they become separated or their contractual obligations to each other are weakened. If partners *think ahead* to Time 2 while still in Time 1, then they avoid rigid specialization and opt instead for greater flexibility. Thus, women's multiple roles, to the extent that they allow both men and women to respond more flexibly to unforeseen events in work and family life, can be interpreted as one of the major adaptations to uncertainty in modern life. Or, in the words of Thomas and Znaniecki (1918-1920/1927), "The individual must be trained not for conformity, but for efficiency, not for stability, but for creative evolution" (Volume 2, p. 1906).

Linked Lives: Diversity and Generalization of New Life Patterns

Throughout the new research on life course patterns as adaptation is a dual theme of diversity and generalization. Diversity most often arises in connection with black women's roles. Many observers have noted that black women always have combined family activity with working for a living. Thus, the new feminism associated with white women's emancipation from the home hardly seems that "new"; in fact, black women seem to have pointed the way (Bell, 1974; Giele & Gilfus, 1990). Heilbrun (1988) noted that black women writers escaped the dilemma of achievement versus domesticity. She quoted Toni Morrison:

> It seems to me there's an enormous difference in the writing of black and white women. Aggression is not as new to black women as it is to white women. Black women seem able to combine the nest and the adventure.

They don't see conflicts in certain areas as do white women. They are both
safe harbor and ship: they are both inn and trail. We, black women, do
both. We don't find these places, these roles, mutually exclusive. (p. 61)

Social scientists such as Collins (1990) and Higginbotham and Weber
(1997) have explained the different stance of black women toward multiple
roles as the result of the legacy of slavery and racial discrimination that
always have made the position of black men insecure. Thus, black women
do not expect marriage to support them. Instead, they rely on their own
work to be self-supporting and think of marriage as a separate undertaking.
Latino women, on the other hand, are more likely to be working within the
context of a traditional patriarchal culture that has expected women to be
family caregivers and men to be heads of their families (Segura, 1997).
When Mexican immigrant women go to work, they do so because their
husbands cannot support their families. When Cuban immigrant women
work, it is to help their husbands establish businesses that eventually permit
the wives to stay at home once again (Fernandez-Kelly, 1997). Similarly,
Asian women immigrants work as domestics or service workers in the
context of a traditional patriarchal family system (Chow, 1997; Glenn,
1986). Unlike African American women who seem more independent in
job holding vis-à-vis their men, the Latin American and Asian American
women appear to be following a trajectory of modernization in women's
roles that leads from menial work on behalf of the family to "lady of the
house" when middle class status is first achieved and then perhaps to
professional status in the third generation.
    All of these differences among minority and majority women's role
adaptations are a signal that society comprises various subpopulations who
accommodate to their situations in alternative ways. Thus, although the
modal pattern may shift, a variety of other patterns also can be found. It is
an open question which of these will turn out to be innovations that become
institutionalized and which are transitional adaptations to limited resources
and temporary conditions.
    Another side of the coin, an opposite trend toward a more abstract
sense of self and greater generalization of idealized life patterns, also has
been noted. Meyer (1986) hypothesized that the reason life satisfaction has
become such a general goal in modern society is that the institutionalized
life course that is demanded by the modern state is not necessarily connected to the subjective self. There is less psychological virtue attached to

identification with family, local community, ethnic group, or religious denomination, and the upshot is that individuals are more likely to identify with state, nation, or their work. The principle of the universalized subjective self becomes an integrative mechanism in a complex society that frees the individual from ascribed boundaries of family, ethnicity, religion, and even gender.

In 1996 and 1997, in the context of the new welfare law that imposes time limits on benefits and work requirements even for mothers of young children, the institutionalized life course works against diversity of adaptation and generalizes one pattern to fit all. Thus, a challenge to future life course research is to assess what may be the negative effects of such life course generalizations by investigating overwork, underemployment, and the strains of dealing with contingency work and chronic uncertainty.

Cultural and Temporal Location: Variations in Impact

The effects on the life course of living in one cultural or temporal context rather than another are tested in different ways. Cultural impact is seen by comparing the reactions of people from different backgrounds to similar social and institutional settings. The impact of a historical period, however, is best understood through the adaptations of persons from similar cultural backgrounds who differ by age and cohort.

Cultural location. Cultural influence is evident in cross-national surveys of sex role attitudes and women's labor force behavior. A 1988-1989 survey of attitudes toward women's work in Germany, Great Britain, and the United States found that a majority in all these countries approved so long as the care of children was not an issue. But when asked their opinions about whether a woman should stay home or work if there was a preschool child, the answers varied by country. In Germany, 74% of women answered that the woman should stay home compared to 66% in the United Kingdom and 50% in the United States (Alwin, Braun, & Scott, 1992). Women's labor force behavior shows similar variation in the 12 countries of the European Union (EU). Although roughly 90% of all women with graduate degrees are employed throughout the EU, there is much more variation when it comes to women who have only a compulsory level of education

and a child under age 14 years living at home. More than 50% of such
women in Denmark, Portugal, Belgium, and the United Kingdom are
employed compared to less than 40% in Spain, Greece, the Netherlands,
and Ireland (European Commission, 1995). With Holst, I found in comparisons of American and West German women's levels of employment
that *within* the two countries, the reasons why women were employed were
similar. But *between* the two countries, the 10% to 15% lower employment
rate of German women seemed to be explained by differences in general
cultural and institutional conditions that provided more public benefits to
families and were less favorable to employment of mothers (Giele & Holst,
1997).

   Temporal location. The same historical period and socioeconomic
climate also can have different effects depending on whether it is experienced in childhood, youth, or early adulthood (Ryder, 1965; Stewart &
Healy, 1989). Events during *childhood* shape basic values and attitudes
about gender role that derive primarily from the family of origin. Thus, a
girl growing up in a traditional family with her mother in a traditional
homemaker role is likely to value that role and want to follow in her
mother's footsteps. In *youth,* when the person is constructing an individual
identity, norms define the appropriate work, marital, and civic duties that
are associated with manhood and femininity. These norms vary with the
historical period and have a type of moral force (Stewart & Healy, 1989).
In *adulthood,* economic conditions and employment opportunities shape a
woman's actual marital, maternal, and work behaviors. In good times as
well as hardship, job opportunities can make a woman override her values
derived from childhood about the traditional role of women and encourage
her to follow a new path that departs from that of her mother (Giele, 1993).
   The evolving life patterns of college women display these principles.
Each succeeding age group of women confronted the new life pattern of
women at a younger stage of the life course with different effects on the
model that the women adopted. Thus, women born in the 1910s and 1920s
did not feel the impact of the women's movement of the 1960s until they
already were past age 40 years and so continued the homemaker pattern.
Women born in the 1930s and 1940s still were in their 20s and 30s when
they discovered women's changing roles, so it was possible for them to
forge a new dual-career pattern. But for women born after 1950, the new

women's role was a reality by the time they left high school; they generally delayed marriage and childbearing to establish their careers.

> ## ➢ SUMMARY AND CONCLUSIONS

The importance of life course innovation is that it creates uncertainty and establishes new milestones for individuals living in changing times. At the same time, it demands the adjustment or creation of social policies that will accommodate and institutionalize the new life patterns that have evolved. Although innovation in the life course has not been a clearly recognized object for research, there is considerable knowledge available about changes that have occurred in retirement age, the transition to adulthood, and the roles of women.

Two major conceptual advances have resulted from the analysis of women's changing roles. First, the phenomenon, when reviewed from a life course perspective, began to be defined as innovation rather than deviance. So long as the issue of wives and mothers working was conceived as a problem of role conflict or of a midlife stage, there was little progress in understanding because the problem was located in the women them-selves—their role choices and their development. Only when women's changing life patterns were reconceived as a positive adaptation to several interlocking circumstances (their own needs, the realities of the larger social and economic settings, and the demands of their immediate jobs and families) could the more complex analysis occur that would uncover the reasons that some became pioneers. Second, a specific indicator (the adoption of multiple roles) helped to pinpoint when and in what groups innovation had occurred. The dramatic change was concentrated in the period from the 1940s to the 1980s when women's labor force participation almost doubled from 35% to 67%. The innovating pioneers were concen-trated in a specific cohort born between the 1930s and 1940s; they invented their new life patterns during a particular historical period from the 1960s to 1970s and were in early and middle adulthood at the time.

Using the life course perspective has brought new analytic methods to the study of inventive life patterns. The most useful research design has been age cohort analysis. Comparison *across* cohorts has helped to pinpoint the pioneers. Comparison *within* cohorts between traditionals and innovators has explicated the processes by which innovation comes about. The most illuminating data have been detailed life histories or longitudinal records of major life events. By constructing life histories from matrices or chains of significant life events that contain markers by age or calendar time, the researcher is in a position to analyze the factors in innovation that relate to age of the individual, historical conditions, and the cohort norms that have shaped the person's response.

Out of the various interpretations of why life patterns have changed has come a clear understanding of the ways in which individual motivation, social structure, and cultural and temporal location shape a person's life. There are many rich and persuasive accounts of the role that moral consciousness, economic need, dissatisfaction, and uncertainty have had in motivating individuals to devise new ways in which to live. However, even while norms shift to reflect new ways, there is simultaneous recognition that not everyone takes the same path and that there are important variants among different racial, ethnic, and socioeconomic groups. At the same time, coupled with diversity in modern society, there is a trend toward generalization and institutionalization of some tracks more than others so that, for example, in the scheduling of women's lives, it is becoming ever more common to expect mothers to work and to frame social policy accordingly.

Whether an innovation "takes" by becoming widespread in a given society or group is dependent on cultural and temporal locations. The issue is the degree to which a change in the statistical norm will be converted into a change in normative expectations. Cultural location can either facilitate or retard the conversion. Even highly educated women with children who are very likely to work in some societies are less likely to work in others because of more conservative sex role ideology or the presence of alternative institutional structures such as widespread public benefits that supplement the male breadwinner role. The individuals' temporal location (age at time of exposure to the innovation-producing conditions) also can hasten or retard adoption of new life patterns. Exposure in adolescence or early adulthood to the ferment that produces change is likely to breed a pioneer, whereas for an older person the formative period will already have passed and, for a younger person, will not have yet come.

In the end, one asks how the study of life course innovation can benefit society and social policy so that people can live happier and more productive lives even under conditions of constant change. The research agenda to answer these questions is only now being formulated. What one learns from the remarkable recent changes in women's lives is that multiple roles have brought better health and satisfaction to many. But we have yet to explore fully what also may be some of the less favorable correlates—overwork, less time for family and community, and continuing uncertainty about the future. We also have to expand the study of role innovation to other groups by bringing similar methods and analysis to men's changing lives and the evolving life patterns of children, adolescents, and elders.

➢ NOTES

1. I conceived of the project and chaired the sessions. The members of the seminar were Lotte Bailyn, Rosalind C. Barnett, Grace K. Baruch, Anne Carter, John Demos, Carol Gilligan, Carolyn G. Heilbrun, Hilda Kahne, Jean Baker Miller, Malkah Notman, Samuel D. Osherson, Joseph H. Pleck, Kristine Rosenthal, Barbara Sicherman, and Beatrice B. Whiting.

2. Postgraduate education was counted as an attribute of the individual at age 35 years, not as a current life event.

Chapter 11

Linking History
and Human Lives

GLEN H. ELDER, JR.
LISA A. PELLERIN

No feature of the emerging life course paradigm is more distinctive than its attention to the relation between historical change and life patterns. As Ryder (1965) so aptly noted, "Each new cohort makes fresh contact with the contemporary social heritage and carries the impress of the encounter through life" (p. 844). Environmental variation always implies the potential for life course variation, and the latter in aggregate form has the potential for altering the social order. Each cohort "is a possible intermediary in the [social] transformation process, a vehicle for introducing new postures" (p. 844). From a macro perspective, researchers study the intersection of history with lives to understand not only how the cohort has been shaped by its past but also how the cohort will shape its future. The central task is to move beyond cohort studies to the actual

AUTHORS' NOTE: The senior author acknowledges support by the National Institute of Mental Health (MH 41327, MH 43270, and MH 51361), a contract with the U.S. Army Research Institute, a grant from the Department of Veterans Affairs Merit Review program, research support from the John D. and Catherine T. MacArthur Foundation Research Network on Successful Adolescent Development Among Youth in High-Risk Settings, and a Research Scientist Award (MH 00567).

investigation of a particular form of historical change, both transitory and enduring.

This chapter addresses the task of linking social history and human lives. We begin with a brief description of three strategies that have been used in such work: generational analysis, cohort comparisons, and the assessment of a type or form of social change. This is followed by a detailed discussion of two models of analysis: outcome based and event based. The second model asks how a particular type of social change makes a difference in the life course and thus represents the preferred strategy for specifying linkages between times and lives.

The first and most critical step in designing a study of the impact of historical change is the formulation of the research question and theoretical model, as it is for any study. Questions that do not explicitly include the influence of historical change are not likely to generate research that will illuminate such influence. Following this discussion of historically informed questions, we take up the challenge of constructing a theoretical model of the social process, whether short term and disjunctive or long term and evolutionary.

The second major step addresses a series of conceptual and operational issues in the area of measurement such as conceptualizing the historical change of interest and locating it precisely in historical time. In this chapter, we use the term "event" broadly to include the evolutionary social change process as well as duration- and location-specific transitions within it such as a plant closing in a community within a generalized process of industrial modernization. Hareven's (1982) study of the collapse of the historic Amoskeag textile mill and its human consequences illustrates this type of change. An event-based study always focuses on a definable "event" of social change, be it short term and disjunctive or long term and evolutionary.

In many cases, an existing data set may be the best or only research option. Because these data typically were not collected or archived with current objectives in mind, the challenge for the life course analyst is to fit the research question to the data set through a recasting process (Elder, Pavalko, & Clipp, 1993). We describe the recasting process in detail, the pros and cons of working with both retrospective and prospective data (see Scott & Alwin's chapter in this volume [Chapter 5]), and the decision factors on whether a recasting effort is justified.

The second part of the chapter focuses on the challenges of assessing historical change, using specimen studies of war mobilization and economic decline. We begin with a study of war mobilization based on the Terman study archive (Elder et al., 1993) to illustrate an attempt to assess a change process that was of no theoretical interest to the original investigator. The next specimen includes studies of the effects of the Depression and World War II on two cohorts, using the Oakland and Berkeley study archives (Elder, 1981). These archives included *relevant* historical data that had not been structured or coded for the task of testing the effects of change. The chapter concludes with the Iowa Youth and Families Project (Conger & Elder, 1994) to illustrate the initiation of a social change study in rural America, with emphasis on the 1980s Farm Crisis. This study uses retrospective reports to index prior change (e.g., year in which farm was lost) and also prospective data collection to assess the continuing impact of the change on children's lives.

> ➢ FRAMING THE STUDY

Three issues are central to the task of framing a life course study to investigate historical forces of one type or another. First is the issue of getting the best available handle on the social change of interest. The second issue concerns the value of giving thought to the particular event and change process in the question formulation. This formulation also is influenced by the available data, and thus the third issue concerns the match between research question or analytic model and the data.

Generations, Cohorts, and Social Change

Investigators have used three basic strategies for linking history and lives: (a) compare the generations, (b) compare birth cohorts and the subgroups within them, and (c) measure historical change and assess its effects. Each strategy represents an improvement on the one before in that each new strategy addressed major limitations of its predecessor.

In one of the 20th century's classic studies in the social sciences, *The Polish Peasant in Europe and America,* Thomas and Znaniecki (1918-1920/1927) sought to relate the lives of Polish immigrants to their times through the concept of immigration generation—foreign born as first generation, their native-born children as second generation, and so on. They also used another concept of generation, that of the kinship relation of parents and offspring. Although successful in relating the experiences of one generation to another, they were less successful in relating the lives of the study members to their historical times. The reason stems from the temporal limitations of generational distinctions.

Generation represents a "polysemous" concept (Kertzer, 1983) with diverse definitions that are used even within a single study. These include generation as a position within a continuum of kinship descent, generation as a synonym for birth cohort (e.g., the baby boom generation), generation as a synonym for life stage (e.g., the college student generation), and generation as a label for a historical period (a cultural generation). Of these, all but the first are imprecise and colloquial.

Even when the term "generation" is carefully focused on kinship, the imprecise temporality of generational location is problematic. Members of a specific generation may vary in age by as much as 40 years (Figure 11.1). When three-generation families are sampled at a point in time, a sizable proportion of the parent and grandparent generations will have the same ages. The same overlap in ages applies to members of the parent and child generations. Such age similarity implies a common historical location and a corresponding temporal relation to major historical events.

Generational membership or position may be less influential on beliefs or behavior than are shared historical location and related experiences. The differing influence of generation and age status becomes especially confusing when the two rank orders yield opposing results, as when some members of a parent generation are younger than some members of the child generation. An example of this type of confusion comes from a study of female lineages in a black community of Los Angeles (Burton & Bengtson, 1985). The birth of a child to the teenage daughter of a young mother created a large disparity between age and kinship status, between being young and facing the prospects of grandparental child care obligations. Four out of five of these young grandmothers actually refused to accept such obligations, shifting the burden up the generational ladder to the great-grandmothers.

The strategy of comparing birth cohorts offers a more precise handle on locating people temporally in relation to social change, but it does no more than locate the change processes. Research based on cohort-sequential designs provides estimates of social change by isolating age, period, and cohort effects (Schaie, 1965; cf. Schaie, 1984). Of these, cohort and period effects are historical in nature. History takes the form of a period

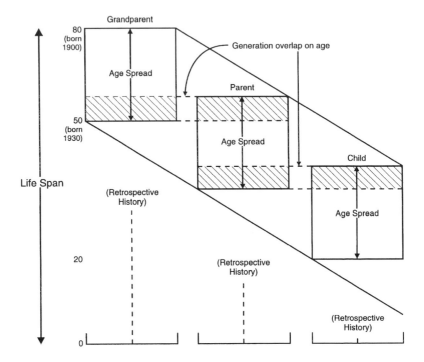

Figure 11.1. Three Generations in a Survey: Cross-Sectional

effect when the influence of a social change or event is relatively uniform across successive cohorts. Secular trends in the scheduling of marriages and first births across the 20th century are largely an expression of large-scale period effects. History takes the form of a cohort effect when social change differentiates the life patterns of successive cohorts. Thus, Americans who were born just before the 1930s were affected by Depression hardships more adversely than were those who were 10 years older (Elder, 1979). Age effects occur through the process of maturation or aging.

A cohort-sequential design allows estimation of the relative influence of historical effects but generally leaves the meaning of these estimated effects open to speculation. This inability to induce the meaning of effects typically is based on uncertainty regarding the more potent aspects of the environment. Without being certain about which aspects of the environment are salient, it is impossible to be certain about the mechanism by which the environment alters the course and substance of lives. For example, a study of first births in America concludes that "period factors increase or decrease childbearing at all ages and for all subgroups" (Rindfuss, Morgan, & Swicegood, 1984, p. 368), but the range of potential influences under the "period" umbrella is so great that no conclusion can be drawn about specific factors or causal processes.

Another limitation to the comparison of birth cohorts is the implicit assumption of intracohort homogeneity. As Mannheim (1952b) warned, "The fact that people are born at the same time . . . does not in itself involve similarity of location; what does create a similar location is that they are in a position to experience the same events" (p. 297). Within each cohort, class, race, and gender are likely to differentiate experience, as are geographic location and other variables. Depression hardship varied greatly between the 1930s middle and working classes (Elder, 1974).

The third strategy, measurement of historical change and assessment of its effects, directly addresses the need for contextual understanding. All three approaches have value, but the most critical in linking history to human lives is a measure of the change process itself. Longitudinal data offer rich opportunities for this type of assessment. We now turn to the design of studies that directly assess the effects of historical change.

Stating the Research Question and Theoretical Model

There are two basic models for studying social change in the life course. The first, which is referred to here as Model A (Figure 11.2), focuses on an outcome of interest. The research task is to assess the influence of distal and proximal antecedent variables that are theoretically relevant to this outcome. A historical event may be included as one of these antecedent variables, but the research effort will not assess all primary aspects of the change. Consequently, the change's impact will be underestimated.

The process by which a historical change influences lives is not a focus in this model. As such, the likelihood of uncovering the specifics of this process is small. In addition, because only one outcome is studied, the design fails to capture the full range of influences that stem from a particular type of social change, from change in work to change in family. A single social change may have multiple and diverse effects. Thus, drastic

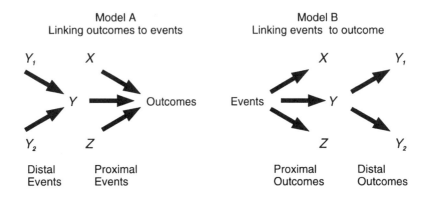

Figure 11.2. Studying Social Change in the Life Course: Two Models

income loss in the Depression exposed children to greater household responsibilities, increased the emotional salience of mothers, and accelerated the social independence of boys (Elder, 1974).

In *The Civic Culture*, Almond and Verba (1963) used a cross-national sample to study the antecedents of political competence in adults. With an age range of at least 40 years in each sample, the authors could have indexed exposure to major events of the 20th century such as the two world wars and the Depression. Instead, they focused on modernization and civic culture. Involvement in decision making within the family, school, and workplace, along with with formal education, stood out as the primary antecedent factors in the life histories of politically competent citizens. Historical forces, such as increasing levels of participation in formal education and the influences of wartime patriotism, were unstudied. Model B, by contrast, begins with the historical event or change process of interest and traces its influence through proximal and distal outcomes. By focusing on the consequences of a type of social change for the life course, an event design pursues the implications of change wherever they may lead. Consequences typically branch out across time, generating a number of outcomes. Proximal consequences tend to emerge from an account of the change itself and then produce consequences of their own for the life course.

The event design relates history and social change to lives and personalities, outlining the flow of influence from macrohistorical developments to the world of the individual, the family, and the peer group. Thomas and Znaniecki (1918-1920/1927) followed this approach, as did the senior author of this chapter in *Children of the Great Depression* (Elder, 1974). For example, Thomas and Znaniecki (1918-1920/1927) showed that emigration and resettlement of Polish immigrants in urban centers initiated a breakdown of traditional norms and a period of family disorganization. These family dynamics, in turn, had consequences for individual behavior. Promiscuity and juvenile delinquency were common among the adolescent children of disorganized families.

Model B requires special sensitivity on the researcher's part to the possible impact of historical forces. However, the outcome perspective of Model A could be used as the initial step in a discovery process. Like a large fishing net, Model A research may collect a variety of influences on the selected outcome without the researcher having to anticipate them. A historical change found to be influential in an outcome study could then be used as the basis for an event-based study. Unfortunately, this two-step strategy seldom is followed.

Use of Model B both generates and requires a theoretical model for the microprocesses that carry the influence of events into lives. Each of these microprocesses could be elaborated by adding other factors, as in a Model A design. In *Children of the Great Depression,* the senior author investigated the relationship between drastic family income loss and children's behavioral outcomes. The microprocesses at work within the family were (a) a change in the household economy (more labor intensive), (b) a change in relationships (the husband-wife balance of power), and (c) a change in social expectations (social strains, anomie). These three adaptations were mediated by resources brought to the crisis situation by family members, both personal and social. Similar models were developed for the Berkeley study of Depression influences and the Iowa study of the 1980s Farm Crisis.

Five concepts are useful in thinking about the interaction between social change and lives: (a) control cycles, (b) situational imperatives, (c) the accentuation principle, (d) the life stage distinction, and (f) the concept of interdependent lives. The first three concepts refer to the correspondence between a changing environment and the life course. Using the terminology of Murray, Barrett, and Homburger (1938), this correspondence refers to the environmental press–individual need relationship between the situation and person. A control cycle involves attempts to regain control of one's situation across life changes. Situational imperatives represent the behavioral requirements or demands of the new situation. The accentuation principle refers to an amplification of individual and relationship attributes, such as coping skills and marital quality, during transitional periods. Poor coping skills and low marital quality often are accentuated during times of stress.

The life stage distinction implies that the effects of social change are likely to vary in type and relative influence, depending on where people find themselves in their lives. The concept of interdependent lives sensitizes analysis to the indirect experience of social change via family members such as children's experience of war mobilization via the enlistment of older brothers.

Conceptual and Measurement Issues

Once a decision has been made to use a social change framework, the investigator is faced with decisions concerning the type of data that will be needed to address the research question (Figure 11.3). The options depend in part on the elapsed time between the event of interest and the time of data collection.

If the event is current or anticipated, new prospective longitudinal data may be collected. This is the ideal situation because the research question informs the entire process. Although ideal, launching a longitudinal study has its costs. Because the full extent of outcomes is unknown, data across many domains are needed to capture the broad range of effects. These data also will need to be collected over a long time span to capture the distal effects.

Needless to say, such projects are extremely expensive and complex. Both time and labor requirements often are so demanding that the originating investigator collects the data but is unable to carry out the actual analysis. (This is, in fact, why there are massive data archives, such as the Berkeley Guidance Study, in which whole categories of data were left uncoded.) The result of this effort, however, is a rich source for addressing research questions, some of which transcend the original purpose of the study.

If the social change of interest is recent or memorable (e.g., wartime experience), then new retrospective data may be collected about the event along with retrospective and current data on outcomes. A major disadvan-

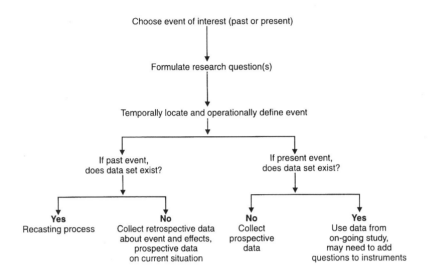

Figure 11.3. Steps in the Design of Event-Based Research

tage of retrospective data concerns their accuracy or general quality, particularly regarding emotional states or behavior. Respondents either do not accurately remember this information or what they do remember are recent constructions of the past states. Retrospective data on work, family, and residential histories are more reliable, especially when techniques are used that maximize the accuracy of recalled facts such as the life history calendar (Freedman, Thornton, Camburn, Alwin, & Young-DeMarco, 1988).

Numerous longitudinal data archives (including both prospective and retrospective data) are available for life course research, but many of these were collected by investigators who had no interest in the historical context (social change), an element essential to life course study. These archives still may be used profitably if reformulated by recasting, a process that involves both coding and recoding of archival data and, if necessary, adjustment of the research question to better fit the data available. A data archive may provide an option for recasting when answers to open-ended questions, letters, and marginal comments are stored (such materials can be coded for the first time) or if original detailed responses are available (including previously coded material that can be recoded).

Investigators seek to maximize the fit between their research questions and the best available data at hand, but there is generally some disparity between questions and data. As noted earlier, the process of working with archival data typically involves adjustments on both questions and data. We reformulate questions in light of the data at hand and frequently recast data for a better fit with our questions.

The process of working with archival data entails a series of steps. As noted, the first step is *problem specification* because it is essential to have a well-honed sense of the problem before beginning the *search for an appropriate data set or archive.* With the options surveyed, the stage is set for *preparing a research proposal* that makes the very best case for the goodness of fit between data and question. *Initial analysis of the data* may be carried out in preparation for a research proposal along with a thorough inventory of at least the coded data. This overview can provide evidence for why a *recasting* effort must be made, and it might indicate the need to seek other data.

Even if an archive seems well matched for the desired analysis, the extent of the match and the coding requirements can only be determined through an inventory of both coded and uncoded data. Interviews, home observations, and letters may provide a source of uncoded data and allow lines of inquiry not anticipated by the originating investigator. In addition to its usefulness in deciding to use an archive, preparation of the inventory can be considered the first step in the actual recasting process. The inventory establishes a map of the archival territory in relation to research objectives and enables more effective use of resources. It answers the following questions. What relevant materials are uncoded? What data are coded but not prepared for analysis? What coded data are useful as they are?

As strange as it may seem, many longitudinal data sets were not originally archived to be analyzed longitudinally. Instead, the data were structured for cross-sectional analyses at each wave. The second step in recasting, then, is to assemble the social data in life records. A life record is a chronology of major life events and experiences including trajectories of interest to the researcher such as the socioeconomic career of a family, the work histories of family members, household composition over time, and the quality of relationships over time.

Life records have been compiled using three basic methods. In the first, a life record is produced by the respondent from a personal perspective, as in oral histories (Hareven, 1982). In the second, a life record for one person is produced from the perspective of an informant or a knowledgeable other such as a spouse or confidant. Finally, a life record may be synthesized by a third party, such as a clinician or researcher, using a wide array of materials including written and oral reports from the respondent, vital records, observations, and public documents (see Clausen, 1993, for examples). An advantage of this method is that equivalent data from multiple sources may be compared and discrepancies resolved, resulting in a historically accurate record.

Large data archives often lend themselves to this last method. For example, the Berkeley Guidance Study archive includes data from numerous sources. The intensively studied families were contacted many times each year by a fieldworker, whose field notes became part of the archive. Other data sources include reports by the target children and their mothers, teacher ratings, and letters from various agencies. Once structured into life records, these data are ready for any necessary recoding.

In the next section, we illustrate these processes using as specimens several major studies conducted by the senior author. The specimens represent a range of challenges and adaptive strategies in conducting contextual life course research.

➤ MEASURING HISTORICAL INFLUENCES

Over the past three decades, the senior author has sought ways of addressing the challenging issues of analytic strategy, problem formulation and model construction in life studies, and the fit between question and data in studies of historical change in lives. We provide examples of the path followed in accounts of three different projects: (a) war mobilization and the Terman data archive, (b) the Depression in birth cohorts of the Oakland Growth Study and Berkeley Guidance Study, and (c) a contemporary economic crisis in the lives of rural youths from the Iowa Youth and Families Project.

World War II and the Terman Data Archive

Our use of the Terman data stemmed from an interest in the effects of military experience during World War II on the life course of men, focusing on their emotional and physical health immediately after the return to civilian life and on their long-term patterns of health and aging. With birth years across the first two decades of the 20th century, the Terman sample was especially promising for addressing these interests because 45% of the men reported service in the military.

A psychologist at Stanford University, Lewis Terman launched his study in 1921-1922 to investigate the maintenance of early intellectual superiority over a 10-year period. He selected 857 boys and 671 girls ages 3 to 19 years who had IQs above 135 (Terman & Oden, 1959). The original 10-year study was extended into the adult years for the purpose of determining the life paths of these gifted Californians. A total of 13 waves of data collection have been carried out up to 1992, beginning with interviews of parents and the study members plus an array of tests and inventories (Table 11.1). Data collection in later waves has been accomplished mainly through the use of survey forms mailed to the study members. Primary topics have been education, work, military experience, marriage and family, and achievements.

In addition to completed surveys, an inventory of the files revealed that they contain a rich selection of other data such as news clippings, interviews with parents, questionnaires from spouses, letters from study members, and birth and death certificates. The letters, in particular, add a great deal beyond the often narrow structure of the survey forms. Men shared work and military experience with Terman, frequently in requests for letters of recommendation to prospective employers or for advice on personal matters. The wealth of these materials in the study files provides an opportunity for the user who is not satisfied with the machine-readable data to develop new codes for qualitative analysis.

As mentioned in the previous section, most longitudinal data archives have been organized cross-sectionally as the data waves are completed. The Terman archive is one of these. Thus, recasting the archive for life course use entailed preparation of life records on work, earnings, marriage, parenthood, and health from the computerized data. This work was supplemented with a series of new codes on the life course and historical experience, a task requiring a number of weeks of archival research at the Terman Study Center at Stanford.

A useful first step in historical analysis entails the identification of birth cohorts and their relation to specific events and experiences. By locating study members in history, birth year enables the researcher to place

TABLE 11.1 Terman Longitudinal Sample and Data

Survey Wave	Number of Respondents	Primary Topics
1922	1,528: 857 men, 671 women	Home and school
1928		
1936	1,256: 699 men, 557 women	Education, work, marriage
1940		
1945	1,334: 749 men, 585 women	Military experience
1950	1,271: 716 men, 555 women	
1955	1,286: 716 men, 570 women	Work, marriage, achievements
1960	1,127: 616 men, 511 women	
1972	927: 497 men, 430 women	
1977	812: 426 men, 386 women	Aging, work and retirement, life review
1982	813: 415 men, 398 women	
1986	805: 404 men, 401 women	
1991-1992	Follow-up in progress	

lives in relation to specific conditions and changes such as the onset of World War II. All men in a birth cohort may not have been exposed to similar conditions and changes, but cohorts generally tell us something about the risk of exposure. An analysis of the Terman sample by birth cohort shows that the men were ages 19 to 40 years at the start of war mobilization, with most subject to the draft (Table 11.2). Fewer than half actually served in the military in World War II—50% of the younger men and 35% of the older men—but this enabled service-nonservice comparisons.

Based on this analysis, the archive appeared to be suitable for a study of the effects of wartime mobilization on men's lives. Two problem foci and their research questions were identified. The first concerned time of entry as a problem in men's lives. Both life course theory and empirical findings (Elder, 1987) predicted more disruption and socioeconomic costs from the service for men who entered the war beyond age 30 years. The second line of questions addressed the stressfulness of wartime service and its life course and health effects. Exposure to heavy combat increased the risk of posttraumatic stress symptoms and the likelihood of enduring relationships with fellow veterans (Elder & Clipp, 1988).

The major challenge in using the Terman archive to study the effects of war mobilization stems from Terman's near-total lack of interest in

TABLE 11.2 Age of Terman Men Respondents by Birth Cohorts and by Historical Events

		Age by Birth Cohort (years)	
Year(s)	Event	1900-1910	1911-1920
1914-1918	World War I	4-18	0-7
1921-1922	1920s depression	11-22	1-11
1923-1929	General economic boom	13-29	3-18
1929-1933	Great Depression onset	19-33	9-22
1933-1936	Partial recovery	23-36	13-25
1937-1938	Economic slump	27-38	17-27
1939-1940	Start of war mobilization	29-40	19-29
1941-1943	Major growth of armed forces and war industries	31-43	21-32
1945	End of World War II	35-45	25-34
1950-1953	Korean War	40-53	30-42
1957	Peak of baby boom	47-57	37-46
1963-1973	Vietnam War	53-73	43-62
1973	End of postwar affluence	63-73	53-62

historical influences. Several questions on the duration, timing, and branch of service were included on the information blanks, but no direct questions on war mobilization or experiences were asked in the 1945 or 1950 updates. The questions that were asked did not capture diversity in experience such as the intensity and duration of any combat exposure, location and nature of assignment, or reactions to service. Fortunately, many study members supplemented their survey forms with letters and marginal comments addressing this oversight and volunteering relevant data.

Given that useful data existed, a crucial next step involved a conceptualization of World War II mobilization for the purposes of the study (Elder et al., 1993). With military service and homefront employment as elements of two historical boundaries for World War II, it made sense to define the beginning of the nation's war mobilization with the enactment of the Selective Service Act on September 16, 1940, and the end beyond the formal end of the war in January 1948. The second set of boundaries marks the formal entry of the United States into the war in December 1941 and the Japanese surrender on August 14, 1945 (Figure 11.4). Work histories on the Terman men respondents provided data on pre- and postmobilization employment as well as on their wartime activities.

Military service was only *part* of war mobilization during World War II and did not directly involve the majority of Terman men respondents. Most remained civilians but may have been affected by mobilization in other ways. The Terman life records showed that some men on the homefront were subject to greater stresses and opportunities than they would have experienced in peacetime. For some the war meant long hours, radical occupational shifts, and cross-country relocations, whereas for others it produced relatively little change.

In what way, then, could mobilization be defined? The answer lay in policy documents of the War Manpower Commission and the Selective Service Administration. To achieve goals in wartime, these agencies made explicit determinations as to what constituted mobilization activity. These lists of essential activities formed the basis of coding categories for two levels of civilian mobilization:

1. *civilian activities necessary to war production:* processing or production of materials directly used in conducting war or civilian employment with war agencies or the armed forces; and

2. *civilian activities supporting the war effort:* employment in activities deemed essential for the national health, safety, or interest (other than war production) that supported the war effort including occupations that produced for both civilian and military needs such as mining and agriculture.

The addition of nonmilitary mobilization categories provided an opportunity to investigate the impact of different wartime experiences using a more historically informed coding scheme. Exploring homefront and military mobilization would result in a much broader concept of the original study and a rare opportunity to investigate these competing processes in men's lives.

To achieve this end, usable measures of military service were needed from the follow-up of 1945-1946, a data collection not addressed to wartime experience in a comprehensive manner. As noted previously, the men were not asked directly about their exposure to combat, although they often reported such experiences when answering other questions. We chose to develop suitable codes and apply them to an enriched file of life history

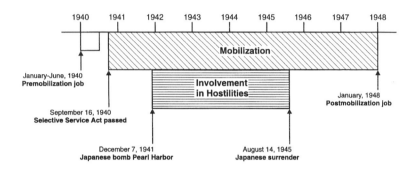

Figure 11.4. U.S. Mobilization and Involvement in Hostilities: World War II

material on the study members. This required permission to photocopy all relevant material in the Terman archive at Stanford. Developing a codebook and applying it to the data would follow. The actual project eventually required four trips to Stanford of about 2 weeks each and nearly a full year of coding.

The extra effort and expense proved worthwhile, however, because recasting the Terman archive for the purposes of this study allowed the proposed research to be carried out at a level beyond that anticipated during the planning stage. This was so because the new coding on combat experiences and homefront employment made more sense when included in a multifaceted account of wartime experience.

From the very beginning, this account included both military and homefront mobilization. A study of this type calls for detailed coding of occupations during the war and its demobilization phase. Despite questions about the completeness and overall quality of work histories across the war years, the Terman data on occupational change stand at the center of the individual files, generously supplemented by letters to and from the Terman staff, career advice from Terman, and news clippings.

Measuring Wartime Experience

Laufer (1985) explored three dimensions of war stress in a study of Vietnam that bear on subsequent symptomatology and behavioral problems—exposure to life-threatening situations, exposure to abusive violence, and participation in episodes of abusive violence. Our conceptual and measurement approach borrowed from this line of thinking by defining combat experience by prolonged exposure to the dying, wounded, and dead and to incoming and outgoing gunfire.

We reviewed the files of a veteran subgroup for the purpose of constructing a military service codebook on six topics:

1. *lifetime military and military-related experiences:* veteran status and type; service before, during, and after World War II; entry and exit information; service career, branch, and unit; medals and education linked to the service (e.g., ROTC, G.I. Bill);

2. *overseas experience before World War II or U.S. involvement:* duty for government, volunteer agency;

3. *homefront experience during World War II:* deferments, conscientious objector status, service with government;

4. *wartime stress:* combat duration in weeks and months; experience of firing at the enemy and of being fired on; exposure to wounded and dead (Allies and enemy); experiences of being wounded, held prisoner, and missing in action (also identified men killed in action [3% of the total sample]);

5. *postwar experiences linked to the war:* civil administration duties during military occupation, medical care for the Allied wounded, medical evaluation for repatriation or emigration; and

6. *domestic exposure to the care of American wounded and the dying:* experience of medical personnel in the sample, separated from those on the front line.

Before coding began, a summary sheet was constructed for each case. This organized all relevant information in a standard format and was necessary because the data were found on numerous documents and were not systematically ordered in any way. An initial draft of the codebook was then applied to a set of cases. Codesheets were then checked, and disparities were discussed. Five such trials led to revisions in the codes that, in turn, produced an improved fit with the data.

Descriptive statistics show that 71% of World War II veterans served overseas and that more than four out of five of them served in a combat theater with some exposure to gunfire and death. Most veterans who served in a combat zone showed evidence of involvement in combat, defined for this study as exposure to gunfire and death or dying. Consistent with the literature, combat veterans were recruited disproportionately from men who entered in the youngest age category. Combat exposure increased the risk of impaired physical health after the war, especially among men who ranked below average on self-esteem and self-confidence before the war, and it markedly increased memories of the war as a highly influential experience in life among men in old age (Elder, Shanahan, & Clipp, 1997). Although combat is less common among late entrants, and although their prewar health equaled that of the early entrants, late mobilization also placed an unusual number at risk of postwar physical decline (Elder, Shanahan, & Clipp, 1994). All of these initial effects have consequences for the later years of health and retirement and, thus, begin to suggest valuable returns from our recasting efforts on health, late-life careers, and wartime experience.

The original decision to develop new codes on wartime experience led to a greatly enlarged set of variables for analysis that extends well beyond combat. For the first time, we had information on the life experiences men brought to World War II and could show that adverse military influences continued for some men well after the end of hostilities. However, military service is only one part of war mobilization, and most of the Terman men respondents remained at work on the homefront. We now turn to efforts to develop occupational codes for these men.

Indexing Homefront Mobilization

Nearly 500 Terman men respondents remained civilians for the entire war period, and a substantial number of the men who entered the service spent time in the civilian workforce. Occupational histories during the years of war mobilization proved to be sufficiently detailed for charting careers across this period and classifying each job in the occupational sequence on mobilization status and other defining characteristics.

Initial reviews of the work histories suggested that it would be possible to identify men directly involved in war-related work from descriptions of their jobs and employers and that life changes due to mobilization might be estimated from evidence of change in work life (e.g., switches in jobs, occupations, and employment sectors) and in work characteristics (from total hours at work per day and week to supervisory responsibility and geographic mobility). This led to the development of codes for six attributes of a job.

The distinction between employment by private business and employment by government is critical in time of war mobilization. Hence, the first category was employer classification. The industrial sector category enabled us to capture changes in type of industry. The occupation category relied on the 1980 U.S. Census procedures for coding industry and occupation. In times of labor shortage, opportunities for advancement and managerial responsibility increase, hence the code for supervision. Because wartime production demands tend to lead to increased work hours, a code for time was included. The sixth job attribute category, war mobilization, was constructed using government policy mandates that distinguish three possibilities: nonmobilized, directly mobilized, and indirectly mobilized.

In addition to these job attributes, codes for job and employer changes and the dates of these changes were included. This information was required for event history analyses on the process of war mobilization. Given the nature of the data archive, the coders have to use their best judgment on whether a job or employer change had occurred, drawing on all available information from the job attributes and related data.

The coding form was designed to capture all job changes for the war period, defined as between September 1940 and December 1947, as well as pre- and postmobilization jobs on both ends of this interval. For the purposes of the study, premobilization refers to the last job held between January and June 1940, and postmobilization refers to the job held in January 1948. Premobilization employment was used as a baseline for assessing changes across the war years. An example is a Terman male respondent who was a nonsupervisory assistant professor of foreign relations in a west coast university before mobilization. During mobilization, he did social science research for the federal government in a national security agency, a directly mobilized position. By war's end, he had moved to a high-level administrative position, from which he took a postmobilization job as a high-level administrator with a private philanthropic foundation. The war clearly had changed his occupational trajectory.

An analysis of the coded data showed that the percentage of Terman male respondents in uniform increased dramatically across the war years, especially between 1942 and 1943, as did the percentage of men who were engaged in civilian activities deemed essential to war production. Still, less than a fifth of the Terman men respondents were involved in such activity. Younger men were more likely than older men to be mobilized directly, either in the military or on the homefront. Mobilization is socially defined as a young person's activity. In terms of military service, draft eligibility favored younger men without family responsibilities. In civilian mobilization, this selection of younger men may reflect the life stage characteristic of being in the market for new opportunities and having less to lose in giving up a current job. It also may reflect family and career barriers to life course change among the older men. Manpower pressures from the top also may have favored the selection of highly educated younger men.

The Terman data archive clearly presented a demanding challenge to our research team, in large part because Terman had little, if any, appreciation for the relevance of historical change as a shaper of human lives. This meant he did not seek to collect data on the historical forces of the 1920s or depressed 1930s. Indeed, even most of the wartime experiences of the men and women were not assessed through appropriate questions.

By contrast, our next empirical specimen, the Oakland Growth Study and Berkeley Guidance Study, illustrates a rich collection of data on environmental changes, but one that was generally ignored by longitudinal research over the years. There was no methodology at the time for drawing on such information; more important, historical change was simply not an appealing topic for study in the general field of developmental, personality, and clinical psychology.

"Depression Children" and the
Berkeley Data Archives

The Oakland Growth Study and Berkeley Guidance Study archives were used by the senior author in studies of "children of the Great Depression" and their adult lives (Elder, 1974, 1979, 1981). Archival data in the Oakland Growth Study, located at the University of California (Institute of Human Development), offered a unique opportunity to identify economic change in family life and its consequences for persons born before the Depression. Did economic deprivation have an effect on adult life chances? If so, then how can the effect be explained? What is the process from deprivation to outcome?

The project was launched in 1931 to study the physical, intellectual, and social development of boys and girls, and it commenced data collection in 1932. The 167 children who were studied intensively from 1932 to 1939 initially were selected from the fifth and sixth grades of five elementary schools in Oakland. Adult follow-ups were conducted in 1958-1960 (at approximately age 40 years) and in 1968-1970 (at approximately age 50 years). From its inception, the Oakland study focused more on the biological and psychological aspects of human development than on sociocultural phenomena, yet the files contained substantial information on family life, school and social experiences, and the larger milieu of the 1930s.

The Berkeley Guidance Study was launched in 1928 with every third birth in Berkeley over 18 months. The original sample includes an intensive group, which provided information on family patterns across the 1930s, and a less intensively studied group, which was matched on social and economic characteristics in 1929. The archive includes family demographic information, income loss in the Depression, annual teacher ratings, annual interviews with mother and child, observation reports, and psychological testing. Most of the study members participated in adult follow-ups in 1959-1960 (age 30 years) and 1969-1970 (age 40 years), which entailed lengthy interviews and a battery of psychological, medical, and mental tests.

An analysis of the relationship between historical events and the life stages of these cohorts reveals marked differences in the exposure of each cohort to historical influences (Table 11.3). For the Oakland cohort, childhood was paired with the prosperity of the 1920s, adolescence with Depression hardship, and young adulthood with the war. By contrast, the Berkeley cohort, only about 8 years younger, experienced the hardship of the Depression in the vulnerable childhood years, spent adolescence on the homefront, and entered adulthood just in time for an economic boom. Interestingly, the Oakland men respondents, most of whom served in World War II, tended to be pacifists as adolescents in the isolationist 1930s, whereas the Berkeley men respondents, a smaller number of whom served in the Korean War, spent their adolescences preoccupied with matters of war and military service (Elder, 1981).

Unlike the Terman study, both the Oakland Growth Study and the Berkeley Guidance Study included data on the historical context of participating families, in this case, socioeconomic data for at least two points, 1929 and 1933. This made the archives useful for study of the long-term effects of the Depression, the micro-level impact of which could be measured using family socioeconomic data. These data were collected by the original investigators as part of thorough family assessments and, therefore, were included in all the case files.

TABLE 11.3 Age of Oakland Growth Study and Berkeley Guidance
Study Members by Historical Events

| | | Age of Study Members (years) | |
Year(s)	Event	Oakland Growth Study	Berkeley Guidance Study
1880-1900	Birth years of Oakland Growth Study parents		
1890-1910	Birth years of Berkeley Guidance Study parents		
1921-1922	Depression	Birth (1920-1921)	
1923	Great Berkeley Fire	2-3	
1923-1929	General economic boom: Growth of "debt pattern" way of life, cultural change in sexual mores	1-9	Birth (1928-1929)
1929-1930	Onset of Great Depression	9-10	1-2
1932-1933	Depth of Great Depression	11-13	3-5
1933-1936	Partial recovery, increasing cost of living, labor strikes	12-16	4-8
1937-1938	Economic slump	16-18	8-10
1939-1940	Incipient stage of wartime mobilization	18-20	10-12
1941-1943	Major growth of war industries (e.g., shipyards, munitions plants) and of military forces	20-23	12-15
1945	End of World War II	24-25	16-17
1950-1953	Korean War	29-33	21-25

The major challenge in working with the Oakland and Berkeley study archives was that much of the contextual data were uncoded. The data also were organized cross-sectionally by age for each wave of collection. Thus, we could not pull together the life history of any individual or family or select cases by some life-long criterion. These challenges were met through recasting efforts, which we describe subsequently.

All of the machine-readable data were organized according to age and/or grade by particular inventory. Most previous analyses had correlated items from inventories at different time points. The intervening span was largely uncharted. No data set had information on the socioeconomic careers of families or on the timetable of adult events in the lives of the Oakland study members. Men who had served in the military could not be identified. After an inventory of the archive, the next steps in preparing the data for life course use involved coding the essential uncoded data and assembling life histories for work, marital, and family trajectories.

The life course of the study members was divided into *pre-adult* and *adult* phases for coding purposes. The pre-adult phase focused extensively on the social and economic careers of families; the adult phase included major events, roles, and achievements in marriage, parenthood, work life, and community. From a detailed chronology of adult work life, it was possible to construct measures that were truly temporal. A good example is a measure of work life fluctuation—the up-and-down status cycles within an occupational career.

After completing analyses of the long-term effects of economic deprivation with the Oakland cohort (Elder, 1974), the senior author turned to the Berkeley Guidance Study archive to compare the differential effects of deprivation experienced at different life stages (Elder, 1979, 1981). Archival work with the Berkeley study was structured by the requirements of a comparative design. At first glance, the archive seemed well suited for such analysis, although the extent of the match and the coding requirements could only be determined through an on-site inventory of coded and uncoded data.

A fresh inventory of the archive revealed new possibilities for lines of inquiry. For example, the very first interviews conducted with the Berkeley study parents during the study children's infancies included recollections and contemporaneous reports of their own mothers and fathers. These reports were structured by the same measurement categories used on the parents and, thus, could be used to explore intergenerational continuity and change. Some of these data actually had been dropped from the archive's list of materials and likely would not have been found without a new inventory.

As in the Oakland Growth Study archive, the inventory seldom found social data that were coded and structured in life record form. All families were assessed on socioeconomic status in 1929 and again in 1945-1946, but the intervening years of hard times and war were largely uncharted. The appropriate data were available, but they simply had not been viewed as an essential part of the picture. The same blindspot was found in the adult years, from the study children's departure from high school in 1945-1946 to 1970. The archive contained records of their marital, educational, and occupational statuses, but these data were coded at only one or two points in their life course. Before coding could begin, this information had to be arranged in chronological form as life records. Codebooks were then developed using the same methods described for the Terman study.

With recasting, the archival data were profitably analyzed to address the questions on economic deprivation. The Oakland boy and girl respondents became competent adults, in part as a result of their roles as contributors to the household economy during hard times. This experience of responsibility at an early age led to strong career orientations among the boys and to domestic preferences among the girls (Elder, 1974). The Berkeley girl respondents also did well in adulthood. By contrast, the Berkeley boy respondents from hard-pressed families expressed higher levels of self-inadequacy, passivity, and helplessness and did poorly in school (Elder, 1979). The costs of hardship were concentrated among these boys.

The Farm Crisis and the Iowa Project

Our final specimen is based on the Iowa Youth and Families Project, a panel study *designed* to investigate the social and psychological consequences of the 1980s Farm Crisis. It is unlike the other specimens in precisely this respect: The data were collected specifically for the purpose of studying the effects of a historical event, the Farm Crisis, on lives.

The Farm Crisis marked the end of prosperity, expansion, high land values, and high debt loads in the late 1970s. Land values plummeted and interest rates soared in the early 1980s. The result often was financial ruin for the overextended farm families. During the 1980s, the state of Iowa, for example, saw 20% of its farmers lose their operations, 75 of its banks and savings and loans close their doors, 41% of its rural gas stations go out of business, and a staggering 46% increase in bankruptcies in 1985 alone (Conger & Elder, 1994). Many families felt the pain of these events directly through the loss of farms, the loss of jobs, or decreased wages. Others maintained their levels of living but saw friends and relatives financially decimated by a depression almost as severe as that of the 1930s.

In the midst of the Farm Crisis, a research team, headed by Rand Conger at Iowa State University, proposed a panel study of families and adolescents that would investigate the effects of the economic changes underway. The state of Iowa proved to be an excellent research site because it ranks second only to California in the value of farm produce and was deeply mired in the economic crisis. Indeed, no state in the Midwest was harder hit by the declining value of arable land and high interest rates.

The research plan at the time was to design the Iowa study as a contemporary version of *Children of the Great Depression* (Elder, 1974). Because of this, the senior author was invited to join the project as a principal investigator with a research team at the University of North Carolina at Chapel Hill.

Two related changes were identified as focal points: changing rural ecologies (the experience of leaving agriculture and the land) and the linking processes and mechanisms (the impact of economic decline on children through financial pressures, parents' emotional distress and negativity, marital conflict, and ineffective parenting). These linkages were modeled such that analysis could be conducted in three phases (Figure 11.5).

The first wave of data was collected in an eight-county study area in north-central Iowa. A sample consisted of 451 families, each with two parents, a seventh grader, and a sibling within 4 years of age. The inclusion of the sibling provided an opportunity to observe sibling relationships and to determine whether economic hardships are expressed differently among children of different ages within the same family. Of the 451 families, 30% were involved in farming. Another 60% were nonfarm (although many were involved in agriculture-related businesses), and the remainder had given up farming as a result of the Farm Crisis, most in the early 1980s.

During two home visits, study members completed several extensive questionnaires covering family background, family life and finances, friends, physical and mental health, values and beliefs, and important events in their lives. The children answered additional questions about their goals and values, performance in school, and nonschool activities. Because data collection was begun after the height of the crisis, retrospective questions covering the onset and depth of the crisis were included, thus capturing data on events such as farm loss or bankruptcy. Family members also were videotaped engaging in task-oriented discussions in several combinations—all members, parents only, and children only. The taped observations were evaluated on levels of cooperation or hostility, quality

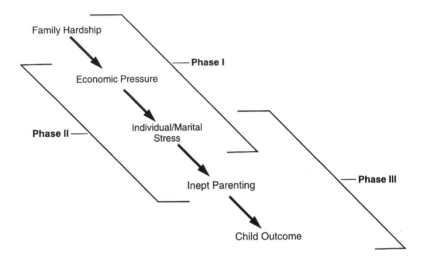

Figure 11.5. Three Analytic Phases

of relationships, problem-solving skills, and personal attributes, among other factors.

The project families have been followed up with questionnaires, video-taped interactions, and interviews in 1990, 1991, 1992, and 1994. Phone interviews were conducted in 1993. The target children, therefore, have been studied extensively from 7th through 12th grades. From these data, coding categories were developed for family types that represent poten-tially significant ecological variation. The categories are farm, part-time farm, displaced, nonfarm but grew up on farm, and neither living on farm nor farm reared.

An analysis revealed economic distress in 1988-1989 to be greatest among the displaced families, followed by nonfarm households and then by farm families. It is not surprising, then, that rates of adolescent distress and maladjustment were highest in displaced families, followed by non-farm households and then by farm families. These differences based on first-wave data remained even with contemporary income controlled, an outcome that reflects the harsh legacy of the Farm Crisis and displacement from the land. It was the influence of strong marriages and fathers who proved to be effective problem solvers that tended to minimize these effects.

Interestingly, little evidence of the differences in adolescent well-being by family type remains at the end of the high school years. Instead of stressing the strong connection between family hardship and adolescent distress, we may need to give more attention to the loose connection, that is, to the fact that many families in hard-pressed circumstances manage to survive very well over the long term. This finding certainly underscores the value of conducting prospective longitudinal research because proximal and distal outcomes may differ considerably.

Although the Iowa Youth and Families Project was designed to be historically aware, a major historical influence did escape our attention at the outset. Preoccupied with the recent Farm Crisis, we almost overlooked the fact that most of the fathers in the study families were young men during the Vietnam War. In fact, 40% of the fathers are Vietnam veterans. Data about their experiences were found in answers to open-ended questions. This situation clearly demonstrates the usefulness of including open-ended questions (qualitative items) as a means of capturing unanticipated data.

The Iowa Project represents a nearly ideal means by which to study the proximal and distal effects of historical change. It is, however, a massive undertaking, requiring a great deal in terms of funding, talent, and commitment. New data can be collected in a more restricted but nevertheless effective way. Consider, for example, a study of the effects of rustication in Shanghai, the People's Republic of China (Elder, Wu, & Yuan, 1993). "Rustication" refers to the forced relocation of urban young people (Figure 11.6) to the countryside during the Cultural Revolution, from 1966 to 1980.

The sample for this study consisted of one respondent each from 1,320 randomly selected households in urban Shanghai. A life calendar (Freedman et al., 1988) was the primary data collection instrument, supplemented by pop-out probes on major life events and transitions. This technique enables an interviewer to maximize the accuracy of the data because it allows the respondent to cross-check information from various domains and make corrections as necessary. For example, a respondent may remember that he or she had, in fact, moved to a different village after the birth of her first child and not before. Data were collected on marriage/divorce, births, deaths, changes in residence, education, work, and standard of living (see also Chapter 7, this volume).

These data were sufficient for cross-cohort analyses that showed, for example, that (a) the rusticates were drawn primarily from the cohort of people born in 1948-1955, (b) the cohort members who experienced

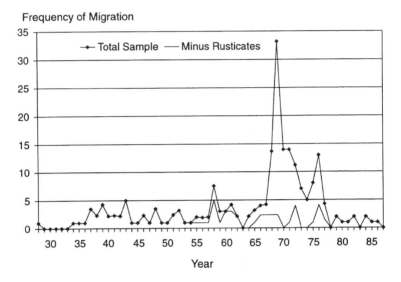

Figure 11.6a. Out-Migration of 1988 Shanghai Residents: Impact of
Rustication Program
SOURCE: Elder, Wu, & Yuan (1993).

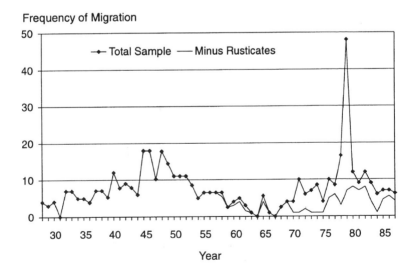

Figure 11.6b. In-Migration of 1988 Shanghai Residents: Impact of
Rustication Program
SOURCE: Elder, Wu, & Yuan (1993).

rustication suffered long-term deficits in education, and (c) the rusticates were more likely than nonrusticates to view the years of the Cultural Revolution as the "worst of times" of their lives. Rustication also delayed the marital timing of women and the births of their children.

➤ CONCLUSION

Growing awareness of an ever-changing environment is giving overdue visibility to matters of time, context, and social dynamics. Problems of social change and human development have gained significance as research foci along with the concept that people make social history even as they are influenced by it. The dialectical perspective of life course analysis, relating social history and life history, brings a number of issues to the fore that call for fresh research approaches.

The first and most basic of these is that the relationship between social history and life history must be studied deliberately and directly to be studied well. We have argued that the most satisfactory strategy is the use of an event-based model—focusing on a historical event or process and following its effects over the short and long term and in several domains of life. An outcome-based model is less satisfactory because it limits the analysis to only one of several outcomes and because a critically important change event may not even be included as an antecedent variable in the analysis.

It is equally important to remain open to the totality of history and to not be too narrowly focused on the target event or change process. As noted earlier, we nearly overlooked the distal effects of the Vietnam War in the Iowa Project while focusing on the proximal impact of the Farm Crisis. Ignoring one salient event while focusing on another can be almost as limiting as ignoring the effects of history altogether. A helpful strategy for avoiding this is to always prepare a table linking the cohorts in a proposed study with the major historical markers of their lifetimes.

Finally, life course analysis requires that the researcher operate on both macro and micro levels simultaneously. In spite of the tendency in quantitative research to analyze lives in the aggregate—comparing farm and nonfarm families, for example, or comparing veterans and nonveterans—it is essential to remain mindful of the individual. History makes its impress on a cohort one individual at a time. Without an understanding of the process by which that impress is made and a direct effort to model this process, studies may result only in tables of inexplicable correlations.

This chapter is by no means a manual for conducting life course research. Our goal, instead, has been to argue for the advantages of an event-based approach in linking history with human lives and to lay out a general strategy for this research. Beyond a few common steps, every research project, like every life, follows a unique trajectory.

References

Abbott, A. (1992). From causes to events: Notes on narrative positivism. *Sociological Methods and Research, 20,* 428-455.

Abbott, A., & Hrycak, A. (1990). Measuring resemblance in sequence data: An optimal matching analysis of musicians' careers. *American Journal of Sociology, 96,* 144-185.

Abeles, R. P., & Riley, M. W. (1977). A life-course perspective on the later years of life: Some implications for research. In *Social Science Research Council annual report, 1976-1977* (pp. 1-16). New York: Social Science Research Council.

Adorno, T. W., Frenkel-Brunswik, E., Levinson, D. J., & Sanford, R. N., with Aron, B., Levinson, M. H., & Morrow, W. (1950). *The authoritarian personality* (Studies in Prejudice). New York: Harper.

Allison, P. D. (1984). *Event history analysis: Regression for longitudinal event data* (Sage University Papers, Quantitative Applications in the Social Sciences No. 07-046). Beverly Hills, CA: Sage.

Allmendinger, J. (1989). *Career mobility dynamics: A comparative analysis of the United States, Norway, and West Germany* (Studien und Berichte No. 49). Berlin: Max-Planck-Institut für Bildungsforschung.

Allmendinger, J. (1994). *Lebensverlauf und Sozialpolitik: Die Ungleichheit von Mann und Frau und ihr öffentlicher Ertrag.* Frankfurt am Main, Germany: Campus.

Allmendinger, J., Brückner, H., & Brückner, E. (1991). Arbeitsleben und Lebensarbeitsentlohnung im Ruhestand. In K. U. Mayer, J. Allmendinger, & J. Huinink (Eds.), *Vom Regen in die Traufe: Frauen zwischen Beruf und Familie* (pp. 423-469). Frankfurt am Main, Germany: Campus.

Allmendinger, J., Brückner, H., & Brückner, E. (1993). The production of gender disparities over the life course and their effects in old age: Results from the West German Life History Study. In A. B. Atkinson & M. Rein (Eds.), *Age, work, and social security* (pp. 189-223). New York: St. Martin's.

Allport, G. W. (1942). *The use of personal documents in psychological science* (Social Science Research Council Bulletin No. 49). New York: Social Science Research Council.

Almond, G. A., & Verba, S. (1963). *The civic culture: Political attitudes and democracy in five nations.* Princeton, NJ: Princeton University Press.

Alter, G. (1988). *Family and the female life course: The women of Verviers, Belgium, 1849-1880* (Life Course Studies). Madison: University of Wisconsin Press.

Alwin, D. F. (1989). Problems in the estimation and interpretation of the reliability of survey data. *Quality and Quantity, 23,* 277-331.

Alwin, D. F. (1994). Aging, personality and social change: The stability of individual differences over the adult life-span. In D. L. Featherman, R. M. Lerner, & M. Perlmutter (Eds.), *Life-span development and behavior* (Vol. 12, pp. 136-185). Hillsdale, NJ: Lawrence Erlbaum.

Alwin, D. F., Braun, M., & Scott, J. (1992). The separation of work and the family: Attitudes toward women's labor force participation in Germany, Great Britain, and the United States. *European Sociological Review, 8,* 13-37.

Alwin, D. F., Cohen, R. L., & Newcomb, T. M. (1991). *Political attitudes over the life-span: The Bennington women after fifty years* (Life Course Series). Madison: University of Wisconsin Press.

Alwin, D. F., & Krosnick, J. A. (1991a). Aging, cohorts, and the stability of sociopolitical orientations over the life span. *American Journal of Sociology, 97,* 169-195.

Alwin, D. F., & Krosnick, J. A. (1991b). The reliability of survey attitude measurement: The influence of question and respondent attributes. *Sociological Methods and Research 20,* 139-181.

Anderson, B. A., Silver, B. D., & Abramson, P. A. (1988). The effects of race of the interviewer on measures of electoral participation by blacks in SRC national election studies. *Public Opinion Quarterly, 52,* 53-83.

Andorka, R. (1971). Social mobility and economic development in Hungary. *Acta Economica, 7*(1), 25-45.

Antler, J. (1981). Feminism as life-process: The life and career of Lucy Sprague Mitchell. *Feminist Studies, 7,* 134-157.

Ariès, P. (1962). *Centuries of childhood: A social history of family life* (R. Baldick, Trans.). London: Cape.

Auriat, N. (1993). "My wife knows best": A comparison of event dating accuracy between the wife, the husband, the couple, and the Belgian Population Register. *Public Opinion Quarterly, 57,* 165-190.

Axinn, W. G., & Thornton, A. (1992). The relationship between cohabitation and divorce: Selectivity or causal influence? *Demography, 29,* 357-371.

Back, K. W. (1994). Accuracy, truth, and meaning in autobiographical reports. In N. Schwarz & S. Sudman (Eds.), *Autobiographical memory and the validity of retrospective reports* (pp. 39-53). New York: Springer-Verlag.

Back, K., & Bourque, L. B. (1970). Life graphs: Aging and cohort effects. *Journal of Gerontology, 25,* 249-255.

Back, K. W., & Gergen, K. J. (1963). Apocalyptic and serial time orientations and the structure of opinions. *Public Opinion Quarterly, 27,* 427-442.

Bailar, B. A. (1989). Information needs, surveys, and measurement errors. In D. Kasprzyk, G. J. Duncan, G. Kalton, & M. Singh (Eds.), *Panel surveys* (pp. 1-24). New York: John Wiley.

Baker, T. L., & Sween, J. A. (1982). Synchronizing postgraduate career, marriage, and fertility. *Western Sociological Review, 13*(1), 69-86.

Balán, J., Browning, H. L., Jelin, E., & Litzler, L. (1969). A computerized approach to the processing and analysis of life histories obtained in sample surveys. *Behavioral Science, 14,* 105-120.

Baltes, P. B. (1968). Longitudinal and cross-sectional sequences in the study of age and generation effects. *Human Development, 11,* 145-171.

Baltes, P. B. (1993). The aging mind: Potential and limits. *The Gerontologist, 33,* 580-594.

Barnett, R. C., Kibria, N., Baruch, G. K., & Pleck, J. H. (1991). Adult daughter-parent relationships and their associations with daughters' subjective well-being and psychological distress. *Journal of Marriage and Family, 53,* 29-43.

Barnett, R. C., & Rivers, C. (1996). *She works/he works: How two-income families are happier, healthier, and better off.* San Francisco: Harper.

Baruch, G. K., Barnett, R. C., & Rivers, C. (1983). *Lifeprints: New patterns of love and work for today's women.* New York: McGraw-Hill.

Bateson, M. C. (1989). *Composing a life.* New York: Atlantic Monthly.

Bauer, R. A., Inkeles, A., & Kluckhohn, C. (1956). *How the Soviet system works: Cultural, psychological, and social themes* (Russian Research Center Studies No. 24). Cambridge, MA: Harvard University Press.

Becker, H. S. (1966). Introduction. In C. R. Shaw, *The jack-roller: A delinquent boy's own story.* Chicago: University of Chicago Press. (Originally published 1930)

Bell, D. (1974). Why participation rates of black and white wives differ. *Journal of Human Resources, 9,* 465-479.

Bell, W. (1979). Roosevelt High School class of 1942. *Yale Review, 69,* 151-60.

Ben-David, J., & Collins, R. (1966). Social factors in the origins of a new science: The case of psychology. *American Sociological Review, 31,* 451-465.

Bengston, V. L. (1975). Generation and family effects in value socialization. *American Sociological Review, 40,* 358-371.

Bennett, J. (1981). *Oral history and delinquency: The rhetoric of criminology.* Chicago: University of Chicago Press.

Bennett, S. K., & Elder, G. H., Jr. (1979). Women's work in the family economy: A study of depression hardship in women's lives. *Journal of Family History, 4,* 153-176.

Bertaux, D. (1981). Introduction. In D. Bertaux (Ed.), *Biography and society: The life history approach in the social sciences* (pp. 5-15, Sage Studies in International Sociology No. 23). Beverly Hills, CA: Sage.

Bertaux, D., & Kohli, M. (1984). The life story approach: A continental view. *Annual Review of Sociology, 10,* 215-237.

Bielby, D. D. V. (1978). Maternal employment and socioeconomic status as factors in daughters' career salience: Some substantive refinements. *Sex Roles, 4,* 249-265.

Bielby, W. T., Hauser, R. M., & Featherman, D. L. (1977). Response errors of black and nonblack males in models of the intergenerational transmission of socioeconomic status. *American Journal of Sociology, 82,* 1242-1288.

Blair-Loy, M. F. (1996, August). *Career and family patterns of executive women in finance: Evidence of structural and cultural change.* Paper presented at the meeting of the American Sociological Association, New York.

Blalock, H. M., Jr. (1967). Status inconsistency, social mobility, status integration and structural effects. *American Sociological Review, 32,* 790-801.

Blau, P. M., & Duncan, O. D., with Tyree, A. (1967). *The American occupational structure.* New York: John Wiley.

Blossfeld, H.-P. (1990). Berufsverläufe und Arbeitsmarktprozesse: Ergebnisse sozial-strukureller Längsschnittuntersuchungen. In K. U. Mayer (Ed.), *Lebensverläufe und sozialer Wandel* (Sonderheft 31/1990 der Kölner Zeitschrift für Soziologie und Sozialpsychologie, pp. 118-145). Opladen: Westdeutscher Verlag.

Blum, Z. D., Karweit, N. L., & Sørensen, A. B. (1969). *A method for the collection and analysis of retrospective life histories* (Center for the Study of Social Organization of Schools Report No. 48). Baltimore, MD: Johns Hopkins University.

Blumer, H. (1939). *An appraisal of Thomas and Znaniecki's* The Polish Peasant in Europe and America (Critiques of Research in the Social Sciences 1, Social Science Research Council Bulletin No. 44). New York: Social Science Research Council.

Blumer, H. (1969). *Symbolic interactionism: Perspective and method.* Englewood Cliffs, NJ: Prentice Hall.

Blumstein, A., Cohen, J., Roth, J., & Visher, C. (Eds.). (1986). *Criminal careers and "career criminals."* Washington, DC: National Academy Press.

Boocock, S. S. (1978). Historical and sociological research on the family and the life cycle: Methodological alternatives. In J. Demos & S. S. Boocock (Eds.), *Turning points: Historical and sociological essays on the family* (pp. S366-S394). Chicago: University of Chicago Press. (*American Journal of Sociology, 84*[Suppl.])

Booth, A., & Johnson, D. R. (1985). Tracking respondents in a telephone interview panel selected by random digit dialing. *Sociological Methods and Research, 14,* 53-64.

Bradburn, E. M., Moen, P., & Dempster-McClain, D. (1995). Women's return to school: Following the transition to motherhood. *Social Forces, 73,* 1517-1551.

Brewer, W. F. (1994). Autobiographical memory and survey research. In N. Schwarz & S. Sudman (Eds.), *Autobiographical memory and the validity of retrospective reports* (pp. 11-20). New York: Springer-Verlag.

Brim, O. G., Jr., & Kagan, J. (Eds.). (1980). *Constancy and change in human development.* Cambridge, MA: Harvard University Press.

Brim, O. G. Jr., & Wheeler, S. (Eds.). (1966). *Socialization after childhood: Two essays.* New York: John Wiley.

Bronfenbrenner, U. (1979). *The ecology of human development: Experiments by nature and by design.* Cambridge, MA: Harvard University Press.

Brückner, E. (1985). *Methodenbericht zur Pilotstudie 1984.* Unpublished manuscript. Berlin: Max-Planck-Institut für Bildungsforschung.

Brückner, E. (1993). *Lebensverläufe und gesellschaftlicher Wandel: Konzeption, Design und Methodik der Erhebung von Lebensverläufen der Geburtsjahrgänge 1919-1921* (5 vols., Materialien aus der Bildungsforschung No. 44). Berlin: Max-Planck-Institut für Bildungsforschung.

Brückner, E., Hoffmeyer-Zlotnik, J., & Tölke, A. (1983). Die Daten-Edition als notwendige Ergänzung der Datenerhebung bei retrospektiven Langzeitstudien. *ZUMA-Nachrichten, 13,* 73-83.

Bruckner, H. (1995). *Surveys don't lie, people do? An analysis of data quality in a retrospective life course study* (Materialien aus der Bildungsforschung Nr. 50). Berlin: Max-Planck-Institut für Bildungsforschung.

Brückner, H., & Mayer, K. U. (1995). *Lebensverläufe und gesellschaftlicher Wandel: Konzeption, Design und Methodik der Erhebung von Lebensverläufen der Geburtsjahrgänge 1954-1956, 1959-1961* (3 vols., Materialien aus der Bildungsforschung No. 48). Berlin: Max-Planck-Institut für Bildungsforschung.

Buck, N., Gershuny, J., Rose, D., & Scott, J. (1994). *Changing households: The BHPS 1990 to 1992.* Colchester, UK: University of Essex, ESRC Research Centre on Micro-Social Change.

Buck, N., & Scott, J. (1993). She's leaving home, but why? An analysis of young people leaving the parental home. *Journal of Marriage and the Family, 55,* 863-874.

Bungard, W. (1979). Methodische Probleme bei der Befragung älterer Menschen. *Zeitschrift für experimentelle und angewandte Psychologie, 26,* 211-237.

Burstein, P., Bricher, R. M., & Einwohner, R. L. (1995). Policy alternatives and political change: Work, family, and gender on the congressional agenda. *American Sociological Review, 60,* 67-83.

Burton, L. M., & Bengtson, V. L. (1985). Black grandmothers: Issues of timing and continuity of roles. In V. L. Bengtson & J. F. Robertson (Eds.), *Grandparenthood* (pp. 61-77, Sage Focus Editions Vol. 74). Beverly Hills, CA: Sage.

Busse, E. W., & Maddox, G. W., with associates. (1985). *The Duke Longitudinal Studies of Normal Aging 1955-1980: Overview of history, design, and findings.* New York: Springer.

Butler, R. (1963). The life review: An interpretation of reminiscence in the aged. *Psychiatry, 26,* 65-76.

Cain, G. G. (1966). *Married women in the labor force: An economic analysis* (Studies in Economics of the Economics Research Center of the University of Chicago). Chicago: University of Chicago Press.

Cain, L. D., Jr. (1964). Life course and social structure. In R. E. L. Faris (Ed.), *Handbook of modern sociology* (pp. 272-309, Rand McNally Sociology Series). Chicago: Rand McNally.

Cairns, R. B. (1986). Phenomena lost: Issues in the study of development. In J. Valsiner (Ed.), *The individual subject and scientific psychology* (pp. 97-111). New York: Plenum.

Cairns, B. D., Neckerman, H. J., Flinchum, T. R., & Cairns, R. B. (1992). *Lost and found: I. Recovery of subjects in longitudinal research.* Working paper, University of North Carolina at Chapel Hill.

Call, V. R. A., Otto, L. B., & Spenner, K. I. (1982). *Tracking respondents: A multi-method approach* (Entry Into Careers Series, Vol. 2). Lexington, MA: Lexington Books.

Callon, M. (1995). Four models for the dynamics of science. In S. Jasanoff, G. E. Markle, J. C. Petersen, & T. Pinch (Eds.), *Handbook of science and technology studies* (pp. 29-63). Thousand Oaks, CA: Sage.

Campbell, M. L., & Richards, L. (1985). Summary of sample location and data collection procedures in the Longitudinal Study of Three Generations, Appendix A, *Progress Report for Year 2, the Longitudinal Study of Aging Parents.* Los Angeles: University of Southern California, Andrus Gerontology Center.

Campbell, R. T. (1994). A data-based revolution in the social sciences. *ICPSR Bulletin, 14*(3), 1-4.

Campbell, R. T., & O'Rand, A. M. (1988). Settings and sequences: The heuristics of aging research. In J. E. Birren & V. L. Bengtson (Eds.), *Emergent theories of aging* (pp. 58-79). New York: Springer.

Carr, D., Ryff, C. D., Singer, B., & Magee, W. J. (1995, August). *Bringing the "life" back into life course research: A "person-centered" approach to studying the life course.* Paper presented at the meeting of the American Sociological Association, Washington, DC.

Carroll, L. (1952). *Alice through the looking glass.* New York: Collier.

Center for Human Resource Research. (1989). *NLS annotated bibliography: 1968-1989—The National Longitudinal Surveys of Labor Market Experience.* Columbus: Ohio State University, Center for Human Resource Research.

Chow, E. N.-L. (1997). Asian American women at work. In M. B. Zinn, P. Hondagneu-Sotelo, & M. A. Messner (Eds.), *The prism of difference: Readings on sex and gender* (pp. 408-417). Boston: Allyn & Bacon.

Clark, R., Ghent, L. S., & Headen, A. (1994). Retiree health insurance and pension coverage: Variations by firm characteristics. *Journals of Gerontology: Social Sciences, 49*(2), S53-S61.

Clarridge, B. R., Sheehy, L. L., & Hauser, T. S. (1978). Tracing members of a panel: A 17-year follow-up. *Sociological Methodology, 10,* 185-203.

Clausen, J. A. (1972). The life course of individuals. In M. W. Riley, M. E. Johnson, & A. Foner (Eds.), *Aging and society,* Vol. 3: *A sociology of age stratification* (pp. 457-514). New York: Russell Sage.

Clausen, J. A. (1983). Sex roles, marital roles, and response to mental disorder. In J. Greenly (Ed.), *Research in community and mental health* (Vol. 3, pp. 165-208). Greenwich, CT: JAI.

Clausen, J. A. (1984). Mental illness and the life course. *Life-Span Development and Behavior, 6,* 203-242.

Clausen, J. A. (1986). A 15- to 20-year follow-up of married adult psychiatric patients. In L. Erlenmeyer-Kimling & N. E. Miller (Eds.), *Life span research on the prediction of psychopathology* (pp. 175-194). Hillsdale, NJ: Lawrence Erlbaum.

Clausen, J. A. (1990, August). *Turning point as a life course concept: Meaning and measurement.* Paper presented at the meeting of the American Sociological Association, Washington, DC.

Clausen, J. A. (1991). Adolescent competence and the shaping of the life course (marriage, family, and the life course). *American Journal of Sociology, 96,* 805-842.

Clausen, J. A. (1993). *American lives: Looking back at the children of the Great Depression.* New York: Free Press.

Clausen, J. A. (1995). Gender, contexts, and turning points in adult lives. In P. Moen, G. H. Elder, Jr., & K. Lüscher (Eds.), with H. E. Quick, *Examining lives in context: Perspectives on the ecology of human development* (pp. 365-389, APA Science Volumes). Washington, DC: American Psychological Association.

Clausen, J. A., & Yarrow, M. R. (Eds.). (1955). The impact of mental illness on the family. *Journal of Social Issues, 11*(4), 1-65.

Cline, H. F. (1980). Criminal behavior over the life span. In O. G. Brim, Jr., & J. Kagan (Eds.), *Constancy and change in human development* (pp. 641-674). Cambridge, MA: Harvard University Press.

Clipp, E., & Elder, G. H., Jr. (1987). Elderly confidantes in geriatric assessment. *Comparative Gerontology, 1,* 35-40.

Cohler, B. J. (1982). Personal narrative and the life course. *Life Span Development and Behavior, 4,* 205-241.

Cohn, R. (1972). On interpretation of cohort and period analyses: a mathematical note. In M. W. Riley, M. E. Johnson, & A. Foner (Eds.), _Aging and society,_ Vol. 3: _A sociology of age stratification_ (pp. 85-88). New York: Russell Sage.

Coleman, J. S. (1981). _Longitudinal data analysis._ New York: Basic Books.

Coleman, J. S. (1990). _Foundations of social theory._ Cambridge, MA: Harvard University Press.

Colerick, E. J. (1985). Stamina in later life. _Social Science and Medicine, 21,_ 997-1006.

Collins, H. M. (1974). The TEA set: Tacit knowledge and scientific networks. _Science Studies, 4,_ 165-186.

Collins, P. H. (1990). _Black feminist thought: Knowledge, consciousness, and the politics of empowerment._ Boston: Unwin Hyman.

Collins, R. (1994). _Four sociological traditions._ New York: Oxford University Press.

Conger, R. D., & Elder, G. H., Jr., with Lorenz, F. O., Simons, R. L., & Whitbeck, L. B. (1994). _Families in troubled times: Adapting to change in rural America._ New York: Aldine de Gruyter.

Cook, T. D. (1985). Postpositivist critical multiplism. In R. L. Shotland & M. M. Mark (Eds.), _Social science and social policy_ (pp. 21-62). Beverly Hills, CA: Sage.

Corsaro, W. A. (1994). Introduction of Glen H. Elder, Jr. for the Cooley-Mead Award. _Social Psychology Quarterly, 57,_ 1-3.

Crider, D. M., & Willits, F. K. (1973). Respondent retrieval bias in a longitudinal survey. _Sociology and Social Research, 58,_ 56-65.

Crider, D. M., Willits, F. K., & Bealer, R. C. (1971). Tracking respondents in longitudinal surveys. _Public Opinion Quarterly, 35,_ 613-620.

Crider, D. M., Willits, F. K., & Bealer, R. C. (1973). Panel studies: Some practical problems. _Sociological Methods and Research, 2,_ 3-19.

Dannefer, D. (1984). Adult development and social theory: A paradigmatic reappraisal. _American Sociological Review, 49,_ 100-116.

Dannefer, D. (1992). On the conceptualization of context in developmental discourse: Four meanings of context and their implications. _Life-Span Development and Behavior, 15,_ 83-110.

Davis, N. J., & Bumpass, L. L. (1976). The continuation of education after marriage among women in the United States: 1970. _Demography, 13,_ 161-174.

Dean, J. P., & Williams, R. M., Jr. (1956). _Social and cultural factors affecting role-conflict and adjustment among American women: A pilot investigation._ Progress report submitted to the National Institute of Mental Health.

Demos, J. (1970). _A little commonwealth: Family life in Plymouth Colony._ New York: Oxford University Press.

Denzin, N. K. (1970). _The research act: A theoretical introduction to sociological methods._ Chicago: Aldine.

Denzin, N. K. (1989). _Interpretive biography_ (Qualitative Research Methods No. 17). Newbury Park, CA: Sage.

Dex, S. (1984). Work history analysis, women and large scale data sets. _Sociological Review, 32,_ 637-661.

Dex, S. (1991). _Life and work history analyses: Qualitative and quantitative developments_ (Sociological Review Monograph No. 37). London: Routledge.

Dex, S. (1995). The reliability of recall data: A literature review. _Bulletin de Methodologie Sociologique, 49,_ 58-89.

DiPrete, T. A., & Forristal, J. D. (1994). Multilevel models: Methods and substance. *Annual Review of Sociology, 20,* 331-357.

Dollard, J. (1935). *Criteria for the life history with analyses of six notable documents.* New Haven, CT: Yale University Press for the Institute of Human Relations.

Duncan, G. J. (1992). *Household panel studies: Prospects and problems* (Working Papers of the ESF Network on Household Panel Studies No. 54). Colchester, UK: University of Essex.

Duncan, G. J., & Kalton, G. (1987). Issues of design and analysis of surveys across time. *International Statistical Review, 55,* 97-117.

Duncan, G. J., Smeeding, T. M., & Rodgers, W. (1993). W(h)ither the middle class? A dynamic view. In D. B. Papadimitriou & E. N. Wolff (Eds.), *Poverty and prosperity in the USA in the late twentieth century* (pp. 240-271). New York: St. Martin's.

Duncan, O. D. (1975). Measuring social change via replication of surveys. In K. C. Land & S. Spilerman (Eds.), *Social indicator models* (pp. 105-127). New York: Russell Sage.

Durkheim, É. (1933). *The division of labor in society* (G. Simpson, Ed. & Trans.). New York: Macmillan. (Originally published 1893)

Easterlin, R. A. (1978). What will 1984 be like? Socioeconomic implications of recent twists in age structure. *Demography, 15,* 397-432.

Easterlin, R. A. (1980). *Birth and fortune: The impact of numbers on personal welfare.* New York: Basic Books.

Edge, D. O., & Mulkay, M. J. (1976). *Astronomy transformed: The emergence of radio astronomy in Britain* (Science, Culture, and Society). New York: John Wiley.

Eichorn, D. H. (1981a). Acknowledgements. In D. H. Eichorn, J. A. Clausen, N. Haan, M. P. Honzik, & P. H. Mussen (Eds.), *Present and past in middle life* (pp. xvii-xviii). New York: Academic Press.

Eichorn, D. H. (1981b). Sample and procedures. In D. H. Eichorn, J. A. Clausen, N. Haan, M. P. Honzik, & P. H. Mussen (Eds.), *Present and past in middle life* (pp. 33-51). New York: Academic Press.

Elder, G. H., Jr. (1974). *Children of the Great Depression: Social change in life experience.* Chicago: University of Chicago Press.

Elder, G. H., Jr. (1975). Age differentiation and the life course. *Annual Review of Sociology, 1,* 165-190.

Elder, G. H., Jr. (1979). Historical change in life patterns and personality. *Life-Span Development and Behavior, 2,* 117-159.

Elder, G. H., Jr. (1981). Social history and life experience. In D. H. Eichorn, J. A. Clausen, N. Haan, M. P. Honzik, & P. H. Mussen (Eds.), *Present and past in middle life* (pp. 3-31). New York: Academic Press.

Elder, G. H., Jr. (1985). Perspectives on the life course. In G. H. Elder, Jr. (Ed.), *Life course dynamics: Trajectories and transitions, 1968 to 1980* (pp. 23-49). Ithaca, NY: Cornell University Press.

Elder, G. H., Jr. (1986). Military times and turning points in men's lives. *Developmental Psychology, 22,* 233-245.

Elder, G. H., Jr. (1987). War mobilization and the life course: A cohort of World War II veterans. *Sociological Forum, 2,* 449-472.

Elder, G. H., Jr. (1992). Life course. In E. F. Borgatta & M. L. Borgatta (Eds.), *Encyclopedia of sociology* (Vol. 3, pp. 1120-1130). New York: Macmillan.

Elder, G. H., Jr. (1994). Time, human agency, and social change: Perspectives on the life course. *Social Psychology Quarterly, 57,* 4-15.

Elder, G. H., Jr. (1995). The life course paradigm: Social change and individual development. In P. Moen, G. H. Elder, Jr., & K. Lüscher (Eds.) with H. E. Quick, *Examining lives in context: Perspectives on the ecology of human development* (pp. 101-139). Washington, DC: American Psychological Association.

Elder, G. H., Jr. (1998). The life course and human development. In R. M. Lerner (Ed.), *Handbook of child psychology,* Vol. 1: *Theoretical models of human development* (5th ed., pp. 939-991). New York: John Wiley.

Elder, G. H., Jr., & Caspi, A. (1990). Studying lives in a changing society. In A. I. Rabin, R. A. Zucker, R. A. Emmons, & S. Frank (Eds.), *Studying persons and lives* (pp. 201-247). New York: Springer.

Elder, G. H., Jr., & Clipp, E. C. (1988). Wartime losses and social bonding: Influences across 40 years in men's lives. *Psychiatry, 51,* 177-198.

Elder, G. H., Jr., & Clipp, E. C. (1989). Combat experience and emotional health: Impairment and resilience in later life. *Journal of Personality, 57,* 311-341.

Elder, G. H., Jr., Conger, R. D., Foster, E. M., & Ardelt, M. (1992). Families under economic pressure. *Journal of Family Issues, 13,* 5-37.

Elder, G, H., Jr., Modell, J., & Parke, R. E. (Eds.). (1993). *Children in time and place: Developmental and historical insights* (Cambridge Studies in Social and Emotional Development). Cambridge, UK: Cambridge University Press.

Elder, G. H., Jr., & O'Rand, A. M. (1995). Adult lives in a changing society. In K. S. Cook, G. A. Fine, & J. S. House (Eds.), *Sociological perspectives on social psychology* (pp. 452-475). Boston: Allyn & Bacon.

Elder, G. H., Jr., Pavalko, E. K., & Clipp, E. C. (1993). *Working with archival data: Studying lives* (Sage University Papers Series, Quantitative Applications in the Social Sciences, No. 07-088). Newbury Park, CA: Sage.

Elder, G. H., Jr., Pavalko, E. K., & Hastings, T. J. (1991). Talent, history, and the fulfillment of promise. *Psychiatry, 54,* 251-267.

Elder, G. H., Jr., & Rockwell, R. C. (1979). Economic depression and postwar opportunity in men's lives: A study of life patterns and mental health. In R. G. Simmons (Ed.), *Research in community and mental health* (Vol. 1, pp. 249-303). Greenwich, CT: JAI.

Elder, G. H., Jr., Shanahan, M. J., & Clipp, E. C. (1994). When war comes to men's lives: Life-course patterns in family, work, and health. *Psychology and Aging, 9,* 5-16.

Elder, G. H., Jr., Shanahan, M. J., & Clipp, E. C. (1997). Linking combat and physical health: The legacy of World War II in men's lives. *American Journal of Psychiatry, 154,* 330-336.

Elder, G. H., Jr., Wu, W., & Yuan, J. (1993). *State-initiated change and the life course in Shanghai, China.* Unpublished manuscript, Carolina Population Center, University of North Carolina at Chapel Hill.

Elias, P. (1991). Methodological, statistical and practical issues arising from the collection and analysis of work history information by survey techniques. *Bulletin de Methodologie Sociologique, 31,* 3-31.

Elias, P. (1996). *Who forgot they were unemployed?* Working paper, Institute for Employment Research, University of Warwick, UK.

Erikson, E. H. (1950). *Childhood and society.* New York: Norton.

Erikson, E. H. (1958). *Young man Luther: A study in psychoanalysis and history* (Austin Riggs Monograph No. 4). New York: Norton.

Erikson, E. H. (1969). *Gandhi's truth: On the origins of militant nonviolence.* New York: Norton.

Erikson, R., & Goldthorpe, J. H. (1992). *The constant flux: A study of class mobility in industrial societies.* Oxford, UK: Clarendon.

Esterberg, K. G., Moen, P., & Dempster-McClain. D. (1994). Transition to divorce: A life-course approach to women's marital duration and dissolution. *Sociological Quarterly, 35,* 289-307.

European Commission. (1995). *Bulletin on women and employment in the EU* (Industrial Relations and Social Affairs, No. 6). Brussels: Directorate General for Employment.

Featherman, D. L. (1980). Retrospective longitudinal research: Methodological considerations. *Journal of Economics and Business, 32,* 152-169.

Featherman, D. L. (1986). Biography, society and history: Individual development as a population process. In A. B. Sørensen, F. E. Weinert, & L. R. Sherrod (Eds.), *Human development and the life course: Multidisciplinary perspectives* (pp. 99-149). Hillsdale, NJ: Lawrence Erlbaum.

Featherman, D. L., & Hauser, R. M. (1978). *Opportunity and change.* New York: Academic Press.

Featherman, D. L., & Lerner, R. W. (1985). Ontogenesis and sociogenesis: Problematics for theory and research about development and socialization across the lifespan. *American Sociological Review, 50,* 659 676.

Featherman, D. L., Selbee, L. K., & Mayer, K. U. (1989). Social class and the structuring of the life course in Norway and West Germany. In D. I. Kertzer & K. W. Schaie (Eds.), *Age structuring in comparative perspective* (pp. 55-93). Hillsdale, NJ: Lawrence Erlbaum.

Featherman, D. L., & Sørensen, A. (1983). Societal transformation in Norway and change in the life course transition into adulthood. *Acta Sociologica, 26,* 105-126.

Felmlee, D. H. (1988). Returning to school and women's occupational attainment. *Sociology of Education, 61,* 29-41.

Fernandez-Kelly, M. P. (1997). Delicate transactions: Gender, home, and employment among Hispanic women. In M. B. Zinn, P. Hondagneu-Sotelo, & M. A. Messner (Eds.), *The prism of difference: Readings on sex and gender* (pp. 313-322). Boston: Allyn & Bacon.

Fleming, D., & Bailyn, B. (Eds.). (1969). *The intellectual migration: Europe and America, 1930-1960.* Cambridge, MA: Belknap Press of Harvard University Press.

Forest, K. B., Moen, P., & Dempster-McClain, D. (1995). Cohort differences in the transition to motherhood: The variable effects of education and employment before marriage. *Sociological Quarterly, 36,* 315-336.

Forest, K. B., Moen, P., & Dempster-McClain, D. (1996). The effects of childhood family stress on women's depressive symptoms: A life course approach. *Psychology of Women Quarterly, 20,* 81-100.

Forster, R., & Ranum, O. (1976). *Family and society: Selections from the Annales, Économies, Sociétés, Civilisations* (E. Forster & P. M. Ranum, Trans., Biology of Man in History). Baltimore, MD: Johns Hopkins University Press.

Freedman, D., Thornton, A., Camburn, D., Alwin, D. F., & Young-DeMarco, L. (1988). The life history calendar: A technique for collecting retrospective data. *Sociological Methodology, 18,* 37-68.

Friedan, B. (1963). *The feminine mystique.* New York: Norton.

Fuchs, W. (1984). *Biographische Forschung: Eine Einführung in Praxis und Methoden.* Opladen, Germany: Westdeutscher Verlag.

Gallie, D., Marsh, C., & Vogler, C. (Eds.). (1994). *Social change and the experience of unemployment* (Social Change and Economic Life Initiative). Oxford, UK: Oxford University Press.

Gergen, K. J., & Gergen, M. M. (1987). The self in temporal perspective. In R. P. Abeles (Ed.), *Life-span perspectives and social psychology* (pp. 121-137). Hillsdale, NJ: Lawrence Erlbaum.

Gerson, K. (1985). *Hard choices: How women decide about work, career, and motherhood.* Berkeley: University of California Press.

Giele, J. Z. (1978). *Women and the future: Changing sex roles in modern America.* New York: Free Press.

Giele, J. Z. (1980). Adulthood as transcendence of age and sex. In N. J. Smelser & E. H. Erikson (Eds.), *Themes of work and love in adulthood* (pp. 151-173). Cambridge, MA: Harvard University Press.

Giele, J. Z. (1982a). Cohort variation in life patterns of educated women, 1911-1960. *Western Sociological Review, 13*(1), 1-24.

Giele, J. Z. (Ed.). (1982b). *Women in the middle years: Current knowledge and directions for research and policy.* New York: John Wiley.

Giele, J. Z. (1987). Coeducation or women's education: A comparison of alumnae from two colleges. In C. Lasser (Ed.), *Educating men and women together: Coeducation in a changing world* (pp. 91-109). Urbana: University of Illinois Press.

Giele, J. Z. (1988). Gender and sex roles. In N. J. Smelser (Ed.), *The handbook of sociology* (pp. 291-323). Newbury Park, CA: Sage.

Giele, J. Z. (1993). Women's role change and adaptation, 1920-1990. In K. D. Hulbert & D. T. Schuster (Eds.), *Women's lives through time: Educated American women of the twentieth century* (pp. 32-60, Jossey-Bass Social and Behavioral Science Series and Jossey-Bass Adult and Higher Education Series). San Francisco: Jossey-Bass.

Giele, J. Z. (1995). *Two paths to women's equality: Temperance, suffrage, and the origins of modern feminism* (Social Movements Past and Present). New York: Twayne.

Giele, J. Z., & Gilfus, M. (1990). Race and college differences in life patterns of educated women, 1934-82. In J. Antler & S. K. Biklen (Eds.), *Changing education: Women as radicals and conservators* (pp. 179-197). Albany: State University of New York Press.

Giele, J. Z., & Holst, E. (1997). Dynamics of women's labor force participation in the U.S. and Germany, 1983-1990. *Vierteljahrshefte zur Wirtschaftsforschung,* No. 1, 55-61.

Giele, J. Z., & Pischner, R. (1994). The emergence of multiple role patterns among women: A comparison of Germany and the United States. *Vierteljahrshefte zur Wirtschaftsforschung,* Nos. 1/2, 97-103.

Giele, J. Z., & Smock, A. C. (Eds.). (1977). *Women: Roles and status in eight countries.* New York: John Wiley.

Gilligan, C. (1982). *In a different voice: Psychological theory and women's development.* Cambridge, MA: Harvard University Press.

Giordano, P. C. (1989). Confronting control theory's negative cases. In S. F. Messner, M. D. Krohn, & A. E. Liska (Eds.), *Theoretical integration in the study of deviance and crime* (pp. 261-278, SUNY Series in Critical Issues in Criminal Justice and SUNY Series in Deviance and Social Control). Albany: State University of New York Press.

Glenn, E. N. (1986). *Issei, Nisei, war bride: Three generations of Japanese American women in domestic service.* Philadelphia: Temple University Press.

Glueck, S., & Glueck, E. (1930). *500 criminal careers.* New York: Knopf.

Glueck, S., & Glueck, E. (1934a). *Five hundred delinquent women.* New York: Knopf.

Glueck, S., & Glueck, E. (1934b). *One thousand juvenile delinquents.* Cambridge, MA: Harvard University Press.

Glueck, S., & Glueck, E. (1950). *Unraveling juvenile delinquency.* New York: Commonwealth Fund.

Glueck, S., & Glueck, E. (1968). *Delinquents and nondelinquents in perspective.* Cambridge, MA: Harvard University Press.

Goldin, C. D. (1995). *Career and family: College women look to the past* (NBER Working Paper Series No. 5188). Cambridge, MA: National Bureau of Economic Research.

Gottfredson, M. R., & Hirschi, T. (1990). *A general theory of crime.* Stanford, CA: Stanford University Press.

Gottschalk, L. R., Kluckhohn, C., & Angell, R. C. (1945). *The use of personal documents in history, anthropology, and sociology* (Social Science Research Council Bulletin No. 53). New York: Social Science Research Council.

Gould, R. L. (1978). *Transformations: Growth and change in adult life.* New York: Simon & Schuster.

Graaf, P. de (1987). Intergenerationale klassenmobiliteit in Nederland tussen 1970 en 1986. *Mens en Maatschappij, 62,* 209-221.

Groves, R. M., Blemer, P. P., Lyberg, L. E., Massey, J. T., Nichols, W. L., II, & Walksberg, J. (1988). *Telephone survey methodology* (Wiley Series in Probability and Mathematical Statistics, Applied Probability and Statistics, No. 0271-6356). New York: John Wiley.

Gunderson, T. L., with McGovern, R. (1989). *How to locate anyone anywhere without leaving home.* New York: Dutton.

Halbwachs, M. (1925). *Les cadres sociaux de la mémoire.* Paris: Alcan.

Handl, J. (1988). *Berufschancen und Heiratsmuster von Frauen: Empirische Untersuchungen zu Prozessen sozialer Mobilität.* Frankfurt am Main, Germany: Campus.

Hareven, T. K. (1982). *Family time and industrial time: The relationship between family and work in a New England industrial community* (Interdisciplinary Perspectives on Modern History). Cambridge, UK: Cambridge University Press.

Hareven, T. K., & Masaoka, K. (1988). Turning points and transitions: Perceptions of the life course. *Journal of Family History, 13,* 271-289.

Harris, P. M. G. (1969). The social origins of American leaders: The demographic foundations. *Perspectives in American History, 3,* 157-344.

Hauser, R. M., Tsai, S.-L., & Sewell, W. H. (1983). A model of stratification with response error in social and psychological variables. *Sociology of Education, 56,* 20-46.

Heilbrun, C. G. (1988). *Writing a woman's life.* New York: Norton.

Helson, R., & Picano, J. (1990). Is the traditional role bad for women? *Journal of Personality and Social Psychology, 59,* 311-320.

Henry, B., Moffitt, T. E., Caspi, A., Langley, J., & Silva, P. A. (1994). On the "Remembrance of Things Past": A longitudinal evaluation of the retrospective method. *Psychological Assessment, 6,* 92-101.

Henz, U. (1996). *Intergenerationale Mobilität: Methodische und empirische Analysen* (Studien und Berichte Nr. 63). Berlin: Max-Planck-Institut für Bildungsforschung.

Herzog, A. R., & Rodgers, W. L. (1988). Interviewing older adults: Mode comparison using data from a face-to-face survey and a telephone resurvey. *Public Opinion Quarterly, 52,* 84-99.

Heyde, C. A. von der (1988). *InfraScope: Der neue Standard für CATI in Deutschland.* Munich: Infratest.

Higginbotham, E., & Weber, L. (1997). Moving up with kin and community: Upward social mobility for black and white women. In M. B. Zinn, P. Hondagneu-Sotelo, & M. A. Messner (Eds.), *The prism of difference: Readings on sex and gender* (pp. 337-345). Boston: Allyn & Bacon.

Hill, D. H. (1987). Response errors around the seam: Analysis of change in a panel with overlapping reference periods. In *American Statistical Association 1987 Proceedings of the Section on Survey Research Methods* (pp. 210-215). Washington, DC: American Statistical Association.

Hill, D. H., & Hill, M. S. (1986). Labor force transitions: A comparison of unemployment estimates from two longitudinal surveys. In *American Statistical Association 1986 proceedings of the Section on Survey Research Methods* (pp. 220-225). Washington, DC: American Statistical Association.

Hill, M. S. (1992). *The Panel Study of Income Dynamics: User's guide.* Newbury Park, CA: Sage.

Hill, R., with Foote, N. (1970). *Family development in three generations: A longitudinal study of changing family patterns of planning and achievement.* Cambridge, MA: Schenkman.

Hogan, D. P. (1978). The variable order of events in the life course. *American Sociological Review, 43,* 573-586.

Hogan, D. P. (1981). *Transitions and social change: The early lives of American men.* New York: Academic Press.

Hogan, D. P., & Kertzer, D. I. (1985a) Longitudinal approaches to migration in social history. *Historical Methods, 18,* 20-30.

Hogan, D. P., & Kertzer, D. I. (1985b). Migration patterns during Italian urbanization, 1865-1921. *Demography, 22,* 309-325.

Hormuth, S. E. (1990). *The ecology of the self: Relocation and self concept change* (European Monographs in Social Psychology). Cambridge, UK: Cambridge University Press.

Hormuth, S. E., & Brückner, E. (1985). Telefoninterviews in Sozialforschung und Sozialpsychologie: Ausgewählte Probleme der Stichprobengewinnung, Kontaktierung und Versuchsplanung. *Kölner Zeitschrift für Soziologie und Sozialpsychologie, 37,* 526-545.

Hormuth, S. E., & Lalli, M. (1988). Skala zur Erfassung der bereichsspezifischen Selbstzufriedenheit. *Diagnostica, 34,* 148-166.

Hout, M. (1989). *Following in father's footsteps: Social mobility in Ireland.* Cambridge, MA: Harvard University Press.

Huinink, J. (1994). Familienentwicklung und Haushaltsgründung in der DDR: Vom traditionellen Muster zur instrumentellen Lebensplanung? In B. Nauck, N. Schneider, & A. Tölke (Eds.), *Familie und Lebensverlauf im gesellschaftlichen Umbruch* (pp. 39-55). Stuttgart, Germany: F. Enke.

Huinink, J., & Mayer, K. U. (1995). Gender, social inequality, and family formation in West Germany. In K. O. Mason & A.-M. Jensen (Eds.), *Gender and family change in industrialized countries* (pp. 168-199). Oxford, UK: Clarendon.

Huinink, J., Mayer, K. U., Diewald, M., Solga, H., Sørensen, A., & Trappe, H. (1995). *Kollektiv und Eigensinn: Lebensverläufe in der DDR und danach.* Berlin: Akademie Verlag.

Hulbert, K. D., & Schuster, D. T. (Eds.). (1993). *Women's lives through time: Educated American women of the twentieth century.* San Francisco: Jossey-Bass.

Hyman, H. H. (1954). *Survey design and analysis: Principles, cases and procedures.* New York: Free Press.

Inkeles, A., & Levinson, D. J. (1954). National character: The study of modal personality and sociocultural systems. In G. Lindzey (Ed.), *Handbook of social psychology* (Vol. 2, pp. 977-1020). Reading, MA: Addison-Wesley.

Inkeles, A., & Smith, D. H. (1974). *Becoming modern: Individual change in six developing countries.* Cambridge, MA: Harvard University Press.

James, W. (1906). *The varieties of religious experience: A study in human nature—Being the Gifford Lectures on Natural Religion delivered at Edinburgh in 1901-1902.* New York: Longman, Green.

Janson, C.-G. (1990). Retrospective data, undesirable behavior, and the longitudinal perspective. In D. Magnusson & L. R. Bergman (Eds.), *Data quality in longitudinal research* (pp. 100-121). Cambridge, UK: Cambridge University Press.

Jick, T. D. (1979). Mixing qualitative and quantitative methods: Triangulation in action. *Administrative Science Quarterly, 24,* 602-611.

Johnson, M. E. (1976). *The role of perceived parental models, expectations and socializing behaviors in the self-expectations of adolescents, from the U.S. and West Germany.* Unpublished doctoral dissertation, Rutgers University.

Jones, J. (1985). *Labor of love, labor of sorrow: Black women, work, and the family from slavery to the present.* New York: Basic Books.

Jöreskog, K. G., & Sörbom, D. (1979). *Advances in factor analysis and structural equation models.* Cambridge, MA: Abt Books.

Jung, C. (1963). *Memories, dreams, reflections* (Aniela Jaffé, Ed., and R. Winston & C. Winston, Trans.). New York: Vintage.

Kahne, H., & Giele, J. Z. (Eds.). (1992). *Women's work and women's lives: The continuing struggle worldwide.* Boulder, CO: Westview.

Kalleberg, A. L., & Rockwell, R. C. (1995). Employers, employees, and work: A research program. In D. B. Bills (Ed.), *The new modern times: Factors reshaping the world of work* (pp. 281-302). Albany: State University of New York Press.

Kanter, R. M. (1977). *Work and family in the United States: A critical review and agenda for research and policy.* New York: Russell Sage.

Karweit, N. L. (1973). Storage and retrieval of life history data. *Social Science Research, 2,* 41-50.

Karweit, N. L., & Kertzer, D. I. (1986). Data base management for life course family research. *Current Perspectives on Aging and the Life Cycle, 2,* 167-188.

Katz, E., & Lazarsfeld, P. F. (1956). *Personal influence: The part played by people in the flow of mass communications* (Foundations of Communications Research). Glencoe, IL: Free Press.

Katz, J. (1988). *Seductions of crime: Moral and sensual attractions in doing evil.* New York: Basic Books.

Kendall, P. L., & Lazarsfeld, P. F. (1950). Problems of survey analysis. In R. K. Merton & P. F. Lazarsfeld (Eds.), *Studies in the scope and method of "The American Soldier"* (pp. 33-196, Perspectives in Social Inquiry). Glencoe, IL: Free Press.

Kertzer, D. I. (1983). Generation as a sociological problem. *Annual Review of Sociology, 9,* 125-149.

Kertzer, D. I. (1986). A life course approach to coresidence. *Current Perspectives on Aging and the Life Cycle, 2,* 1-22.

Kertzer, D. I., & Hogan, D. P. (1985). On the move: Migration in an Italian community, 1865-1921. *Social Science History, 9,* 1-23.

Kertzer, D. I., & Hogan, D. P. (1986). The social bases of declining infant mortality: Lessons from a nineteenth-century Italian community. *European Journal of Population, 2,* 361-386.

Kertzer, D. I., & Hogan, D. P. (1989). *Family, political economy, and demographic change: The transformation of life in Casalecchio, Italy, 1861-1921.* Madison: University of Wisconsin Press.

Kertzer, D. I., & Hogan, D. P. (1990). Household organization and migration in nineteenth-century Italy. *Social Science History, 14,* 483-505.

Kertzer, D. I., Hogan, D. P., & Karweit, N. L. (1992). Kinship beyond the household in a nineteenth-century Italian town. *Continuity and Change, 7,* 1-19.

Kertzer, D. I., & Karweit, N. L. (1991). Living with grandparents: The tenacity of three-generational households in an industrializing Italian community (1871-1921). *Annales de Démographie Historique 1991,* pp. 91-102.

Kertzer, D. I., & Karweit, N. L. (1994). The life course of widows and widowers in nineteenth-century Italy. In D. I. Kertzer & P. Laslett, (Eds.), *Aging in the past: Demography, society, and old age* (Studies in Demography No. 7). Berkeley: University of California Press.

Kertzer, D. I., & Schiaffino, A. (1983). Industrialization and coresidence: A life-course approach. *Life-Span Development and Human Behavior, 5,* 359-391.

Kessler, R. C., & Greenberg, D. F. (1981). *Linear panel analysis: Models of quantitative change.* New York: Academic Press.

Kessler, R. C., Mroczek, D. K., & Belli, R. F. (1994). Retrospective adult assessment of childhood psychopathology. In D. Shaffer & J. Richters (Eds.), *Assessment in child and adolescent psychopathology.* New York: Guilford.

Kidder, L. H., & Fine, M. (1987). Qualitative and quantitative methods: When stories converge. *New Directions for Program Evaluation, 35,* 57-75.

King, D. (1992). *Get the facts on anyone.* Englewood Cliffs, NJ: Prentice Hall.

Kirschner, H.-P., & Wiedenbeck, M. (1989). Methodenreport: Stichprobe. In K. U. Mayer & E. Brückner (Eds.), *Lebensverläufe und Wohlfahrtsentwicklung: Konzeption, Design und Methodik der Erhebung von Lebensverläufen der Geburtsjahrgänge*

1929-1931, 1939-1941, 1949-1951—Teil I, p. 83, Materialien aus der Bildungsforschung No. 35. Berlin: Max-Planck-Institut für Bildungsforschung.

Knorr-Cetina, K. D. (1982). Scientific communities or transepistemic arenas of research? A critique of quasi-economic models of science. *Social Studies of Science, 12,* 101-130.

Kohlberg, L. (1969). Stage and sequence: The cognitive-developmental approach to socialization. In D. A. Goslin (Ed.), *Handbook of socialization theory and research* (pp. 347-480, Rand McNally Sociology Series). Chicago: Rand McNally.

Kohli, M. (1986). The world we forgot: A historical review of the life course. In V. W. Marshall (Ed.), *Later life: The social psychology of aging* (pp. 271-303). Beverly Hills, CA: Sage.

Kohli, M. (1987). Retirement and the moral economy: An historical interpretation of the German case. *Journal of Aging Studies, 1,* 125-144.

Kohli, M., Rein, M., Guillemard, A.-M., & Van Gunsteren, H. (Eds.). (1991). *Time for retirement: Comparative studies of early exit from the labor force* (pp. 90-105). Cambridge, UK: Cambridge University Press.

Kohn, M. L., & Schooler, C. (1983). *Work and personality: An inquiry into the impact of social stratification* (Modern Sociology). Norwood, NJ: Ablex.

Komarovsky, M. (1982). Female freshmen view their future: Career salience and its correlates. *Sex Roles, 8,* 299-314.

Körmendi, E., Esgsmose, L., & Noordhoek, J. (1986). *Datakvalitet ved telefoninterview: En sammenlignende undersogelse af besogs- og telefoninterviewing* (Studie/Socialforskningsinstituttet No. 52). Copenhagen: Socialforskingsinstituttet.

Kotlowitz, A. (1991). *There are no children here: The story of two boys growing up in the other America.* New York: Doubleday.

Ladurie, E. L. R. (1976). A system of customary law: Family structures and inheritance customs in sixteenth-century France. In R. Forster & O. Ranum (Eds.), *Family and society: Selections from the Annales, Économies, Sociétés, Civilisations* (pp. 75-103, E. Forster & P. M. Ranum, Trans., Biology of Man in History). Baltimore, MD: Johns Hopkins University Press. (Originally published 1972)

Laslett, P. (1972). The comparative history of household and family. In M. Gordon (Ed.), *The American family in social-historical perspective* (pp. 19-33). New York: St. Martin's.

Laslett, P. (1991). *A fresh map of life: The emergence of the third age.* London: Weidenfeld & Nicholson.

Latour, B. (1987). *Science in action: How to follow scientists and engineers through society.* Cambridge MA: Harvard University Press.

Laub, J. H., & Sampson. R. J. (1988). Unraveling families and delinquency: A reanalysis of the Gluecks' data. *Criminology, 26,* 355-380.

Laub, J. H., & Sampson, R. J. (1993). Turning points in the life course: Why change matters to the study of crime. *Criminology, 31,* 301-325.

Laub, J. H., & Sampson, R. J. (1995). Crime and context in the lives of 1,000 Boston men, circa 1925-1955. In Z. S. Blau & J. H. Hagan (Eds.), *Current Perspectives on Aging and Life Cycle, Vol. 4: Delinquency and disrepute in the life course* (pp. 119-139). Greenwich, CT: JAI Press.

Laub, J. H., Sampson, R. J., & Kiger, K. (1990). Assessing the potential of secondary data analysis: A new look at the Gluecks' data. In K. L. Kempf (Ed.), *Measurement issues in criminology* (pp. 241-257). New York: Springer-Verlag.

Laufer, R. S. (1985). War trauma and human development: The Viet Nam experience. In S. M. Sonnenberg, A. S. Blank, Jr., & J. A. Talbot (Eds.), *The trauma of war: Stress and recovery in Viet Nam veterans* (pp. 33-56). Washington, DC: American Psychiatric Press.

Lazarsfeld, P. F. (1948). The use of panels in social research. *Proceedings of the American Philosophical Society, 92,* 405-410.

Lazarsfeld, P. F., Berelson, B., & Gaudet, H. (1944). *The people's choice: How the voter makes up his mind in a presidential campaign* (Columbia University, Bureau of Applied Social Research, No. B-3). New York: Duell, Sloane, & Pierce.

Lazarsfeld, P. F., & Fiske, M. (1938). The "panel" as a new tool for measuring opinion. *Public Opinion Quarterly, 2,* 596-612.

Lazarsfeld, P. F., & Thielens, W., Jr. (1958). *The academic mind: Social scientists in a time of crisis.* Glencoe, IL: Free Press.

Levinson, D. J., with Darrow, C. N., Klein, E. B., Levinson, M. H., & McKee, B. (1978). *The seasons of a man's life.* New York: Knopf.

Lévi-Strauss, C. (1969). *The elementary structures of kinship* (rev. ed., J. H. Bell, J. R. von Sturmer, & R. Needham, Eds. and Trans.). Boston: Beacon. (Originally published 1949)

Lillard, L. A. (1989). Sample dynamics: Some behavioral issues. In D. Kasprzyk, G. J. Duncan, G. Kalton, & M. Singh (Eds.), *Panel surveys* (pp. 497-511, Wiley Series in Probability and Mathematical Statistics, Applied Probability and Statistics Section). New York: John Wiley.

Lillard, L. A., & Waite, L. J. (1989). Panel versus retrospective data on marital histories: Lessons from PSID. In H. Beaton, D. Ganni, & D. Frankel (Eds.), *Individuals and families in transition: Understanding change through longitudinal data* (pp. 243-253). Washington, DC: U.S. Department of Commerce, Bureau of the Census.

Loeber, R., & Stouthamer-Loeber, M. (1986). Family factors as correlates and predictors of juvenile conduct problems and delinquency. In M. H. Tonry & N. Morris (Eds.), *Crime and justice* (Vol. 7, pp. 29-149). Chicago: University of Chicago Press.

Lowenthal, M. F., Thurnher, M., & Chiriboga, D. (1975). *Four stages of life* (Jossey-Bass Behavioral Science Series). San Francisco: Jossey-Bass.

Lykken, D. T. (1968). Statistical significance in psychological research. *Psychological Bulletin, 70,* 151-159.

Mach, B. W., Mayer, K. U., & Pohoski, M. (1994). Job changes in the Federal Republic of Germany and Poland: A longitudinal assessment of the impact of welfare-capitalist and state-socialist labour-market segmentation. *European Sociological Review, 10,* 1-28.

Maddox, G. L. (1962). A longitudinal multidisciplinary study of human aging: Selected methodological issues. In *1962 Proceedings of the Social Statistics Section of the American Statistical Association* (pp. 280-285). Washington, DC: American Statistical Association.

Maddox, G. L. (1993). Foreword: Special issue on the Berlin Aging Study. *Ageing and Society, 13,* 475-482.

Maddox, G. L., & Wiley, J. (1976). Scope, concepts and methods in the study of aging. In R. H. Binstock & E. Shanas (Eds.), with V. L. Bengtson, G. L. Maddox, & D. Wedderburn, *Handbook of aging and the social sciences* (pp. 3-34, Handbooks of Aging). New York: Van Nostrand Reinhold.

Magnusson, D., & Bergman, L. R. (1988). Individual and variable-based approaches to longitudinal research on early risk factors. In M. Rutter (Ed.), *Studies of psychosocial risk: The power of longitudinal data* (pp. 45-61). Cambridge, UK: Cambridge University Press.

Magnusson, D., & Bergman, L. R. (1990). A pattern approach to the study of pathways from childhood to adulthood. In L. N. Robins & M. Rutter (Eds.), *Straight and devious pathways from childhood to adulthood* (pp. 101-115). Cambridge, UK: Cambridge University Press.

Maines, D. R. (1992). Life history. In E. F. Borgatta & M. L. Borgatta (Eds.), *Encyclopedia of sociology* (Vol. 3, pp. 1134-1137). New York: Macmillan.

Mannheim, K. (1952a). *Essays on the sociology of knowledge.* New York: Oxford University Press. (Originally published 1929)

Mannheim, K. (1952b). The problem of generations. In P. Kecskemeti (Ed. and Trans.), *Essays on the sociology of knowledge* (pp. 276-322). New York: Oxford University Press.

Marini, M. M. (1984). The order of events in the transition to adulthood. *Sociology of Education, 57,* 63-84.

Marini, M. M., Shin, H.-C., & Raymond, J. (1989). Socioeconomic consequences of the process of transition to adulthood. *Social Science Research, 18,* 89-135.

Marks, S. R. (1977). Multiple roles and role strain: Some notes on human energy, time and commitment. *American Sociological Review, 42,* 921-936.

Markus, G. B. (1986). Stability and change in political attitudes: Observed, recalled and "explained." *Political Behavior, 8,* 21-44.

Marshall, V. W. (1975). Age and awareness of finitude in developmental gerontology. *Omega, 6,* 113-129.

Mauss, M. (1967). *The gift: Forms of exchange and function in archaic societies.* New York: Norton. (Originally published 1925)

Mayer, K. U. (1977). *Fluktuation und Umschichtung. Empirische Untersuchungen zu Strukturen sozialer Ungleichheit und Prozessen sozialer Mobilität in der Bundesrepublik Deutschland* (Habilitationsschrift). Mannheim, Germany: Universität Mannheim.

Mayer, K. U. (1980). *Amtliche Statistik und Umfrageforschung als Datenquellen der Soziologie.* Mannheim, Germany: VASMA-Arbeitspapier.

Mayer, K. U. (1989). Die Mikrodatenstrategie des Sonderforschungsbereichs 3 "Mikroanalytische Grundlagen der Gesellschaftspolitik." In G. Wagner, N. Ott, & H.-J. Hoffmann-Nowotny (Eds.), *Familienbildung und Erwerbstätigkeit im demographischen Wandel: Proceedings der 23. Arbeitstagung der Deutschen Gesellschaft für Bevölkerungswissenschaft am 28. Februar-3. März 1989 in Bad Homburg v.d.H.* (pp. 47-69). Berlin: Springer-Verlag.

Mayer, K. U. (1995). Gesellschaftlicher Wandel, Kohortenungleichheit und Lebensverläufe. In P. A. Berger & P. Sopp (Eds.), *Sozialstruktur und Lebenslauf* (pp. 27-47). Opladen, Germany: Leske & Budrich.

Mayer, K. U., Allmendinger, J., & Huinink, J. (Eds.). (1991). *Vom Regen in die Traufe: Frauen zwischen Beruf und Familie.* Frankfurt am Main, Germany: Campus.

Mayer, K. U., & Baltes, P. B. (Eds.). (1996). *Die Berliner Altersstudie.* Berlin: Akademie Verlag.

Mayer, K. U., & Brückner, E. (1989). *Lebensverläufe und Wohlfahrtsentwicklung: Konzeption, Design und Methodik der Erhebung von Lebensverläufen der Geburtsjahrgänge 1929-1931, 1939-1941, 1949-1951* (3 vols., Materialien aus der Bildungsforschung No. 35). Berlin: Max-Planck-Institut für Bildungsforschung.

Mayer, K. U., & Carroll, G. R. (1987). Jobs and classes: Structural constraints on career mobility. *European Sociological Review, 3,* 14-38.

Mayer, K. U., & Huinink, J. (1990). Age, period, and cohort in the study of the life course: A comparison of the classical A-P-C analysis with event history analysis or farewell to Lexis? In D. Magnusson & L. R. Bergman (Eds.), *Data quality in longitudinal research* (pp. 211-232). Cambridge, UK: Cambridge University Press.

Mayer, K. U., & Müller, W. (1986). The state and the structure of the life course. In A. B. Sørensen, F. E. Weinert, & L. R. Sherrod (Eds.), *Human development and the life course: Multidisciplinary perspectives* (pp. 217-245). Hillsdale, NJ: Lawrence Erlbaum.

Mayer, K. U., & Solga, H. (1994). Mobilität und Legitimität: Zum Vergleich der Chancenstrukturen in der alten DDR und der alten BRD oder—Haben Mobilitätschancen zu Stabilität und Zusammenbruch der DDR beigetragen? *Kölner Zeitschrift für Soziologie und Sozialpsychologie, 46,* 193-208.

Mayer, K. U., & Tuma, N. B. (1990). *Event history analysis in life course research* (Life Course Studies). Madison: University of Wisconsin Press.

Mayer, K. U., & Wagner, M. (1996). Lebenslagen und soziale Ungleichheit im hohen Alter. In K. U. Mayer & P. B. Baltes (Eds.), *Die Berliner Altersstudie* (pp. 251-275). Berlin: Akademie Verlag.

McAdams, D. P. (1985). *Power, intimacy and the life story: Personological inquiries into identity.* Homewood, IL: Dorsey.

McAllister, R. J., Butler, E. W., & Goe, S. J. (1973). Evolution of a strategy for the retrieval of cases in longitudinal survey research. *Sociology and Social Research, 58,* 37-47.

Mead, G. H. (1934). *Mind, self, and society from the standpoint of a social behavioralist* (C. W. Morris, Ed.). Chicago: University of Chicago Press.

Mead, M. (1949). *Male and female: A study of the sexes in a changing world.* New York: William Morrow.

Merriam, S. (1980). The concept and function of reminiscence: A review of the research. *The Gerontologist, 20,* 604-609.

Merton, R. K. (1948). The bearing of empirical research upon the development of social theory. *American Sociological Review, 13,* 505-515.

Merton, R. K. (1956). *The focused interview.* Glencoe, IL: Free Press.

Merton, R. K. (1959). Notes on problem-finding in sociology. In R. K. Merton, L. Broom, & L. S. Cottrell, Jr. (Eds.), *Sociology today: Problems and prospects* (pp. ix-xxxiv). New York: Basic Books.

Merton, R. K. (1973). *The sociology of science: Theoretical and empirical investigations* (N. K. Storer, Ed.). Chicago: University of Chicago Press.

Merton, R. K. (1981). Remarks on theoretical pluralism. In P. M. Blau & R. K. Merton (Eds.), *Continuities in structural inquiry* (pp. i-vii). Beverly Hills, CA: Sage.

Merton, R. K. (1984). Socially expected durations: A case study of concept formation in sociology. In W. W. Powell & R. Robbins (Eds.), *Conflict and consensus: A festschrift in honor of Lewis A. Coser* (pp. 262-283). New York: Free Press.

Merton, R. K. (1987). Three fragments from a sociologist's notebooks: Establishing the phenomenon, specified ignorance, and strategic research materials. *Annual Review of Sociology, 13,* 1-28.

Merton, R. K., Fiske, M., & Kendall, P. L. (1990). *The focused interview: A manual of problems and procedures* (2nd ed.). New York: Free Press.

Meyer, J. W. (1986). The self and the life course: Institutionalization and its effects. In A. B. Sørensen, F. E. Weinert, & L. R. Sherrod (Eds.), *Human development and the life course: Multidisciplinary perspectives* (pp. 199-216). Hillsdale, NJ: Lawrence Erlbaum.

Mill, J. S. (1909). *The subjection of women* (S. Coit, Ed., with introductory analysis). London: Longman, Green. (Originally published 1869)

Miller, M., Moen, P., & Dempster-McClain, D. (1991). Motherhood, multiple roles, and maternal well-being: Women of the 1950s. *Gender & Society, 5,* 565-582.

Mills, C. W. (1959). *The sociological imagination.* New York: Oxford University Press.

Mincer, J. (1962). Labor force participation of married women: A study of labor supply. In *Aspects of labor economics: A report of the National Bureau of Economic Research* (pp. 63-106, National Bureau of Economic Research Special Conference Series, Vol. 00014). Princeton, NJ: Princeton University Press.

Mishler, E. G. (1986). *Research interviewing: Context and narrative.* Cambridge, MA: Harvard University Press.

Modell, J. (1989). *Into one's own: From youth to adulthood in the United States 1920-1975.* Berkeley: University of California Press.

Modell, J. (1994). Review of *Crime in the Making: Pathways and Turning Points Through Life. American Journal of Sociology, 99,* 1389-1391.

Modell, J., Furstenberg, F. F., & Hershberg, T. (1976). Social change and transitions in adulthood in historical perspective. *Journal of Family History, 1,* 7-32.

Moen, P. (1992). *Women's two roles: A contemporary dilemma.* New York: Auburn House.

Moen, P., & Dempster-McClain, D. (1990). Constructing life histories of women and their daughters. *Human Ecology Forum: A Cornell University Magazine, 18*(4), 19-24.

Moen, P., Dempster-McClain, D., & Williams, R. M., Jr. (1989). Social integration and longevity: An event history analysis of women's roles and resilience. *American Sociological Review, 54,* 635-647.

Moen, P., Dempster-McClain, D., & Williams, R. M., Jr. (1992). Successful aging: A life-course perspective on women's multiple roles and health. *American Journal of Sociology, 97,* 1612-1638.

Moen, P., & Erickson, M. A. (1995). Linked lives: A trans-generational approach to resiliency. In P. Moen, G. H. Elder, Jr., & K. Lüscher (Eds.), with H. E. Quick, *Examining lives in context: Perspectives on the ecology of human development* (pp. 169-210, APA Science Volumes). Washington, DC: American Psychological Association.

Moen, P., Erickson, M. A., & Dempster-McClain, D. (1997). Their mothers' daughters? The intergenerational transmission of gender orientations. *Journal of Marriage and the Family, 59,* 281-293.

Moen, P., Robison, J., & Dempster-McClain, D. (1995). Caregiving and women's well-being: A life course approach. *Journal of Health and Social Behavior, 36,* 259-273.

Moen, P., Robison, J., & Fields, V. (1994). Women's work and caregiving roles: A life course approach. *Journals of Gerontology: Social Sciences, 49,* S176-S186.

Moen, P., & Williams, R. M., Jr. (1986). *Women's roles and well-being: A two generation study* (National Institute on Aging Research Grant No. R01-AG05450). Unpublished manuscript, Cornell University.

Moffitt, T. E., Caspi, A., Henry, B., Langley, J., & Silva, P. A. (1992). *On the "Remembrance of Things Past." I: A longitudinal evaluation of the retrospective method.* Unpublished manuscript, University of Wisconsin.

Molinari, V., & Reichlin, R. E. (1984-1985). Life review reminiscence in the elderly: A review of the literature. *International Journal of Aging & Human Development, 20,* 81-92.

Mroz, T. A. (1987). The sensitivity of an empirical model of married women's hours of work to economic and statistical assumptions. *Econometrica, 55,* 765-799.

Mullins, N. C. (1972). The development of a scientific specialty: The phage group and the origins of molecular biology. *Minerva, 10,* 51-82.

Müller, W. (1978). *Klassenlage und Lebenslauf* (Habilitationsschrift). Mannheim, Germany: Universität Mannheim.

Murray, H. A., Barrett, W. G., & Homburger, E. (1938). *Explorations in personality: A clinical and experimental study of fifty men of college age by the workers at the Harvard Psychological Clinic.* New York: Oxford University Press.

Myrdal, A. R., & Klein, V. (1956). *Women's two roles: Home and work* (International Library of Sociology and Social Reconstruction). London: Routledge & Kegan Paul.

Nasar, S. (1992, October 18). Women's progress stalled? It just isn't so. *The New York Times,* p. C1.

Neugarten, B. L. (1968a). Adult personality: Toward a social psychology of the life cycle. In B. L. Neugarten (Ed.), *Middle age and aging: A reader in social psychology* (pp. 137-147). Chicago: University of Chicago Press.

Neugarten, B. L. (Ed.). (1968b). *Middle age and aging: A reader in social psychology.* Chicago: University of Chicago Press.

Neugarten, B. L. (1979). Time, age, and the life cycle. *American Journal of Psychiatry, 136,* 887-894.

Neugarten, B. L. (1987). Kansas City Studies of Adult Life. In G. L. Maddox (Ed.), *The encyclopedia of aging* (pp. 372-373). New York: Springer.

Neugarten, B. L., & Datan, N. (1973). Sociological perspectives on the life cycle. In P. B. Baltes & K. W. Schaie (Eds.), *Life-span developmental psychology: Personality and socialization* (pp. 53-69). New York: Academic Press.

Neugarten, B. L., & Hagestad, G. O. (1976). Age and the life course. In R. H. Binstock & E. Shanas (Eds.), *Handbook of aging and the social sciences* (pp. 35-55). New York: Van Nostrand Reinhold.

Neugarten, B. L., Moore, J. W., & Lowe, J. C. (1965). Age norms, age constraints, and adult socialization. *American Journal of Sociology, 70,* 710-717.

Neugarten, B. L., & Peterson, W. A. (1957). A study of the American age-grade system. *Proceedings of the 4th Congress of the International Association of Gerontology, 3,* 497-502.

Newcomb, T. (1943). *Personality and social change: Attitude formation in a student community.* New York: Dryden.

Newcomb, T., Koenig, K., Flacks, R., & Warwick, D. (1967). *Persistence and change: Bennington College and its students after 25 years.* New York: John Wiley.

Oppenheimer, V. K. (1970). *The female labor force in the United States: Demographic and economic factors governing its growth and changing composition* (Population Monograph Series, No. 5). Berkeley: University of California, Institute of International Studies.

Oppenheimer, V. K. (1979). Structural sources of economic pressure for wives to work: An analytical framework. *Journal of Family History, 4,* 177-197.

Oppenheimer, V. K. (1982). *Work and the family: A study in social demography* (Studies in Population). New York: Academic Press.

O'Rand, A. M. (1992). Mathematizing social science in the 1950s: The early development and diffusion of game theory. In E. R. Weintraub (Ed.), *Toward a history of game theory* (pp. 177-204). Durham, NC: Duke University Press. (Annual supplement to Vol. 24 of *History of Political Economy*)

O'Rand, A. M., & Ellis, R. A. (1974). Social class and social time perspective. *Social Forces, 53,* 53-62.

O'Rand, A. M., & Krecker, M. L. (1990). Concepts of the life cycle: Their history, meanings and uses in the social sciences. *Annual Review of Sociology, 16,* 241-262.

Ott, N. (1992). *Intrafamily bargaining and household decisions* (Microeconomic Studies). Berlin: Springer-Verlag.

Otto, L. B., & Call, V. R. A. (1990). Managing family data on multiple roles and changing statuses over time. *Journal of Marriage and the Family, 52,* 243-248.

Otto, L. B., Call, V. R. A., & Spenner, K. I. (1981) *Design for a study of entry into careers* (Entry Into Careers Series, Vol. 1). Lexington, MA: Lexington Books.

Papastefanou, G. (1980). *Zur Güte von retrospektiven Daten: Eine Anwendung gedächtnispsychologischer Theorie und Ergebnisse einer Nachbefragung* (Arbeitspapier No. 29). Frankfurt am Main, Germany: Sonderforschungsbereich 3 der Johann Wolfgang Goethe-Universität.

Parsons, T. (1961). An outline of the social system. In T. Parsons, E. Shils, K. D. Naegele, & J. R. Pitts (Eds.), *Theories of society: Foundations of modern sociological theory* (Vol. 1, pp. 30-79). New York: Free Press.

Parsons, T. (1966). *Societies: Evolutionary and comparative perspectives* (Foundations of Modern Sociology Series). Englewood Cliffs, NJ: Prentice Hall.

Parsons, T., & Bales, R. F. (1955). *Family, socialization and interaction process.* Glencoe, IL: Free Press.

Pearson, R. W., Ross, M., & Dawes, R. M. (1992). Personal recall and the limits of retrospective questions in surveys. In J. Tanur (Ed.), *Questions about questions: Inquiries into the cognitive bases of surveys* (pp. 65-94). New York: Russell Sage.

Perun, P. J., & Giele, J. Z. (1982). Life after college: Historical links between women's education and women's work. In P. J. Perun (Ed.), *The undergraduate woman: Issues in educational equality* (pp. 375-398). Lexington, MA: Lexington Books.

Peters, H. E. (1988). Retrospective versus panel data in analyzing lifecycle events. *Journal of Human Resources, 13,* 487-513.

Plummer, K. (1983). *Documents of life: An introduction to the problems and literature of a humanistic method* (Contemporary Social Reseach Series No. 7). London: Allen & Unwin.

Presser, S. (1982). Studying social change with survey data: Examples from Louis Harris surveys. *Social Indicators Research, 10,* 407-422.

Rabb, T. K., & Rotberg, R. I. (Eds.). (1971). *The family in history: Interdisciplinary essays.* New York: Harper & Row.

Ramsøy, N. R. (1984). *Codebook and documentation of the Norwegian Life History Study.* Oslo: University of Oslo.

Ramsøy, N. R., & Clausen, S. (1977, October). *Events as units of analysis in life history studies.* Paper presented at the Social Science Research Council Conference on National Longitudinal Surveys, Washington, DC.

Ravetz, J. R. (1971). *Scientific knowledge and its social problems.* Oxford, UK: Clarendon.

Rhodes, R. (1990). *A hole in the world: An American boyhood.* New York: Simon & Schuster.

Riley, M. W. (1963). *Sociological research* (2 vols.). New York: Harcourt Brace & World.

Riley, M. W. (1973). Aging and cohort succession: Interpretations and misinterpretations. *Public Opinion Quarterly, 37,* 35-49.

Riley, M. W. (1978, Fall). Aging, social change, and the power of ideas. *Daedalus, 107,* 39-52.

Riley, M. W. (Ed.). (1979). *Aging from birth to death, Vol. 1: Interdisciplinary perspectives* (AAAS Selected Symposium No. 30). Boulder, CO: Westview.

Riley, M. W. (1987). On the significance of age in sociology: American Sociological Association 1986 presidential address. *American Sociological Review, 52,* 1-14.

Riley, M. W. (Ed.). (1988). *Sociological lives.* Newbury Park, CA: Sage.

Riley, M. W. (1990). The influence of sociological lives: Personal reflections. *Annual Review of Sociology, 16,* 1-25.

Riley, M. W. (1994a). Aging and society: Past, present and future—The 1993 Kent Lecture. *The Gerontologist, 34,* 436-446.

Riley, M. W. (1994b). Data on age-related structural change: Challenges to ICPSR. *ICPSR Bulletin, 15*(1), 1-6.

Riley, M. W., & Abeles, R. P. (Eds.). (1990). *The behavioral and social research program at the National Institute on Aging: History of a decade.* Working document prepared by Behavioral and Social Research Program, National Institute on Aging, National Institutes of Health.

Riley, M. W., Abeles, R. P., & Teitelbaum, M. S. (Eds.). (1982). *Aging from birth to death, Vol. 2: Sociotemporal perspectives* (AAAS Selected Symposium No. 79). Boulder, CO: Westview.

Riley, M. W., Cohn, R., Toby, J., & Riley, J. W., Jr. (1954). Interpersonal orientations in small groups: A consideration of the questionnaire approach. *American Sociological Review, 19,* 715-724.

Riley, M. W., & Foner, A. (1968-1972). *Aging and society* (3 vols.). New York: Russell Sage.

Riley, M. W., Foner, A., Moore, M. E., Hess, B., & Roth, B. K. (1968). *Aging and society,* Vol. 1: *An inventory of research findings.* New York: Russell Sage.

Riley, M. W., Foner, A., & Waring, J. (1988). Sociology of age. In N. J. Smelser (Ed.), *Handbook of sociology* (pp. 243-290). Newbury Park, CA: Sage.

Riley, M. W., Johnson, M. E., & Boocock, S. S. (1963). Women's changing occupational role: A research report. *American Behavioral Scientist, 6,* 33-37.

Riley, M. W., Johnson, M. E., & Foner, A. (1972a). *Aging and society,* Vol. 3: *A sociology of age stratification.* New York: Russell Sage.

Riley, M. W., Johnson, M. E., & Foner, A. (1972b). Elements in a model of age stratification. In M. W. Riley, M. E. Johnson, & A. Foner (Eds.), *Aging and society,* Vol. 3: *A sociology of age stratification* (pp. 3-25). New York: Russell Sage.

Riley, M. W., Kahn, R. L., & Foner, A. (Eds.). (1994). *Age and structural lag: Society's failure to provide meaningful opportunities in work, family, and leisure.* New York: John Wiley.

Riley, M. W., & Nelson, E. E. (1971). Research on stability and change in social systems. In B. Barber & A. Inkeles (Eds.), *Stability and social change: A volume in honor of Talcott Parsons* (pp. 407-449). Boston: Little, Brown.

Riley, M. W., & Riley, J. W., Jr. (1959). Scaling and the clarification of concepts. In A. W. Shyne (Ed.), *Use of judgments as data in social work research* (pp. 79-88, proceedings of a conference held by the Research Section of the National Association of Social Workers). New York: National Association of Social Workers.

Riley, M. W., & Riley, J. W., Jr. (1994). Age integration and the lives of older people. *The Gerontologist, 34,* 110-115.

Riley, M. W., & Waring, J. (1976). Age and aging. In R. K. Merton & R. Nisbet. *Contemporary social problems* (4th ed., pp. 357-410). New York: Harcourt Brace Jovanovich.

Rindfuss, R. R., Morgan, S. P., & Swicegood, C. G. (1984). The transition to motherhood: The intersection of structure and temporal dimension. *American Sociological Review, 49,* 359-372.

Rindfuss, R. R., Swicegood, C. G., & Rosenfeld, R. (1987). Disorder in the life course: How common and does it matter? *American Sociological Review, 52,* 785-801.

Robins, L. N. (1966). *Deviant children grown up: A sociological and psychiatric study of sociopathic personality.* Baltimore, MD: Williams & Wilkins.

Robins, L. N., Schoenberg, S. P., Holmes, S. J., Ratcliff, K. S., Benham, A., & Works, J. (1985). Early home environment and retrospective recall: A test for concordance between siblings with and without psychiatric disorders. *American Journal of Orthopsychiatry, 55,* 27-41.

Robison, J., Moen, P., & Dempster-McClain, D. (1995). Women's caregiving: Changing profiles and pathways. *Journals of Gerontology: Social Sciences, 50B,* S362-S373.

Rodgers, W. L. (1982). Estimable functions of age, period, and cohort effects. *American Sociological Review, 47,* 774-787.

Rosow, I. (1967). *Social integration of the aged.* New York: Free Press.

Ross, M. (1988). The relation of implicit theories to the construction of personal histories. *Psychological Review, 96,* 341-357.

Rossi, A. S. (1980). Life-span theories and women's lives. *Signs: Journal of Women in Culture and Society, 6,* 4-32.

Rossi, A. S. (1983). *Seasons of a woman's life: A self-reflective essay on love and work in family, profession, and politics.* Amherst: University of Massachusetts, Social and Demographic Research Institute.

Rossi, A. S., & Rossi, P. E. (1977). Body time and social time: Mood patterns by menstrual cycle phase and day of the week. *Social Science Research, 6,* 273-308.

Rubin, D. C. (Ed.). (1986). *Autobiographical memory.* Cambridge, UK: Cambridge University Press.

Rubin, D. C., & Baddeley, A. D. (1989). Telescoping is not time compression: A model of the dating of autobiographical events. *Memory and Cognition, 17,* 653-661.

Ryder, N. B. (1965). The cohort as a concept in the study of social change. *American Sociological Review, 30,* 843-861.

Ryder, N. B. (1979). *Commentary on cohorts, periods, and ages.* Paper presented at a conference sponsored by the Social Science Research Council, Aspen, CO.

Ryder, N. B. (1992). Cohort analysis. In E. F. Borgatta & M. L. Borgatta (Eds.), *Encyclopedia of sociology* (Vol. 1, pp. 227-231). New York: Macmillan.

Sampson, H., Messinger, S. L., & Towne, R. (1964). *Schizophrenic women: Studies in marital crisis* (Atherton Press Behavioral Science Series). New York: Atherton.

Sampson, R. J., & Laub, J. H. (1993). *Crime in the making: Pathways and turning points through life.* Cambridge, MA: Harvard University Press.

Sampson, R. J., & Laub, J. H. (1997). A life-course theory of cumulative disadvantage and the stability of delinquency. In T. P. Thornberry (Ed.), *Developmental theories of crime and delinquency* (pp. 133-161, Advances in Criminological Theory, Vol. 7). New Brunswick, NJ: Transaction Publishers.

SanGiovanni, L. (1978). *Ex-nuns: A study of emergent role passages* (Modern Sociology). Norwood, NJ: Ablex.

Sarbin, T. R. (1986). The narrative as a root metaphor for psychology. In T. R. Sarbin (Ed.), *Narrative psychology: The storied nature of human conduct* (pp. 3-21). New York: Praeger.

Schaie, K. W. (1965). A general model for the study of developmental problems. *Psychological Bulletin, 64,* 92-107.

Schaie, K. W. (1977). Quasi-experimental research designs in the psychology of aging. In J. E. Birren & K. W. Schaie (Eds.), *Handbook of the psychology of aging* (pp. 39-58, Handbooks of Aging). New York: Van Nostrand Reinhold.

Schaie, K. W. (1984). Historical time and cohort effects. In K. A. McCluskey & H. W. Reese (Eds.), *Life-span developmental psychology: Historical and generational effects* (pp. 1-15). Orlando, FL: Academic Press.

Schaie, K. W. (1989). The hazards of cognitive aging. *The Gerontologist, 29,* 484-493.

Schaie, K. W., Willis, S., & O'Hanlon, A. (1994). Perceived intellectual performance change over seven years. *Journals of Gerontology: Psychological Sciences, 49,* 108-118.

Schlossman, S., & Cairns, R. B. (1993). Problem girls: Observations on past and present. In G. H. Elder, Jr., J. Modell, & R. D. Parke (Eds.), *Children in time and place: Developmental and historical insights* (pp. 110-130). Cambridge, UK: Cambridge University Press.

Schuman, H., & Rieger, C. (1992). Historical analogies, generational effects, and attitudes towards war. *American Sociological Review, 57,* 315-326.

Schuman, H., Reiger, C., & Gaidys, V. (1994). Collective memories in the United States and Lithuania. In N. Schwarz & S. Sudman (Eds.), *Autobiographical memory and the validity of retrospective reports* (pp. 313-333). New York: Springer-Verlag.

Schuman, H., & Scott, J. (1989). Generations and collective memories. *American Sociological Review, 54,* 359-381.

Schwarz, N., & Sudman, S. (1994). *Autobiographical memory and the validity of retrospective reports.* New York: Springer-Verlag.

Scott, J. (1995). Using household panel studies to study micro-social change. *Innovation, 8,* 61-74.

Scott, J., & Alwin, D. F. (1993, August). *The reliability of retrospective life history data: Implications for integrating methods.* Paper presented at the meeting of the American Sociological Association, Miami, FL.

Scott, J., & Zac, L. (1993). Collective memories in the United States and Britain. *Public Opinion Quarterly, 57,* 315-331.

Sears, D. O. (1983). On the persistence of early political predispositions: The roles of attitude object and life stage. *Review of Personality and Social Psychology, 4,* 79-116.

Segura, D. A. 1997. Working at motherhood: Chicana and Mexican immigrant mothers and employment. In M. B. Zinn, P. Hondagneu-Sotelo, & M. A. Messner (Eds.), *The prism of difference: Readings on sex and gender* (pp. 276-290). Boston: Allyn & Bacon.

Shanas, E. (1968). *Old people in three industrial societies.* New York: Atherton.

Shaw, C. R. (1930). *The jack-roller: A delinquent boy's own story* (Behavior Research Fund Monographs). Chicago: University of Chicago Press.

Shaw, C. R. (1931). *The natural history of a delinquent career* (Behavior Research Fund Monographs). Chicago: University of Chicago Press.

Shaw, C. R., with McKay, H. D., & McDonald, J. F. (1938). *Brothers in crime.* Chicago: University of Chicago Press.

Sheehy, G. (1976). *Passages: Predictable crises of adult life.* New York: Dutton.

Sieber, S. D. (1974). Toward a theory of role accumulation. *American Sociological Review, 39,* 567-578.

Smelser, N. J., & Erikson, E. H. (Eds.). (1980). *Themes of work and love in adulthood.* Cambridge, MA: Harvard University Press.

Smith, B. (1987). Foreword. In R. P. Abeles (Ed.), *Life-span perspectives and social psychology* (pp. xi-xiv). Hillsdale, NJ: Lawrence Erlbaum.

Smith, M. C. (1994). *Social science in the crucible: The American debate over objectivity and purpose, 1918-1941.* Durham, NC: Duke University Press.

Smith, R. E. (Ed.). (1979). *The subtle revolution: Women at work.* Washington, DC: Urban Institute.

Solga, H. (1995). *Auf dem Weg in eine klassenlose Gesellschaft? Klassenlagen und Mobilität zwischen Generationen in der DDR.* Berlin: Akademie Verlag.

Sørensen, A. B. (1991). Symposium: Robert K. Merton in review—Merton and methodology. *Contemporary Sociology, 20,* 516-519.

Sørensen, A., & Trappe, H. (1994). *Life course convergence and gender inequality in the German Democratic Republic* (Arbeitsbericht No. 6 aus dem Projekt Lebensverläufe und historischer Wandel in der ehemaligen DDR). Berlin: Max-Planck-Institut für Bildungsforschung.

Spain, D., & Bianchi, S. M. (1996). *Balancing act: Motherhood, marriage, and employment among American women*. New York: Russell Sage.

Stewart, A. J., & Healy, J. M., Jr. (1989). Linking individual development and social changes. *American Psychologist, 44,* 30-42.

Stinchcombe, A. L. (1968). *Constructing social theories.* New York: Harcourt Brace & World.

Stouffer, S. A., Suchman, E. A., DeVinney, L. C., Star, S. A., & Williams, R. M., Jr. (1949). *The American soldier: Adjustment during army life* (Studies in Social Psychology in World War II, Vol. 1). Princeton, NJ: Princeton University Press.

Streib, G. F. (1993). The life course of activities and retirement communities. In J. R. Kelly (Ed.), *Activity and aging: Staying involved in later life* (pp. 246-263, Sage Focus Editions No. 161). Newbury Park, CA: Sage.

Susser, M. (1969). Aging and the field of public health. In M. W. Riley, J. W. Riley, Jr., & M. E. Johnson (Eds.), *Aging and society,* Vol. 2: *Aging and the professions* (pp. 114-160). New York: Russell Sage.

Sutherland, E. H. (Annotator and Interpreter). (1937). *The professional thief by a professional thief* (University of Chicago Sociological Series). Chicago: University of Chicago Press.

Swedberg, R. (1990). *Economics and sociology: Redefining their boundaries—Conversations with economists and sociologists.* Princeton, NJ: Princeton University Press.

Swidler, A. (1986). Culture in action: Symbols and strategies. *American Sociological Review, 51,* 273-286.

Tåhlin, M. (1991). *Work-life class mobility in post-industrial Sweden.* Paper prepared for the workshop on Life Course and Social Inequality at the European research conference, "European Society or European Societies?," Gausdal, Norway.

Teachman, J. D. (1982). Methodological issues in the analysis of family formation and dissolution. *Journal of Marriage and the Family, 20,* 1037-1051.

Teachman, J. D. (1983). Analyzing social processes: Life tables and proportional hazards models. *Social Science Research, 12,* 263-301.

Terman, L. M. (1925). *Genetic studies of genius,* Vol. 1: *Mental and physical traits of a thousand gifted children.* Stanford, CA: Stanford University Press.

Terman, L. M., & Oden, M. H. (1947). *Genetic studies of genius,* Vol. 4: *The gifted child grows up: Twenty-five years' follow-up of a superior group.* Stanford, CA: Stanford University Press.

Terman, L. M., & Oden, M. H. (1959). *Genetic studies of genius,* Vol. 5: *The gifted group at mid-life: Thirty-five years' follow-up of the superior child.* Stanford, CA: Stanford University Press.

Thoits, P. (1983). Multiple identities and psychological well-being: A reformulation and test of the social isolation hypothesis. *American Sociological Review, 48,* 174-187.

Thoits, P. (1987). Negotiating roles. In F. J. Crosby (Ed.), *Spouse, parent, worker: On gender and multiple roles* (pp. 11-22). New Haven, CT: Yale University Press.

Thomas, W. I. (1966). *W. I. Thomas on social organization and social personality* (M. Janowitz, Ed.). Chicago: University of Chicago Press.

Thomas, W. I., & Znaniecki, F. (1927). *The Polish peasant in Europe and America*. New York: Knopf. (Originally published 1918-1920)

Thompson, P. R. (1978). *The voice of the past: Oral history*. Oxford, UK: Oxford University Press.

Thorne, B. (1994). *Gender play: Girls and boys in school*. New Brunswick, NJ: Rutgers University Press.

Tilly, C. (1992). *History and sociological imagining* (Working Paper Series No. 134). New York: New School for Social Research.

Tilly, L. A., & Scott, J. W. (1978). *Women, work and family*. New York: Holt, Rinehart & Winston.

Tölke, A. (1989). Möglichkeiten und Grenzen einer Edition bei retrospektiven Verlaufsdaten. In K. U. Mayer & E. Brückner (Eds.), *Lebensverläufe und Wohlfahrtsentwicklung: Konzeption, Design und Methodik der Erhebung von Lebensverläufen der Geburtsjahrgänge 1929-1931, 1939-1941, 1949-1951—Teil I* (pp. 173-226, Materialien aus der Bildungsforschung Nr. 35). Berlin: Max-Planck-Institut für Bildungsforschung.

Trappe, H. (1995). *Emanzipation oder Zwang? Frauen in der DDR zwischen Beruf, Familie und Sozialpolitik*. Berlin: Akademie Verlag.

Tuma, N. B., & Hannan, M. T. (1984). *Social dynamics: Models and methods*. Orlando, FL: Academic Press.

Uchitelle, L. (1994, November 28). Women in their 50's follow many paths into workplace. *The New York Times*, p. A1.

Uhlenberg, P. R. (1969). A study of cohort life cycles: Cohorts of native-born Massachusetts women, 1830-1920. *Population Studies, 23*, 407-420.

Uhlenberg, P. R. (1979). Older women: The growing challenge to design constructive roles. *The Gerontologist, 19*, 236-241.

University of Michigan Survey Research Center. (1972-1990). *A Panel Study of Income Dynamics: Procedures and tape-codes—Wave I-XX*. Ann Arbor: University of Michigan, Survey Research Center/Inter-University Consortium for Political and Social Research, Institute for Social Research.

Upchurch, D. M., Lillard, L. A., & Panis, C. W. A. (1995). *Updating women's life courses: Theoretical and methodological considerations* (Labor and Population Working Paper Series No. 95-18). Santa Monica, CA: RAND.

Urban, D. (1982). Mobility and the growth of science. *Social Studies of Science, 12*, 409-433.

Vaillant, G. E. (1977). *Adaptation to life*. Boston: Little, Brown.

Vaillant, G. E. (1983). *The natural history of alcoholism*. Cambridge, MA: Harvard University Press.

Vaillant, G. E. (1993). *The wisdom of the ego*. Cambridge, MA: Harvard University Press.

Van der Klaauw, W. (1996). Female labour supply and marital status decisions: A life-cycle model. *Review of Economic Studies, 63*, 199-235.

Vaughan, D. (1986). *Uncoupling: Turning points in intimate relationships*. New York: Oxford University Press.

Veroff, J., Hatchett, S., & Douvan, E. (1992). Consequences of participating in a longitudinal study of marriage. *Public Opinion Quarterly, 56*, 315-327.

Voges, W. (Ed.). (1987). *Methoden der Biographie- und Lebenslaufforschung* (Biographie und Gesellschaft, Vol. 1). Opladen, Germany: Leske & Budrich.

Wagner, M. (1989). *Räumliche Mobilität im Lebenslauf: Eine empirische Untersuchung sozialer Bedingungen der Migration.* Stuttgart, Germany: F. Enke.

Wallace, J. B. (1992). Reconsidering the life review: The social construction of talk about the past. *The Gerontologist, 32,* 120-125.

Wandersee, W. D. (1988). *On the move: American women in the 1970s.* Boston: Twayne.

Waring, J. M. (1975). Social replenishment and social change: The problem of disordered cohort flow. *American Behavioral Scientist, 19,* 237-256.

Waring, J. M. (1978). *The middle years: A multidisciplinary view.* New York: Academy for Educational Development.

Weiss, R. S. (1994). *Learning from strangers: The art and method of qualitative interview studies.* New York: Free Press.

Welter, B. (1976). *Dimity convictions: The American woman in the nineteenth century.* Athens: Ohio University Press.

Wexler, S. (1997). Work/family policy stratification: The examples of family support and family leave. *Qualitative Sociology, 20,* 311-322.

White, R. W. (1960). Competence and the psychosexual stages of development. In *Nebraska Symposium on Motivation, 1960* (pp. 97-141). Lincoln: University of Nebraska Press.

Williams, R. M., Jr. (1970). *American society: A sociological interpretation.* New York: Knopf.

Williams, R. M., Jr., & Suchman, E. A. (1964). *Strangers next door: Ethnic relations in American communities.* Englewood Cliffs, NJ: Prentice Hall.

Willigan, J. D., & Lynch, K. A. (1982). *Sources and methods of historical demography* (Studies in Social Discontinuity). New York: Academic Press.

Winston, G. C. (1988). Three problems with the treatment of time in economics: Perspectives, repetitiveness and time units. In G. C. Winston & R. F. Teichgraeber, III (Eds.), *The boundaries of economics* (pp. 30-52, Murphy Institute Series in Political Economy). Cambridge, UK: Cambridge University Press.

Wolfgang, M. E., Thornberry, T., & Figlio, R. (1987). *From boy to man: From delinquency to crime* (Studies in Crime and Justice). Chicago: University of Chicago Press.

Wrigley, E. A. (1969). *Population and history* (World University Library). New York: McGraw-Hill.

Yahraes, H. C. (1969). The effect of childhood influence upon intelligence, personality and mental health. *Mental Health Program Reports,* No. 3.

Yamaguchi, K. (1991). *Event history analysis* (Applied Social Research Methods Series, Vol. 28). Newbury Park, CA: Sage.

Yarrow, M. R., Campbell, J. D., & Burton, R. V. (1970). *Recollections of childhood: A study of the retrospective method* (Monographs of the Society for Research in Child Development, Vol. 35, No. 5, Serial No. 138). Chicago: University of Chicago Press.

Young, C. H., Savola, K. L., & Phelps, E. (1991). *Inventory of longitudinal studies in the social sciences.* Newbury Park, CA: Sage.

Young, C. M. (1978). Work sequences of women during the family life cycle. *Journal of Marriage and the Family, 40,* 401-411.

Name Index

Subject Index

Adaptation, ix, 253, 257
Adaptation to Life (Vaillant), 18
Adult development, 237-238
African American women, 257-258, 267
Age:
    childhood, 35-36, 65
    generation, in contrast to, 23-24
    middle years, 37, 238
    multilevel phenomenon, aging process as
      a, 62
    old age, 35-36
    social meanings of, 29-34
    sociology of, 2, 11, 15-17
Aging and Society (Riley, Johnson, &
    Foner), 32, 34
Aging From Birth to Death, 33
Alice Through the Looking Glass (Carroll),
    125
American Association for the Advancement
    of Science, 33
American Lives (Clausen), 19, 34, 40, 104,
    208, 211
*American Society: A Sociological Interpre-
    tation* (Williams), 130
American Sociological Association, xv
American Soldier, The (Stouffer, Suchman,
    DeVinney, Star, & Williams), 5
Analysis and interpretation of life course
    data, 90-91, 183-187, 274
    See also History and human lives,
      linking; Innovation in the typical life
      course; Life reviews and life studies;

Quantitative and qualitative data,
    integrating
Analytical time, 72-73
Archival data, x-xi, 216-218, 273-275
Association of German Market Research In-
    stitutions, 168
Asynchrony, understanding, 49-50
Autobiographical notes, 28
    cohort analyses, 41-43
    future agenda, 50-51
    phases of the life course, 34-41
    social meanings of age, 29-34
    structures, combining studies of lives and
      social, 43-50

Bengston's Longitudinal Study of Three
    Generations, 141-143
Bennington Studies of Persistence and
    Change in Attitudes and Values, 68-
    69, 113-115
Berkeley Guidance Study, 68, 144-145,
    275, 284-288
Bidirectional model of interrelated life
    course, 8
Biography and history, intersection of, x,
    64-66
Birth cohorts as population units, 160, 267-
    269
British Household Panel Study (PHPS), 109
Bureau of Applied Social Research, 57

331

About the Contributors

DUANE F. ALWIN is Professor of Sociology and Senior Research Scientist in the Survey Research Center of the Institute for Social Research at the University of Michigan. He received a Ph.D. in sociology from the University of Wisconsin in 1972. Over the past two decades, his work has focused on human development, the family, socialization, and social change. He is particularly well known for innovative contributions to the study of the role of life course factors in the development of attitudes, beliefs, and values.

ERIKA BRÜCKNER studied psychology in Leipzig and Münster, Germany. She worked as a clinical psychologist in Potsdam and as an assistant professor in Münster before founding her own institute for research in the social sciences in 1965. In 1974, she became the chief of the field department of ZUMA (National Center for Survey Research, Methodology, and Data Analysis). In 1984, she moved to the Max Planck Institute for Human Development and Education in Berlin and concentrated her activities on the design and realization of the German Life History Study (principal investigator: Karl Ulrich Mayer). Her publications are mainly in the field of data collection methodology including telephone interviewing and retrospective data collection. In recent years, however, she has published a number of articles and research reports on social inequality in old age. Since her retirement in 1992, she continues to work freelance on several projects.

JOHN A. CLAUSEN, who died in 1996, was Professor Emeritus of Sociology at the University of California, Berkeley. In the early 1950s, he established the Laboratory of Socioenvironmental Studies at the National Institute of Mental Health and provided an intellectual home for Erving Goffman, Morris Rosenberg, and others. In 1960, he accepted an invitation to become the third director of the Institute of Human Development at Berkeley, where for 33 years he managed the important Berkeley longitudinal studies of infants and children born in the 1920s. Trained as a social psychologist at the University of Chicago, he brought his long-standing interest in individual life history to his magnum opus, *American Lives: Looking Back at the Children of the Great Depression* (1993).

ANNE COLBY, Director of the Henry Murray Research Center at Radcliffe College and Senior Scholar at the Carnegie Foundation for the Advancement of Teaching, is a developmental psychologist working in the field of moral and social development. Her research focuses on the development of moral judgment, moral commitment, and social responsibility. She is the principal author of *A Longitudinal Study of Moral Judgment* (1983), *The Measurement of Moral Judgment* (1987), and *Some Do Care: Contemporary Lives of Moral Commitment* (1992) and is coeditor of *Ethnography and Human Development: Context and Meaning in Social Inquiry* (1996) and *Competence and Character Through Life* (in press).

DONNA DEMPSTER-McCLAIN is Associate Director of the Bronfenbrenner Life Course Center and Senior Lecturer in the Department of Human Development at Cornell University. Her research and teaching interests focus on social gerontology and the life course. She served as Project Director for the Cornell Women's Roles and Well-Being Study from 1985 to 1992 and was an associate professor of child and family development at California State University, Long Beach, from 1970 to 1983. She received an M.S. degree from Ohio University in 1969 and a Ph.D. from Cornell University in 1985.

GLEN H. ELDER, JR. is Howard W. Odum Distinguished Professor of Sociology and Research Professor of Psychology at the University of North Carolina at Chapel Hill, where he codirects the Carolina Consortium on Human Development and manages a research program on life course studies. He also has served on the faculties of the University of California,

Berkeley, and Cornell University. His books (authored, coauthored, and edited) include *Children of the Great Depression* (1974), *Life Course Dynamics* (1985), *Children in Time and Place* (1993), *Families in Troubled Times* (1995), and *Developmental Science* (1996). His contributions to life course theory and studies began in Clausen's Institute of Human Development in the early 1960s.

JANET ZOLLINGER GIELE is Professor of Sociology at the Heller School at Brandeis University, where she founded the Family and Children's Policy Center. Her main research interests are the historic women's movement, changing life patterns of women, and the growth of family policy. She is the author of *Women and the Future* (1978) and *Two Paths to Women's Equality: Temperance, Suffrage, and the Origins of Modern Feminism* (1995). Her edited works include *Women: Roles and Status in Eight Countries* (1977), *Women in the Middle Years* (1982), and *Women's Lives and Women's Work: The Continuing Struggle Worldwide* (1992).

NANCY KARWEIT received her Ph.D. in sociology at Johns Hopkins University, where she currently is Principal Research Scientist at the Center for Research on the Education of Students Placed at Risk. Her work has focused primarily on issues in sociology of education including research on the effects of school, classroom, and curricular organization on disadvantaged children and on the development and evaluation of school-based intervention programs. In addition, she has had extensive experience in the processing and management of large data sets and has developed procedures for the processing and manipulation of life history data.

DAVID J. KERTZER is Paul Dupee University Professor of Social Science at Brown University, where he also is Professor of Anthropology and History. He is the author of many books including, most recently, *Sacrificed for Honor* (1993), *Politics and Symbols* (1996), and *The Kidnapping of Edgardo Mortara* (1997). He has edited or coedited numerous books including *Age and Anthropological Theory* (1983), *Age Structuring in Comparative Perspective* (1989), *The Family in Italy From Antiquity to the Present* (1991), *Aging in the Past* (1995), and *Anthropological Demography* (1997).

JOHN H. LAUB is Professor in the College of Criminal Justice at Northeastern University and Visiting Scholar at the Murray Research Center at Radcliffe College. He is the former editor of the *Journal of Quantitative Criminology* and recently served as vice president of the American Society of Criminology. His areas of research include crime and deviance over the life course, juvenile justice, and the history of criminology. He has published widely including, most recently, *Crime in the Making: Pathways and Turning Points Through Life* (with Robert Sampson) (1993). He is working on a study (with Sampson) of criminal careers over the life span.

KARL ULRICH MAYER has been codirector of the Max Planck Institute for Human Development and Education in Berlin, where he heads the Center for Sociology and the Study of the Life Course, since 1983. He was one of the founding editors of the *European Sociological Review* and currently is one of the coeditors of the *Kölner Zeitschrift für Soziologie und Sozialpsychologie* and an active member in the German Science Council (Wissenschaftsrat). In the 1996-1997 academic year, he was a scholar at the Robert Schuman Centre of the European University Institute in Florence, Italy. He recently has coedited and coauthored several books including *Die Berliner Altersstudie* (1996), *Zwischenbilanz der Wiedervereinigung* (1996), and *Kollektiv und Eigensinn: Lebensverläufe in der DDR und danach* (1995). His main research interests include social stratification and mobility, comparative social structure analysis, occupational careers and labor markets, and the sociology of the life course.

PHYLLIS MOEN is Ferris Family Professor of Life Course Studies and Professor of Sociology and of Human Development at Cornell University, where she is a founding director of the Bronfenbrenner Life Course Center. Her research focuses on gender and aging over the life course including work/family transitions and trajectories. She has received funding from the National Institute on Aging and the Alfred P. Sloan Foundation for life course research. Her books include *Working Parents* (1989), *Women's Two Roles* (1992), and (as coauthor) *Examining Lives in Context* (1995), and *The State of Americans* (1996).

ANGELA M. O'RAND is on the faculty of the Department of Sociology at Duke University, where she also is affiliated with the Center for the

Study of Aging and Human Development and the Center for Demographic Studies. Her research on aging has focused primarily on aging and stratification, particularly on the labor market effects of pensions on retirement timing and retirement economic status among women and men. In addition, she frequently applies ideas from the sociology of science to her analysis of the state of life course research.

LISA PELLERIN is an advanced graduate student in the sociology graduate program at the University of North Carolina at Chapel Hill. She has pursued research on the psychological aspects of social change beginning with rural change in the Midwest and continuing with the process of status crystallization in periods of rapid change.

MATILDA WHITE RILEY is Professor Emerita of Sociology at Rutgers University and Bowdoin College. She also has been president of the American Sociological Association and chair of key committees of the Social Science Research Council, the American Association for the Advancement of Science, and the Gerontological Society. A member of the National Academy of Sciences and the American Academy of Arts and Sciences, she is the recipient of countless awards and honorary degrees, the latest from the State University of New York at Albany in 1997. The best known of her publications is *Sociological Research* (1963). She currently is senior social scientist at the National Institute on Aging, National Institutes of Health.

ROBERT J. SAMPSON is Professor of Sociology at the University of Chicago and Research Fellow at the American Bar Foundation. His major research interests include crime, deviance, and social control; community/urban sociology; and the life course. His most recent book (with John Laub), *Crime in the Making: Pathways and Turning Points Through Life* (1993), received outstanding book awards from the American Society of Criminology; the Academy of Criminal Justice Sciences; and the Crime, Law, and Deviance Section of the American Sociological Association.

JACQUELINE SCOTT is a member of the Faculty of Social and Political Sciences at the University of Cambridge and a Fellow of Queens'

College. She formerly was director of research for the British Household Panel at Essex University. Her current research interests are in household and family change in a cross-national perspective and inequality in childhood.